Rick Steves®

Kraków, Warsaw & Gdańsk

CONTENTS

Central Warsaw

MIĘDZYPARKOWA

Rondo Babka

Z. SŁOMIŃSKIEGO

PARKING LOT WITH FORMER GHETTO WALL

STAWKI

KONWIKTORSKA SANGUSZKI

UMSCHLAGPLATZ MONUMENT

MURANÓW (Former Jewish Ghetto)

FORMER SS HQ

NISKA

DUBOIS

FRANCISZKAŃSKA

OKOPOWA

AL. JANA PAWŁA II

STAWKI

BUNKER

ZAMENHOFA

MUSEUM OF THE HISTORY OF POLISH JEWS

MIŁA

GHETTO HEROES SQUARE

Muranów

Plac Krasińskich

M. ANIELEWICZA

(B) Nalewki

GEN. WŁ. ANDERSA

Krasińskich Garden

Accommodations

1. Hotel Indigo
2. Between Us B&B
3. Chopin Boutique B&B
4. Zgoda by DeSilva
5. Apple Inn
6. Oki Doki City Hostel
7. Hotel Bristol
8. Hotel Le Régina
9. Castle Inn
10. Duval Apartments

Eateries

11. Kamanda Lwowska
12. Bibenda
13. Butchery & Wine
14. A. Blikle
15. E. Wedel Pijalnia Czekolady
16. Odette
17. Warszawa Powiśle
18. Kawiarnia Kafka
19. Restauracja pod Samsonem
20. Freta 33
21. Zapiecek (5)

KARMELICKA

Ratusz M

Plac Bankowy

SOLIDARNOŚCI

ELEKTORALNA

PTASIA

PL. MIROWSKI

AL. JANA PAWŁA II

GRZYBOWSKA

Plac Grzybowski

WALICÓW

CIEPŁA

TWARDA

ŚWIĘTOKRZYSKA

GRZYBOWSKA

ŁUCKA

ŻELAZNA

PROSTA

Muzeum (B) Powstania Warszawskiego

WARSAW UPRISING MUSEUM

TOWAROWA

WRONIA

PAŃSKA

SIENNA

ZŁOTA

ZŁOTE TARASY MALL

PRZYKOPANA

Rondo Daszyńskiego M (B) Rondo Daszyńskiego

PROSTA

MIEDZIANA

CHMIELNA

ZŁOTA

Dworzec Centralny Bus #160 (B)

CENTRAL TRAIN STATION

Dw. Centralny

Dworzec Centralny Bus #175 (B)

400 Meters

400 Yards

Other
- ㉒ Observation Deck Entrance
- ㉓ Canaletto Paintings (3)
- ㉔ Mysia 3 (Mini-Mall)
- ㉕ Jazz Club Akwarium

Kraków's Old Town

OLD MARKET

BAŁOREGO

DŁUGA

PADEREWSKIEGO

ŁOBZOWSKA

ASNYKA

KARMELICKA

GARBARSKA

Planty

PIJARSKA

ŚW. MARKA

SŁAWKOWSKA

WALK BEGINS

BARBICAN

FLORIAN GATE

DUNAJEWSKIEGO

SZCZEPAŃSKA

ŚW. JANA

ŚW. MARKA

CZARTORYSKI MUSEUM

FLORIAŃSKA

SZPITALNA

KRUPNICZA

#24 Teatr Bagatela

OLD

P

STUDENSKA

PODWALE

SZEWSKA

SZOŁAYSKI HOUSE

ŚW. TOMASZA

ŚW. ANNY

JAGIELLOŃSKA

Main Market Square

CLOTH HALL ⑩ ⑨

ST. MARY'S

COLLEGIUM MAIUS

⑧

Small Market Square

JABŁONOWSKICH

MICKIEWICZ STATUE

ST. MARY'S TICKETS

SIENNA

SIENNA

⑯ TOWN HALL TOWER

COLLEGIUM NOVUM

GOŁĘBIA

BRACKA

PIŁSUDSKIEGO

OLSZEWSKIEGO

WIŚLNA

⑪ ARCH-BISHOP'S MANSION

PASAŻ 13 MALL

P

#8 plac Wszystkich Świętych

⑮

GRODZKA

STOLARSKA

DOMINICAN CHURCH

WC

To Airport, Auschwitz & Kościuszko Mound

SMOLEŃSK

FRANCISZKAŃSKA

ST. FRANCIS

WYSPIAŃSKI PAVILION

DOMINIKAŃSKA

TOWN

Planty

STRASZEWSKIEGO

POSELSKA

MILK BAR

SENACKA

MILK BAR

STS. PETER & PAUL

FELICJANEK

ZWIERZYNIECKA

⑫

⑭

Mary Mag. Square

ST. ANDREW'S

SAREGO

BISHOP ERAZM CIOŁEK PALACE

ARCHDIOCESAN MUSEUM

GRODZKA

ŚW. GERTRUDY

POWIŚLE

WALK ENDS

KANONICZA

PODZAMCZE

Vistula River

CATHEDRAL ①

⑤ ⑥

④

③

INNER COURTYARD

ST. IDZIEGO

STRADOMSKA

WAWEL HILL

WC

⑦

WC

②

DRAGON STATUE

BERNARDYŃSKA

ST. BERNARDINO'S

KONOPNICKIEJ

KOLETEK

To St. John Paul II Sanctuary

Sights

1 John Paul II Wawel Cathedral Museum

2 Sandomierska Tower

3 Royal State Rooms

4 Royal Private Apartments

5 Oriental Art

6 Crown Treasury & Armory

7 Lost Wawel Museum

8 Gallery of 19th-Century Polish Art (Entrance)

9 Rynek Underground Museum Entrance

Services & Other

10 Kraków City Museum Visitors Center

11 Wieliczka Promotion Office

12 Massolit Books

13 Frania Café/Laundry

14 Betty Clean Laundry

15 Kraków Bike Tours & Rental

16 KRK Bike Rental

17 Trams #3 & #24 to/from Kazimierz (3)

KURNIKI

B Kurniki

GALERIA KRAKOWSKA MALL

TRAIN STN.

B BUS STATION

#3 Dworzec Główny Zachód

Plac Matejki

ZACISZE

#24 Basztowa

BASZTOWA

PAWIA

Plac Jana Jeroziorańskiego

BOSACKA

POST OFFICE

LUBICZ

To Nowa Huta

SŁOWACKI THEATER

Planty

ŚW. KRZYŻA

WESTERPLATTE

PEDESTRIAN UNDERPASS

#3 & 24 Dworzec Główny

RADZIWIŁŁOWSKA

MIKOŁAJSKA

ŻYBLIKIEWICZA

17

#3 & 24 Poczta Główna

KOPERNIKA

BLICH

MAIN POST OFFICE

WIELOPOLE

GRZEGÓRZECKA

STAROWIŚLNA

DIETLA

#3 & 24 Dietla

17

13

200 Meters

200 Yards

ŚW. SEBASTIANA

See Kazimierz map

B. JÓSELEWICZA

KAZIMIERZ

17

#3 & 24 Miodowa

New Cemetery

DIETLA

PODBRZEZIE

MIODOWA

Old Cemetery

POST

STAROWIŚLNA

DAJWÓR

GALERIA KAZIMIERZ

REMU'H SYNAGOGUE

Plac Nowy

MARKET HALL

To Podgórze & Wieliczka Salt Mine

INTRODUCTION

This Snapshot guide, excerpted from my guidebook *Rick Steves Eastern Europe,* introduces you a trio of grand Polish cities: historic Kraków, thriving Warsaw, and gorgeous Gdańsk. Covering the best of Poland, this book offers an enjoyable cross-section of this proud nation.

Poland's historical capital, Kraków, clusters around one of Europe's biggest and most inviting market squares. Explore Kraków's picture-perfect Old Town—filled with museums, restaurants, university life, and Old World charm—and head to the Kazimierz neighborhood to learn about Poland's Jewish story. Side-trip to the world's most powerful memorial to the victims of the Holocaust at Auschwitz-Birkenau concentration camp.

For a look at today's Poland, visit Warsaw—leveled in World War II, rebuilt soon after, and now rapidly gentrifying. Stroll through Warsaw's reconstructed Old Town, promenade along newly spiffed-up boulevards, gape up at the communist-style Palace of Culture and Science, and dip into engaging museums on WWII history, native son Fryderyk Chopin, Polish painters, and much more.

On the Baltic Coast, Gdańsk offers a vibrantly colorful main drag fronted by opulent old Hanseatic facades, plus inspiring tales from the toppling of communism at the shipyard where the Solidarity trade union was born. Nearby in Pomerania is a pair of medieval red-brick sights: the imposing Gothic headquarters of the Teutonic Knights, Malbork Castle; and the appealing, gingerbread-scented town of Toruń.

To help you have the best trip possible, I've included the following topics in this book:

• **Planning Your Time,** with advice on how to make the most of your limited time

• **Orientation,** including tourist information offices (abbreviated as TI), tips on public transportation, local tour options, and helpful hints

• **Sights** with ratings:

▲▲▲—Don't miss

▲▲—Try hard to see

▲—Worthwhile if you can make it

No rating—Worth knowing about

• **Sleeping** and **Eating,** with good-value recommendations in every price range

• **Connections,** with tips on trains, buses, and boats

Practicalities, near the end of this book, has information on money, staying connected, lodging, restaurants, transportation, and more, plus Polish survival phrases.

To travel smartly, read this little book in its entirety before you go. It's my hope that this guide will make your trip more meaningful and rewarding. Traveling like a temporary local, you'll get the absolute most out of every mile, minute, and dollar.

Szczęśliwej podróży—Happy travels!

POLAND

POLAND

Polska

Poland is a land of surprises. Some travelers imagine Poland as a backwards, impoverished land of rusting factories, smoggy cities, and gloomy citizens—only to be left speechless when they step into Kraków's vibrant main square, Gdańsk's colorful Royal Way, or Warsaw's trendy hipster zones. Today's Poland has a vibrant urbanity, an enticing food and design culture, dynamic history, and kindhearted natives.

The Poles are a proud people—as moved by their spectacular failures as by their successes. Their quiet elegance has been tempered by generations of abuse by foreign powers. In a way, there are two Polands: lively, cosmopolitan urban centers, and countless tiny farm villages in the countryside. A societal tension exists between city-dwelling progressives and what they call the "simple people" of Poland: hardworking small-town Poles descended from generations of farmers, who still live an uncomplicated, agrarian lifestyle. There's a large contingent of these salt-of-the-earth folks, who tend to be politically conservative and staunchly Euroskeptic.

Poland is arguably Europe's most devoutly Catholic country. Their profound faith has united the Poles through many tough times.

Squeezed between Protestant Germany (originally Prussia) and Eastern Orthodox Russia, Poland wasn't even a country for generations (1795-1918)—but its Catholicism helped keep its spirit alive. Under communism, Poles found their religion a source of strength as well as rebellion—they could express dissent against the atheistic regime by going to church. Be sure to step into some serene church interiors. These aren't museums—you'll almost certainly see locals engrossed in prayer. (Visit with respect: Maintain silence, and if you want to take pictures, do so discreetly.)

Much of Poland's story is a Jewish story. Before World War

II, 80 percent of Europe's Jews lived in Poland. Warsaw was the world's second-largest Jewish city (after New York), with 380,000 Jews (out of a total population of 1.2 million). Poland was a magnet for Jewish refugees because of its relatively welcoming policies. Still, Jews were forbidden from owning land; that's why they settled mostly in cities.

But the Holocaust (and a later Soviet policy of sending "troublemaking" Jews to Israel) decimated the Jewish population. This tragic chapter, combined with postwar border shifts and population movements, made Poland one of Europe's most ethnically homogeneous countries. Today, virtually everyone in the country is an ethnic Pole, and only a few thousand Polish Jews remain.

Poland has long been staunchly pro-America. Of course, their big neighbors (Russia and Germany) have been their historic enemies. And when Hitler invaded in 1939, the Poles felt let down by their supposed European friends (France and Britain), who declared war on Germany but provided virtually no military support to the Polish resistance. America, meanwhile, is seen as the big ally from across the ocean—and the home of the largest population of Poles outside of Poland.

On my first visit to Poland, I had a poor impression of Poles, who seemed brusque and often elbowed ahead of me in line. I've since learned that all it takes is a smile and a cheerful greeting—preferably in Polish—to break through the thick skin that helped these kind people survive the difficult communist times. With a friendly *Dzień dobry!*, you'll turn any grouch into an ally.

It may help to know that, because of the distinct cadence of Polish, Poles speaking English sometimes sound more impatient, gruff, or irritated than they actually are. Part of the Poles' charm

POLAND

Poland Almanac

Official Name: Rzeczpospolita Polska (Republic of Poland), or Polska for short.

Snapshot History: This thousand-year-old country has been dominated by foreign powers for much of the past two centuries, finally achieving true independence (from the Soviet Union) in 1989.

Population: 38.5 million people, slightly less than California. About 97 percent are ethnic Poles who speak Polish (though English is also widely spoken). Four out of every five Poles are practicing Catholics. The population is relatively young compared to most European countries, with an average age of 41 (Germany's is 47).

Latitude and Longitude: 52°N and 20°E (similar latitude to Berlin, London, and Edmonton, Alberta).

Area: 121,000 square miles, the same as New Mexico (or Illinois and Iowa put together).

Geography: Because of its overall flatness, Poland has been a corridor for invading armies since its infancy. The Vistula River (650 miles) runs south-to-north up the middle of the country, passing through Kraków and Warsaw, and emptying into the Baltic Sea at Gdańsk. Poland's climate is generally cool and rainy—40,000 storks love it.

Biggest Cities: Warsaw (the capital, 1.7 million), Kraków (767,000), and Łódź (747,000).

Economy: The Gross Domestic Product is $1.1 trillion, with a GDP per capita of $29,500. The 1990s saw an aggressive and successful transition from state-run socialism to privately owned capitalism. Only five percent of Poles are unemployed, but one in five lives below the poverty line (mostly low-income farmers).

is that they're not as slick and self-assured as many Europeans: They're kind, soft-spoken, and quite shy. On a recent train trip in Poland, I offered my Polish seatmate a snack—and spent the rest of the trip enjoying a delightful conversation with a new friend.

HELPFUL HINTS

Restroom Signage: To confuse tourists, the Poles have devised a secret way of marking their WCs. You'll see doors marked with *męska* (men) and *damska* (women)—but even more often, you'll simply see a triangle (for men) or a circle (for women).

Train Station Lingo: "PKP" is the abbreviation for Polish National Railways ("PKS" is for buses). In larger towns with several train stations, you'll normally use the one called Główny (meaning "Main"—except in Warsaw, where it's Centralna).

Currency: 1 złoty (zł, or PLN) = 100 groszy (gr) = about 25 cents; 4 zł = about $1.

Government: Poland's mostly figurehead president selects the prime minister and cabinet, with legislators' approval. They govern along with a two-house legislature (Sejm and Senat) of 560 seats. Prime Minister Mateusz Morawiecki represents the majority political party, the right-wing Law and Justice (Prawo i Sprawiedliwość, or PiS for short). President Andrzej Duda, formerly of the Law and Justice party (but currently a conservative-leaning independent), began his five-year term in 2015.

Flag: The upper half is white, and the lower half is red—the traditional colors of Poland. Poetic Poles claim the white represents honor, and the red represents the blood spilled by the Poles to protect that honor. The flag sometimes includes a coat of arms with a crowned eagle (representing Polish sovereignty). Under Soviet rule, the crown was removed from the emblem, and the eagle's talons were trimmed. On regaining its independence, Poland coronated its eagle once more.

Not-so-Average Poles: Poland's three big airports offer a rundown of just a few of the country's biggest names: St. John Paul II (in Kraków), Fryderyk Chopin (in Warsaw), and Lech Wałęsa (in Gdańsk). And, despite the many "Polack jokes" you've heard, you're already familiar with many other famous Polish intellectuals—you just don't realize they're Polish. The "Dumb Polack" Hall of Fame includes Mikołaj Kopernik **(Nicolas Copernicus),** scientist **Marie Curie** (née Skłodowska), writer Teodor Józef Korzeniowski (better known as **Joseph Conrad,** author of *Heart of Darkness*), architect **Daniel Libeskind** (known for redeveloping One World Trade Center in New York City)...and one of this book's co-authors.

Dworzec główny means "main train station." Most stations have several platforms *(peron)*, each of which has two tracks *(tor)*. Departures are generally listed by the *peron*, so keep your eye on both tracks for your train. Arrivals are *przyjazdy*, and departures are *odjazdy*. Left-luggage counters or lockers are marked *przechowalnia bagażu*. *Kasy* are ticket windows. These can be marked (sometimes only in Polish) for specific needs—domestic tickets, international tickets, and so on; ask fellow travelers to be sure you select the right line. The line you choose will invariably be the slowest one—leave plenty of time to buy your ticket. On arriving at a station, to get into town, follow signs for *wyjście* (sometimes followed by *do centrum* or *do miasta*).

POLAND

Top 10 Dates that Changed Poland

AD 966: The Polish king, Mieszko I, is baptized a Christian, symbolically uniting the Polish people and founding the nation.

1385: The Polish queen (called a "king" by sexist aristocrats of the time) marries a Lithuanian duke, starting the two-century reign of the Jagiełło family.

1410: Poland defeats the Teutonic Knights at the Battle of Grunwald, part of a Golden Age of territorial expansion and cultural achievement.

1572: The last Jagiellonian king dies, soon replaced by bickering nobles and foreign kings. Poland declines.

1795: In the last of three Partitions, the country is divvied up by its more-powerful neighbors: Russia, Prussia, and Austria.

1918: Following World War I, Poland finally reclaims its land and sovereignty.

1939: The Free City of Danzig (today's Gdańsk) is invaded by Nazi Germany, starting World War II. At war's end, the country is "liberated" (i.e., occupied) by the Soviet Union.

1980: Lech Wałęsa leads a successful strike, demanding more freedom from the communist regime.

1989: Poland gains independence under its first president—Lech Wałęsa. Fifteen years later, Poland joins the European Union.

2010: President Lech Kaczyński and 95 other high-level government officials are killed in a plane crash in Russia.

Transit Route Planner: For a good public transit route planner for most Polish cities, try www.jakdojade.pl.

Busy May: May 1 is May Day and May 3 is Constitution Day, when the entire country closes up for several days. Later in the month, younger kids get out of school, so families go on vacation (and Kraków is one of the most popular domestic destinations).

Telephones: Remember these Polish prefixes: 800 is toll-free, and 70 is expensive (like phone sex). Many Poles use mobile phones (which come with the prefix 50, 51, 53, 60, 66, 69, 72, 78, 79, or 88). For tips on dialing to, from, and within Poland, see the Practicalities chapter.

POLISH HISTORY

Poland is flat. Take a look at a topographical map of Europe, and it's easy to see the Poles' historical dilemma: The path of least resistance from northern Europe to Russia leads right through Poland. Over the years, many invaders—from Genghis Khan to Napoleon

to Hitler—have taken ad-
vantage of this fact. The
country has been called
"God's playground" for
the many wars that have
rumbled through its ter-
ritory. Poland has been
invaded by Soviets, Nazis,
French, Austrians, Rus-
sians, Prussians, Swedes,
Teutonic Knights, Tatars,

Bohemians, Magyars—and, about 1,300 years ago, Poles.

Medieval Greatness

The first Poles were the Polonians ("people of the plains"), a Slavic
band that arrived here in the eighth century. In 966, Mieszko I,
duke of the Polonian tribe, adopted Christianity and founded the
Piast dynasty, which would last for more than 400 years. Centuries
before Germany, Italy, or Spain first united, Poland was born.

Poland struggled against two different invaders in the 13th
century: the Tatars (Mongols who ravaged the south) and the Teutonic Knights (Germans who conquered the north). But despite
these challenges, Poland persevered. The last king of the Piast dynasty was also the greatest: Kazimierz the Great, who famously
"found a Poland made of wood and left one made of brick and
stone," and helped bring Poland (and its then-capital, Kraków) to
international prominence. The progressive Kazimierz also invited
Europe's much-persecuted Jews to settle here, establishing Poland
as a haven for the Jewish people, which it would remain until the
Nazis arrived.

Kazimierz the Great died at the end of the 14th century
without a male heir. His grand-niece, Princess Jadwiga, became
"king" (the Poles weren't ready for a "queen") and married Lithuanian Prince Władysław Jagiełło, uniting their countries against a
common enemy, the Teutonic Knights. Their marriage marked the
beginning of the Jagiellonian dynasty and set the stage for Poland's
Golden Age.

During this time, Poland expanded its territory, the Polish nobility began to acquire more political influence, Italy's Renaissance
(and its architectural styles) became popular, and the Toruń-born
astronomer Nicholas Copernicus shook up the scientific world with
his bold new heliocentric theory. Up on the Baltic coast, the port
city of Danzig (today's Gdańsk) took advantage of its Hanseatic
League trading partnership to become one of Europe's most pros-
perous cities.

POLAND

Foreign Kings and Partitions

When the Jagiellonians died out in 1572, political power shifted to the nobility. Poland became a republic of nobles governed by its wealthiest 10 percent—the *szlachta,* who elected a series of foreign kings. In the 16th and 17th centuries—with its territory spanning from the Baltic Sea to the Black Sea—the Polish-Lithuanian Commonwealth was the largest state in Europe.

But over time, many of the elected kings made poor diplomatic decisions and squandered the country's resources. To make matters worse, the nobles' parliament (Sejm) introduced the concept of *liberum veto* (literally "I freely forbid"), whereby any measure could be vetoed by a single member. This policy, which effectively demanded unanimous approval for any law to be passed, paralyzed the Sejm's already-waning power.

Sensing the Commonwealth's weakness, in the mid-17th century forces from Sweden rampaged through Polish and Lithuanian lands in the devastating "Swedish Deluge." While Poland eventually reclaimed its territory, a third of its population was dead. The Commonwealth continued to import self-serving foreign kings, including Saxony's Augustus the Strong and his son, who drained Polish wealth to finance vanity projects in their hometown of Dresden.

By the late 18th century, the Commonwealth was floundering...and surrounded by three land-hungry empires (Russia, Prussia, and Austria). The Poles were unaware that these neighbors had entered into an agreement now dubbed the "Alliance of the Three Black Eagles" (all three of those countries, coincidentally, had that same symbol); like vultures, they began to circle Poland's white eagle. Stanisław August Poniatowski, elected king with Russian support in 1764, would be Poland's last.

Over the course of less than 25 years, Russia, Prussia, and Austria divided Polish territory among themselves in a series of three Partitions. In 1772 and again in 1790, Poland was forced into ceding large chunks of land to its neighbors. Desperate to reform their government, Poles enacted Europe's first democratic constitution (and the world's second, after the US Constitution) on May 3, 1791—still celebrated as a national holiday. This visionary document protected the peasants, dispensed with both *liberum veto* and the election of the king, and set up something resembling a modern nation. But the constitution alarmed Poland's neighbors, who swept in soon after with the third and final Partition in 1795. "Poland" disappeared from Europe's maps, not to return until 1918.

Even though Poland was gone, the Poles wouldn't go quietly. As the Partitions were taking place, Polish soldier Tadeusz Kościuszko (also a hero of the American Revolution) returned home to lead an unsuccessful military resistance against the Russians in 1794.

Napoleon offered a brief glimmer of hope to the Poles in the early 19th century, when he marched eastward through Europe and set up the semi-independent "Duchy of Warsaw" in Polish lands. But that fleeting taste of freedom lasted only eight years; with Napoleon's defeat, Polish hopes were dashed. The Congress of Vienna, which again redistributed Polish territory to Prussia, Russia, and Austria, is sometimes called (by Poles) the "Fourth Partition." In a classic case of "my enemy's enemy is my friend," the Poles still have great affection for Napoleon for how fiercely he fought against their mutual foes.

The Napoleonic connection also established France as a safe haven for refugee Poles. After another failed uprising against Russia in 1830, many of Poland's top artists and writers fled to Paris—including pianist Fryderyk Chopin and Romantic poet Adam Mickiewicz (whose statue adorns Kraków's main square and Warsaw's Royal Way). These Polish artists tried to preserve the nation's spirit with music and words; those who remained in Poland continued to fight with swords and fists. By the end of the 19th century, the image of the Pole as a tireless, idealistic insurgent emerged. During this time, some Romantics—with typically melodramatic flair—dubbed Poland "the Christ of nations" for the way it was misunderstood and persecuted by the world, despite its nobility.

Poles didn't just flock to France during the Partitions. Untold numbers of Polish people uprooted their lives to pursue a better future in the New World. About 10 million Americans have Polish ancestry, and most of them came stateside from the mid-19th to early 20th century. Because the sophisticated and educated tended to remain in Poland, these new arrivals were mostly poor farmers who were (at first) unschooled and didn't speak English, placing them on a bottom rung of American society. It was during this time that the tradition of insulting "Polack jokes" emerged. Some claim these originated in Chicago, which was both a national trendsetter in humor and a magnet for Polish immigrants. Others suggest that German immigrants to America imported insulting stereotypes of their Polish neighbors from the Old World. Either way, the jokes became more vicious through the 20th century, until the Polish government actually lobbied the US State Department to put a stop to them.

As the map of Europe was redrawn following World War I, Poland emerged as a reborn nation, under the war hero-turned-head of state, Marshal Józef Piłsudski. The newly reformed "Second Polish Republic," which patched together the bits and pieces of territory that had been under foreign rule for decades, enjoyed a diverse ethnic mix—including Germans, Russians, Ukrainians,

Lithuanians, and an enormous Jewish minority. A third of Poland spoke no Polish.

This interwar period was particularly good to the Jewish people. Jews were, for the first time, legally protected citizens of Poland, with full voting rights. Cities like Warsaw, Kraków, and Wilno (today's Vilnius, Lithuania)—where Jews made up a quarter to a third of the population—saw the blossoming of a rich Jewish culture.

Meanwhile, the historic Baltic port city of Gdańsk—which was bicultural (German and Polish)—was granted the special "Free City of Danzig" status to avoid dealing with the prickly issue of whether to assign it to Germany or Poland. But the peace was not to last.

World War II

On September 1, 1939, Adolf Hitler began World War II by attacking Danzig to bring it into the German fold. Before the month was out, Hitler's forces had overrun Poland, and the Soviets had taken over a swath of eastern Poland (today part of Ukraine, Belarus, and Lithuania).

The Nazis considered the Poles *slawische Untermenschen,* "Slavic sub-humans" who were useful only for manual labor. And Poland was also home to a huge population of Jewish people. Nazi Germany annexed Polish regions that it claimed historic ties to, while the rest (including "Warschau" and "Krakau") became a puppet state ruled by the *Generalgouvernement* and Hitler's handpicked governor, Hans Frank. The Nazis considered this area *Lebensraum*—"living space" that wasn't nice enough to actually incorporate into Germany, but served perfectly as extra territory for building things that Germans didn't want in their backyards...such as the notorious death camp, Auschwitz-Birkenau.

The Poles anxiously awaited the promised military aid of France and Britain; when help failed to arrive, they took matters into their own hands, forming a ragtag "Polish Home Army" and staging incredibly courageous but lopsided battles against their powerful German overlords (such as the Warsaw Uprising). Throughout the spring of 1945, as the Nazis retreated from their failed invasion of the Soviet Union, the Red Army gradually "liberated" the rubble of Poland from Nazi oppression—guaranteeing it another four decades of oppression under another regime.

During World War II, occupied Poland had the strictest laws in the Nazi realm: This was the only place where, if you were caught trying to help Jews escape, your entire family could be executed. And yet, many Poles risked their lives to help escapees.

With six million deaths over six years—including both Polish Jews and ethnic Poles—Poland suffered the worst per-capita

WWII losses of any nation. By the war's end, one out of every five Polish citizens was dead—and 90 percent of those killed were civilians. While the human and infrastructure loss of World War II was incalculable, that war's cultural losses were also devastating—for example, some 60,000 paintings were lost.

At the war's end, the victorious Allies shifted Poland's borders significantly westward—folding historically German areas into Polish territory and appropriating previously Polish areas for the USSR. This prompted a massive movement of populations—which today we'd decry as "ethnic cleansing"—as Germans were forcibly removed from western Poland, and Poles from newly Soviet territory were transplanted to Poland proper. Entire cities were repopulated (such as the formerly German metropolis of Breslau, which was renamed Wrocław and filled with refugee Poles from Lwów, now Lviv, in Ukraine). After millions died in the war, millions more were displaced from their ancestral homes. When the dust settled, Poland was almost exclusively populated by Poles.

Saddle on a Cow: Poland Under Communism

Poland suffered horribly under the communists. A postwar intimidation regime was designed to frighten people "on board" and coincided with government seizure of private property, rationing, and food shortages. The country enjoyed a relatively open society under Premier Władysław Gomułka in the 1960s, but the impractical, centrally planned economy began to unravel in the 1970s. Stores were marked by long lines stretching around the block.

The little absurdities of communist life—which today seem almost comical—made every day a struggle. For years, every elderly woman in Poland had hair the same strange magenta color. There was only one color of dye available, so if you had dyed hair, the choice was simple: Let your hair grow out (and look clownishly half red and half white), or line up and go red.

During these difficult times, the Poles often rose up—staging major protests in 1956, 1968, 1970, and 1976. Stalin famously noted that introducing communism to the Poles was like putting a saddle on a cow.

When an anticommunist Polish cardinal named Karol Wojtyła (later known as St. John Paul II) was elected pope in 1978, then visited his homeland in 1979, it was a sign to his countrymen that change was in the air. In 1980, Lech Wałęsa, an electrician at the shipyards in Gdańsk, became the leader of the Solidarity movement, the first workers' union in communist Eastern Europe. After an initial 18-day strike at the Gdańsk shipyards, the communist regime gave in, legalizing Solidarity.

But the union grew too powerful, and the communists felt their control slipping away. On Sunday, December 13, 1981, Po-

The Heritage of Communism

While communism is an ugly memory for most Poles, those who were teenagers when it ended—with only gauzy memories of communist times, and no experience grappling with its adult realities—have some nostalgia. A friend who was 13 in 1989 recalled those days this way:

"My childhood is filled with happy memories. Under communism, life was family-oriented. Careers didn't matter. There was no way to get rich, no reason to rush, so we had time. People always had time.

"But there were also shortages. We stood in line not knowing what would be for sale. We'd buy whatever shoes were available and then trade for the right size. At grocery stores, vinegar and mustard were always on the shelf, along with plastic cheese to make it seem less empty. We had to carry ration coupons, which we'd present when buying a staple that was in short supply. We didn't necessarily buy what we needed—just anything that could be bartered on the black market. I remember my mother and father had to 'organize' for special events...somehow find a good sausage and some Coca-Cola.

"Instead of a tidy roll of toilet paper, bathrooms came with a wad of old newspapers. Sometimes my uncle would bring us several toilet paper rolls, held together with a string—the best gift anyone could give.

"Boys in my neighborhood collected pop cans. Cans from other countries represented a world of opportunities beyond our borders. Parents could buy these cans on the black market, and the few families who were allowed to travel returned home with a treasure trove of cans. One boy up the street from me went to Italy, and proudly brought home a Pepsi can. Everyone wanted to see this huge status symbol. But a month later, communism ended, you could buy whatever you wanted, and everyone's can collections were worthless.

"We had real chocolate only for Christmas. The rest of the year, we got something called 'chocolate-like product,' which was sweet, dark, and smelled vaguely of chocolate. And we had oranges from Cuba for Christmas, too. Everybody was excited when the newspapers announced, 'The boat with the oranges from Cuba is just five days away.' The smell of Christmas was so special: chocolate and oranges. Now we have that smell every day. Still, my happiest Christmases were under communism."

land's head of state, General Wojciech Jaruzelski, declared martial law in order to "forestall Soviet intervention." (Whether the Soviets actually would have invaded remains a hotly debated issue.) Tanks ominously rolled through the streets of Poland on that snowy December morning, and the Poles were terrified.

Martial law lasted until 1983. Each Pole has chilling memories of this frightening time. During riots, the people would flock into churches—the only place they could be safe from the ZOMO (riot police). People would go for their evening walks during the 19:30 government-sanctioned national news as a sign of protest. But Solidarity struggled on, going underground and becoming a united movement of all demographics, 10 million members strong (more than a quarter of the population).

In July 1989, the ruling Communist Party agreed to hold open elections (reserving 65 percent of representatives for themselves). Their goal was to appease Solidarity, but the plan backfired: Communists didn't win a single contested seat. These elections helped spark the chain reaction across Eastern Europe that eventually tore down the Iron Curtain. Lech Wałęsa became Poland's first post-communist president.

Poland in the 21st Century

When 10 new countries joined the European Union in May 2004, Poland was the most ambivalent of the bunch. After centuries of being under other empires' authority, the Poles were hardly eager to relinquish some of their hard-fought autonomy to Brussels. Many Poles thought that EU membership would make things worse (higher prices, a loss of traditional lifestyles) before they got better. But most people agreed that their country had to join to survive in today's Europe.

The most obvious initial impact of EU membership was the droves of job-seeking young Poles who migrated to other EU countries (mostly Britain, Ireland, and Sweden, which were the first to waive visa requirements for Eastern European workers). Many found employment at hotels and restaurants. In the mid-aughts, visitors to London and Dublin noticed a surprising language barrier at hotel front desks, and Polish-language expat newspapers joined British gossip rags on newsstands. Those who remained in Poland were concerned about the "brain drain" of bright young people flocking out of their country. But with the economic crisis, quite a few Polish expats returned home. And as Britain moves to leave the EU (Brexit), Poland will likely see another wave of returnees.

Poland is by far the most populous of the Eastern European EU members, with nearly 39 million people (about the same as Spain, or about half the size of Germany). This makes Poland the

POLAND

Polish Jokes

Through the dreary communist times, the Poles managed to keep their sense of humor. A popular target of jokes was the riot police, called the ZOMO. Here are just a few of the things Poles said about these unpopular cops:

- ZOMO police are hired based on the 90-90 principle: They have to weigh at least 90 kilograms (200 pounds), and their I.Q. must be less than 90.
- ZOMO are dispatched in teams of three: one who can read, one who can write, and a third to protect those other two smart guys.
- A ZOMO policeman was sitting on the curb, crying. Someone came up to him and asked what was wrong. "I lost my dog!" he said. "No matter," the person replied. "He's a smart police dog. I'm sure he can find his way back to the station." "Yes," the ZOMO said. "But without him, I can't!"

The communists gave their people no options at elections: If you voted, you voted for the regime. Poles liked to joke that in some ways, this made communists like God—who created Eve, then said to Adam, "Now choose a wife." It was said that communists could run a pig as a candidate, and it would still win; a popular symbol of dissent became a pig painted with the words "Vote Red."

There were even jokes about jokes. Under communism, Poles noted that there was a government-sponsored prize for the funniest political joke: 15 years in prison.

sixth largest of the 26 EU member states—giving it serious political clout, which it has already asserted...sometimes to the dismay of the EU's more established powers.

On the American political spectrum, Poland may be the most conservative country in Europe. Poles are phobic when it comes to "big government"—likely because they've been subjugated and manipulated by so many foreign oppressors over the centuries. For most of the 2000s, the country's right wing was represented by a pair of twin brothers, Lech and Jarosław Kaczyński. (The Kaczyński brothers were child actors who appeared in several popular movies together.) Their conservative Law and Justice Party (PiS for short) is pro-tax cuts, fiercely Euroskeptic (anti-EU), and very Catholic. In the 2005 presidential election, Lech Kaczyński emerged as the victor; several months later, he took the controversial step of appointing his identical twin brother Jarosław as Poland's prime minister.

The political pendulum swung back toward the center in October 2007, when the Kaczyński brothers' main political rival, the pro-EU Donald Tusk, led his Civic Platform Party to victory in the parliamentary elections. The name Kaczyński loosely means "duck"—so the Poles quipped that they were led by "Donald and the Ducks."

Tragically, the levity wasn't to last. On April 10, 2010, a plane carrying President Lech Kaczyński crashed in a thick fog near the city of Smolensk, Russia. All 96 people on board—including top government, military, and business officials, high-ranking clergy, and others—were killed, plunging the nation into a period of stunned mourning. Poles wondered why, yet again, an unprecedented tragedy had befallen their nation. (Ironically, the group's trip was intended to put a painful chapter of Poland's history to rest: a commemoration of the Polish officers and enlisted men killed in the Soviet massacre at Katyń.)

Meanwhile, Poland's economy kept chugging along, even as the rest of Europe and much of the world were bogged down by the economic crisis. More than a quarter of Poland's trade is with neighboring Germany—another of Europe's healthiest economies—and Poland was the only European Union country that didn't have a recession in 2009. Why? Poland is a big, self-sustaining, insular economy. (Although in recent years, Poland's relatively weak currency—"cheaper" than the euro, yet also shielded from euro volatility—and robust economy have lured foreign investment, paradoxically threatening that autonomy.)

Over the last decade, the political pendulum has just kept on swinging, as key governmental posts have gone back and forth between the two dominant parties—the Civic Platform (which controlled parliament 2007-2015) and Law and Justice (2015-present).

Since taking power, Law and Justice—chaired by Jarosław Kaczyński—has come under fire for policies that many observers have termed "nationalistic" and borderline-authoritarian (in the vein of Viktor Orbán's Fidesz in Hungary, or Donald Trump in the US). They've packed the ostensibly autonomous Constitutional Tribunal with party loyalists, purged opposition civil servants and military leaders, levied fines against critical news coverage in a manner that threatens freedom of the press, and removed the director of the brand-new Museum of the Second World War in Gdańsk—deeming the exhibit "not Polish enough" and installing a new director who altered many of the exhibits. Because of these and other concerns, in late 2017, the EU initiated Article 7 of the EU Treaty for the first time—stripping Poland of some of its voting rights within the EU. (Hungary has sided with Poland in the dispute, triggering the invocation of Article 7 against itself as well.)

In a high-profile act that drew vocal international criticism, in summer 2018, Law and Order removed 27 long-serving judges (approximately one-third of the top judiciary) from Poland's Supreme Court. While the party insisted they were simply rooting out corruption (claiming those judges were holdovers of the communist

POLAND

Bar Mleczny (Milk Bar)

When you see a "bar" in Poland, it doesn't mean alcohol—it means cheap grub. Eating at a *bar mleczny* (bar MLECH-neh) is an essential Polish sightseeing experience. These cafeterias, which you'll see all over the country, are an incredibly cheap way to get a good meal...and, with the right attitude, a fun cultural experience.

In the communist era, the government subsidized the food at milk bars, allowing workers to enjoy a meal out. The name comes from the cheese cutlets that were sold here, back in a time when good meat was rare. The tradition continues today, as milk-bar prices remain astoundingly low: about $5 for a filling meal. And, while communist-era fare was gross, today's milk-bar cuisine is usually quite tasty.

Milk bars usually offer many of the traditional tastes listed in the "Polish food" section. Common items are soups (such as *żurek* and *barszcz*), a variety of cabbage-based salads, *kotlet* (fried pork chops), pierogi (similar to ravioli, with various fillings), and *naleśniki* (pancakes). You'll see glasses of juice and (of course) milk, but most milk bars also stock bottles of water and Coke.

There are two types of milk bars: updated, modern cafeterias that cater to tourists (English menus), add some modern twists to their traditional fare, and charge about 50 percent more; and time-machine dives that haven't changed for decades. At truly traditional milk bars, the service is aimed at locals, which means no English menu and a confusing ordering system.

Every milk bar is a little different, but here's the general procedure: Head to the counter, wait to be acknowledged, and point to what you want. Handy vocabulary: *to* (sounds like "toe") means "this"; *i* (pronounced "ee") means "and."

If the milk-bar lady asks you any questions, you have three options: Nod stupidly until she just gives you something; repeat one of the things she just said (assuming she's asked you to choose between two options, like meat or cheese in your pierogi); or hope that a kindly English-speaking Pole in line will leap to your rescue. If nothing else, ordering at a milk bar is an adventure in gestures. Smiling seems to slightly extend the patience of milk-bar staffers.

Once your tray is all loaded up, pay the cashier, do a double-take when you realize how cheap your bill is, then find a table. After the meal, bus your own dishes to the little window.

system), tens of thousands of Poles filled the streets of cities and towns in protest. All of this has raised troubling questions about the long-term viability of Polish democracy, and about Poland's role within the EU.

And yet, at the same time, Donald Tusk—Poland's former prime minister and most high-profile left-leaning politician—has become a major player in the EU government; in 2017, he was re-elected to his second term as the president of the European Council. It remains to be seen where the Polish political pendulum swings next. But one thing is clear: The Poles—although a bit late to the party—are making their presence felt in European politics.

POLISH FOOD

Polish food is hearty and tasty. Because Poland is north of the Carpathian Mountains, its weather tends to be chilly, limiting the kinds of fruits and vegetables that flourish here. As in other northern European countries (such as Russia or Scandinavia), dominant staples include potatoes, dill, berries, beets, and rye. Much of what you might think of as "Jewish cuisine" turns up on Polish menus (gefilte

fish, potato pancakes, chicken soup, and so forth)—which makes sense, given that Poles and Jews lived in the same area for centuries.

Polish soups are a highlight. The most typical are *żurek* and *barszcz*. *Żurek* (often translated as "sour soup" on menus) is a thickened, light-colored soup made from a sourdough base, usually containing a hard-boiled egg and pieces of *kiełbasa* (sausage). *Barszcz*, better known to Americans as borscht, is a savory beet soup that you'll see in several varieties: *Barszcz czerwony* (red borscht) is a thin, flavorful broth with a deep red color, sometimes containing dumplings or a hard-boiled egg. *Barszcz ukraiński* (Ukrainian borscht) is thicker, with cream and vegetables (usually cabbage, beans, and carrots). In summer, try the "Polish gazpacho"—*chłodnik*, a savory cream soup with beets, onions, and radishes that's served cold. I never met a Polish soup I didn't like...until I was introduced to *flaki* (sometimes *flaczki*)—tripe soup.

Another familiar Polish dish is pierogi. These ravioli-like dumplings come with various fillings. The most traditional are minced meat, sauerkraut, mushroom, cheese, and blueberry; many restaurants also experiment with more exotic fillings. Pierogi are often served with specks of fatty bacon to add flavor. Pierogi are a

POLAND

budget traveler's dream: Restaurants serving them are everywhere, and they're generally cheap, tasty, and very filling.

Bigos is a rich and delicious sauerkraut stew cooked with meat, mushrooms, and whatever's in the pantry. It's sort of the Polish version of chili—it's a beloved comfort food, especially in the cold of winter, and everyone has their own recipe. *Gołąbki* is a dish of cabbage leaves stuffed with minced meat and rice in a tomato or mushroom sauce. *Kotlet schabowy* (fried pork chop)—once painfully scarce in communist Poland—remains a local favorite to this day.

Kaczka (duck) is popular, as is freshwater fish: Look for *pstrąg* (trout), *karp* (carp, beware of bones), and *węgorz* (eel). On the Baltic Coast (such as in Gdańsk), you'll also see *łosoś* (salmon), *śledź* (herring), and *dorsz* (cod). Poles eat lots of potatoes, which are served with nearly every meal. Look for *placki ziemniaczane*—potato pancakes.

Some dreary old foods are newly hip in today's Poland. Herring-and-vodka bars are trendy, many following the "4/8 model"—4 zł for a shot of vodka, 8 zł for a herring snack. The Polish street food *zapiekanka*—a toasted baguette with melted cheese, rubbery mushrooms from a can, and a drizzle of ersatz ketchup—began life as a "hardship food" under communism, as a pale imitation of pizza. These days it has been reborn as a street-food staple; *zapiekanka* vendors top them with a world of creative flavors. The bagel-like rings you'll see sold on the street, *obwarzanki* (singular *obwarzanek*), are also cheap, and usually fresh and tasty. And, as throughout Europe, gourmet hamburgers are in—including a trend for vegan burgers.

Poland has good pastries—look for a *cukiernia* (pastry shop). The classic Polish treat is *pączki*, glazed jelly doughnuts. They can have different fillings, but most typical is a wild-rose jam. *Szarlotka* is apple cake—sometimes made with chunks of apples (especially in season), sometimes with apple filling. *Sernik* is cheesecake, and *makowiec* is poppy-seed cake. *Winebreda* is an especially gooey Danish. *Babeczka* is like a cupcake filled with pudding. And *Napoleonka* is a French-style treat with layers of crispy wafers and custard.

Lody (ice cream) is popular. The tall, skinny cones of soft-serve ice cream are called *świderki*, sometimes translated as "American ice cream." The most beloved traditional candy is *ptasie mleczko* (birds' milk), which is semisour marshmallow covered with chocolate. E. Wedel is the country's top brand of chocolate, with outlets in all the big cities.

Thirsty? *Woda* is water, *woda mineralna* is bottled water (*gazowana* is with gas, *niegazowana* is without), *kawa* is coffee, *herbata* is tea, *sok* is juice, and *mleko* is milk. Żywiec, Okocim, and Lech are the best-known brands of *piwo* (beer).

Wódka (vodka) is a Polish staple—the word means, roughly, "precious little water." Żubrówka, the most famous brand of vodka, comes with a blade of grass from the bison reserves in eastern Poland (look for the bison on the label). The bison "flavor" the grass...then the grass flavors the vodka. Poles often mix Żubrówka with apple juice, and call this cocktail *szarlotka* ("apple cake"). For "Cheers!" say, *"Na zdrowie!"* (nah ZDROH-vyeh).

Unusual drinks to try if you have the chance are *kwas* (a cold, fizzy, Ukrainian-style nonalcoholic beverage made from day-old rye bread) and *kompot* (a hot drink made from stewed berries). Poles are unusually fond of carrot juice (often cut with fruit juice); Kubuś is the most popular brand.

"Bon appétit" is *"Smacznego"* (smatch-NEH-goh). To pay, ask for the *rachunek* (rah-KHOO-nehk).

POLISH LANGUAGE

Polish is closely related to its neighboring Slavic languages (Slovak and Czech), with the biggest difference being that Polish has lots of fricatives (hissing sounds—"sh" and "ch"—often in close proximity).

Polish intimidates Americans with long, difficult-to-pronounce words. But if you take your time and sound things out, you'll quickly develop an ear for it. One rule of thumb to help you out: The stress is generally on the next-to-last syllable.

Polish has some letters that don't appear in English, and some letters and combinations are pronounced differently than in English:

ć, ci, and **cz** all sound like "ch" as in "church"
ś, si, and **sz** all sound like "sh" as in "short"
ż, ź, zi, and **rz** all sound like "zh" as in "leisure"
dż and **dź** both sound like the "dj" sound in "jeans"
ń and **ni** sound like "ny" as in "canyon"
ę and **ą** are pronounced nasally, as in French: "e*n*" and "a*n*"
c sounds like "ts" as in "cats"
ch sounds like "kh" as in the Scottish "loch"
j sounds like "y" as in "yellow"
w sounds like "v" as in "Victor"
ł sounds like "w" as in "with"

So to Poles, "Lech Wałęsa" isn't pronounced "lehk wah-LEH-sah," as Americans tend to say—but "lehkh vah-WEHN-sah."

The Polish people you meet will be impressed and flattered if you take the time to learn a little of their language. To get started, check out the selection of Polish survival phrases on the following pages.

As you're tracking down addresses, these words will help: *miasto* (mee-AH-stoh, town), *plac* (plahts, square), *rynek* (REE-nehk, big market square), *ulica* (OO-leet-sah, road), *aleja* (ah-LAY-yah, avenue), and *most* (mohst, bridge). And that long word you see everywhere—*zapraszamy*—means "welcome."

POLAND

Polish Survival Phrases

Keep in mind a few Polish pronunciation tips: **w** sounds like "v," **ł** sounds like "w," **ch** is a back-of-your-throat "kh" sound (as in the Scottish "loch"), and **rz** sounds like the "zh" sound in "pleasure." The vowels with a tail (**ą** and **ę**) have a slight nasal "n" sound at the end, similar to French.

English	Polish	Pronunciation
Hello. (formal)	Dzień dobry.	jehn **doh**-brih
Hi. / Bye. (informal)	Cześć.	cheshch
Do you speak English? (asked of a man)	Czy Pan mówi po angielsku?	chih pahn **moo**-vee poh ahn-**gyehl**-skoo
Do you speak English? (asked of a woman)	Czy Pani mówi po angielsku?	chih **pah**-nee **moo**-vee poh ahn-**gyehl**-skoo
Yes. / No.	Tak. / Nie.	tahk / nyeh
I (don't) understand.	(Nie) rozumiem.	(nyeh) roh-**zoo**-myehm
Please. / You're welcome. / Can I help you?	Proszę.	**proh**-sheh
Thank you (very much).	Dziękuję (bardzo).	jehn-**koo**-yeh (**bard**-zoh)
Excuse me. / I'm sorry.	Przepraszam.	psheh-**prah**-shahm
(No) problem.	(Żaden) problem.	(**zhah**-dehn) **proh**-blehm
Good.	Dobrze.	**dohb**-zheh
Goodbye.	Do widzenia.	doh veed-**zay**-nyah
one / two / three	jeden / dwa / trzy	**yeh**-dehn / dvah / tzhih
four / five / six	cztery / pięć / sześć	**chteh**-rih / pyench / sheshch
seven / eight	siedem / osiem	**shyeh**-dehm / **oh**-shehm
nine / ten	dziewięć / dziesięć	**jeh**-vyench / **jeh**-shench
hundred / thousand	sto / tysiąc	stoh / **tih**-shants
How much?	Ile?	**ee**-leh
local currency	złoty (zł)	**zwoh**-tih
Write it.	Napisz to.	**nah**-peesh toh
Is it free?	Czy to jest za darmo?	chih toh yehst zah **dar**-moh
Is it included?	Czy jest to wliczone?	chih yehst toh vlee-**choh**-neh
Where can I find / buy...?	Gdzie mogę dostać / kupić...?	guh-**dyeh** moh-geh **doh**-statch / **koo**-peech
I'd like... (said by a man)	Chciałbym...	**khchaw**-beem
I'd like... (said by a woman)	Chciałabym...	**khchah**-wah-beem
We'd like...	Chcielibyśmy...	**khchehl**-ee-bish-mih
...a room.	...pokój.	**poh**-kooy
...a ticket to ___.	...bilet do ___.	**bee**-leht doh ___
Is it possible?	Czy jest to możliwe?	chih yehst toh mohzh-**lee**-veh
Where is...?	Gdzie jest...?	guh-**dyeh** yehst
...the train station	...dworzec kolejowy	**dvoh**-zhehts koh-leh-**yoh**-vih
...the bus station	...dworzec autobusowy	**dvoh**-zhehts ow-toh-boos-**oh**-vih
...the tourist information office	...informacja turystyczna	een-for-**maht**-syah too-ris-**titch**-nah
...the toilet	...toaleta	toh-ah-**leh**-tah
men / women	męska / damska	**mehn**-skah / **dahm**-skah
left / right / straight	lewo / prawo / prosto	**leh**-voh / **prah**-voh / **proh**-stoh
At what time...?	O której godzinie...?	oh kuh-**too**-ray gohd-**zhee**-nyeh
...does this open / close	...będzie otwarte / zamknięte	**bend**-zheh oht-**vahr**-teh / zahm-**knyehn**-teh
Just a moment.	Chwileczkę.	khvee-**letch**-keh
now / soon / later	teraz / niedługo / później	**teh**-rahz / nyed-**woo**-goh / **poozh**-nyey
today / tomorrow	dzisiaj / jutro	**jee**-shigh / **yoo**-troh

POLAND

In a Polish Restaurant

English	Polish	Pronunciation
I'd like to reserve... (said by a man)	Chciałbym zarezerwować...	khchaw-beem zah-reh-zehr-voh-vahch
I'd like to reserve... (said by a woman)	Chciałabym zarezerwować...	khchah-wah-beem zah-reh-zehr-voh-vahch
We'd like to reserve...	Chcielibyśmy zarezerwować...	khchehl-ee-bish-mih zah-reh-zehr-voh-vahch
...a table for one person / two people.	...stolik na jedną osobę / dwie osoby.	stoh-leek nah yehd-now oh-soh-beh / dvyeh oh-soh-bih
Is this table free?	Czy ten stolik jest wolny?	chih tehn stoh-leek yehst vohl-nih
Can I help you?	W czym mogę pomóc?	vchim moh-geh poh-moots
The menu (in English), please.	Menu (po angielsku), proszę.	meh-noo (poh ahn-gyehl-skoo) proh-sheh
service (not) included	usługa (nie) wliczona	oos-woo-gah (nyeh) vlee-choh-nah
cover charge	wstęp	vstenp
"to go"	na wynos	nah vih-nohs
with / without	z / bez	z / behz
and / or	i / lub	ee / loob
milk bar (cheap cafeteria)	bar mleczny	bar mletch-nih
fixed-price meal (of the day)	zestaw (dnia)	zehs-tahv (dih-nyah)
specialty of the house	specjalność zakładu	speht-syahl-nohshch zah-kwah-doo
half portion	pół porcji	poow ports-yee
daily special	danie dnia	dah-nyeh dih-nyah
appetizers	przystawki	pshih-stahv-kee
bread	chleb	khlehb
cheese	ser	sehr
sandwich	kanapka	kah-nahp-kah
soup	zupa	zoo-pah
salad	sałatka	sah-waht-kah
meat / poultry	mięso / drób	myehn-soh / droob
fish / seafood	ryba / owoce morza	rih-bah / oh-voht-seh moh-zhah
fruit / vegetables	owoce / warzywa	oh-voht-seh / vah-zhih-vah
dessert	deser	deh-sehr
(tap) water	woda (z kranu)	voh-dah (skrah-noo)
mineral water	woda mineralna	voh-dah mee-neh-rahl-nah
carbonated / not carbonated	gazowana / niegazowana	gah-zoh-vah-nah / nyeh-gah-zoh-vah-nah
milk	mleko	mleh-koh
(orange) juice	sok (pomarańczowy)	sohk (poh-mah-rayn-choh-vih)
coffee / tea	kawa / herbata	kah-vah / hehr-bah-tah
wine	wino	vee-noh
red / white	czerwone / białe	chehr-voh-neh / bee-ah-weh
sweet / dry / semi-dry	słodkie / wytrawne / półwytrawne	swoht-kyeh / vih-trahv-neh / poow-vih-trahv-neh
glass / bottle	szklanka / butelka	shklahn-kah / boo-tehl-kah
beer	piwo	pee-voh
vodka	wódka	vood-kah
Cheers!	Na zdrowie!	nah zdroh-vyeh
Enjoy your meal.	Smacznego.	smatch-neh-goh
More. / Another.	Więcej. / Inny.	vyehnt-say / ee-nih-nih
The same.	Taki sam.	tah-kee sahm
the bill	rachunek	rah-khoo-nehk
I'll pay.	Ja płacę.	yah pwaht-seh
tip	napiwek	nah-pee-vehk
Delicious!	Pyszne!	pish-neh

KRAKÓW

Kraków is easily Poland's best destination: a beautiful, old-fashioned city buzzing with history, enjoyable sights, tourists, and college students. Even though the country's capital moved from here to Warsaw 400 years ago, Kraków remains Poland's cultural and intellectual center. Increasingly (and justifiably) popular, Kraków is giving Prague a run for its money on the "must visit" tourist route.

What's so special about it? First off, Kraków is simply charming; more than any town in Europe, it seems made for aimless strolling. And its historic walls and former moat corral an unusually full range of activities and interests: bustling university life; thought-provoking museums; breathtaking churches that evoke a powerful faith (and include many sights relating to Poland's favorite son, St. John Paul II); sprawling parks that invite you to just relax; vivid Jewish heritage sights; a burgeoning foodie and nightlife scene; and compelling side trips to the most notorious Holocaust site anywhere (Auschwitz-Birkenau), a communist-planned workers town, and a mine filled with salty statues. With so many opportunities to learn, to have fun, or to do both at once, it's no surprise that Kraków has become a world-class destination.

PLANNING YOUR TIME

Don't skimp on your time in Kraków. It takes a minimum of two days to experience the city, and a third (or even a fourth) day lets you dig in and consider a world of fascinating side trips.

Almost everyone coming to Kraków also visits the Auschwitz-Birkenau Concentration Camp Memorial—and should. As it's about an hour and a half away, this demands the better part of a day to fully appreciate (either as a round-trip from Kraków, or en route to or from another destination). Visiting Auschwitz requires a reservation, which should be arranged long in advance.

If you have only two full days (the "express plan"), start off with my self-guided walk through the Old Town and a quick stroll up to Wawel Castle, then head over to the Schindler's Factory Museum and wind down your day in Kazimierz. Your second day is for a side trip to Auschwitz. This plan gives you a once-over-lightly look at Kraków, but leaves almost no time for entering the sights.

More time buys you the chance to relax, enjoy, and linger: Tackle the Old Town and Wawel Castle on the first day, Kazimierz and museums of your choice on the second day, and Auschwitz (and other side trips) with additional days. If you have a special interest, you could side-trip to the St. John Paul II pilgrimage sites on the outskirts of town, or to the communist architecture of the Nowa Huta suburb. Wieliczka Salt Mine is another crowd-pleasing, half-day option.

Regardless of how long you stay, your evening choices are many and varied: Savor the Main Market Square over dinner or a drink, take in a jazz show, do a pub crawl through the city's many youthful bars and clubs (best in Kazimierz), or enjoy traditional Jewish music and cuisine (also in Kazimierz).

Orientation to Kraków

Kraków (Poles say KROCK-oof, but you can say KRACK-cow; it's sometimes spelled "Cracow" in English) is mercifully compact, flat, and easy to navigate. While the urban sprawl is big (with 767,000 people), the tourist's Kraków feels small—from the main square, you can walk to just about everything of interest in less than 15 minutes. Just to the south is Poland's main river, the Vistula (Wisła, VEES-wah).

Most sights—and almost all recommended hotels and restaurants—are in the **Old Town** (Stare Miasto, STAH-reh mee-AH-stoh), which is surrounded by a greenbelt called the Planty (PLAHN-tee). In the center of the Old Town lies the Main Market Square (Rynek Główny, REE-nehk GWOHV-nee)—it's such an important landmark, I call it simply "the Square." At the Old Town's northeast corner, just outside the ring road, is the main train station. And at the southern end of the Old Town, on the riverbank, is the hill called **Wawel** (VAH-vehl)—with a historic castle, museums, and Poland's national church.

About a 20-minute walk (or quick tram/taxi ride) southeast of the Square is the neighborhood called **Kazimierz** (kah-ZHEE-mehzh)—with Jewish landmarks and Holocaust sites (including the Schindler's Factory Museum) and the city's best foodie and nightlife area.

A few more attractions are just beyond the core, including the St. John Paul II pilgrimage sites (in the Łagiewniki neighborhood), the communist-planned town of Nowa Huta, Wieliczka Salt Mine, and the Kościuszko Mound.

TOURIST INFORMATION

Kraków has many helpful TIs, called InfoKraków (*www.infokrakow.pl*). Five branches are in or near the Old Town (all open daily May-Sept 9:00-19:00, Oct-April until 17:00, unless otherwise noted):

• In the **Planty** park, between the main train station and Main Market Square (in round kiosk at ulica Szpitalna 25, tel. 12-354-2720)

• On **ulica Św. Jana,** just north of the Main Market Square (specializes in concert tickets, daily year-round 9:00-19:00, at #2, tel. 12-354-2725)

• In the **Cloth Hall** right on the Main Market Square (tel. 12-354-2716)

• In the **Wyspiański Pavilion,** just south of the Square on ulica Grodzka (daily 9:00-17:00, plac Wszystkich Świętych 3, not at the window but inside the building, tel. 12-354-2723)

• Just west of **Wawel Hill** (also covers the entire region, Powiśle 11, tel. 12-354-2710)

Other TI branches are in **Kazimierz** (daily 9:00-17:00, ulica Józefa 7, tel. 12-354-2728) and the **airport** (daily 9:00-19:00, tel. 12-285-5341).

Note that the TIs sell tickets for *only* one tour company, See Kraków; for additional options, see "Tours in Kraków," later, and look around online.

Sightseeing Pass: The TI's **Kraków Tourist Card** includes admission to 40 city museums (basically everything except the Wawel Hill sights and Wieliczka Salt Mine)—but admissions are so cheap, it's unlikely you'd save money with the card. Given how walkable Kraków is, the version that does not include public transit is a better value than the one that does.

Warning: Many private travel agencies, room-booking services, and tour operators masquerade as TIs, with deceptive blue-and-white *i* signs. If I haven't listed them in this section, they're not a real TI.

Kraków City History Museum's Visitors Center: Tucked in the Cloth Hall (on the quiet western side) is a little information office operated by the Kraków City History Museum, where you can book tickets, without a line, for the popular Schindler's Factory Museum and Rynek Underground Museum. If you anticipate

KRAKÓW

Kraków's Old Town

Sights
1. John Paul II Wawel Cathedral Museum
2. Sandomierska Tower
3. Royal State Rooms
4. Royal Private Apartments
5. Oriental Art
6. Crown Treasury & Armory
7. Lost Wawel Museum
8. Gallery of 19th-Century Polish Art (Entrance)
9. Rynek Underground Museum Entrance

Services & Other
10. Kraków City Museum Visitors Center
11. Wieliczka Promotion Office
12. Massolit Books
13. Frania Café/Laundry
14. Betty Clean Laundry
15. Kraków Bike Tours & Rental
16. KRK Bike Rental
17. Trams #3 & #24 to/from Kazimierz (3)

KRAKÓW

Don't Miss Out!
Book Key Sights in Advance

A few popular Kraków attractions can fill up at busy times, and it pays to reserve ahead. If you're going to **Auschwitz,** book as far in advance as possible—ideally three months ahead (details in the next chapter). In Kraków, during very busy times you'll want to reserve several days ahead for **Schindler's Factory Museum,** the **Wieliczka Salt Mine,** and the **Rynek Underground Museum** (in roughly that order of popularity). You can only book up to three days in advance online—but in person, you can prebook even the same day for Schindler and Rynek, at the ticket office in the Cloth Hall—see "Tourist Information," earlier.

What constitutes **"busy times"?** Summers and weekends are the most crowded, reaching a peak during Poland's many long summer holiday weekends (Labor Day and Constitution Day, May 1-3; Corpus Christi, usually in late May or early June; and Assumption, Aug 15). If coming at these times, anticipate crowds and book well ahead.

crowds at either museum—particularly likely on the free day for each one (Mon and Tue, respectively), or on summer weekends—drop by this office to book an entry time (daily 10:00-19:00, until 20:00 in summer, at #1).

ARRIVAL IN KRAKÓW
By Train

Kraków's main train station (called "Kraków Główny," KROCK-oof GWOHV-nee) sits just northeast of the Old Town, adjoining the sprawling Galeria Krakowska shopping mall. The station and the mall face a broad plaza (plac Dworcowy) across the ring road from the Planty park and Old Town. My recommended Old Town hotels are within about a 15- to 20-minute walk, or a quick tram or taxi ride. (If you're staying in the Old Town, the tram doesn't save you much time; for those staying in Kazimierz—a 30-minute walk away—the tram is definitely worthwhile.)

The main concourse has all of the amenities: ATMs, lockers (under the big schedule board between the ticket windows), WCs, takeaway coffee, and a handy Biedronka minisupermarket. From this area, five numbered escalators lead up to the corresponding train platforms. If you need to buy tickets, tucked under the escalators is a long row of numbered ticket windows (some for domestic tickets only, others for domestic and international—check signs before you line up; a few are marked with UK flags to denote English-speaking staff). In the middle of the ticket windows (between #11 and #12) is the PKP Passenger Service Center, which may have a longer wait but is more likely to have staff who speak English (no extra fee). Remember, you can also buy most tickets online (*www.rozklad-pkp.pl*)—saving you a trip to the station or a long wait in line.

Getting Between the Station and Downtown: The easiest option is to take a **taxi** (they wait in the parking lot on the station's rooftop—go up the stairs or elevator from your platform). The usual metered rate to downtown is a reasonable 10-15 zł; only take a taxi marked with a company name and telephone number. You can also order an **Uber,** which is often cheaper (see "Getting Around Kraków," later).

If you prefer to walk or take a tram, you first must navigate the Galeria Krakowska shopping mall. Begin by following *Exit to the City* signs. Once inside the mall, continue straight ahead. To **walk,** follow *Old Town* signs, which eventually route you to the left. You'll pop out at a big plaza where you'll continue straight, taking the broad ramp down into a pedestrian underpass beneath the ring road. Emerging at the other side, bear right up the ramp into the Planty. The Main Market Square is straight ahead (you'll see the twin spires of St. Mary's Church).

If you'd rather take a **tram,** continue straight ahead through the mall, following signs to *Pawia street.* Emerging here, you'll see the Dworzec Główny Zachód tram stop. Buy a ticket from the machine and hop on tram #3 in the direction of Nowy Bieżanów. This tram stops at the eastern edge of the Old Town (Poczta Główna stop) before continuing to Kazimierz (Miodowa stop). (Note: Avoid the tram stop you'll see signposted inside the station—it's served by trams that don't go anywhere near the Old Town or Kazimierz.)

There is a **shortcut** to avoid going through the sprawling and sometimes congested mall: The modern train station is attached to the old station (the yellow building facing the big plaza, now hosting art exhibitions) by a sidewalk under a green canopy. This can save you a little walking (and a lot of shopping temptations). It's tricky to find from inside the station: Go behind the Biedronka supermarket, near track 1, and exit toward Lubicz street. Walk up the ramp and follow the green canopy to the plaza.

To get **from town to the station** (or to the bus station behind it), head to the northeast corner of the Planty, take the underpass beneath the ring road, walk across the plaza and into the Galeria Krakowska mall, and once inside, follow signs to *Railway Station* and *Station Hall.*

By Bus

The bus station is directly behind the main train station. When arriving by bus, it's easiest to get into town by first heading into the

KRAKÓW

Kraków: A Snapshot History

Kraków grew wealthy from trade in the late 10th and early 11th centuries. Traders who passed through were required to stop here for a few days and sell their wares at a reduced cost. Local merchants turned around and sold those goods with big price hikes...and Kraków thrived. In 1038, it became Poland's capital.

Tatars invaded in 1241, leaving the city in ruins. Krakovians took this opportunity to rebuild their streets in a near-perfect grid, a striking contrast to the narrow, mazelike lanes of most medieval towns. The destruction also paved the way for the spectacular Main Market Square—still Kraków's best feature.

King Kazimierz the Great sparked Kraków's Golden Age in the 14th century (see the "Kazimierz the Great" sidebar, later). In 1364, he established the university that still defines the city (and counts Copernicus and St. John Paul II among its alumni).

But Kraków's power waned as Poland's political center shifted to Warsaw. In 1596, the capital officially moved north. And with the three Partitions of the late 18th century, Poland disappeared from the map and Kraków became a poor provincial backwater of Vienna.

After Napoleon briefly reshuffled Europe in the early 19th century, Kraków was granted the status of a relatively independent city-state for about 30 years. The Free City of Kraków, a tiny sliver wedged between three of Europe's mightiest empires, enjoyed an economic boom that saw the creation of the Planty park, the arrival of gas lighting and trams, and the construction of upscale suburbs outside the Old Town. Only after the unsuccessful Kraków Uprising of 1846 was the city forcefully brought back into the Austrian fold. But despite Kraków's reduced prominence, Austria's comparatively liberal climate allowed the city to become a haven for intellectuals and progressives (including a young revolutionary thinker from Russia named Vladimir Lenin).

The Nazis overran Poland in September of 1939, installing

train station, then continuing through it, following the directions on the previous page.

To get *to* the bus station from the Old Town (for example, if you need to catch a bus to Auschwitz), follow the directions above, then walk all the way through to the far end of the train station area (past platform 5, exit marked for *bus station*). Exiting the train station, escalate up to the bus terminal (marked *MDA Dworzec Autobusowy*). Inside are the standard amenities (lockers and WCs), domestic and international ticket windows, and an electronic board showing the next several departures. Some bus departures, marked on the board with a *G*, leave from the upper *(gorna)* stalls, which you can see out the window. Other bus departures, marked with a *D*, leave from the lower *(dolna)* stalls in the garage beneath your a ruling body called the *Generalgouvernement,* headed by Hans Frank. Germany wanted to quickly develop "Krakau" (as they called it) into the German capital of the nation. They renamed the Main Market Square "Adolf-Hitler-Platz," tore down statues of Polish figures (including the Adam Mickiewicz statue that dominates the Main Market Square today), and invested heavily in construction and industrialization (opening the door for Oskar Schindler to come and take over a factory from its Jewish owners). The German overlords imposed a "New Order" that included seizing businesses, rationing, and a strict curfew for Poles and Jews alike. A special set of "Jewish laws" targeted, then decimated, Poland's huge Jewish population.

Kraków's cityscape—if not its people—emerged from World War II virtually unscathed. But when the communists took over, they decided to give intellectual (and potentially dissident) Kraków an injection of good Soviet values—in the form of heavy industry. They built Nowa Huta, an enormous steelworks and planned town for workers, on Kraków's outskirts, dooming the city to decades of smog.

St. John Paul II was born (as Karol Wojtyła) in nearby Wadowice and served as archbishop of Kraków before being called to Rome. Today, the hometown boy-turned-saint draws lots of pilgrims and is, for many, a big part of the city's attraction. Saintly ties aside, Kraków might be the most Catholic town in Europe's most Catholic country; be sure to visit a few of its many churches.

The story of Kraków continues to play out. In recent years, its Kazimierz district has come back to life—both with Jewish-themed cultural sights and with some of Eastern Europe's best bars, food trucks, and restaurants. This mingling of the historic with the contemporary typifies a city that always has been, and continues to be, Poland's heartbeat.

feet; to find these, use the stairs or the elevator right in the middle of the bus terminal. Note that some minibuses, such as those to Auschwitz, also leave from, or near, this station (though the buses and minibuses that go to the Wieliczka Salt Mine leave from nearby streets—see page 107). Because the bus station area can be challenging to navigate, leave yourself plenty of time before departure.

By Car

Centrum signs lead you into the Old Town—you'll know you're there when you hit the ring road that surrounds the Planty park. Parking garages surround the Old Town. Your hotelier can advise you on directions and parking.

By Plane

The modern **John Paul II Kraków-Balice Airport** is about 10 miles west of the center (airport code: KRK, airport info: tel. 12-295-5800, www.krakowairport.pl). The easiest way downtown is to hop on the slick and speedy **train** (follow signs up the ramp, then across the sky bridge to the parking garage; 9 zł, buy ticket from machine or from conductor on board, 2/hour, 18 minutes to Kraków's main train station—see arrival instructions earlier, under "By Train"). Alternatively, you can take **public bus** #208 or (at night) #902—follow signs to the right end of the building to find the stop (4 zł, goes to main bus station—see arrival instructions earlier, under "By Bus," 50-minute trip depending on traffic). There's also a **taxi** stand in front of the terminal (ask about the fare up front—rates vary, but official cabs should not exceed 90 zł, more expensive at night, about 30 minutes). You can also order an Uber (typically cheaper than a taxi), or arrange a taxi transfer in advance (such as with recommended driver Andrew Durman, listed later, under "Tours in Kraków").

Many budget flights—including those on Wizz Air and Ryanair—use the **International Airport Katowice in Pyrzowice** (Międzynarodowy Port Lotniczy Katowice w Pyrzowicach, airport code: KTW, www.katowice-airport.com). This airport is about 18 miles from the city of Katowice, which is about 50 miles west of Kraków. Direct buses run sporadically between Katowice Airport and Kraków's main train station area (50 zł, trip takes 1.75 hours, generally scheduled to meet incoming flights). You can also take the bus from Katowice Airport to Katowice's train station (hourly, 50 minutes), then take the train to Kraków (hourly, 1.5 hours). Wizz Air's website is useful for figuring out your connection: www.wizzair.com.

HELPFUL HINTS

Exchange Rate: 1 złoty (zł, or PLN) = about 25 cents; 4 zł = about $1.

Sightseeing Tips: Some sights are closed on Monday (including the Gallery of 19th-Century Polish Art, Szołayski House, and a few museums in Kazimierz), but many sights are open (including the churches and Jagiellonian University Museum, and in Kazimierz, all of the Jewish-themed sights). On Saturday, most of Kazimierz's Jewish-themed sights are closed. Before heading out, check the "Kraków at a Glance" sidebar on page 38. Also be aware of days that certain sights are free: On Sunday, the National Museum branches (including the Gallery of 19th-Century Polish Art in the Cloth Hall) are free, but some are open limited hours. On Monday, Schindler's Factory Museum is free (and especially crowded), as are two sights at Wawel Castle (open only mornings April-Oct). And on Tuesday, the Rynek Underground Museum is free (and crowded).

Remember: You may want to book ahead for the popular Schindler's Factory Museum, Wieliczka Salt Mine, and Rynek Underground Museum (see details in each listing)—and you definitely need to book well ahead for a visit to Auschwitz (see next chapter).

Bookstore: For an impressive selection of new and used English books, try **Massolit Books,** just west of the Old Town. They also have a café with drinks and light snacks, and a good children's section (daily 10:00-20:00, ulica Felicjanek 4, tel. 12-432-4150, www.massolit.com).

Laundry: Frania Café, halfway between the Old Town and Kazimierz, is an inviting café/pub with ample washers and dryers, relaxing ambience, free Wi-Fi, a full bar serving espresso drinks and laundry-themed hard drinks, long hours, and a friendly staff (you can pay extra for them to do it for you in 2-3 hours—consider dropping it off on your way to Kazimierz and picking it up on the way back, daily 7:30-24:00, ulica Starowiślna 26, mobile 783-945-021).

Betty Clean is a full-service laundry that's slightly closer to the Old Town, but pricey (15 zł/shirt, 27 zł/pants, takes 24 hours, 50 percent more for express 3-hour service, Mon-Fri 7:30-19:30, Sat 8:00-15:30, closed Sun, just outside the Planty park at ulica Zwierzyniecka 6, tel. 12-423-0848).

GETTING AROUND KRAKÓW

Kraków's top sights and best hotels are easily accessible by foot. You'll need wheels only if you're going to outlying areas (Kazimierz, Nowa Huta, John Paul II pilgrimage sites, and so on).

By Public Transit

Trams and buses zip around Kraków's urban sprawl. The same tickets work system-wide and can be purchased at most kiosks, or at the machines you'll see at most stops (these accept coins and small bills). You can also buy tickets on board—most trams have machines (coins only); otherwise, buy your ticket from the driver for a bit more. If your coin won't work in the machine, do as the locals do and rub it against the metal, then try inserting it again. For a good route planner, see www.jakdojade.pl.

A *bilet jednoprzejazdowy*, which covers any single journey (including transfers), costs 3.80 zł. However, many journeys you're likely to take—such as between the Old Town and Kazimierz—are likely to be brief, so you'll save by buying a 20-minute ticket *(20-minutowy)* for 2.80 zł. You can also get longer-term tickets for

24 hours (15 zł), 48 hours (24 zł), and 72 hours (36 zł). These prices are for a "one-zone" ticket, which covers almost everything of interest in Kraków (including Nowa Huta, the St. John Paul II pilgrimage sites, and the Kościuszko Mound)—unless you're headed for the airport or Wieliczka Salt Mine, which are beyond the city limits and require a slightly more expensive *aglomeracyjny* ticket (4 zł for a single journey). Always validate your ticket when you board the bus or tram (24-, 48-, and 72-hour tickets must be validated only the first time you use them).

Tram #3 is particularly handy. It goes from the side of the train station (Dworzec Główny Zachód) to the ring road in front of the station (Dworzec Główny), then stops at the eastern edge of the Old Town (Poczta Główna, at the main post office) before continuing to Kazimierz (Miodowa is at the north end, near ulica Szeroka; Św. Wawrzyńca is at the south end, near the old tram depot) and Podgórze, near Schindler's Factory Museum (plac Bohaterow Getta). **Tram #24** is also useful: It stops at the western edge of the Old Town (Teatr Bagatela), then loops around the northern edge to stop near the Barbican (Stary Kleparz) before meeting up with tram #3 in front of the train station (Dworzec Główny) and continuing on to Kazimierz and Podgórze (same stops as listed above).

By Taxi or Uber
Only take cabs that are clearly marked with a company logo and telephone number. Legitimate Kraków taxis start at 7 zł and charge about 3 zł per kilometer (while unofficial taxis charge whatever they like). Rides generally cost less than 20 zł, but can take longer than you'd expect: Due to the Old Town's many traffic restrictions and pedestrian zones, a "short ride across town" may require looping all the way around the ring road. You're more likely to get the fair metered rate by calling or hailing a cab, rather than taking one waiting at tourist spots. To call a cab, try **Radio Taxi** (tel. 19191).

Uber is typically cheaper than Kraków's official taxis (though prices can spike during busy "surge" periods). In my experience, Polish Uber drivers (and their cars) are a bit less polished and professional than those back home—but they're cheap, usually friendly, and handy.

By Bike
The riverfront bike path is enticing on a nice day; the Planty park, while inviting, can be a bit crowded for biking. **Kraków Bike Tours** rents a wide variety of new, good-quality bikes (10 zł/first hour, cheaper per hour for longer rentals, 50 zł/day, 60 zł/24 hours; they also have electric bikes for about double these prices; daily 9:30-19:00, until 15:00 off-season, just off the Square at Grodzka 2; see listing later, under "Tours in Kraków"). Nearby, **KRK Bike Rental**

rents basic, cheaper bikes (9 zł/hour, 50 zł/24 hours, daily 9:00-21:00, less in bad weather, closed Nov-March, ulica Św. Anny 4, mobile 509-267-733, www.krkbikerental.pl).

Tours in Kraków

Local Guides

Hiring a guide in Kraków is fun and affordable, and makes a huge difference in your experience. I've enjoyed working with three in particular, any of whom can show you the sights in Kraków and also have cars for day-tripping into the countryside: **Tomasz Klimek** (400 zł/half-day, 800 zł/day, slightly more with a car, mobile 605-231-923, tomasz.klimek@interia.pl); **Anna Bakowska** (400 zł/4 hours, 600 zł/day, mobile 604-151-293, www.leadertour.eu, leadertour@wp.pl); and **Marta Chmielowska** (350 zł/4 hours, 600 zł/day, same prices by foot or car, can be more for larger groups and for long-distance trips, mobile 603-668-008, martachm7@gmail.com). I wouldn't bother hiring a guide for the trip to Auschwitz (which generally costs 600-700 zł)—only official Auschwitz guides can legally give tours onsite, so you'll wind up joining one of the tours once there; instead, it's a better value to hire a driver (like Andrew, listed next).

Drivers

Since Kraków is such a useful home base for day trips, it can be handy to splurge on a private driver for door-to-door service. **Andrew (Andrzej) Durman,** a Pole who lived in Chicago and speaks fluent English, is a gregarious driver, translator, miracle worker, and all-around great guy. While not a licensed tour guide, Andrew is an eager conversationalist and loves to provide lively commentary while you roll. Although you can hire Andrew for a simple airport transfer or an Auschwitz day trip, he also enjoys tackling more ambitious itineraries, from helping you track down your Polish roots to taking you on multiple-day journeys around Poland and beyond. These prices are transportation only for up to 4 people: 400 zł to Auschwitz, 250 zł to Wieliczka Salt Mine, 80 zł for transfer from Kraków-Balice Airport, 500 zł for transfer from Katowice Airport, or 600 zł for an all-day trip into the countryside—such as into the High Tatras or to track down your Polish roots near Kraków (more to cover gas costs for trips longer than 100 km one-way; long-distance transfers for up to 4 people to Prague, Budapest, Vienna, or Berlin for 1,800 zł—or 200 zł extra if he picks you up there; also available for multiday trips—price negotiable, all prices higher for bigger van, tel. 12-411-5630, mobile 602-243-306, www.tour-service.pl, andrew@tour-service.pl). If he's busy, Andrew may send you with one of his English-speaking colleagues, such as Lucas or Matthew.

KRAKÓW

Kraków at a Glance

▲▲▲**Main Market Square** Stunning heart of Kraków and a people magnet any time of day. See page 47.

▲▲▲**Schindler's Factory Museum** Building where Oskar Schindler saved over 1,000 Jewish workers, now an engaging exhibit about Kraków's WWII experience. **Hours:** April-Oct Mon 10:00-16:00 (closes at 14:00 first Mon of month), Tue-Sun 9:00-20:00; Nov-March Mon 10:00-14:00, Tue-Sun 10:00-18:00. See page 96.

▲▲**Planty** Once a moat, now a scenic park encircling the city. See page 42.

▲▲**St. Mary's Church** Landmark church with extraordinary wood-carved Gothic altarpiece. **Hours:** Mon-Sat 11:30-18:00, Sun from 14:00. See page 45.

▲▲**Cloth Hall** Fourteenth-century market hall with souvenirs. **Hours:** Summer Mon-Fri 9:00-18:00, Sat-Sun until 15:00 or later; winter Mon-Fri 9:00-16:00, Sat-Sun until 15:00. See page 50.

▲▲**St. Francis Basilica** Lovely Gothic church with some of Poland's best Art Nouveau. **Hours:** Mon-Sat 10:00-16:00, Sun 13:00-15:30; open longer hours for services and prayer. See page 53.

▲▲**Wawel Cathedral** Poland's national church, with tons of tombs, a crypt, and a climbable tower. **Hours:** Mon-Sat 9:00-17:00, Sun from 12:30; Oct-March daily until 16:00. See page 60.

▲▲**Wawel Castle Grounds** Historic hilltop with views, castle, cathedral, courtyard with chakras, and a passel of museums. **Hours:** Grounds open daily 6:00 until dusk, but many of the museums closed Mon, and Sun in winter. See page 65.

▲▲**Gallery of 19th-Century Polish Art** Worthwhile collection of paintings by should-be-famous artists, upstairs in the Cloth Hall. **Hours:** Tue-Fri 9:00-17:00, Sat 10:00-18:00, Sun 10:00-16:00, closed Mon. See page 71.

Local guide Marta Chmielowska's husband, **Czesław** (a.k.a. Chester), can also drive you to nearby locations (350 zł for all-day trip to Auschwitz for 1-3 people, 450 zł for 4-8 people; 250 zł to Wieliczka Salt Mine, including waiting time, or a very long day combining Wieliczka and Auschwitz for 600 zł; 1,700 zł for a transfer to Prague; to book, see Marta's contact information, earlier).

▲▲**Rynek Underground Museum** Exhibit on medieval Kraków filling excavated cellars beneath the Main Market Square. **Hours:** Mon 10:00-20:00 (closed second Mon of each month), Tue until 16:00, Wed-Sun until 22:00, shorter hours in winter. See page 78.

▲▲**Old Jewish Cemetery** Poignant burial site in Kazimierz, with graves from 1552 to 1800. **Hours:** Sun-Fri 9:00-16:00, sometimes until 18:00 May-Sept, closes earlier in winter and by sundown on Fri, closed Sat. See page 85.

▲**Czartoryski Museum** Varied collection, with European paintings and Polish armor, handicrafts, and decorative arts. **Hours:** Likely closed for restoration. See page 76.

▲**Jagiellonian University Museum Collegium Maius** Proud collection of historic university, surrounding a tranquil courtyard where medieval professors lived. **Hours:** Entry with 30-minute guided tour Mon-Fri 10:00-14:20, Tue and Thu until 17:20 in April-Oct, no tours Sat-Sun; one-hour version in English usually Mon-Fri at 13:00, no tours Sat-Sun; free entry without tour Sat 10:00-13:30. See page 80.

▲**New Jewish Cemetery** Graveyard with tombs from after 1800, partly restored after Nazi desecration. **Hours:** Sun-Fri 8:00-16:00, closed Sat. See page 93.

▲**Ethnographic Museum** Traditional rural Polish life on display. **Hours:** Tue-Sun 10:00-19:00, closed Mon. See page 91.

▲**Pharmacy Under the Eagle** Small exhibit about the Holocaust in Kraków, including three evocative films. **Hours:** Mon 10:00-14:00, Tue-Sun 9:00-17:00; closed second Tue of each month. See page 95.

▲**Museum of Contemporary Art in Kraków** Today's thought-provoking art, displayed in renovated old warehouses behind Schindler's Factory Museum. **Hours:** Tue-Sun 11:00-19:00, closed Mon. See page 101.

Walking Tours

Various companies run daily city walking tours in English in summer. Most do a three-hour tour of the Old Town as well as a three-hour tour of Kazimierz, the Jewish district (most charge about 50 zł per tour, depending on company). Three people can hire their own great private local guide for about the same amount of money they'd spend on a group walking tour.

Because the scene is continually evolving, it's best to pick up local fliers (the TI works exclusively with one company, See Kraków, but hotel reception desks generally have more options), then choose the one that fits your interests and schedule. You'll also see ads for "free" tours—which are, of course, not really free (the guide gets paid only if you tip generously).

Food Tours
In this stealth-foodie city, you have multiple good options. **Eat Polska**—which does a marvelous job of connecting food to culture and history, making the experience equal parts informative and delicious—does top-notch, insightful food tours (at 13:00, 290 zł, 4 hours) and vodka tours with food pairings (at 17:00, 290 zł, 3.5 hours; for details on either, and other culinary experiences, see www.eatpolska.com). **Urban Adventures,** more casual and locally based, does evening food walks that basically assemble a full meal with a little sightseeing thrown in (at 18:00, 310 zł, RS%—email to ask for discount code, 3 hours, www.urbanadventures.com, info@urbanadventures.com).

Crazy Guides
This irreverent company offers tours to the communist suburb of Nowa Huta and other outlying sights. For details, see page 111.

Bike Tours
Kraków Bike Tours is a well-established operation that runs daily four-hour bike tours in English, with 25 stops in the Old Town, Kazimierz, and Podgórze (90 zł, May-Sept daily at 10:00 and 15:00, spring and fall only 1/day at 12:00, confirm schedule and meet tour at their office down the passage at Grodzka 2—right at the bottom of the Square, mobile 510-394-657, www.krakowbiketour.com).

Bus Tours to Auschwitz or Wieliczka
As Kraków is so easily enjoyed on foot, taking a bus tour doesn't make much sense in town. But they can be handy for reaching outlying sights. Various tour companies run big-bus itineraries to Auschwitz (6 hours), Wieliczka Salt Mine (4 hours), and other regional side trips (each itinerary around 150-180 zł).

Given the difficulty of reserving your own appointment at Auschwitz (explained in the next chapter), one of these bus tours—which include a guided tour of the camp—may be your most convenient option. **See Kraków** (which has a monopoly at the TI, www.seekrakow.com) and **Discover Cracow** (www.discovercracow.com) both use smaller 19-seat minibuses. They sometimes offer hotel pickup, which seems convenient, but you'll waste a lot of time driving around the city to other hotels. **Cracow City Tours** (www.cracowcitytours.com) uses larger 50-seat buses with a central pickup point (on plac Matejki, across the ring road from the Barbican, at the north end of the Old Town).

At any company, the on-bus guiding is hit-or-miss but largely irrelevant—since you'll be handed off to an official Auschwitz guide once at the camp. Note that the many tour offices and faux-TIs you'll see around town simply sell tickets for these companies. If you waited too long to reserve at Auschwitz and are desperate to get in at short notice, try dropping in to various agencies around town to see if anyone has space.

Buggy Tours
You'll see (and hear) horse-drawn buggies that trot around Kraków from the Main Market Square. The going rate is a hefty 200 zł for a 30-minute tour to the castle and back. After dark, they're lit up like fanciful Cinderella coaches—a memorable scene, all lined up in front of St. Mary's Church.

Golf-Cart Tours
Several outfits around town (including on the Square) offer tours on a golf cart with recorded commentary. Given the limits on car traffic in the old center, this can be a handy way to connect the sights for those with limited mobility. Generally you'll pay about 180 zł for a 30-minute tour around the Old Town; to extend the trip to Kazimierz, it's 360 zł; and adding the Podgórze former Jewish ghetto and Schindler's Factory Museum costs a total of 540 zł (these prices are for the entire golf cart, up to 5 people).

Kraków's Royal Way Walk

This self-guided walk is designed to link up most of Kraków's major sights. Most of the walk follows a route called the "Royal Way," because the king used to follow this same path when he returned to Kraków after a journey. After the capital moved to Warsaw, most kings still used Wawel Cathedral for important events. In fact, from 1320 to 1795, nearly every Polish king traversed Kraków's Royal Way at least twice: on the day he was crowned and on the day he was buried. You could sprint through this walk in about an hour and a half (less than a mile altogether), but it's much more fun if you take it like the kings did...slowly.
• *Begin just outside the main gate (the Florian Gate) at the north end of the Old Town. Face the tall, rectangular tower.*

▲Barbican (Barbakan) and City Walls
Tatars—those mysterious and terrifying invaders from Central Asia—destroyed Kraków in 1241. To better defend their rebuilt city, Krakovians built this wall. The original rampart had 47 watch-

towers and eight gates. (You can see a bronze model of the wall just to the right of the tower.)

Now turn around. The big, round defensive fort standing outside the wall is the **Barbican,** built to provide extra fortification to weak sections—namely, the gates. Imagine how it looked in 1500, when the Barbican stood outside the town moat with a long bridge leading to the Florian Gate—the city's main entryway. Today you can pay to scramble along the passages and fortifications of the Barbican, though there's little to see inside, other than a small but good exhibit giving you a sense of how the walls were designed (9 zł, April-Oct daily 10:30-18:00, closed Nov-March). The same ticket also lets you climb up onto the surviving stretch of Old Town walls flanking the Florian Gate (entry from inside walls).

• *The greenbelt within which the Barbican sits is called the...*

▲▲Planty

By the 19th century, Kraków's no-longer-necessary city wall had fallen into disrepair. As the Austrian authorities were doing all

over their empire, they decided to tear down what remained, fill in the moat, and plant trees. (The name comes not from the English "plant" but from the Polish *plantovac,* or "flat"—because they flattened out this area to create it.) Today, the Planty is a beautiful park that stretches 2.5 miles around the entire perimeter of Kraków's Old Town. To give your Kraków visit an extra dimension, consider a quick bike ride around the Planty (best early in the morning, when it's less crowded) with a side trip along the parklike riverbank near Wawel Castle; you'll see bike-rental places around the Old Town, including the two mentioned on page 36.

Circle around the left side of the Barbican. On your left, keep an eye out for a unique monument depicting an elderly, bearded man in the corner of a huge frame. This honors **Jan Matejko,** arguably Poland's most beloved painter, who specialized in giant-scale epic historical scenes several times larger than this frame. We'll hear Matejko's name many more times on this walk.

As you continue around the Barbican, look down to see the

much lower ground level around its base—making it easy to imagine that the Planty was once anything but flat.

• *Across the busy street from the Barbican, standing in the middle of the long park, is the...*

Grunwald Monument

This memorial honors one of the most important battles in the history of a nation that has seen more than its share: the Battle of Grunwald on July 15, 1410, when Polish and Lithuanian forces banded together to finally defeat the Teutonic Knights, who had been running roughshod over the lands along the Baltic. (For more on the battle and the knights, see page 303.) Lying dramatically slain at the base of this monument, like a toppled Goliath, is the defeated Grand Master of the Teutonic Knights—German crusaders who had originally been brought to Poland as mercenaries. It's easy to see this vanquished statue as a thinly veiled metaphor for one of Poland's powerful, often domineering neighbors. When the Nazis took power here, this statue was one of the first things they tore down. When they left, it was one of the first things the Poles put back up.

• *If you'd like to see a slice of Krakovian life, side-trip one block to the left of the monument, to the local farmers market.*

The Old Market (Stary Kleparz)

The colorful Old Market offers a refreshing dash of Kraków that has nothing to do with history or tourism. It's just lots of hardscrabble people selling what they grow or knit, and lots of others buying. Wander around as if on a cultural scavenger hunt. Find the freshest doughnuts *(pączki)*, the most popular bakery, the villager selling slippers she knitted, the smelliest smoked-fish stand, and the old man with the smoked cheese (Mon-Sat 7:00-18:00—but busiest and most interesting in the morning, closed Sun).

• *Now retrace your steps to the Barbican, and enter the Old Town by walking through the...*

Florian Gate (Brama Floriańska)

As you approach the gate, look up at the **crowned white eagle**—representing courage and freedom—the historic symbol of the Polish people.

Inside the gate, notice the little chapel on the right with a replica of the famous **Black Madonna of Częstochowa,** the most important religious symbol among Polish Catholics. The original, located in Częstochowa (70 miles north of Kraków), is an Eastern Orthodox-style icon of mysterious origin with several mystical legends attached to it. After the icon's believed role in protecting a monastery from Swedish invaders in the mid-17th century, it was named "Queen and Protector of Poland."

Once through the gate, look back at it. High above is **St. Florian,** patron of the fire brigade. As fire was a big concern for a wooden city of the 15th century, Florian gets a place of honor.

You'll often see traditionally clad **musicians** near the gate, performing their lilting folk melodies for tips.

• *You're standing at the head of Kraków's historic (and now touristic) gamut...*

▲Floriańska Street (Ulica Floriańska)

Hanging on the inside of the city wall in both directions is a makeshift **art gallery,** where—traditionally—starving students hawk

the works they've painted at the Academy of Fine Arts (across the busy street from the Barbican). These days, the art is so kitschy, this stretch of the town's fortification is nicknamed "The Wailing Wall." The entrance to get on top of the wall—covered by the Barbican ticket—is at the left end of this starving artists' gallery. If you detoured even farther along the wall, soon you'd reach the Czartoryski Museum, an eclectic collection of artifacts that's due to reopen any year now (see page 76).

Now begin strolling down **Floriańska street** (floh-ree-AHN-skah). Notice that all over town, storefronts advertising themselves as "tourist information" offices are actually tourist sales agencies (legitimate TIs are listed on page 27). Along with the fast-food joints, also notice some uniquely Polish snacks: The various pizza and kebab windows also sell *zapiekanka*—a toasted baguette with toppings, similar to a French bread pizza. Or, for an even quicker bite, buy an *obwarzanek* (ring-shaped, bagel-like roll, typically fresh) from a street vendor; many still use their old-fashioned blue carts.

About halfway down the first block, on the left (at #45, round green sign), look for **Jama Michalika** ("Michael's Cave"). Around the turn of the 20th century, this dark, atmospheric café was a hangout of the *Młoda Polska* (Young Poland) movement—the Polish answer to Art Nouveau (explained on page 49). The walls are papered with sketches from poor artists—local bohemians who couldn't pay their tabs. Today it hosts a folk troupe that performs traditional music and dance with dinner many evenings (see listing under "Entertainment in Kraków," page 120). Poke around inside this circa-1900 time warp and appreciate this unique art gallery.

About a block farther down, at #20 (on the right), **Staropolskie Trunki** ("Old Polish Drinks") offers an education in vodka, with a long bar and countless local vodkas and liquors—all open and ready to be tasted (four tastes for 10 zł with an explanation from the bartender, daily 10:00-late).

• *Continue into the Main Market Square, where you'll run into...*

▲▲St. Mary's Church (Kościół Mariacki)

A church has stood on this spot for 800 years. The original church was destroyed by the first Tatar invasion in 1241, but all subsequent versions—including the current one—have been built on the same foundation. You can look down the sides to see how the Main Market Square has risen about seven feet over the centuries.

How many church towers does St. Mary's have? Technically, the answer is one. The shorter tower belongs to the church; the taller one is a municipal watchtower, from which you'll hear a bugler playing the hourly *hejnał* song. According to Kraków's favorite legend, during that first Tatar invasion, a town watchman saw the enemy approaching and sounded the alarm. Before he could finish the tune, an arrow pierced his throat—which is why, even today, the *hejnał* stops suddenly partway through. Today's buglers—12 in all—are firemen first, musicians second. Each one works a 24-hour shift up there, playing the *hejnał* four times on the hour—with one

bugle call for each direction. (It's even broadcast on national Polish radio at noon.) While you're in Kraków, you'll certainly hear one of these tiny, hourly, broken performances.

To see one of the most finely crafted Gothic altarpieces anywhere, it's worth paying admission to enter the church. The front door is open 14 hours a day and is free to those who come to pray, but tourists use the door around the right side (buy your ticket across the little square from this door).

Cost and Hours: 10 zł, Mon-Sat 11:30-18:00, Sun from 14:00.

Visiting the Church: Inside, you're struck by the lavish decor. This was the church of the everyday townspeople, built out of a spirit of competition with the royal high church at Wawel Castle.

At the altar is one of the best medieval woodcarvings in existence—the exquisite, three-part altarpiece by German Veit Stoss (Wit Stwosz in Polish). Carved in 12 years and completed in 1489, it's packed with emotion rare in Gothic art. Get as close as you can and study the remarkable details. Stoss used oak for the structural parts and linden trunks for the figures. The open altar depicts the Dormition (death—or, if splitting theological hairs, heavenly sleep) of the Virgin. The artist catches the apostles around Mary, reacting in the seconds after she collapses. Mary is depicted in three stages: life leaving her earthly body, being escorted to heaven by Jesus, and (at the very top) being crowned in heaven. The six scenes on the sides are the Annunciation, birth of Jesus, visit by the Three Magi, Jesus' Resurrection, his Ascension, and Mary becoming the mother of the apostles at Pentecost.

There's more to St. Mary's than the altar. While you're admiring this church's art, notice the flowery Neo-Gothic painting covering the choir walls. Stare up into the starry, starry blue ceiling. As you wander around, consider that the church was renovated a century ago by three Polish geniuses from two very different artistic generations: the venerable positivist Jan Matejko and his Art Nouveau students, Stanisław Wyspiański and Józef Mehoffer (we'll learn more about these two later on our walk). The huge silver bird under the organ loft in back is that symbol of Poland, the crowned white eagle.

Tower Climb: You may be able to climb up the 271 stairs to the top of the taller tower to visit the *hejnał* fireman. While it's a huff—with some claustrophobic stone stairs, followed by some steep, acrophobic wooden ones—the view up top is the best you'll find of the Square (15 zł, pay at the ticket office for the church, departs at :10 and :40 past each hour, Tue-Sat 9:10-11:40 & 13:10-17:40, Sun 13:10-17:40 only, closed Mon; March and Nov-Dec open only good-weather Thu-Sat; closed Jan-Feb).

• *Leaving the church, notice the neck clamps dangling from the exterior walls near the side door. If you were leaving Mass in centuries past,*

Kazimierz the Great (1333-1370)

Out of the many centuries of Polish kings, only one earned the nickname "great," and he's the only one worth remembering: Kazimierz the Great.

K. the G., who ruled Poland from Kraków in the 14th century, was one of those larger-than-life medieval kings who left his mark on all fronts—from war to diplomacy, art patronage to womanizing. His scribes bragged that Kazimierz "found a Poland made of wood, and left one made of brick and stone." He put Kraków on the map as a major European capital. He founded many villages (some of which still bear his name—including one that's an important neighborhood of Kraków) and replaced wooden structures with stone ones (such as Kraków's Cloth Hall). Kazimierz also established the Kraków Academy (today's Jagiellonian University), the second-oldest university in Central Europe. And to protect all of these new building projects, he heavily fortified Poland by building a series of imposing forts and walls around its perimeter. If you have a 50-zł note, take a look at it: That's Kazimierz the Great on the front, and on the back you'll see his capital, Cracovia, and the most important town he founded, Casmirus.

Most of all, Kazimierz is remembered as a progressive, tolerant king. In the 14th century, other nations were deporting—or even interning—their Jewish subjects, who were commonly scapegoated for anything that went wrong. But the enlightened Kazimierz created policies that granted Jews more opportunities (often related to banking and trade) and allowed them a chance for higher social standing—establishing the country as a safe haven for Jews in Europe.

Kazimierz the Great was the last of Poland's long-lived Piast dynasty. Although he left no male heir—at least, no legitimate one—Kazimierz's advances set the stage for Poland's Golden Age (14th-16th century). After his death, Poland united with Lithuania (against the common threat of the Teutonic Knights), the Jagiellonian dynasty was born, and Poland became one of Europe's mightiest medieval powers.

there would be criminals chained here for public humiliation. You'd spit on them before turning right and stepping into one of the biggest market squares anywhere.

▲▲▲Main Market Square (Rynek Główny), a.k.a. "The Square"

Kraków's marvelous Square, one of Europe's most gasp-worthy public spaces, bustles with street musicians, colorful flower stalls, cotton-candy vendors, loitering teenagers, the local breakdancing troupe, businesspeople commuting by foot, gawking tourists, soap-balloon-blowers, and the lusty coos of pigeons. The Square is where

Kraków lives. It's often filled with various special events, markets, and festivals. The biggest are the seasonal markets before Easter and Christmas, but you're likely to stumble on something special going on just about any time of year (especially June through Aug).

The Square was established in the 13th century, when the city had to be rebuilt after being flattened by the Tatars. At the time,

it was the biggest square in medieval Europe. It was illegal to sell anything on the street, so everything had to be sold here on the Main Market Square. It was divided into smaller markets, such as the butcher stalls, the ironworkers' tents, and the still-standing Cloth Hall (described later).

Notice the modern **fountain** with the glass pyramid at this end of the Square. A major excavation of the surrounding area created a museum of Kraków's medieval history that literally sprawls beneath the Square (for more on the recommended **Rynek Underground Museum,** see page 78).

The statue in the middle of the Square is a traditional meeting place for Krakovians. It depicts Romantic poet **Adam Mickiewicz** (1789-1855), who's considered the "Polish Shakespeare." His epic masterpiece, *Pan Tadeusz,* is still regarded as one of the greatest works in Polish literature. A wistful, nostalgic tale of Polish-Lithuanian nobility, *Pan Tadeusz* stirred patriotism in a Poland that had been dismantled by surrounding empires through a series of three Partitions.

If you survey the Square from here, you'll notice that the Old Town was spared the bombs of World War II. The Nazis considered Kraków a city with Germanic roots and wanted it saved. But they were quick to destroy any symbols of Polish culture or pride. The statue of Adam Mickiewicz, for example, was pulled down immediately after occupation.

Near the end of the Square, you'll see the tiny, cubical, copper-domed **Church of St. Adalbert,** one of the oldest churches in Kraków (10th century). This Romanesque structure predates the Square. Like St. Mary's (described earlier), it seems to be at an angle because it's aligned east-west, as was the custom when it was built. (In other words, the churches aren't crooked—the Square is. Any other "crooked" building you see around town predates the 13th-century grid created during the rebuilding of Kraków.)

Drinks are reasonably priced at cafés on the Square (most around 10-15 zł). Find a spot where you like the view and the

The Młoda Polska (Young Poland) Art Movement

Polish art in the late 19th century was ruled by positivism, a school with a very literal, straightforward focus on Polish his-

tory (Jan Matejko led the charge; see page 195). But when the new generation of Kraków's artists came into their own in the early 1900s, they decided that the old school was exactly that. Though moved by the same spirit and goals as the previous generation—evoking Polish patriotism at a time when their country was being occupied—these new artists used very different methods. They were inspired by a renewed appreciation of folklore and peasant life. Rather than being earnest and literal (an 18th-century Polish war hero on horseback), the new art was playful and highly symbolic (the artist frolicking in a magical garden in the idyllic Polish countryside). This movement became known as Młoda Polska (Young Poland)—Art Nouveau with a Polish accent.

Stanisław Wyspiański (vees-PAYN-skee, 1869-1907) was the leader of Młoda Polska. He produced beautiful artwork, from simple drawings to the stirring stained-glass images in Kraków's St. Francis Basilica. Wyspiański was an expert at capturing human faces with realistic detail, emotion, and personality. The versatile Wyspiański was also an accomplished stage designer and writer. His patriotic play *The Wedding*—about the nuptials of a big-city artist and a peasant girl—is regarded as one of Poland's finest dramas. You'll find excellent examples of Wyspiański's art in Kraków's St. Francis Basilica and Szołayski House, and in Warsaw's National Museum.

Józef Mehoffer (may-HOH-fehr), Wyspiański's good friend and rival, was another great Młoda Polska artist. Mehoffer's style is more expressionistic and abstract than Wyspiański's, often creating an otherworldly effect. See Mehoffer's work in Kraków's St. Francis Basilica and at the artist's former residence (see the Józef Mehoffer House); and in Warsaw, at the National Museum.

Other names to look for include **Jacek Malczewski** (mahl-CHEHV-skee), who specialized in self-portraits, and **Olga Boznańska** (bohz-NAHN-skah), the movement's only prominent female artist. Both are featured in Warsaw's National Museum; Malczewski's works also appear in Kraków's Gallery of 19th-Century Polish Art.

chairs, then sit and sip. Order a coffee, Polish *piwo* (beer, such as Żywiec, Okocim, or Lech), or a shot of *wódka* (Żubrówka is a quality brand; for more on Polish drinks, see page 20). For a higher vantage point, the Cloth Hall's **Café Szał terrace**—overlooking the Square and St. Mary's Church—offers one of the best views in town (open daily until 24:00, affordable drinks, some light meals, slow service, enter through Gallery of 19th-Century Polish Art entrance).

As the Square buzzes around you, imagine this place before 1989. There were no outdoor cafés, no touristy souvenir stands, and no salespeople hawking cotton candy or neon-lit whirligigs. The communist government shut down all but a handful of the businesses. They didn't want people to congregate here—they should be at home, because "a rested worker is a productive worker." The buildings were covered with soot from the nearby Lenin Steelworks in Nowa Huta. The communists denied the pollution, and when the student "Green Brigades" staged a demonstration in this Square to raise awareness in the 1970s, they were immediately arrested. How things have changed.

• *The huge, yellow building right in the middle of the Square is the...*

▲▲Cloth Hall (Sukiennice)

In the Middle Ages, this was the place where cloth sellers had their market stalls. Kazimierz the Great turned the Cloth Hall into a permanent structure in the 14th century. In 1555, it burned down and was replaced by the current building. The crowned letter *S* (at the top of the gable above the entryway) stands for King Sigismund the Old, who commissioned this version of the hall. As Sigismund fancied all things Italian (including women—he married an Italian princess), this

structure is in the Italianate Renaissance style. Sigismund kicked off a nationwide trend, and you'll still see Renaissance-style buildings like this one all over the country, making the style typically Polish. We'll see more works by Sigismund's imported Italian architects at Wawel Castle.

The Cloth Hall is still a functioning market—selling mostly souvenirs, including wood carvings, chess sets, jewelry (especially amber), painted boxes, and trinkets (see hours under "Shopping in Kraków," page 114). Cloth Hall prices are slightly inflated, but still cheap by American standards. You're paying a little extra for the convenience and the atmosphere, but you'll see locals buying gifts here, too.

Pay WCs are at each end of the Cloth Hall. The upstairs of the Cloth Hall is home to the excellent **Gallery of 19th-Century Polish Art** (enter behind the statue of Adam; for a self-guided tour, see page 71).

• *Browse through the Cloth Hall passageway. As you emerge into the sleepier half of the Square, the big tower on your left is the...*

Town Hall Tower

This is all that remains of a town hall building from the 14th century—when Kraków was the powerful capital of Poland. After the 18th-century Partitions of Poland, Kraków's prominence took a nosedive. As the town's importance crumbled, so did its town hall. It was cheaper to tear down the building than to repair it, and all that was left standing was this nearly 200-foot-tall tower. In summer, you can climb the tower, stopping along the way to poke around an exhibit on Kraków history, but the views from up top are disappointing (9 zł, free on Mon, open March-Oct daily 10:30-18:00—except closed first Tue of each month, Nov-Dec 11:00-17:00, closed Jan-Feb).

Nearby: The **gigantic head** at the base of the Town Hall Tower is a sculpture by contemporary artist Igor Mitoraj, who studied here in Kraków. Typical of Mitoraj's works, the head is an empty shell that appears to be wrapped in cloth. While some locals enjoy having a work by their fellow Krakovian in such a prominent place, others disapprove of its sharp contrast with the Square's genteel Old World ambience. Tourists

enjoy playing peek-a-boo with the head's eyes.

• *When you're finished on the Square, we'll head toward Wawel Hill. The official Royal Way makes a beeline for the castle, but we'll take a scenic detour to see some less touristy back streets, visit Kraków's historic university and one of its best churches, and go for a quick walk through the Planty park.*

KRAKÓW

Exit the square at the corner nearest the Town Hall Tower, down ulica Św. Anny. After one block, turn left onto Jagiellońska street. Enter the courtyard of the big, red-brick building on your right.

Jagiellonian University and the Collegium Maius

Kraków had the second university in Central Europe (founded in 1364, after Prague's). Over the centuries, Jagiellonian U. has

boasted such illustrious grads as Copernicus and St. John Paul II. And today, the city's character is still defined largely by its huge student population (numbering around 150,000). Many of the university buildings fill the area to the west of the Old Town, so you'll see more students (and fewer tourist traps) in this part of town than elsewhere.

This building—called the Collegium Maius—is the historic heart of Kraków's university culture. It dates from the 15th century. In the Middle Ages, professors were completely devoted to their scholarly pursuits. They were unmarried and lived, ate, and slept here in an almost monastic environment. They taught downstairs and lived upstairs. In many ways, this building feels more like a monastery than a university. While this courtyard is the most interesting part, you can also tour the interior (for details, see page 80). The courtyard also hosts free temporary exhibits; look for posters.

The university also comes with some chilling history. On November 6, 1939, the occupying Nazis called all professors together for a meeting. With 183 gathered unknowingly in a hall, they were unceremoniously loaded into trucks and sent to their deaths in concentration camps. Hitler knew: If you want to decapitate a culture, you kill its intelligentsia.

Before you leave, if you're a fan of rich, thick hot chocolate, enjoy a cup at **Kawiarnia U Pęcherza** (down the stairs near the entrance)—widely regarded as the best in town.

Head down the *sgraffito*-lined passage on the side of the courtyard (it's the first door on your left as you entered the courtyard—just past the little security office). You'll emerge into the **Professors' Garden,** a tranquil space filled with red brick, ivy, stony statues, and inviting benches (open daily 9:00-18:30 or until dusk, closed in winter).

• *Exit the garden through the fancy gate and turn right on Jagiellońska. Spot any students? You'll follow this for two more blocks, passing the much larger and newer, but still red-brick, **Collegium Novum** build-*

ing—the modern administrative headquarters of Jag U., built in the late 19th century to commemorate the 500th anniversary of the building we just left.

*Jagiellońska dead-ends at a dynamic statue on a pillar. Turn left into the inviting **Planty**—the ring park we saw at the start of this walk. You'll stroll about five minutes through the Planty—dodging bikes and hearing the rattle of trams through the trees—with the Old Town buildings on your left and the ring road through the park on your right. When you reach a street with tram tracks, cross it and turn left. Pause in the park just before the church, and take note of the light-yellow building on the left (across the street), with a picture of St. John Paul II smiling down from above the stone doorway.*

KRAKÓW

Archbishop's Palace

This building was St. John Paul II's residence when he was the archbishop of Kraków. And even after he became pope, it remained

his home-away-from-Rome for visits to his hometown. After a long day of saying formal Mass during his visits to Kraków, he'd wind up here. Weary as he was, before going to bed he'd stand in the window above the entrance for hours, chatting casually with the people assembled below— about religion, but also about sports, current events, and whatever was on their minds.

In 2005, when the pope's health deteriorated, this street filled with his supporters, even though he was in Rome. For days, somber locals focused their vigil on this same window, their eyes fixed on a black crucifix that had been placed here. At 21:37 on the night of April 2, 2005, the pope passed away in Rome. Ten thousand Krakovians were on this street, under this window, listening to a Mass broadcast on loudspeakers from the church. When the priest announced the pope's death, every single person simultaneously fell to their knees in silence. For the next several days, thousands of the faithful continued to stand on this street, staring intently at the window where they last saw the man they considered to be the greatest Pole.

• *Now go through the back door of one of Kraków's finest churches...*

▲▲St. Francis Basilica (Bazylika Św. Franciszka)

This beautiful Gothic church, which was St. John Paul II's home church while he was archbishop of Kraków, features some of Poland's best Art Nouveau in situ (in the setting for which it was intended). After an 1850 fire, it was redecorated by the two leading members of the Młoda Polska (Young Poland) movement: Stanisław Wyspiański and Józef Mehoffer. The glorious decorations inside this church are the result of their great rivalry run amok.

Cost and Hours: Free; open for visitors Mon-Sat 10:00-16:00, Sun 13:00-15:30; longer hours for services and prayer.

Visiting the Basilica: Step through the door and let your eyes adjust to the low light. Take a few steps up the nave, pausing at the third pew on the left. On the back of this pew, notice the **silver plate** labeled "Jan Paweł II"—marking JPII's favorite place to pray when he lived in the Archbishop's Palace across the street.

Now walk another 20 feet down the nave, and notice the painting on the right, with an orange-and-blue background. This depicts **St. Maksymilian Kolbe,** the Catholic priest who sacrificed his own life to save a fellow inmate at Auschwitz in 1941 (notice the *16670*—his concentration camp number—etched into the background; read his story on page 152). Kolbe is particularly beloved here, as he actually served at this church.

Now turn around and look up above the door you entered. There, in all its glory, is the stained-glass window titled *God the Father Let It Be,* created by the great Art Nouveau artist Stanisław Wyspiański—and regarded by some as his finest masterpiece. (For more on Wyspiański, see page 49.) The colors beneath the Creator change from yellows and oranges (fire) to soothing blues (water), depending on the light. Wyspiański was supposedly inspired by Michelangelo's vision of God in the Sistine Chapel, though he used a street beggar to model God's specific features. Wyspiański also painted the delightful floral stained-glass windows that line the nave, high up—fitting for a church dedicated to a saint so famous for his spiritual connection to nature.

Now turn back around to face the main altar, and head into the **chapel** on the left (marked *Całun Turyński*). This important chapel houses a replica of the Shroud of Turin—which, since it touched the original shroud, is also considered a holy relic (displayed along the side of the chapel). At the main altar in this chapel, notice the plaques honoring Michał Tomaszek and Zbigniew Strzałkowski. These two Polish priests traveled to Peru as missionaries. There, they (along with an Italian priest) were murdered by communist guerrillas calling themselves the Shining Path. Today they are considered martyrs.

Before leaving this chapel, look high on the walls at the glorious Stations of the Cross. These are painted by **Józef Mehoffer**—a friend and rival of Wyspiański—as a response to Wyspiański's work.

Now head back into the nave, turn left, and walk toward the main altar. (If a service is going on, you may not be able to get very far—just look from here.) On the walls, notice Wyspiański's gorgeous Art Nouveau floral patterns.

Up in the apse, take a moment to appreciate the Wyspiański-designed **stained-glass windows** flanking the high altar. On the right is St. Francis, the church's namesake. On the left is the Blessed Salomea—a medieval Polish woman who became queen of Hungary but later returned to Poland and entered a convent after her husband's death. Notice she's dropping a crown—repudiating the earthly world and giving herself over to the simple, stop-and-smell-God's-roses lifestyle of St. Francis. Salomea (who's buried in a side chapel) founded this church. Notice also the Mucha-like paintings by Wyspiański on the pilasters between the windows...yet one more sumptuous Art Nouveau detail in this church that's so rich with them.

• *Head back outside. If no services are going on, you can slip out the side door, to the left of the altar. Otherwise, head back out the way you came and hook right. Either way, you're heading to the right along Franciszkańska street. After passing a few monuments and a tram stop, turn right down busy...*

Grodzka Street

Now you're back on the Royal Way proper. At the corner of Grodzka street stands the modern, copper-colored **Wyspiański Pavilion.** Step inside (daily 9:00-17:00), past the little TI, to see three recent stained-glass windows based on designs Wyspiański once submitted for a contest to redecorate Wawel Cathedral. Although these designs were rejected back then, they were finally realized on the hundredth anniversary of his death (in 2007). Visible from inside the building during the day, and gloriously illuminated to be seen outside the building at night, they represent three Polish historical figures: the gaunt St. Stanisław (Poland's first saint), the skel-

Karol Wojtyła (1920-2005): The Greatest Pole

The man who became St. John Paul II began his life as Karol Wojtyła, born to a humble family in the town of Wadowice near Kraków on May 18, 1920. Karol's mother died when he was a young boy. When he was a teenager, he moved with his father to Kraków to study philosophy and drama at Jagiellonian University. Young Karol was gregarious and athletic—an avid skier, hiker, swimmer, and soccer goalie. During the Nazi occupation in World War II, he was forced to work in a quarry. In defiance of the Nazis, he secretly studied theology and appeared in illegal underground theatrical productions. When the war ended, he resumed his studies, now at the theology faculty.

After graduating in 1947, Wojtyła swiftly rose through the ranks of the Catholic Church hierarchy. By 1964, he was archbishop of Kraków, and just three years later, he became the youngest cardinal ever. Throughout the 1960s, he fought an ongoing battle with the regime when they refused to allow the construction of a church in the Kraków suburb of Nowa Huta. After years of saying Mass for huge crowds in open fields, Wojtyła finally convinced the communists to allow the construction of the Lord's Ark Church in 1977. A year later, Karol Wojtyła was called to the papacy—the first non-Italian pope in more than four centuries. In 1979, he paid a visit to his native Poland. In a series of cautiously provocative speeches, he demonstrated to his countrymen the potential for mass opposition to communism.

Imagine you're Polish in the 1970s. Your country was devastated by World War II and has struggled under an oppressive regime ever since. Food shortages are epidemic. Lines stretch around the block even to buy a measly scrap of bread. Life is bleak, oppressive, and hopeless. Then someone who speaks your language—someone you've admired your entire life, and one of the only people you've seen successfully stand up to the regime—becomes one of the world's most influential people. A Pole like you is the leader of a billion Catholics. He makes you believe that

etal Kazimierz the Great (in the middle), and the swooning King Henry the Pious.

If you're not churched out, you can dip into the **Dominican Church**—just a block away, to your left (described on page 80).

Now continue down Grodzka street. This lively thoroughfare, connecting the Square with Wawel, is teeming with shops—and some of Kraków's best restaurants (see "Eating in Kraków," later). Survey your options now, and choose (and maybe reserve) your favorite for dinner tonight. This street is also characterized by its fine arcades over the sidewalks. While this might seem like a charming Renaissance feature, the arcades were actually added by the Nazis the impossible can happen. He says to you again and again: "*Nie lękajcie się*"—"Have no fear." And you begin to believe it.

From his bully pulpit, the pope had a knack for cleverly challenging the communists—just firmly enough to get his point across, but stopping short of jeopardizing the stature of the Church in Poland. Gentle but pointed wordplay was his specialty. The inspirational role he played in the lives of Lech Wałęsa and the other leaders of Solidarity emboldened them to rise up; it's no coincidence that the first successful trade union strikes in the Soviet Bloc took place shortly after John Paul II became pope. Many people (including Mikhail Gorbachev) credit John Paul II for the collapse of Eastern European communism.

Even as John Paul II's easy charisma attracted new worshippers to the Church (especially young people), his conservatism on issues such as birth control, homosexuality, and female priests pushed away many Catholics. Under his watch, the Church struggled with pedophilia scandals. Many still fault him for turning a blind eye and not putting a stop to these abuses much earlier. By the end of his papacy, John Paul II's failing health and conservatism had caused him to lose stature in worldwide public opinion.

And yet, approval of the pope never waned in Poland. His compatriots—even the relatively few atheists and agnostics—saw John Paul II both as the greatest hero of their people...and as a member of the family, like a kindly grandfather. When Pope John Paul II died on April 2, 2005, the mourning in his homeland was particularly deep and sustained. Musical performances of all kinds were canceled, and the irreverent MTV-style music channel simply went off the air out of respect.

A speedy nine years after his death, Karol Wojtyła became St. John Paul II in April of 2014. Out of 265 popes, only two have been given the title "great." There's already talk in Rome of increasing that number to three. Someday soon we may speak of this man as "St. John Paul the Great." His fellow Poles already do.

after they invaded in 1939; they wanted to convert Kraków into a city befitting its status as the capital of their Polish puppet state.

This is also a good street to find some of Kraków's **milk bars** (two are listed on page 135). The most traditional one is about two blocks down, on the right (at #45), with a simple *Bar Mleczny* sign. These government-subsidized cafeterias are the locals' choice for a quick, cheap, filling, lowbrow lunch. Prices are deliriously cheap (soup costs about a dollar), and the food isn't bad. For more on milk bars, see page 18.

• *One more block ahead, the small square on your right is...*

Mary Magdalene Square
(Plac Św. Marii Magdaleny)

This square offers a great visual example of Kraków's deeply religious character. In the Middle Ages, Kraków was known as "Small Rome" for its many churches. Today, there are 142 churches and monasteries within the city limits (32 in the Old Town alone)—more per square mile than anywhere outside of Rome. You can see several of them from this spot: The nearest, with the picturesque white facade and row of saints out front, is the **Church of Saints Peter and Paul** (Poland's first Baroque church, and a popular tourist concert venue). The statues lining this church's facade are the 11 apostles (minus Judas), plus Mary Magdalene, the square's namesake. The next church to the right, with the twin towers, is the Romanesque **St. Andrew's** (now with a Baroque interior). Dating from the rough-and-tumble 11th century, it was designed to double as a place of last refuge—notice the arrow slits around the impassable lower floor. According to legend, a spring inside this church provided water to citizens who holed up here during the Tatar invasions. The church was spared, but that didn't save the rest of Kraków from being overrun by marauding armies. Imagine this stone fortress of God being the only building standing amid a smoldering and flattened Kraków after the 13th-century destruction.

If you look farther down the street, you can see three more churches. And even the square next to you used to be a church, too—it burned in 1855, and only its footprint survives.

• *Go through the square and turn left down...*

Kanonicza Street (Ulica Kanonicza)

With so many churches around here, the clergy had to live somewhere. Many lived on this well-preserved street—supposedly the oldest street in Kraków. As you walk, look for the cardinal hats over three different doorways. The **Hotel Copernicus,** on the left at #16, is named for a famous guest who stayed here five centuries ago. Directly across the street at #17, the **Bishop Erazm Ciołek Palace** hosts a good exhibit of medieval art and Orthodox icons. Next door, the yellow house at #19 is where Karol Wojtyła lived for 10 years after World War II—long before he became St. John Paul II. Today this building houses the **Archdiocesan Museum,** which is the top spot in the Old Town to learn about Kraków's favorite son. Both of these sights are described later, under "Sights in Kraków."

• *This marks the end of Kanonicza street—and the end of our self-guided walk. But there's still much more to see. Across the busy street, a ramp leads up to the most important piece of ground in all of Poland: Wawel (described next).*

Sights in the Old Town

WAWEL HILL

Wawel (VAH-vehl), a symbol of Polish royalty and independence, is sacred territory to every Polish person. A castle has stood here since the beginning of Poland's recorded history. Today, Wawel—awash in tourists—is the most visited sight in the country. Crowds and an overly complex admissions system for the hill's many historic sights can be exasperating. Thankfully, a stroll through the cathedral and around the castle grounds requires no tickets, and—

with the help of the following commentary—is enough. I've described these sights in the order of a handy self-guided walk. The many museums on Wawel (all described in this section) are mildly interesting but can be skipped (grounds open daily from 6:00 until dusk, inner courtyard closes 30 minutes earlier). In May and June, it's mobbed with students, as it's a required field trip for Polish schoolkids.

Wawel Sights: The sights you'll enter at Wawel are divided into two institutions: church and castle, each with separate tickets. Tickets for the castle sights are sold at two points (at the long line at the top of the ramp, or with no line at the top of the hill, across the central square). The most important church sight—the cathedral—is mostly free, but to enter the paid sights inside (or the museum), get a ticket at the office across from the cathedral entrance.

• *From Kanonicza street—where my self-guided walk ends—head up the long ramp to the castle entry.*

Entry Ramp

Huffing up this ramp, it's easy to imagine how this location—rising above the otherwise flat plains around Kraków—was both strategic and easy to defend. When Kraków was part of the Habsburg Empire in the 19th century, the Austrians turned this castle complex into a fortress, destroying much of its delicate beauty. When Poland regained its independence after World War I, the castle was returned to its former glory. The bricks you see on your left as you climb the ramp bear the names of Poles from around the world who donated to the cause.

The jaunty equestrian statue ahead is **Tadeusz Kościuszko**

(1746-1817). If that name seems familiar, it's because Kościuszko was a hero of the American Revolution and helped design West Point. When he returned to his native Poland, he fought bravely but unsuccessfully against the Russians (during the Partitions that would divide Poland's territory among three neighboring powers). Kościuszko also gave his name to several American towns, a county in Indiana, a brand of mustard from Illinois, and the tallest mountain in Australia.

• *Hiking through the Heraldic Gate next to Kościuszko, you pass the ticket office (if you'll be going into the museums, use the other ticket office, with shorter lines, on the top of the hill—see "Tickets and Reservations," later). As you crest the hill and pass through the stone gate, on your left is...*

▲▲Wawel Cathedral

Poland's national church is its Westminster Abbey. While the history buried here is pretty murky to most Americans, to Poles, this

church is the national mausoleum. It holds the tombs of nearly all of Poland's most important rulers and greatest historical figures.

Cost and Hours: It's usually free to walk around the main part of the church. You must buy a 12-zł ticket to climb up the tallest tower; visit the crypt, the royal tombs, and some

of the lesser chapels; and tour the John Paul II Wawel Cathedral Museum. Buy this ticket at the house across from the cathedral entry—marked *KASA*—where you can also rent an audioguide (7 zł). The cathedral is open Mon-Sat 9:00-17:00, Sun from 12:30, Oct-March daily until 16:00 (tel. 12-429-9516, www.katedrawawelska.pl). Note that the cathedral's museum (described later) is closed on Sunday.

Cathedral Exterior

Before entering, go around to the far side of the cathedral to take in its profile. This uniquely eclectic church is the product of centuries of haphazard additions...yet somehow, it works. It began as a simple, stripped-down Romanesque church in the 12th century. (The white base of the nearest tower is original. Anything at Wawel that's made of white limestone like this was probably part of the earliest Romanesque structures.) Kazimierz the Great and his predecessors gradually surrounded the cathedral with some 20 chapels, which were further modified over the centuries, making this beautiful church a happy hodgepodge of styles. To give you a sense of the historical sweep, scan the chapels from left to right: 14th-century Gothic, 12th-century Romanesque (the base of the tower), 17th-century Baroque (the inside is Baroque, though the exterior is a copy of its Renaissance neighbor), 16th-century Renaissance, and 18th- and 19th-century Neoclassical. (This variety in styles is even more evident in the chapels' interiors, which we'll see soon.)

Pay attention to the two particularly interesting domed chapels to the right of the tall tower. The gold one is the Sigismund Chapel, housing memorials to the Jagiellonian kings—including Sigismund the Old, who was responsible for Kraków's Renaissance renovation in the 16th century. The Jagiellonian Dynasty was a high point in Polish history. During that golden 16th century, Poland was triple the size it is today, stretching all the way to the Ottoman Empire and the Black Sea. Poles consider the Sigismund Chapel, made with 80 pounds of gold, to be the finest Renaissance chapel north of the Alps. The copper-domed chapel next to it, home to the Swedish Vasa dynasty, resembles its neighbor (but it's a copy built 150 years later, and without all that gold).

Go back around and face the church's **front entry** for more architectonic extravagance. The tallest tower, called the Sigismund

Tower, has a clock with only an hour hand. Climbing a few steps into the entry, you see Gothic chapels (with pointy windows) flanking the door, a Renaissance ceiling, lavish Baroque decoration over the door, and some big bones (a simple whale rib and two vertebrae). In the Middle Ages, these were thought to have been the bones of the mythic Wawel dragon and put here as an oddity to be viewed by the public. (Back

then, there were no museums, so unusual items like these were used to lure people to the church.) The door is the original from the 14th century, with fine wrought-iron work. The K with the crown stands for Kazimierz the Great. The black marble frame is made of Kraków stone from nearby quarries.

Cathedral Interior

The cathedral interior is slathered in Baroque memorials and tombs, decorated with tapestries, and soaked in Polish history. The ensemble was designed to help keep Polish identity strong through the ages. It has...and it still does.

After you step inside, you'll follow the one-way, clockwise route that leads you through the choir, then around the back of the apse, then back to the entry.

At the entry, look straight ahead to see the silver tomb under a **canopy,** inspired by the one in St. Peter's Basilica at the Vatican. It contains the remains of the first Polish saint, Stanisław (from the 11th century). In front of the canopy, look for a metallic reliquary that's shaped like a book with its pages being ruffled by the wind (labeled, in Latin, *Sanctus Johannes Paulus II*). The glass capsule in the reliquary holds a drop of St. John Paul II's blood. It takes this shape because of what believers consider a highly significant moment during his memorial service: Before a crowd of thousands on St. Peter's Square in Rome, a book was placed on John Paul II's simple wooden coffin. As the service processed, its pages were ruffled back and forth by the wind, until they were finally slammed shut...as if the Holy Spirit were "closing the book" on his life.

Go behind this canopy into the ornately carved **choir** area. For 200 years, the colorful chair to the right of the high altar has been the seat of Kraków's archbishops, including Karol Wojtyła, who served here for 14 years before becoming pope. It's here that Polish royal coronations took place.

Now you'll continue into the left aisle. From here, if you have a ticket, you can enter two of the optional attractions: Seventy claustrophobic wooden stairs lead up to the 11-ton **Sigismund Bell** and pleasant views of the steeples and spires of Kraków. Then, to the left (closer to where you entered), descend into the little **crypt** (with a rare purely Romanesque interior), which houses the remains of Adam Mickiewicz, the Romantic poet whose statue dominates the Main Market Square, and another beloved Romantic poet and playwright, Juliusz Słowacki. You'll also find a white marble monument to Fryderyk Chopin (who's buried in Paris), put here on the 200th anniversary of his birth in 2010.

Now continue around the apse (behind the main altar). After curving around to the right, look for the red-marble tomb (on the right) of The Great One—**Kazimierz,** of course. Look for *Kazimierz Wielki*—at his feet you can see a little beaver. This is an allusion to a famous saying about Kazimierz, the nation-builder: He found a Poland made of wood, and left one made of brick and stone.

You may notice that there's one VIP (Very Important Pole) who's missing...Karol Wojtyła, a.k.a. John Paul II. Even so, a few more steps toward the entrance, on the left, is the **Chapel of St.**

John Paul II. The late pontiff left no specific requests for his body, and the Vatican controversially (to Poles, at least) chose to entomb him in Vatican City, instead of sending him back home to Wawel. While Karol Wojtyła's remains are in St. Peter's Basilica, this chapel was recently converted to honor him—with a plaque in the floor and an altar with his picture. Someday, Poles hope, he may be moved here (but, the Vatican says, don't hold your breath).

Directly opposite the chapel, you'll see the rusty funeral regalia (orb and scepter) of **St. Jadwiga;** ten steps farther is her white sarcophagus (with a dog

at her feet). This 14th-century "king" of Poland advanced the fortunes of her realm by partnering with the king of Lithuania. The resulting Jagiellonian dynasty fought off the Teutonic Knights, helped Christianize Lithuania, and oversaw a high-water mark in Polish history. (Despite the queen's many contributions, the sexism of the age meant that she was considered a "king" rather than a "queen.") She was sainted by Pope John Paul II in 1997.

Across from Jadwiga, peek into the gorgeous 16th-century **Sigismund Chapel,** with its silver altar (this is the gold-roofed chapel you just saw from outside). Locals consider this the "Pearl of the Polish Renaissance" and the finest Renaissance building outside Italy.

Just beyond is a door leading back outside. If you don't have a ticket, your tour is finished—head out here. But those with a ticket can keep circling around.

Next, look into the **Vasa Chapel:** Remember that its exterior matches the restrained, Renaissance style of the Sigismund Chapel, but the interior is clearly Baroque, slathered with gold and silver—quite a contrast.

To the left of the main door, take a look at the Gothic **Holy Cross Chapel,** with its seemingly Orthodox-style 14th-century frescoes.

In the back corner of the church—on the other side of the main door—is the entrance to the **royal tombs.** (You'll exit outside the church, so be sure you're done in here first.) Once downstairs, the first big room, an original Romanesque space called St. Leonard's Crypt, houses Poland's greatest war heroes: Kościuszko (of American Revolution fame), Jan III Sobieski (who successfully defended Vienna from the Ottomans; he's in the simple black coffin with the gold inscription *J III S*), Sikorski, Poniatowski, and so on.

Poles consider this room highly significant as the place where St. John Paul II celebrated his first Mass after becoming a priest (in November of 1946). Then you'll wander through several rooms of second-tier Polish kings, queens, and their kids. Head down more stairs to find the plaque honoring the Polish victims of the Katyń massacre in the USSR during World War II. Stepping into the next room, you'll see the cathedral's newest tomb: President Lech Kaczyński and his wife Helena, who were among the 96 Polish politicians killed in a tragic 2010 plane crash—which was delivering those diplomats to a ceremony memorializing the Katyń massacre. Up a few stairs is the final grave, belonging to Marshal Józef Piłsudski, the WWI hero who later seized power and was the de facto ruler of Poland from 1926 to 1935. His tomb was moved here so the rowdy soldiers who came to pay their respects wouldn't disturb the others.

• *Nearby (and covered by the same ticket as the tower and crypt) is the cathedral's museum.*

John Paul II Wawel Cathedral Museum

This small museum, up the little staircase across from the cathedral entry, was recently spiffed up and rededicated to Kraków's favorite archbishop. It fills four rooms with artifacts relating to both the cathedral and St. John Paul II.

Downstairs is the Royal Room, with vestments, swords, regalia, coronation robes, and items that were once buried with the kings, as well as early treasury items (from the 11th through 16th century). Upstairs is the "Papal Room" with items from St. John Paul II's life: his armchair, vestments, caps, shoes, and miter (pointy pope hat), plus souvenirs from his travels. (If you're into papal memorabilia, the collection at the nearby Archdiocesan Museum—described later—is better.) The adjoining room holds a later treasury collection (17th through 20th century).

Cost and Hours: Admission to this museum is included with your ticket to the cathedral's special options (Sigismund Bell tower, plus crypt and royal tombs); open Mon-Sat 9:00-17:00, Oct-March until 16:00, closed Sun year-round; tel. 12-429-3321.

• *When you're finished with the cathedral sights, stroll around the...*

▲▲Wawel Castle Grounds

In the rest of the castle, you'll uncover more fragments of Kraków's history and have the opportunity to visit several museums. I con-

sider the museums skippable, but if you want to visit them, buy tickets before you enter the inner courtyard. Read the descriptions on page 68 to decide which museums appeal to you.

Read the descriptions on page 68 to decide which museums appeal to you.

❍ **Self-Guided Tour:** This guided stroll, which doesn't enter any of the admission-charging attractions, is plenty for most visitors.

• *For a historical orientation, stand with the cathedral to your back, and survey the empty field between here and the castle walls.*

Gothic Church Ruins: This hilltop has seen lots of changes over the years. Kazimierz the Great turned a small fortress into a mighty Gothic castle in the 14th century. But that original fortress burned to the ground in 1499, and ever since, Wawel has been in flux. For example, in the grassy field, notice the foundations of two Gothic churches that were destroyed when the Austrians took over Wawel in the 19th century and needed a parade ground for their troops. (They built the red-brick hospital building beyond the field, now used by the Wawel administration.)

• *Facing the cathedral, look right to find a grand green-and-pink entryway. Go through here and into the palace's dramatically Renaissance-style...*

Inner Courtyard: If this space seems to have echoes of Florence, that's because it was designed and built by young Florentines

after Kazimierz's original castle burned down. Notice the three distinct levels: The ground floor housed the private apartments of the higher nobility (governors and castle administrators); the middle level held the private apartments of the king; and the top floor—much taller, to allow more light to fill its large spaces—were the public state rooms of the king. The ivy-covered wing to the right of where you entered is Fascist in style, built as the headquarters of the notorious Nazi governor of German-occupied Poland, Hans

Frank. (He was tried and executed in Nürnberg after the war.) At the far end of the courtyard is a false wall, designed to create a pleasant Renaissance symmetry, and also to give the illusion that the castle is bigger than it is. Looking through the windows, notice that there's nothing but air on the other side. When foreign dignitaries visited, these windows could be covered to complete the illusion. The entrances to most Wawel museums are around this courtyard, and some believe that you'll find something even more special: chakra.

Adherents to the Hindu concept of **chakra** believe that a powerful energy field connects all living things. Some believe that, mirroring the seven chakra points on the body (from head to groin), there are seven points on the surface of the earth where this energy is most concentrated: Delhi, Delphi, Jerusalem, Mecca, Rome, Velehrad...and Wawel Hill—specifically over there in the corner (immediately to your left as you enter the courtyard—the stretches of wall flanking the door to the baggage-check room). Look for peaceful people (here or elsewhere on the castle grounds) with their eyes closed. One thing's for sure: They're not thinking of Kazimierz the Great. The smudge marks on the wall are from people pressing up against this corner, trying to absorb some good vibes from this chakra spot.

The Wawel administration seems creeped out by all this. They've done what they can to discourage this ritual (such as putting up information boards right where the power is supposedly most focused), but believers still gravitate from far and wide to hug the wall. Give it a try...and let the chakra be with you. (Just for fun, ask a Wawel tour guide about the chakra, and watch her squirm—they're forbidden to talk about it.)

• *If you want to visit some of the* **castle museums** *(you can enter four of the five from this courtyard), you'll first need to buy tickets elsewhere. Stick with me for a little longer to finish our tour of the grounds, and we'll wind up near a ticket office.*

Head downhill through the square, across to the gap in the buildings beyond the field, to the...

Viewpoint over the Vistula: Belly up to the wall and enjoy the panorama over the **Vistula River** and Kraków's outskirts. The "Polish Mississippi"—which runs its entire course in Polish lands—is the nation's artery for trade and cultural connection. It stretches 650 miles from the foothills of the Tatra Mountains in southern Poland, through most of the country's major cities (Kraków, Warsaw, Toruń), before emptying into the Baltic Sea in Gdańsk.

From this viewpoint, you can see some unusual landmarks, including the odd wavy-roofed building just across the river (which houses the Manggha Japanese art gallery) and the biggest conference center in Poland (opened in 2015, to the left of the wavy building). A bit farther to the left is an eyesore of a communist concrete hotel, now used as a billboard. In the summer, you'll see a popular and very cool "beach bar" filling the field in front of the building (the Forum Przestrzenie, described later). To the right, the suspiciously symmetrical little bulge that tops the highest hill on the horizon is the artificial Kościuszko Mound (described later). And on a particularly crisp day, far in the distance (beyond the wavy building), you can see the Tatra Mountains marking the border of Slovakia.

Now look directly below you, along the riverbank (to the left), to find a fire-belching monument to the **dragon** that was instrumental in the founding of Kraków. Once upon a time, a prince named Krak founded a town on Wawel Hill. It was the perfect location—except for the fire-breathing dragon that lived in the caves under the hill and terrorized the town. Prince Krak had to feed the dragon all of the town's livestock to keep the monster from going after the townspeople. But Krak, with the help of a clever shoemaker, came up with a plan. They stuffed a sheep's skin with sulfur and left it outside the dragon's cave. The dragon swallowed it and, before long, developed a terrible case of heartburn. To put the fire out, the dragon started drinking water from the Vistula. He kept drinking and drinking until he finally exploded. The town was saved, and Kraków thrived. Today visitors enjoy watching the dragon blow fire into the air (about every four minutes, but can vary from a big plume to a tiny puff).

If you'd like a higher viewpoint on the riverfront, you can pay 4 zł to climb 137 stairs to the top of **Sandomierska Tower** (at the far end of the hill, past the visitors center, no elevator). But I'd skip it—the view from up top is only through small windows (May-June daily 10:00-18:00, June-Aug until 19:00, Sept-Oct until 17:00, closed Nov-April).

• *Our Wawel tour is finished. If you'd like to explore some of the museums, you can buy your tickets in the nearby visitors center (head back into the main Wawel complex—with the empty field—and turn right); here you'll also find WCs, a café, a gift shop, and other amenities. Or go down to the riverfront park: Walk downhill (through the Dragon's Den, or use the main ramp and circle around the base of the hill) to reach the park—one of the most delightful places in Kraków to simply relax, with beautiful views back on the castle complex.*

Wawel Castle Museums

There are five museums and exhibits in Wawel Castle (not includ-ing the cathedral and Cathedral Museum, the Dragon's Den, or Sandomierska Tower—all described earlier).

While the following sights are fascinating to Poles, casual visi-tors often find that the best visit is simply to enjoy the cathedral and the castle grounds (following my self-guided tour, earlier). Each sight has its own admission and slightly different hours. English descriptions are posted, and you can rent an audioguide for 20 zł that covers some of the sights. If you do visit all of the sights, start with the Royal State Rooms and/or Royal Private Apartments (which share an entrance), then—on your way back down—see the Oriental Art exhibit, then the Crown Treasury and Armory. Fi-nally, head back to the outer courtyard for the Lost Wawel exhibit.

Tickets and Reservations: Each sight has separate tickets (prices listed later), which you'll buy at one of two ticket windows. Most people line up at the top of the entry ramp, but it's faster to buy tickets at the visitors center at the far corner of the castle grounds (across the field from the cathedral, near the café). You generally can't buy tickets at the door of each sight, so decide in advance which ones you want to see and buy all your tickets at the start of your visit. A limited number of tickets are sold for each sight; boards show the number of available tickets. Tickets come with an assigned entry time (though you can usually sneak in before your scheduled appointment). In summer, ticket lines can be long, and sights can sell out by midmorning. You can make a reservation for some sights (tel. 12-422-1697, extra fee), but frankly, if they're sold out, you're not missing much.

Hours: Unless otherwise noted, the museums are open April-Oct Tue-Fri 9:30-17:00, Sat-Sun from 10:00, closed Mon; Nov-March Tue-Sat 9:30-16:00, closed Sun-Mon. The last ticket is sold 1.25 hours before closing, and the last entry is one hour before closing.

Exceptions: In summer (April-Oct), Lost Wawel and the Crown Treasury and Armory are free and open on Mondays (9:30-13:00). Off-season (Nov-March), everything is closed on Monday and most are closed on Sunday except Lost Wawel and the Royal State Rooms (Jan-March only).

Information: Tel. 12-422-5155 ext. 219, www.wawel.krakow.pl.

Eating: Various light eateries circle the castle courtyard, but if you just want a drink, it's hard to beat the affordable self-service café next to the Lost Wawel entrance, with fine views across to the cathedral.

▲Royal State Rooms (Komnaty Królewskie)

While precious to Poles, these rooms are mediocre by European standards. Still, this is the best of the Wawel museums. First, climb up to the top floor and wander through some ho-hum halls with antique furniture to reach the Throne Room, with 30 carved heads in the ceiling. According to legend, one of these heads got mouthy when the king was trying to pass judgment—so its mouth has been covered to keep it quiet. Continue into some of the palace's finest rooms, with 16th-century Brussels tapestries (140 of the original series of 300 survive), remarkably decorated wooden ceilings, and gorgeous leather-tooled walls. Wandering these halls (with their period furnishings), you get a feeling for the 16th- and 17th-century glory days of Poland, when it was a leading power in Eastern Europe. The Senate Room, with its throne and elaborate tapestries, is the climax. On your way back down to the courtyard, you'll walk right past the Oriental Art exhibit.

KRAKÓW

Cost and Hours: 20 zł, see hours listed earlier, Nov-March also open—and free—Sun 10:00-16:00, enter through courtyard.

Royal Private Apartments (Prywatne Apartamenty Królewskie)

The rooms, which look similar to the State Rooms, can only be visited with a guided (and included) 45-minute tour. As spaces are strictly limited, these tend to sell out the fastest (on busy days, they may book up by around 10:00).

Cost and Hours: 25 zł, request English tour when buying your ticket—they depart 3/hour, see hours listed earlier, enter through courtyard.

Oriental Art (Sztuka Wschodu)

Though small, this exhibit displays swords, carpets, banners, vases, and other items dating from the 1683 Battle of Vienna, in which the Ottoman army attempted to capture the Austrian capital. A painting in the entrance room sets the stage. These are trophies of Jan III Sobieski, the Polish king who led a pan-European army to victory in that battle.

Cost and Hours: 8 zł, see hours listed earlier, enter through courtyard; don't miss entry on your way back downstairs from Royal State Rooms.

KRAKÓW

Crown Treasury and Armory (Skarbiec i Zbrojownia)

This is a decent collection of swords, saddles, and shields; ornately decorated muskets, crossbows, and axes; and cannons in the basement. In the room with the suits of armor, look on the right wall for the winged armor of the Hussars—Polish warriors who made a terrifying noise when riding at top speed on horseback. Back upstairs is the smaller treasury section. From the central room of precious tankards and platters, smaller adjoining rooms hold the most precious items. Up two stairs, look for the regalia given to Jan III Sobieski as thanks for his defeat of the Ottoman invaders in the Battle of Vienna: giant swords consecrated by the pope and the mantle (robe) of the Order of the Holy Ghost from France's King Louis XIV. Nearby is the 13th-century coronation sword of the Polish kings.

Cost and Hours: 20 zł, see hours listed earlier, April-Oct also open—and free—Mon 9:30-13:00, enter through courtyard.

Lost Wawel (Wawel Zaginiony)

This exhibit traces the history of the hill and its various churches and castles. On your way in, view the model of the entire castle complex in the 18th century (pre-Austrian razing). From here, the one-way route leads through scarcely explained excavations of a 10th-century church. On the way, you'll see models of the cathedral at various historical stages (originally Romanesque—much simpler, before all the colorful, bulbous domes, chapels, and towers were added—then Gothic, and so on). Then you'll loop through a collection of architectural decorations, ending with a display of tiles from 16th-century stoves that once heated the place.

Cost and Hours: 10 zł, see hours listed earlier; April-Oct also open—and free—Mon 9:30-13:00; Nov-March also open—and free—Sun 9:30-13:00; enter near snack bar across from side of cathedral.

NATIONAL MUSEUM BRANCHES

Kraków's National Museum (Muzeum Narodowe) is made up of a series of small but interesting collections scattered throughout the city (www.mnk.pl). I've listed the best of the National Museum's branches below, and you can find details on current exhibitions at the National Museum website. A 50-zł **combo-ticket** covers the permanent collections in all of these museums (good for your entire stay)—worth considering if you'll be visiting more than three of them. National Museum branches are free to enter on Sunday (but some have reduced hours).

▲▲Gallery of 19th-Century Polish Art
(Galeria Sztuki Polskiej XIX Wieku)

This small and surprisingly enjoyable collection of works by obscure Polish artists fills the upper level of the Cloth Hall. While you probably won't recognize any of the Polish names in here—and this collection isn't quite as impressive as Warsaw's National Gallery—many of these paintings are just plain delightful. It's worth a visit to see some Polish canvases in their native land, and to enjoy views over the Square from the hall's upper terraces.

Cost and Hours: 20 zł, free on Sun; open Tue-Fri 9:00-17:00, Sat 10:00-18:00, Sun 10:00-16:00, closed Mon; dry 7-zł audioguide, entrance on side of Cloth Hall facing Adam Mickiewicz statue, tel. 12-424-4600.

Background: During the 19th century—when every piece of art in this museum was created—there was no "Poland." The country had been split up among its powerful neighbors in a series of three Partitions and would not appear again on the map of Europe until after World War I. Meanwhile, the 19th century was a period of national revival throughout Europe, when various previously marginalized ethnic groups began to take pride in what made them different from their neighbors. So the artists you see represented here were grappling with trying to forge a national identity at a time when they didn't even have a nation. You'll sense a pessimism that comes from a country that feels abused by foreign powers, mingled with a resolute spirit of national pride.

◉ Self-Guided Tour: The collection fills just four rooms: Two small rooms in the center and two big halls on either side. On a quick visit, focus on the highlights in the big halls I mention here.

Entering the Cloth Hall, buy your ticket and head up the stairs—pausing on the first floor to peek out onto the inviting **café terrace** for a fine view of the Square and St. Mary's. Then continue up to the main exhibit, on the second floor.

The first two small rooms don't feature much of interest. You enter **Room I** (Bacciarelli Room), with works from the Enlightenment; straight ahead is **Room II** (Michałowski Room), featuring Romantic works from 1822 to 1863. The larger, twin halls on either side merit a linger.

Siemiradzki Room (Room III, on the right): This features art of the Academy—that is, "conformist" art embraced by the art critics of the day. Entering the room, turn right and survey the canvases counterclockwise. The space is dominated by the works of Jan

Matejko, a remarkably productive painter who specialized in epic historical scenes that also commented on his own era (for more on Matejko, see page 195).

• *Circling the room, look for these paintings.*

Jan Matejko, *Wenyhora*: The first big canvas is Matejko's depiction of Wenyhora, a late-18th-century Ukrainian soothsayer who, according to legend, foretold Poland's hardships—the three Partitions, Poland's pact with Napoleon, and its difficulties regaining nationhood. Like many Poles of the era, Matejko was preoccupied with Poland's tragic fate, imbuing this scene with an air of inevitable tragedy.

Jacek Malcezewski, *Death of Ellenai*: A similar gloominess is reflected in this canvas. The main characters in a Polish Romantic poem, Ellenai and Anhelli, have been exiled to a remote cabin in Siberia (in Russia, one of the great powers occupying Poland). Just when they think things can't get worse...Ellenai dies. Anhelli sits immobilized by grief.

• *A few canvases down, dominating the right side of the hall, is...*

Jan Matejko, *Tadeusz Kościuszko at Racławice*: One of the heroes of the American Revolution, now back in his native Poland fighting the Russians, doffs his hat after his unlikely victory at the Battle at Racławice. In this battle (which ultimately had little bearing on Russia's drive to overtake Poland), a ragtag army of Polish peasants defeated the Russian forces. Kościuszko is clad in an American uniform, symbolizing Matejko's respect for the American ideals of democracy and self-determination.

• *Dominating the far wall is...*

Henryk Siemiradzki, *Nero's Torches*: On the left, Roman citizens eagerly gather to watch Christians being burned at the stake (on the right). The symbolism is clear: The meek and downtrodden (whether Christians in the time of Rome, or Poles in the heyday of Russia and Austria) may be persecuted now, but we have faith that their noble ideals will ultimately prevail.

• *On the next wall, find...*

Pantaleon Szyndler, *Bathing Girl*: This piece evokes the orientalism popular in 19th-century Europe, when romanticized European notions of the Orient (such as harem slave girls) were popular artistic themes. Already voyeuristic, the painting was originally downright lewd until Szyndler painted over a man leering at the woman from the left side of the canvas.

• *The huge canvas on this wall is...*

Jan Matejko, *The Prussian Homage:* The last Grand Master of the fearsome Teutonic Knights swears allegiance to the Polish king in 1525. This historic ceremony took place in the Main Market Square in Kraków, the capital at the time. Notice the Cloth Hall balustrade and the spires of St. Mary's Church in the background. Matejko has painted his own face on one of his favorite historical figures, the jester Stańczyk at the foot of the throne (for more on Stańczyk, see page 195).

• *Continue the rest of the way around the room. Keep an eye out for Tadeusz Ajdukiewicz's portrait of Helena Modrzejewska, a popular actress of the time, attending a party in this very building. Finally, backtrack through Room I and continue into the...*

Chełmoński Room (Room IV): Featuring works of the late 19th century, this section includes Realism and the first inklings of Symbolism and Impressionism. Just as elsewhere in Europe (including Paris, where many of these artists trained), artists were beginning to throw off the conventions of the Academy and embrace their own muse.

• *As you turn right and proceed counterclockwise through the room, the first stretch of canvases features landscapes and genre paintings. Among these, a particularly fine canvas is...*

Wladyslaw Malecki, *A Gathering of Storks:* The majestic birds stand under big willows in front of the setting sun. Even seemingly innocent wildlife paintings have a political message: Storks are particularly numerous in Poland, making them a subtle patriotic symbol.

• *A few canvases down, find...*

Józef Brandt, *A Meeting on a Bridge:* This dramatic painting shows soldiers and aristocrats pushing a farmer into a ditch—a comment on the state of the Polish people at that time. Just to the right, see Brandt's Fight for a Turkish Standard. This artist specialized in battle scenes, frequently involving a foe from the East—as was often the reality here along Europe's buffer zone with Asia.

• *Just to the left of Brandt's works is...*

Samuel Hirszenberg, *School of Talmudists:* Young Jewish students pore over the Talmud. One of them, deeply lost in thought, may be pondering more than ancient Jewish law. This canvas suggests the inclusion of Jews in Poland's cultural tapestry during this age. While still subject to pervasive bigotry here, many Jewish refugees found Poland to be a relatively welcoming, tolerant place to settle on a typically hostile continent.

• *Dominating the end of the room is...*

Józef Chełmoński, Four-in-Hand: In this intersection of worlds, a Ukrainian horseman gives a lift to a pipe-smoking nobleman. Feel the thrilling energy as the horses charge directly at you through splashing puddles.

• *Heading back toward the entrance, on the right wall, watch for...*

Witold Pruszkowski, *Water Nymphs:* Based on Slavic legends (and wearing traditional Ukrainian costumes), these mischievous, siren-like beings have just taken one victim (see his hand in the foreground) and are about to descend on another (seen faintly in the upper-right corner). Beyond this painting are some travel pictures from Italy and France (including some that are very Impressionistic, suggesting a Parisian influence).

• *Flanking the entrance/exit door are two of this room's best works. First, on the right, is...*

Władysław Podkowiński, *Frenzy:* This gripping painting's title *(Szał)*, tellingly, has been translated as either Ecstasy or Insanity. A pale, sensuous woman—possibly based on a socialite for whom the artist fostered a desperate but unrequited love—clutches an all-fired-up black stallion that's frothing at the mouth. This sexually charged painting caused a frenzy indeed at its 1894 unveiling, leading the unbalanced artist to attack his own creation with a knife (you can still see the slash marks in the canvas).

• *And finally, on the other side of the door is...*

Jacek Malczewski, *Introduction:* A young painter's apprentice on a bench contemplates his future. Surrounded by nature and with his painter's tools beside him, it's easy to imagine this as a self-portrait of the artist as a young man...wondering if he's choosing the correct path. Malczewski was an extremely talented Młoda Polska artist who tends to be overshadowed by his contemporary, Wyspiański. Viewing this canvas—and others by him—makes me feel grateful that he decided to stick with painting.

Szołayski House (Kamienica Szołayskich)

This restored mansion, just one block from the Main Market Square, features high-quality temporary exhibits, most often with artists from the early 20th century. Recent exhibits have featured "Kraków in 1900" and French sculptor Auguste Rodin; many have showcased Art Nouveau works by the Młoda Polska movement (for more on this movement and its members, see the sidebar earlier in this chapter). In the past, the museum featured that movement's prodigiously talented headliner, Stanisław Wyspiański—and in the future, he may be back here. But in the meantime, find out what's on, and if the artist or theme interests you, check it out.

Cost and Hours: 20 zł—but varies with exhibits, Tue-Fri 9:00-17:00, Sat 10:00-18:00, Sun 10:00-16:00, closed Mon, one block northwest of the Square at plac Szczepański 9, tel. 12-433-5450.

Nearby: The charming and stately square that Szołayski House faces, **plac Szczepański,** is a hub for youthful, cutting-edge, artistic types. Tucked in a corner of the Old Town, just away from the Square, it's a strange and wonderful little oasis of urban sophistication holding out against the rising tide of tacky tourism. In addition to Szołayski House itself, the square has several bohemian cafés (including the recommended Charlotte). If you follow Szczepańska street one more block out to the Planty, then turn left, you'll find **Bunkier Sztuki,** an art gallery that fills an unfortunate communist-era building that really does feel like a bunker. But this conformist architecture is filled with quite the opposite: changing exhibitions of contemporary art (12 zł, free on Tue, open Tue-Sun 11:00-19:00, closed Mon, http://bunkier.art.pl). The gallery's fine café, under a delightfully airy canopy facing the Planty, has a Parisian ambience—a great place to escape the crowds and/or rain (see "Eating in Kraków," later).

Bishop Erazm Ciołek Palace
(Pałac Biskupa Erazma Ciołka)

This branch of the National Museum features two separate art collections. Upstairs, the extensive "Art of Old Poland" section shows off works from the 12th through the 18th century, with room after room of altarpieces, sculptures, paintings, and more. The "Orthodox Art of the Old Polish Republic" section on the ground floor offers a taste of the remote Eastern reaches of Poland, with icons and other ecclesiastical art from the Orthodox faith. You'll see a sizeable section of the iconostasis (wall of icons) from the town of Lipovec. Both collections are covered by the same ticket and are very well presented in a modern facility. Items are labeled in English, but there's not much description beyond the 7-zł audioguide.

Cost and Hours: 10 zł, free on Sun; open Tue-Fri 9:00-16:00, Sat 10:00-18:00, Sun 10:00-16:00, closed Mon; Kanonicza 17, tel. 12-424-9371.

Kraków's Homeless Masterpieces

Kraków is home to a few priceless paintings—and one in particular, an exquisite Leonardo da Vinci—that officially belong to the Czartoryski Museum. However, that museum has been closed for renovation for several years, and there's no confident ETA for its reopening. In the meantime, these magnificent paintings have been shuffled around the city, displayed here and there, making them tricky to track down. Art lovers will want to get the latest on where to see these masterpieces. At last sighting, the Leonardo was being displayed at the Main Branch of the National Museum, while the Rembrandt was at the National Museum's Europeum gallery (for details on both, see "More National Museum Branches," later).

When you find them, here are the details:

Leonardo da Vinci's *Lady with an Ermine*

This small (21 x 16 inches) but magnificently executed portrait of a teenage girl is a rare surviving work by one of history's greatest minds. Spend some time lingering over the canvas (dating from 1489 or 1490). The girl is likely Cecilia Gallerani, the young mistress of Ludovico Sforza, the duke of Milan and Leonardo's employer. The ermine (white during winter) suggests chastity (thus bolstering Cecilia's questioned virtue) but is also a naughty reference to the duke's nickname, Ermellino—notice that his mistress is sensually, um, "stroking the ermine."

Painted before the *Mona Lisa*, the portrait was immediately recognized as revolutionary. Cecilia turns to look at someone, her gaze directed to the side. Leonardo catches this unguarded, informal moment, an unheard-of gesture in the days of the posed, front-facing formal portrait. Her simple body language and faraway gaze speak volumes about her inner thoughts and personality. Leonardo tweaks the generic Renaissance "pyramid" composition, turning it to a three-quarters angle, and softens it with curved lines that trace from Cecilia's eyes and down her cheek and slop-

▲Czartoryski Museum (Muzeum Czartoryskich)

This eclectic collection, displaying armor, handicrafts, decorative arts, and paintings, has been closed for a years-long renovation, and its reopening date is unclear. When it does open, it should once again display priceless paintings by Leonardo da Vinci and Rembrandt (see sidebar).

Beyond the famous paintings, the rest of the collection in-

ing shoulders before doubling back across her folded arms. The background—once gray and blue—was painted black in the 19th century.

In a recent high-tech analysis using special lights and cameras, conservators were able to virtually peel back layers of paint to see earlier "drafts" of the painting (Leonardo was known to tinker with his works over time). They've revealed that the ermine was likely not included in the original version. Perhaps Leonardo added it later as a nod to the duke.

Lady with an Ermine is a rare surviving portrait in oil by Leonardo. It's better preserved than her famous cousin in Paris (*Mona Lisa*), and—many think—simply more beautiful. Can we be sure it's really by the enigmatic Leonardo? Yep—the master's fingerprints were found literally pressed into the paint (he was known to work areas of paint directly with his fingertips).

Other Masterpieces

Rembrandt van Rijn's *Landscape with the Good Samaritan* (1638) is a small, detailed painting depicting the popular parable. It is one of only a few known landscapes by Rembrandt. On the right, the samaritan helps the wounded man onto his horse (as a little boy watches). To the left, much farther down the road (just beyond the waterfall), find the two tiny figures walking—the priest and the Levite who passed the injured man by.

The museum technically owns a third masterpiece, **Raphael's *Portrait of a Young Man,*** but its whereabouts are unknown. Arguably one of the most famous and most valuable stolen paintings of all time, it's quite likely a self-portrait (but possibly a portrait of Raphael by another artist), depicting a Renaissance dandy, clad in a fur coat, with a self-satisfied smirk. Painted (perhaps) by the Renaissance master in 1513 or 1514, and purchased by a Czartoryski prince around the turn of the 19th century, the work was seized by the occupying Nazis during World War II. Along with the paintings by Leonardo and Rembrandt, this Raphael decorated the Wawel Castle residence of Nazi governor Hans Frank. But when Frank and the Nazis fled the invading Red Army at the end of the war, many of their pilfered artworks were lost—including the Raphael.

cludes ornate armor (including a ceremonial Turkish tent from the 1683 siege of Vienna, plus feathered Hussar armor), tapestries, treasury items, majolica pottery, Meissen porcelain figures, an impressive painting gallery (including Italian, French, and Dutch High Renaissance and Baroque, as well as Czartoryski family portraits), and ancient art (mostly sculptures and vases).

The museum's collection came about, in part, thanks to Poland's 1791 constitution (Europe's first), which inspired Princess Izabela Czartoryska to begin gathering bits of Polish history and culture. She fled with the collection to Paris after the 1830 insurrection, and 45 years later, her grandson returned it to its present Kraków location. When he ran out of space, he bought part of the monastery across the street, joining the buildings with a fancy passageway. During World War II, the Nazis hauled the collection to Germany; although most of it has been returned, some pieces are still missing.

Cost and Hours: Get the latest from the TI about when the museum will reopen, or check www.mnk.pl/branch. It's 2 blocks north of the Main Market Square and a short walk from the Florian Gate at ulica Św. Jana 19.

More National Museum Branches

While less interesting than the branches listed earlier, the National Museum's **Main Branch** (Gmach Główny) is worth a visit for museum completists. It features 20th-century Polish art and temporary exhibits (10 zł, more for special exhibits, a few blocks west of the Main Market Square at aleja 3 Maja 1). It regularly hosts compelling special exhibits, and until the Czartoryski Museum (described earlier) reopens, this is where you'll most likely find Leonardo da Vinci's *Lady with an Ermine.* The **Europeum** collection, housed in a restored granary, features works by European masters, including Breughel and Veneziano, along with a range of lesser-known artists; until the Czartoryski Museum reopens, it's the most likely place you'll find Rembrandt's *Landscape with the Good Samaritan* (just west of the Old Town at plac Sikorskiego 6). For more branches, and to confirm the location of these masterpieces, see www.mnk.pl.

OTHER OLD TOWN ATTRACTIONS
▲▲Rynek Underground Museum (Podziemia Rynku)

Recent work to renovate the Square's pavement unearthed a wealth of remains from previous structures. Now you can do some urban spelunking with a visit to this high-tech medieval-history museum, which is literally underground—beneath all the photo-snapping tourists on the Square above.

Cost and Hours: 21 zł, free on Tue; open Mon 10:00-20:00 (but closed second Mon of each month), Tue until 16:00, Wed-Sun until 22:00, shorter hours Nov-March; last entry 1.25 hours before closing, enter at north end of Cloth Hall, Rynek Główny

1, tel. 12-426-5060, www. podziemiarynku.com.

Crowd-Beating Tips: This museum can sell out on very busy days (especially on Tuesdays—when it's free— and on summer weekends). It's possible to book ahead online up to three days in advance; alternatively, you can buy advance tickets in person around the opposite side of the Cloth Hall, at the Kraków City History Museum's visitors center (see "Tourist Information," earlier). If you've reserved a ticket, just go straight to the museum's main entrance. To try visiting spontaneously, show up at the entrance; if immediate tickets are available, they'll send you down to buy them. If not, you can circle around to the visitors center to buy a ticket for later during your visit.

Visiting the Museum: You'll enter through a door near the north end of the Cloth Hall (close to the fountain, facing St. Mary's). Climb down a flight of stairs and follow the numbered panels—1 to 70—through the exhibit (all in English). Cutting-edge museum technology illuminates life and times in medieval Kraków: Touchscreens let you delve into topics that intrigue you, 3-D virtual holograms resurrect old buildings, and video clips illustrate everyday life on unexpected surfaces (such as a curtain of fog).

All of this is wrapped around large chunks of early structures that still survive beneath the Square; several "witness columns" of rock and dirt are accompanied by diagrams helping you trace the layers of history. Interactive maps emphasize Kraków's Europe-wide importance as an intersection of major trade routes, and several models, maps, and digital reconstructions give you a good look at Kraków during the Middle Ages—when the Old Town looked barely different from today. You'll see a replica of a blacksmith's shop and learn how "vampire prevention burials" were used to ensure that the suspected undead wouldn't return from the grave. In the middle of the complex, look up through the glass of the Square's fountain to see the towers of St. Mary's above. Under the skylight is a model of medieval Kraków. While it looks much the same as today, notice a few key changes: the moat ringing the Old Town, where the Planty is today; and the several smaller market halls out on the Square.

Deeper in the exhibit, explore the long corridors of ruined

buildings that once ran alongside the length of the Cloth Hall. There are many intriguing cases showing artifacts that shops would have sold (jewelry, tools, amber figurines, and so on). Also in this area, you'll find a corridor with images of the Square all torn up for the recent renovation, plus a series of five modern brick rooms, each showing a brief, excellent film outlining a different period of Kraków's history. These "Kraków Chronicles" provide a big-picture context to what otherwise seems like a loose collection of cool museum gizmos, and also help you better appreciate what you'll see outside the museum's doors.

▲Jagiellonian University Museum: Collegium Maius

Kraków's historic university building can be toured with a student guide. While the courtyard itself (described earlier, in "Kraków's

Royal Way Walk") is the best part, the musty interior is mildly interesting. You'll choose between two different guided tours: 30 minutes (very popular) or one hour. It's smart to call ahead to find out when the shorter tour is scheduled in English, and to reserve for either tour (tel. 12-663-1307 for advance reservations, or tel. 12-663-1521 for same day, www.maius.uj.edu.pl). The building is two short blocks west of the Main Market Square, at ulica Jagiellońska 15.

The **30-minute tour** covers the "main exhibition" route: the library, refectory (with a gorgeously carved Baroque staircase), treasury (including Polish filmmaker Andrzej Wajda's honorary Oscar), assembly hall, and some old scientific instruments (12 zł, a few tours per day in English, 20 people maximum, leaves every 20 minutes Mon-Fri 10:00-14:20, Tue and Thu until 17:20 in April-Oct, these are the last tour times, no tours Sun). On Saturday mornings, you can see the route on your own, for free (10:00-13:30).

The **one-hour tour** adds some more interiors, room after room of more old scientific instruments, medieval art (mostly church sculptures), a Rubens, a small landscape from the shop of Rembrandt, and Chopin's piano (16 zł, usually in English Mon-Fri at 13:00, no tours Sat-Sun).

Dominican Church, a.k.a. Holy Trinity Church (Bazylika Trójcy Świętej)

In most towns, this church would be something special. In church-crazy Kraków, it's an also-ran. Still, it's easy to see (just a couple of blocks south of the Square) and worth a peek.

KRAKÓW

Cost and Hours: Free but donation requested, daily 6:30-13:00 & 16:00-20:00, facing plac Dominikański at Stolarska 12.

Visiting the Church: Inside, you'll find a Neo-Gothic space that was rebuilt after a devastating 1850 fire. You may be approached and offered an audioguide to tour the church, in exchange for a donation; it's a good little tour and worth doing, if you have the time.

Or, for a quick visit, tune in to just a few details: The unique metal chandeliers are one of many modern flourishes added during the late-19th-century restoration of the church. Climb the staircase in the left aisle to reach the chapel of St. Hyacinth. Locally known as St. Jacek, this early Dominican leader—called the "Apostle of the North"—is also the patron saint of pierogi (stuffed dumplings, similar to ravioli). During a famine, St. Jacek supposedly invented pierogi and—in a loaves-and-fishes-type miracle—produced plateful after plateful, feeding the desperate locals. His image adorns Kraków's annual Pierogi Cup contest, and to this day, when old-fashioned Poles are surprised, they might exclaim, *"Święty Jacek z pierogami!"* ("St. Hyacinth and his pierogi!"). Back down in the main part of the church, stroll slowly past the gorgeously carved wooden seats of the choir area (behind the altar); then, at the main altar, identify the three parts of the Trinity: Jesus (short beard), God (long beard), and Holy Spirit (beardless dove).

Archdiocesan Museum (Muzeum Archidiecezjalne)

This museum, in a building where St. John Paul II lived both as a priest and as a bishop, is the best place in town to learn more about Kraków's favorite son (without making the long trip to the St. John Paul II Sanctuary on the outskirts—described later). The exhibition includes John Paul II's personal effects, including clothes, handwritten notes, travel gear, bike, kayak, and skis—reminding visitors that he was one sporty pope. Then you'll tour the lavish private apartments where he lived from 1958 until 1967, as archbishop of Kraków. Throughout the collection are many portraits and photographs of the late pontiff—making his cult of personality almost palpable.

Cost and Hours: 5 zł, Tue-Sun 10:00-17:00, closed Mon, Kanonicza 19-21, tel. 12-421-8963, www.muzeumkra.diecezja.pl.

Sights in Kazimierz

The neighborhood of Kazimierz (kah-ZHEE-mehzh), 20 minutes by foot southeast of Kraków's Old Town, is the historic heart of Kraków's once-thriving Jew-

ish community. After years of neglect, the district began a rejuvenation in the early 2000s. Today, while not quite as slick and polished as Prague's Jewish Quarter, Kazimierz's assortment of synagogues, cemeteries, and museums helps visitors appreciate the neighborhood's rich Jewish history. At the same time, Kazimierz also happens to be the city's edgy, hipster culture center—jammed with colorful bars, creative eateries, and designer boutiques. This unlikely combination—where somber synagogues coexist with funky food trucks—makes Kazimierz a big draw for travelers both young and old.

Planning Your Visit: Try to visit any day except Saturday, when most Jewish-themed sights are closed (except the Old Synagogue, High Synagogue, and Galicia Jewish Museum). Monday comes with a few closures of non-Jewish sights: the Ethnographic Museum, Museum of Contemporary Art in Kraków, and Museum of Municipal Engineering. On Monday, the Schindler's Factory Museum is free, but it's open shorter hours and is more crowded than usual. It's always smart to book ahead for the Schindler's Factory Museum, which can sell out. For more suggestions on what to do in Kazimierz, see the Shopping, Entertainment, Sleeping, and Eating sections.

Etiquette: To show respect, men cover their heads while visiting a Jewish cemetery or synagogue. Most sights offer loaner yarmulkes, or you can wear your own hat.

Getting to Kazimierz: From Kraków's Old Town, it's about a 20-minute **walk.** From the Main Market Square, head down ulica Sienna (near St. Mary's Church) and through the Planty park. When you hit the busy ring road, bear right and continue down Starowiślna for 15 more minutes. The **tram** shaves off a few minutes: Find the stop along the ring road, on the left-hand side of ulica Sienna (across the street from the Poczta Główna, or main post office). Catch tram #3 or #24, and ride two stops to Miodowa. Walking or by tram, at the intersection of Starowiślna and Miodowa, you'll see a tiny park with food trucks across the street and to the right. To reach the heart of Kazimierz—ulica Sze-

Kazimierz Walk

(#3 & 24 from Old Town) T

New Cemetery ⑥

NEW CEMETERY ENTRANCE

T (#3 & 24 to Old Town)

UL. MIODOWA

④
③
②
①

TEMPEL SYNAGOGUE

KUPA SYNAGOGUE

Old Cemetery

REMU'H SYNAGOGUE

⑤

◆ POST

⑦

⑧

Ulica Szeroka

■WALK BEGINS

PODBRZEZIE

UL. MIODOWA

DIETLA

WARSZAUERA

KUPA

Plac Nowy MARKET HALL ⑫

ISAAC SYNAGOGUE

⑪

ESTERY

IZAAKA

⑩

HIGH SYNAGOGUE

WASKA

OLD SYNAGOGUE

⑨

DAJWOR

WALL

RZESZOWSKA

HALICKA

PRZEMYSKA

STAROWISLNA

#3 & 24

KABINA MEISELSA

⑬

⑭

NOWA

UL. JÓZEFA

⑮

BOŻEGO CIAŁA

BARTOSZA

GALICIA JEWISH MUSEUM

⑳

WALK ENDS

T

ⓘ

CORPUS CHRISTI CHURCH

⑱

⑳

MUSEUM OF MUNICIPAL ENGINEERING

ŚW. WAWRZYNCA

⑲

UL. KRAKOWSKA

SKALECZNA

AUGUSTIANSKA

Plac Wolnica ⑯

⑰

ETHNO-GRAPHIC MUSEUM

BONIFRATERSKA

BOCHENSKA

GAZOWA

KAZIMIERZ

PODGÓRSKA

BULWAR KURLANDZKI

(#6, 8, 10 & 13 to Castle & Old Town) T

MOSTOWA

TRYNITARSKA

SKAWINSKA

Vistula River

① Kazimierz Monument
② Old Jewish Cemetery & Jan Karski Statue
③ Old Shop Fronts
④ Hamsa Rest. & Jarden Bookshop
⑤ Klezmer-Hois Restaurant
⑥ New Jewish Cemetery
⑦ Rubinstein Birthplace
⑧ Popper Synagogue
⑨ Old Synagogue
⑩ Food Trucks
⑪ Isaac Synagogue

⑫ Plac Nowy
⑬ Meiselsa & Bożego Ciała Streets
⑭ "Schindler's List Passage"
⑮ Ulica Józefa
⑯ Plac Wolnica
⑰ Ethnographic Museum
⑱ Old Tram Depot
⑲ Museum of Municipal Engineering
⑳ Judah Square
㉑ Galicia Jewish Museum

KRAKOW

roka—cut through this park. The same trams continue to the sights in Podgórze (including the Schindler's Factory Museum).

To return to the Old Town, catch tram #3 or #24 from the intersection of Starowiślna and Miodowa (kitty-corner from where you got off the tram).

Information: An official **TI** is just a few blocks off the bottom of ulica Szeroka, at ulica Józefa 7 (daily 9:00-17:00, tel. 12-422-0471).

KAZIMIERZ WALK
This self-guided walk, worth ▲▲, is designed to help you get your bearings in Kazimierz, connecting both its Jewish sights (mostly in "Part 1") and its eclectic other attractions, from trendy bars to underrated museums ("Part 2"). Allow about an hour for the entire walk, not counting museum visits along the way. From the end of the walk, you can easily cross the river to this area's biggest sight, the Schindler's Factory Museum.

Part 1: Jewish Heritage on Ulica Szeroka
• *We'll start on ulica Szeroka ("Broad Street")—the center of the neighborhood, which feels like more of an elongated square than a "street." Begin at the bottom (southern) edge of the small, grassy park, near the strip of restaurants. In the park with the tall trees, look for the low-profile, stone...*

Kazimierz Monument
You're standing in the historical heart of Kraków's Jewish community. In the 14th century, King Kazimierz the Great enacted policies that encouraged Jews fleeing other kingdoms to settle in Poland—including in Kraków. He also founded this town, which still bears his name. Originally, Jews lived in the Old Town, but they were scapegoated after a 1495 fire and forced to relocate to Kazimierz. Back then, Kazimierz was still a separate town, divided by a wall into Christian (west) and Jewish (east) neighborhoods. Ulica Szeroka was the main square of the Jewish community. Over time, Jews were more or less accepted into the greater community, and Jewish culture flourished here.

All that would change in the mid-20th century. The **monument** honors the "65 thousand Polish citizens of Jewish nationality from Kraków and its environs"—more than a quarter of the city's pre-WWII population—who were murdered by the Nazis during the Holocaust. When the Nazis arrived, they immediately sent most of Kraków's Jews to the ghetto in the eastern Polish city of Lublin. Soon after, they forced Kraków's remaining 15,000 Jews into a walled ghetto at Podgórze, across the river. The Jews' cemeteries were defiled, and their buildings were ransacked and destroyed. In 1942, the Nazis began transporting Kraków's Jews to death camps (including Płaszów, just on Kraków's outskirts, and Auschwitz).

Only a few thousand Kraków Jews survived the war. During the communist era, this waning population was ignored or mistreated. After 1989, interest in Kazimierz's unique Jewish history was faintly rekindled. But it was only when Steven Spielberg chose to film *Schindler's List* here in 1993 that the world took renewed interest in Kazimierz. (A local once winked to me, "They ought to build a statue to Spielberg on that square.") Although the current Jewish population in Kraków numbers only 200, Kazimierz has become an internationally known destination for those with an interest in Jewish heritage.

• *Facing the park, look to the left. The arch with the Hebrew characters marks the entrance to the...*

▲▲Old Jewish Cemetery (Stary Cmentarz)

This small cemetery was used to bury members of the Jewish community from 1552 to 1800. With more than a hundred of the top

Jewish intellectuals of that age buried here, this is considered one of the most important Jewish cemeteries in Europe.

Cost and Hours: 10 zł includes cemetery and attached Remu'h Synagogue; hours vary with demand—especially outside peak season—but generally open Sun-Fri 9:00-16:00, can be open until 18:00 May-Sept, closes earlier off-season and by sundown on Fri, closed Sat yearround, ulica Szeroka 40.

Visiting the Cemetery: Walk under the arch, pay the admission fee, step into the cemetery, and survey the tidy rows of headstones. This early Jewish resting place (later replaced by the New Cemetery, described later) was desecrated by the Nazis during the Holocaust. In the 1950s, it was discovered, excavated, and put back together as you see here. Shattered gravestones form a mosaic **wall** around the perimeter.

Notice that many graves have a curved top or are engraved with an arch-like pattern—suggesting passage into another realm. As in all Jewish cemeteries

and memorials, you'll see many small stones stacked on the graves. The tradition comes from placing stones—representing prayers—over desert graves to cover the body and prevent animals from disturbing it.

Behind the little synagogue to the left, in the elevated, fenced area near the tree, the tallest **tombstone** belonged to Moses Isserles (a.k.a. Remu'h), an important 16th-century rabbi. He is believed to have been a miracle worker, and his grave was one of the only ones that remained standing after World War II. Notice the written prayers crammed into the cracks and crevices of the tombstone.

Near the gate to the cemetery, step into the tiny **Remu'h Synagogue** (c. 1553, covered by cemetery ticket). Tight and cozy, this has been carefully renovated and is fully active. Notice the original 16th-century frescoed walls and ceilings, and the historic donation box at the door. For more on typical synagogue architecture, see the sidebar.

• *Back outside, turn left and continue up to the top of...*

Ulica Szeroka

Just above the cemetery gate, notice a bronze statue of a gentleman seated on a bench. This is a tribute to **Jan Karski** (1914-2000), a Catholic Pole and resistance fighter who published his eyewitness account *The Story of a Secret State* about the Holocaust in 1944. Karski—the ultimate whistleblower—was one of the first people who spoke out about Nazi atrocities, at a time when even many world leaders had only an inkling about what was happening in Hitler's realm. Karski's revelations, so shocking as to be literally unbelievable to many, went ignored by some key leaders—arguably extending the horrors of the Holocaust.

Just above that, at the top corner of the square, notice the side street with a row of rustic old Jewish **shop fronts,** which evoke the bustle of prewar Kazimierz. The Jewish names—Rattner, Weinberg, Nowak, Holcer—stand testament to the lively soul of this neighborhood in its heyday. This lane leads to Miodowa street, which you can follow left to reach two of Kazimierz's lesser-known synagogues (Tempel and Kupa, both described later).

The building at the top of the square houses the recommended **Hamsa** restaurant (with modern Israeli food) and **Jarden Bookshop,** which serves as an unofficial information point for the neighborhood and sells a wide variety of fairly priced books on Kazimierz and Jewish culture in the region (Mon-Fri 9:00-18:00, Sat-Sun from 10:00, ulica Szeroka 2).

Kitty-corner from the bookshop, notice **Klezmer-Hois**—one of many restaurants offering live traditional Jewish klezmer music nightly in summer (for more on klezmer music, and details on your options, see the sidebar on page 123).

The Synagogue

KRAKÓW

A synagogue is a place of public worship, where Jews gather to pray, sing, and read from the Torah. Most synagogues have similar features, though they vary depending on the congregation.

The synagogue generally faces toward Jerusalem (so in Kraków, worshippers face east). At the east end is an alcove called the **ark,** which holds the Torah. These scriptures (the first five books of the Christian Old Testament) are written in Hebrew on scrolls wrapped in luxuriant cloth. The other main element of the synagogue is the **bema,** an elevated platform from which the Torah is read aloud (the equivalent of a pulpit in a Christian church). In traditional Orthodox synagogues, the bema is near the center of the hall, and the reader stands facing the same direction as the congregation. In other branches of Judaism, the bema is at the front, and the reader faces the worshippers. Orthodox synagogues have separate worship areas for men and women, usually with women in the balcony.

The synagogue walls might be decorated with elaborate patterns of vines or geometric designs, but never statues of people, which could be considered idol worship. A lamp above the ark is always kept lit, as it was in the ancient temple of Jerusalem, and candelabras called menorahs also recall the temple. Other common symbols are the two tablets of the Ten Commandments given to Moses, or a Star of David, representing the Jewish king's shield.

At a typical service, the congregation arrives at the start of Sabbath (Friday evening). As a sign of respect toward God, men don yarmulkes (small round caps). As the cantor leads songs and prayers, worshippers follow along in a book of weekly readings. At the heart of the service, everyone stands as the Torah is ceremoniously paraded, unwrapped, and placed on the bema. Someone—the rabbi, the cantor, or a congregant—reads the words aloud. The rabbi ("teacher") might give a commentary on the Torah passage.

The **New Jewish Cemetery**—less touristed and a striking contrast to the Old Jewish Cemetery we just saw—is a worthwhile detour, about a five-minute walk away (and described earlier in this section). To get there, cut through the grassy little lot between Jarden Bookshop and Klezmer-Hois, turn right, cross the busy street, then go through the railway underpass.

When you're ready to move on, do a 180 and head back downhill on ulica Szeroka. You'll pass the little park again, then come to a row of lively, mostly Jewish-themed **restaurants** with outdoor tables. Several places along here (especially Ester Hotel, at the bottom of the row) feature outdoor klezmer music in good weather—allowing you to get a taste of this unique musical form before committing to a full meal.

Halfway down this side of the square, the green house at #14 is where **Helena Rubinstein** was born in 1870. At age 31, she emigrated to Australia, where she parlayed her grandmother's traditional formula for hand cream into a cosmetics empire. Many cosmetics still used by people worldwide today were invented by Rubinstein, who died at age 92 in New York City as one of the most successful businesswomen of all time—just one of many illustrious Jewish residents of Kazimierz.

Two doors past the Rubinstein house, notice the round arch marking the courtyard of the **Popper Synagogue,** which is now home to an extensive bookstore that's worth a peek.

Continue past the restaurants to the very bottom of ulica Szeroka, and pause at the steps before heading down into the sunken area around the Old Synagogue. To the synagogue's left, notice a short, reconstructed stretch of Kazimierz's 14th-century **town wall.** This is a reminder that medieval Kazimierz was a separate city from Kraków. It's easy to read some history into a map of Kazimierz (you'll find one on the big panel in front of the Old Synagogue, down the stairs): Today's Starowiślna and Dietla streets—which frame off Kazimierz in a triangle of land hemmed in by the riverbank—were once canals (Kazimierz was built on an island). When King Kazimierz the Great—who reportedly didn't care much for Krakovians—founded this district in 1335, he envisioned it as a separate town to rival Kraków. It wasn't until around 1800 that the two towns merged.

• *The building at the bottom of the square is the...*

Old Synagogue (Stara Synagoga)

The oldest surviving Jewish building in Poland (15th century) sits eight steps below street level. Jewish structures weren't allowed to be taller than Christian ones—and so, in order to have the proper proportions, the synagogue's "ground floor" had to be underground. Today the synagogue houses a good three-room museum on local

Jewish culture, with informative English descriptions and a well-preserved main prayer hall (11 zł, free on Mon; Mon 10:00-14:00, Tue-Sun 9:00-17:00; shorter hours off-season; good 50-stop audioguide-10 zł; ulica Szeroka 24, tel. 12-422-0962).

KRAKÓW

• *A few more Jewish sights can be found in the surrounding streets; I'll point these out in "Part 2," though the rest of this walk focuses on a more recent chapter of the neighborhood.*

Part 2: Contemporary Kazimierz

• *Stand with your back to the Old Synagogue, at the top of the stairs, and turn left, heading up the little alley next to Szeroka 28—called Lewkowa.*

Hipster Kazimierz

Follow Lewkowa between some old buildings. When you pop out into an open area, angle right, then continue straight along ulica Ciemna. Soon you'll hit an inviting little **pod of food trucks** (described on page 137). Pause here—perhaps while nursing an açaí smoothie, a Thai-style rolled ice cream, or a taco—and ponder the explosion of youthful culture that's taken place in Kazimierz over the last generation.

At the end of World War II, Kazimierz was badly damaged and depopulated. And so it remained for generations, as the communist authorities brushed Jewish heritage under the rug. By the early 2000s, Kazimierz's artistically dilapidated buildings, low rents, and easy proximity to the Old Town became enticing to creative young people. A variety of artsy entrepreneurs took root here, beginning with a cluster of ramshackle, rustic bars (inspired partly by Budapest's "ruin pub" scene). Today the district has the city's (and probably Poland's) highest concentration of trendy food trucks, cafés, bars, restaurants, and design shops—several of which we'll see as we continue.

• *From the food trucks, continue straight ahead (on Izaaka street). This leads you along the left side of...*

Isaac Synagogue (Synagoga Izaaka)

One of Kraków's biggest synagogues, this was built in the 17th century. Inside, the walls in the prayer hall are decorated with giant paintings of prayers for worshippers who couldn't afford to buy books (with translations posted below). The synagogue also serves as the local center for the Hasidic Jewish group Chabad, with a kosher restaurant and a library (10 zł; Sun-Thu 8:30-20:00, Fri 8:30-14:30, closed Sat year-round, shorter hours off-season; ulica Kupa 18, tel. 12-430-2222). In addition to its Sabbath services, this is Kraków's only synagogue with daily prayers (at 8:30). They also host klezmer music concerts many evenings at 18:00 (60 zł).

• *Just past Isaac Synagogue is the heart of Kazimierz's nightlife zone (also bustling by day). Dive in, passing some characteristic cafés (on your left) and the chic Taawa nightclub (on your right). Then jog right at the glitzy Plac Nowy 1 beer hall to reach...*

Plac Nowy

Kazimierz's endearing "new" market square, plac Nowy (plats NOH-vee), retains much of the gritty flavor of the district before tourism and gentrification. The circular brick building in the center is a slaughterhouse where Jewish butchers would properly kill livestock, kosher-style. Today its windows are filled with little stand-up eateries ranging from burgers and ice cream to the traditional local pizza-like *zapiekanki*. Circle the market hall and browse for a snack (for more on the plac Nowy scene, see "Eating in Kraków," later). Good Lood has Kraków's best artisanal ice cream—if you don't mind the line. This square is also ringed by several fun and funky bars—enjoyable by day, but hopping at night (see page 122).

• *Leave plac Nowy along Meiselsa street (to the left from where you entered, past the yellow Jewish Cultural Center). After one block, pause at the intersection of...*

Meiselsa and Bożego Ciała Streets

The Holocaust was a dark chapter that dominates Kazimierz's history. But this intersection is a reminder that, up until the Nazis arrived, Kazimierz was a place where Jews and Christians lived side by side, in relative harmony.

Notice the street names, which mix Jewish and Catholic namesakes: ulica Meiselsa ("Meisels Street"—honoring a deeply respected 19th-century rabbi) and ulica Bożego Ciała ("Corpus Christi Street"—named for the towering brick church you can see just ahead). As if to celebrate the ecumenism of this intersection, a street artist has painted a graffiti Gene Kelly on the wall... very "happy again" indeed that Kazimierz is blossoming and full of life.

• *Backtrack a few steps up Meiselsa and duck into the courtyard on the right, under the dilapidated arch.*

Schindler's List **Passage**

This courtyard is a popular tourist spot thanks to its brush with fame, as a location for some key scenes in *Schindler's List* (find the black-and-white stills from the movie—and actual historic photos—partway down on the right, just before the arch). Spielberg connection aside, this is a particularly evocative setting to nurse a relaxing drink at the atmospheric café.

• *Carry on all the way through the passage. You'll pop out at...*

Ulica Józefa: **Design Street**

This street has Kazimierz's highest concentration of funky, one-off boutiques: jewelry, fashion, housewares, and more. For a rundown of the best options along here, see the "Shopping in Kraków" section, later. There's also a TI just across the street.

• *When you're ready to move along, take ulica Józefa right a few steps to the intersection with ulica Bożego Ciała, turn left, and follow it a long block. You'll pass Corpus Christi Church on your left, then arrive at...*

Plac Wolnica

Remember that Kazimierz was originally a separate town from Kraków. This was its main market square, designed to one-up its crosstown rival—right down to the dramatic, red-brick Catholic church on the corner (Corpus Christi). If you're still hungry, this square also has good craft beer, good ice cream, and good vegan burgers (see page 139).

The former Kazimierz Town Hall at the far end of the square houses an unusually good **Ethnographic Museum** (Muzeum Etnograficzne)—worth ▲. If you're interested in Polish folk culture, it's worth a visit (13 zł, free on Sun, open Tue-Sun 10:00-19:00, closed Mon, ulica Krakowska 46, tel. 12-430-6023, www. etnomuzeum.eu). On the ground floor, you'll find models of traditional rural Polish homes, as well as musty replicas of the interiors (like an open-air folk museum moved inside). The exhibit continues upstairs, where each in a long lineup of traditional Polish folk costumes is identified by specific region. Follow the one-way route through exhibits on village lifestyles, rustic tools, and musical instruments (including a Polish bagpipe). A highlight is the explanation of traditional holiday celebrations—from elaborate crèche scenes at Christmas, to a wall of remarkably painted Easter eggs. Some items are labeled in English, but it's mostly in Polish. The top floor features temporary exhibits.

- *There's more to see in Kazimierz. But if you're pooped, you could catch tram #6, #8, #10, or #13 back to Wawel Castle, then on to the plac Wszystkich Świętych stop in the heart of the Old Town (catch tram from along Krakowska street, behind the Ethnographic Museum).*

To continue the walk from plac Wolnica, head up ulica Św. Wawrzyńca (at the corner where you entered the square, with the Corpus Christi Church on your left).

Ulica Św. Wawrzyńca: Industrial Kazimierz

By the late 19th century, Kazimierz was not just a Jewish cultural hotspot but also a center of local industry. (It's no coincidence that Oskar Schindler had his factory near here.) After the church, on your left, look for the glass-and-steel arched roof of the Industrial Age **old tram depot,** which now houses a recommended brewpub. In sunny summer weather, the pebbly courtyard is filled with happy drinkers.

Across the street, notice the many tram tracks leading into a courtyard with several more storage sheds for local trams. This gorgeously restored complex now houses the **Museum of Municipal Engineering** (Muzeum Inżynierii Miejskiej). Exhibits include a history of the town's public transit system (including several antique trams), old Polish-made cars and motorcycles (among them the tiny commie-era Polski Fiat), typography and historical printing presses, and a hands-on area for kids (15 zł, family ticket—40 zł, free on Tue; open Tue 10:00-16:00, Wed-Fri 9:00-20:00, Sat-Sun 10:00-20:00, closed Mon; Św. Wawrzyńca 15, tel. 12-421-1242, www.mim.krakow.pl).

Continue along ulica Św. Wawrzyńca a few more steps. At the intersection with Wąska, **Judah Square** (Skwer Judah) is a vacant lot with a gaggle of enticing food carts watched over by a giant mural. Commissioned for Kraków's Jewish Cultural Festival in 2013, the illustration was painted by Israeli street artist Pilpeled. It shows a young boy who feels small and scared, but lionhearted nevertheless—a poignant symbol for the Holo-

caust survivors of Kazimierz. If you're ready for a meal or snack, you'll find several good options here.

- *A half-block farther down ulica Św. Wawrzyńca is another place for refreshment, the recommended Craftownia (Polish microwbrews on tap, on the left at #22). Next you'll reach the intersection with Dajwór street. Turn left here and walk a few steps up the street; on the right, you'll find the...*

Galicia Jewish Museum (Galicja Muzeum)

This museum, worth ▲ and housed in a restored Jewish furniture factory, focuses on the present rather than the past. The permanent "Traces of Memory" photographic exhibit shows today's remnants of yesterday's Judaism in the area around Kraków (a region known as "Galicia"). From abandoned synagogues to old Jewish gravestones flipped over and used as doorsteps, these giant postcards of Jewish artifacts (with good English descriptions) ensure that an important part of this region's heritage won't be forgotten. Good temporary exhibits complement this permanent collection (16 zł, daily 10:00-18:00, one block east of ulica Szeroka at ulica Dajwór 18, tel. 12-421-6842, www.galiciajewishmuseum.org). The museum also serves as a sort of cultural center, with a good bookstore and café.

• *Notice yet another cluster of food trucks across the street from the museum.*

Our Kazimierz orientation walk is finished. From here, you have several options. To **return to ulica Szeroka,** where we began, walk up Dajwór street past the museum, then angle left through the park at the reconstructed chunk of town wall—you'll wind up at the Old Synagogue.

For the next two options, you'll first head back down to ulica Św. Wawrzyńca, turn left, and walk one more block to the intersection with Starowiślna street. Just to the left on Starowiślna, look for the tram stops. The tram stop on the far side of the street takes you **back to the Old Town** (tram #3 or #24). From the tram stop on the near side of the street, tram #3 or #24 zips you to the **sights in Podgórze**—including Ghetto Heroes' Square and the Schindler's Factory Museum (both described later). You can also reach the Podgórze sights on foot by turning right on Starowiślna and crossing the bridge (about a 10-minute walk).

MORE JEWISH SIGHTS IN KAZIMIERZ

In addition to the sights connected by the walk above, here's another cemetery and a few more synagogues to round out your Jewish Kazimierz experience.

▲New Jewish Cemetery (Nowy Cmentarz)

This burial place—much larger than the Old Jewish Cemetery—has graves of those who died after 1800. It was vandalized by the Nazis, who sold many of its gravestones to stonecutters and used others as pavement in their concentration camps. Many have since been cemented back in their original positions, while others—which could not be replaced—have been used to create the moving mosaic wall and Holocaust monument (on the right as you enter). Most gravestones are in one of four languages: Hebrew (generally the oldest, especially if there's no other language, though some are newer "retro" tombstones); Yiddish (sounds like a mix of German and Hebrew and uses the Hebrew alphabet); Polish (Jews who assimilated into the Polish community); and German (Jews who assimilated into the German community). The earliest graves are simple stones, while later ones imitate graves in Polish Catholic cemeteries—larger, more elaborate, and with a long stone jutting out to cover the body. Notice that some new-looking graves have old dates. These were most likely put here well after the Holocaust (or even after the communist era) by relatives of the dead.

Cost and Hours: Free, Sun-Fri 8:00-16:00, closed Sat. It's tricky to find: Go under the railway tunnel at the east end of ulica Miodowa, and jog left as you emerge. The cemetery is to your right (enter through gate with small *cmentarz żydowski* sign).

Synagogues

In addition to the three synagogues mentioned on the Kazimierz Walk (Old Synagogue, Isaac, and Remu'h), others also welcome visitors. Each of these charges a small admission fee and is closed Saturdays (unless noted). The **High Synagogue**—so called because its prayer room is upstairs—displays changing exhibits, most of which focus on the people who lived here before the Holocaust (daily, ulica Józefa 38). **Tempel Synagogue** (Synagoga Templu) has the grandest interior—big and dark, with elaborately decorated, gilded ceilings and balconies (corner of ulica Miodowa and ulica Podbrzezie). The **Jewish Community Centre** next door offers activities both for members of the local Jewish community and for tourists (lectures, genealogical research, Friday-night Shabbat meals, Hebrew and Yiddish classes, and so on; www.jcckrakow. org). Nearly across the street, the smaller **Kupa Synagogue** (Synagoga Kupa)—clean and brightly decorated—sometimes hosts temporary exhibits (Miodowa 27).

NEAR KAZIMIERZ: PODGÓRZE

The neighborhood called Podgórze (POD-goo-zheh), directly across the Vistula from Kazimierz, has one of Kraków's most famous sights: Schindler's Factory Museum. I've listed these sights in the order you'll reach them as you come from Kazimierz or the Old Town.

Background: This is the neighborhood where the Nazis

forced Kraków's Jews into a ghetto in early 1941. (Schindler's List and the films in the Pharmacy Under the Eagle museum depict the sad scene of the Jews loading their belongings onto carts and trudging over the bridge into Podgórze.) Non-Jews who had lived here were displaced to make way for the new arrivals. The ghetto was surrounded by a wall with a fringe along the top that resembled Jewish gravestones—a chilling premonition. A short section of this wall still stands along Lwowska street. The tram continued to run through the middle of Podgórze, without stopping—giving Krakovians a chilling glimpse at the horrifying conditions inside the ghetto.

Getting There: To go directly to Ghetto Heroes' Square, continue through Kazimierz on tram #3 or #24 (described earlier, under "Getting to Kazimierz") to the stop called plac Bohaterow Getta. Or you can ride the tram or walk 10 minutes across the bridge from the end of my Kazimierz Walk.

Ghetto Heroes' Square (Plac Bohaterow Getta)

This unassuming square is the focal point of the visitor's Podgórze. Today the square is filled with a monument consisting of 68 empty

metal chairs—representing the 68,000 people deported from here. This is intended to remind viewers that the Jews of Kazimierz were forced to carry all of their belongings—including furniture—to the ghetto on this side of the river. It was also here that many Jews waited to be sent to extermination camps. The small, gray building at the river end of Ghetto Heroes' Square feels like a train car inside, evocative of the wagons that carried people from here to certain death.

▲Pharmacy Under the Eagle (Apteka pod Orłem)

This small but good museum, on Ghetto Heroes' Square, tells the story of Tadeusz Pankiewicz, a Polish Catholic pharmacist who chose to remain in Podgórze when it became a Jewish ghetto. During this time, the pharmacy was an important meeting point for the ghetto residents, and Pankiewicz and his staff heroically aided and hid Jewish victims of the Nazis. (Pankiewicz survived the war and was later acknowledged by Israel as one of the "Righteous Among the Nations"—non-Jews who risked their lives to help the Nazis' victims during World War II. You'll see his medal on display in the white memorial room at the end of the museum.) Today the pharmacy hosts an exhibit about the Jewish ghetto. You'll enter into the re-created pharmacy, where the "windows" are actually screens that show footage from the era. Push buttons, pull out drawers, answer the phone—it's full of interactive opportunities to better understand what ghetto life was like. You'll learn about people who worked in the pharmacy (including riveting interviews with eye-witnesses—some in English, others subtitled) and hear Pankiewicz telling stories about that tense time. You'll also learn a bit about the pharmacy business from that period.

Cost and Hours: 11 zł; if you're also going to the Schindler's Factory Museum, buy the 32-zł combo-ticket; free on Mon; open Mon 10:00-14:00, Tue-Sun 9:00-17:00, closed the second Tue of each month; plac Bohaterow Getta 18, tel. 12-656-5625, www.mhk.pl/branches/eagle-pharmacy.

▲▲▲Schindler's Factory Museum
(Fabryka Emalia Oskara Schindlera)

One of Europe's best museums about the Nazi occupation fills some of the factory buildings where Oskar Schindler and his Jew-

ish employees worked. The museum tells the story of Schindler and his workers and also broadens its perspective to take in the full experience of all of Kraków during the painful era of Nazi rule. It's loaded with in-depth information (all in English), and touchscreens invite you to learn more and watch eyewitness in-

terviews. Scattered randomly between the exhibits are replicas of everyday places from the age—a photographer's shop, a tram car, a hairdresser's salon—designed to give you a taste of 1940s Kraków. Throughout the museum are calendar pages outlining wartime events and giving a sense of chronology. Note that you'll see nothing of the actual factory or equipment, as the threat of the advancing Red Army forced Schindler to move his operation lock, stock, and barrel to Nazi-occupied Czechoslovakia in 1944.

Cost and Hours: 24 zł, 29-zł combo-ticket with next-door Museum of Contemporary Art, 32-zł "Memory Trail" combo-ticket with Pharmacy Under the Eagle; free on Mon; open April-Oct Mon 10:00-16:00 (except closes at 14:00 first Mon of month), Tue-Sun 9:00-20:00; Nov-March Mon 10:00-14:00, Tue-Sun 10:00-18:00; last entry 1.5 hours before closing, tel. 12-257-1017, www.mhk.pl/branches/oskar-schindlers-factory.

Advance Reservations: Crowds can be a real problem at this popular sight—especially on Mondays (when it's free, and many other museums are closed), during the summer holidays (June-

Aug), and midday (usually worst 11:00-16:00). At busy times, you may have to wait in a long line—an hour or more—just to buy a ticket. And then, once inside, congestion can make it challenging to fully appreciate the place. If you anticipate crowds, you can book tickets for no extra fee up to three days before your visit (www.bilety.mhk.pl); or you can buy tickets anytime (even for later the same day) at the Kraków City Museum visitors center in the Cloth Hall on the Main Market Square (see "Tourist Information" near the beginning of this chapter).

Crowd-Beating Tips: Even if you avoid the ticket line, the museum can still be jammed inside. The best strategy is to arrive early (9:00 or soon after on most days) or late (in summer, arriving by 18:00 gives you two hours to tour the exhibits)—but be warned that if you're arriving late without a reservation, it's possible on very busy days that all tickets could be sold out.

Getting There: It's in a gloomy industrial area a five-minute walk from Ghetto Heroes' Square (plac Bohaterow Getta): Go up Kącik street (to the left of the big, glass skyscraper), go under the railroad underpass, and continue two blocks, past MOCAK (the Museum of Contemporary Art in Kraków, described later) to the second big building on the left (ulica Lipowa 4). Look for signs to *Emalia*.

Visiting the Museum: You'll begin on the ground floor, where you'll buy your ticket and have the chance to tour the special exhibits. There's also a "film café" (interesting for fans of the movie) with refreshments. Then head upstairs to the first floor.

First Floor: The 35-minute **film,** called *Lipowa 4* (this building's address), sets the stage with interviews of both Jews and non-Jews describing their wartime experience (find it just off the museum's first, circular room; subtitled in English, it runs continuously). From here, the one-way route winds through the permanent exhibit, called **"Kraków Under Nazi Occupation 1939-1945."** First, while idyllic music plays, "stereoscopic" (primitive 3-D) photos of prewar Kraków capture an idyllic age when culture flourished and the city's Jews (more than one-quarter of the population) blended more or less smoothly with their Catholic-Pole neighbors. But then, a video explains the Nazi invasion of Poland in early September of 1939: It took them only a few weeks to overrun the coun-

Oskar Schindler (1908-1974) and His List

Steven Spielberg's instant-classic, Oscar-winning 1993 film, *Schindler's List,* brought the world's attention to the inspiring story of Oskar Schindler, the compassionate German businessman who did his creative best to save the lives of the Jewish workers at his factory in Kraków. Spielberg chose to film the story right here in Kazimierz, where the events actually unfolded.

Oskar Schindler was born in 1908 in the Sudetenland (currently part of the Czech Republic, then predominantly German). Early on, he displayed an idiosyncratic interpretation of ethics that earned him both wealth and enemies. As Nazi aggressions escalated, Schindler (who was very much a Nazi) carried out espionage against Poland; when Germany invaded the country in 1939, Schindler smelled a business opportunity. Early in the Nazi occupation of Poland, Schindler came to Kraków and lived in an apartment at ulica Straszewskiego 7 (a block from Wawel Castle). He took over the formerly Jewish-owned Emalia factory at ulica Lipowa 4, which produced metal pots and pans that were dipped into protective enamel; later the factory also began producing armaments for the Nazi war effort. The factory was staffed by about 1,000 Jews from the nearby Płaszów Concentration Camp, which was managed by the ruthless SS officer Amon Göth (depicted in *Schindler's List*—based on real events—shooting at camp inmates for sport from his balcony).

At a certain point, Schindler began to sympathize with his Jewish workers, and he increasingly did what he could to protect them and offer them better lives. Schindler fed them far better than most concentration-camp inmates and allowed them to sell some of the pots and pans they made on the black market to make money. After he saw many of his employees and friends murdered during an SS raid in 1943, he ramped up these efforts. He would come up with bogus paperwork to classify those threat-

try (which desperately awaited the promised help of their British and French allies, who never arrived).

Through the next several rooms, watch the film clip of SS soldiers marching through the Main Market Square—renamed "Adolf-Hitler-Platz"—and read stories about how the Nazis' *Generalgouvernement* attempted to reshape the life of its new capital, "Krakau." (Near the tram car, look for the decapitated head of the Grunwald monument—described on page 43—which had been a powerful symbol of a Polish military victory over German forces.) You'll see the story of a newly German-owned shop selling Nazi propaganda and learn how professors at Kraków's Jagiellonian University were arrested to prevent them from fomenting rebellion among their students. During this time, even Polish secondary schools were closed—effectively prohibiting learning among Poles, ened with deportation as "essential" to the workings of the factory—even if they were unskilled. He sought and was granted permission to build a "concentration camp" barracks for his workers on the factory grounds, where they lived in far better conditions than those at Płaszów. These lucky few became known as *Schindlerjuden*—"Schindler's Jews."

As the Soviet army encroached on Kraków in October of 1944, word came that the factory would need to be relocated west, farther from the front line. While Schindler could easily have simply turned his workers over to the concentration camp system and certain death—as most other industrialists did—he decided to bring them with him to his new factory at Brünnlitz (Brněnec, in today's Czech Republic). He assembled a list of 700 men and 300 women who worked with him, along with 200 other Jewish inmates, and at great personal expense, moved them to Brünnlitz. At the new factory, Schindler and the 1,200 people he had saved produced grenades and rocket parts—virtually all of them, the workers later claimed, mysteriously defective.

After the war, Schindler—who had spent much of his fortune protecting his Jewish workers—hopped around Germany and Argentina, repeatedly attempting but failing to break back into business (often with funding from Jewish donors). He died in poverty in 1974. In accordance with his final wishes, he was buried in Jerusalem, and today his grave is piled high with small stones left there by appreciative Jewish visitors. He has since been named one of the "Righteous Among the Nations" for his efforts to save Jews from the Holocaust. Thomas Keneally's 1982 book *Schindler's Ark* brought the industrialist's tale to a wide audience that included Steven Spielberg, who vaulted Schindler to the ranks of a pop-culture icon.

whom the Nazis considered inferior. But Polish students continued to meet clandestinely with their teachers. You'll also see images of Hans Frank—the hated puppet ruler of Poland—moving into the country's most important symbol of sovereignty, Wawel Castle.

The exhibit also details how early Nazi policies targeted Jews with roundups, torture, and execution. (Down the staircase is an eerie simulation of a cellar prison.) As the Nazis ratcheted up their genocidal activities, troops swept through Kraków on March 3, 1941, forcing all the remaining Jews in town to squeeze into the newly created Podgórze ghetto. At the bottom of the stairs, look for the huge pile of plunder—Jewish wealth stolen by the Nazis.

Second Floor: Climb upstairs using the long **staircase,** which was immortalized in a powerful scene in *Schindler's List*. At the top of the stairs on the right is a small room that served as "Schindler's office" for the film; more recently, it's been determined that his actual office was elsewhere (we'll see it soon).

You'll walk through a corridor lined by a replica of the wall that enclosed the **Podgórze ghetto** and see poignant exhibits about the horrific conditions there (including a replica of the cramped living quarters). The Nazis claimed that Jews had to be segregated here, away from the general population, because they "carried diseases."

Continue into the office of Schindler's secretary, with exhibits about Schindler's life and video touchscreens that play testimonial footage of Schindler's grateful employees. Then proceed into the actual **Schindler's office.**

The big map (with German names for cities) was uncovered only in recent years when the factory was being restored. Because Schindler's short tenure here was the only time in the factory's history that these Polish place names would appear in German, it's believed that this map was hung over his desk. Facing the map is a giant monument of enamel pots and pans, like those that were made in this factory. There are 1,200 pots—one for each Jewish worker that Schindler saved. Inside the monument, the walls are lined with the names on Schindler's famous list. The creaky floorboards are intentional: a reminder that the Nazis knew every step you took.

Proceeding through the exhibit, you'll learn more about everyday life—both for ghetto dwellers and for everyday non-Jewish Krakovians,

including the Polish resistance (see the Home Army's underground print shop). More eyewitness accounts relate the terrifying days of March 13 and 14, 1943, when the Podgórze ghetto was liquidated, sending survivors to the nearby Płaszów Concentration Camp. The replica of the Płaszów quarry, where inmates were forced to work in unimaginably difficult conditions, provides a poignant memorial for those who weren't fortunate enough to wind up on Schindler's list.

Now head all the way back down to the ground floor.

Ground Floor: Exhibits here capture the uncertain days near the end of the war in the summer of 1944, when Nazis arrested between 6,000 and 8,000 suspected saboteurs after the Warsaw Uprising and sent them to Płaszów (see the replica of a basement hideout for 10 Jews who had escaped the ghetto); and later, when many Nazis had fled Kraków, leaving residents to await the Soviet Union's Red Army (see the replica air-raid shelters). The Red Army arrived here on January 18, 1945—at long last, the five years, four months, and twelve days of Nazi rule were over. The Soviets caused their own share of damage to the city before beginning a whole new occupation that would last for generations...but that's a different museum.

Finally, walk along the squishy floor—evoking how life for anyone was unstable and unpredictable during the Nazi occupation—into the **Hall of Choices**. The six rotating pillars tell the stories of people who chose to act—or not to act—when they witnessed atrocities. Think about the ramifications of the choices they made...and what you would have done in their shoes. The final room holds two books: a white book listing those who tried to help, and a black book listing Nazi collaborators. Exiting the museum, notice the portraits of Oscar Schindler's workers who lived long and happy lives after the war.

Nearby: Before heading back to downtown Kraków, consider paying a visit to the superb—and very different—**art museum** that fills the buildings on the factory grounds, behind this main building (described next). Or, for a glass of wine, head just a few doors down from the museum to find the delightful **Krakó Slow Wines** (marked *Lipowa 6F*). This mellow, inviting wine bar and shop is well stocked with wines mostly from Central and Eastern Europe (daily 10:00-22:00, mobile 669-225-222, www.krakoslowwines.pl).

▲Museum of Contemporary Art in Kraków (Muzeum Sztuki Współczesnej w Krakowie)

Called "MOCAK" for short, this museum exhibits a changing array of innovative and thought-provoking works by contemporary artists, often with heavy themes tied to the surrounding Holocaust sites. With the slogan *Kunst macht frei* ("Art will set you free"—a pointed spin on the Nazis' Arbeit macht frei concentration camp motto), the museum occupies warehouse buildings once filled by Schindler's workers.

Now converted to wide-open, bright-white halls, the buildings house many temporary exhibits as well as two permanent ones (the MOCAK Collection in the basement, and the library in the smaller side building). Pick up the floor plan as you enter. It's all well described in English and engaging even for those who don't usually like modern art.

Cost and Hours: 14 zł, 29-zł combo-ticket with next-door Schindler's Factory Museum, free on Tue; open Tue-Sun 11:00-19:00, closed Mon, last entry one hour before closing; Lipowa 4, tel. 12-263-4001, www.mocak.pl.

John Paul II Pilgrimage Sights

Catholics coming to Kraków eager to walk in the footsteps of St. John Paul II appreciate the city's dazzling churches and its Archdiocesan Museum. And for most, that's enough. But true pilgrims head for worthwhile sights outside the city center: two sanctuaries related to John Paul II on the outskirts of Kraków; and the John Paul II Family Home Museum in the town of Wadowice, an hour's drive away (and covered later).

Sanctuaries in Kraków

The two biggest, most impressive JPII destinations are about four miles south of Kraków's Old Town, in the Łagiewniki neighborhood. While the main attraction here for pilgrims is the John Paul II Sanctuary, historically and geographically you'll come first to the Divine Mercy Sanctuary—so I've covered that first. The sights aren't worth the trek for the merely curious, but they offer a glimpse of the deep faith that characterizes the Polish people.

Getting There: A **taxi** or **Uber** from downtown costs around 30-40 zł one-way and takes 20-30 minutes. Public transit connections to this area are still in flux, so ask for advice from the TI. But most likely, the best plan is to take **tram #8** (which loops around the Old Town, including stops next to St. Francis Basilica at plac Wszystkich Świętych, near Wawel Castle, and at plac Wolnica in Kazimierz) to the Divine Mercy Sanctuary (Sanktuarium Bożego Miłosierdzia stop)—about 30 minutes. From the tram stop, take the pedestrian underpass, turn right, cross the train tracks, and huff a few minutes uphill along the wall to find the entrance to the complex. (You can see the glass steeple of the church from the tram stop—a handy visual landmark.)

After touring the Divine Mercy sights, you'll head to the St. John Paul II Sanctuary—a long walk (20-25 minutes) or a short, inexpensive taxi trip (10-15 zł).

Divine Mercy Sanctuary
(Sanktuarium Bożego Miłosierdzia)

This complex, built around a humble red-brick convent, honors the early-20th-century St. Faustina, who saw a miraculous vision of

Jesus that became a powerful religious symbol for many Catholics. Today, pilgrims from around the world come here to revere the relics both of Faustina and of John Paul II (who advocated for her sainthood), and to learn more about her story from the convent's present-day sisters—many of whom speak English.

Background: One cold and blustery evening in 1931, Sister Faustina Kowalska (1905-1938) answered the convent doorbell to find a beggar asking for some food. Faustina brought some soup to the man, who revealed his true nature: a figure of Jesus Christ clad in a white robe, with one hand raised in blessing and the other touching his chest. Emanating from his chest were twin beams of light: red (representing blood, the life of souls) and white (water, which through baptism washes souls righteously clean). Transformed by her experience, Faustina worked with an artist to create a painted version of the image—called the Divine Mercy—which has been embraced by Polish Catholics as one of the most important symbols of their faith.

Always frail in health, Faustina died at 33—the same age as Jesus. The story of Faustina deeply moved a young Karol Wojtyła. When he became pope, he dedicated the first Sunday after Easter as the day of Divine Mercy worldwide. In 2000, he made his fellow Krakovian the first Catholic saint of the third millennium. To properly revere the newly important St. Faustina, a bold, futuristic church and visitors center was built alongside her original convent.

Cost and Hours: All three parts of the complex—the smaller original chapel, a replica of Faustina's cell, and the huge, modern church, with its soaring bell tower—are free to enter, but donations are happily accepted. Each part has slightly different hours (listed later; www.faustyna.pl). Note that the daily 15:00 "Hour of Mercy" service—in both the chapel and the modern church—is worth planning around.

Visiting the Complex: Entering the complex through the side gate, look uphill to find a **walkway** with flags from around the world and plaques translating the Divine Mercy's message—"Jesus, I trust in you"—in dozens of languages.

Just before entering the **original chapel,** look up and to the right—the window with the flowers marks the cell where Faustina died. Inside the chapel (daily 6:00-21:15), the altar to the left of the main altar displays an early copy of Faustina's Divine Mercy painting. Her relics are in the white case just below; in the white kneeler just in front of the chapel, notice the little reliquary holding one of her bones (which worshippers can embrace as they pray).

Leaving the chapel, turn left and go to the far end of the accommodations building. Enter the door on the right to find the **replica of Faustina's cell.** While this is a newer building, here they've created Faustina's convent cell, including many of her personal effects. Drop a coin in the slot for an evocative headphone description of these items, and of the vision of Jesus that put her convent on the map (usually open daily 8:30-18:00).

From here, head downhill and circle around the large brick building—passing (on the right) an area for outdoor Mass.

Dominating the campus is the futuristic, glass-and-steel **main church.** Consecrated by Pope John Paul II on his final visit to Poland in 2002, this build-
ing has several elements (daily 7:00-20:00). The lower level has a variety of small chapels, each one donated by Catholic worshippers in a different country (Germany, Hungary, Slovakia, and so on)—and each with a dramatically different style. The central chapel on this level has a

modern altar and another bone of St. Faustina. Upstairs, the main sanctuary is a sleek cylindrical space with wooden sunbeams sharply radiating from the altar area. That altar—framed by the gnarled limbs of windblown trees, representing the suffering of human existence—contains a replica of the Divine Mercy painting, flanked by the woman who saw the vision (Faustina, on the right) and the Polish pope who made it a worldwide phenomenon (John Paul II, on the left).

Head back out to the terrace surrounding the church. The bold **tower**—as tall as St. Mary's on Main Market Square, and with a statue of John Paul II at the bottom—has an elevator that you can ride up to a glassed-in viewpoint offering panoramas over the Divine Mercy campus, the adjacent John Paul II Sanctuary complex, and—on the distant horizon—the spires of Wawel Cathedral and Kraków's Old Town (daily 8:00-19:00). Near the base of the tower is a **canopy** where Mass is said on Divine Mercy Sunday each year, before a crowd of 100,000 who fill the fields below.

Connecting to the St. John Paul II Sanctuary: You can see the rectangular, brick tower of the JPII Sanctuary from the Divine

Mercy Sanctuary. However, an expressway is being built between the two churches, so access can be tricky (but will improve once the project is complete). Plan on a 20- to 25-minute walk. Better yet, go to the Divine Mercy Sanctuary's hotel (the boxy, white building just uphill from the main church). If no taxis are waiting in the parking lot out front, order an Uber or ask the reception desk to call a taxi for you; the ride should cost only 10-15 zł.

St. John Paul II Sanctuary (Sanktuarium Św. Jana Pawła II)

This new complex, funded entirely by private donors, celebrates the life and sainthood of Kraków's favorite son. Construction is ongoing, but for now there are at least two sections of the complex worth visiting: the sanctuary and museum.

Cost and Hours: Sanctuary—free, daily 7:30-19:00, until 18:00 in winter, www.sanktuariumjp2.pl; museum—10 zł, daily 9:00-17:00.

Sanctuary of St. John Paul II: This hypermodern church is big and splendid. In the **downstairs** area, the central chapel features paintings of JPII's papal visits to various pilgrimage sites, both in Poland (Częstochowa) and abroad (Fátima, Lourdes). Ringing that central area is a variety of interesting smaller chapels.

On the outer wall, look for three in particular: The Kaplica Kapłańska is a replica of the St. Leonard's Crypt under Wawel Cathedral—where a young priest named Karol Wojtyła celebrated his first Mass. In this chapel, you'll see JPII's empty papal tomb from the crypt beneath St. Peter's Basilica at the Vatican. (When he became a saint, his remains—which, controversially, are kept in Rome rather than his homeland—were moved up into the main part of the church, and this simple grave marker was donated to this church.) You'll also see a reliquary in the shape of a book with fluttering pages, holding a small amount of John Paul II's blood (for the story of the book, see page 62). This blood was kept in secret by JPII's personal secretary, only revealed after his death, when it was divvied up among a select few churches. Nearby, another chapel holds the tombs of a few recent cardinals; as they're running out of space below Wawel Cathedral, this chapel is poised to handle the overflow. And the Kaplica Św. Kingi features finely executed reliefs in rock salt, in the style of Wieliczka Salt Mine.

Head upstairs to the sleek, modern **main sanctuary.** The concrete structure supports large walls, providing a canvas for dynamic mosaics of Bible stories. Above the main altar, in the middle, you'll see the Three Kings delivering their gifts to the Baby Jesus and the Virgin Mary—with St. John Paul II serenely overlooking the scene. Other scenes include Adam and Eve, Jesus calming the storm, the wedding feast at Cana, and the Last Supper. In the back-left corner, a smaller chapel has a display case with the blood-spattered vestments that St. John Paul II was wearing on May 13, 1981, when he was shot by a would-be assassin.

The sanctuary anchors a sprawling complex of conference facilities and other attractions for pilgrims. Poke around. The museum, described next (and on the right as you exit the sanctuary's main door), is the sight most worth visiting.

St. John Paul II Museum: This collects the many gifts bestowed on the beloved pope (African carved masks and ivory tusks; Latin American tapestries; the key to the city of Long Branch, New Jersey; a pair of glass doves of peace given to him—perhaps with a touch of irony—by US vice president Dick Cheney); ornate worship aids (chalices, crosses, and so on); and modern art that celebrates the modern pope and his life's work. There are also personal items, from his papal ski and hiking gear to the place settings from his Vatican dinner table to his stylish red leather shoes. You'll also see the throne from his last visit to Poland in 2002, and a replica of the humble room across the street from St. Francis Basilica where he stayed on visits back to his homeland.

Returning to Kraków: Taxis may be waiting at the sanctuary; otherwise, you can ask the museum desk to call one for you (or order an Uber). By public transportation, you can walk about 10 minutes downhill (crossing the white bridge over the railway tracks) to busy Zakopiańska street; near the Cinema City, you'll find a stop for tram #8 back to the Old Town.

John Paul II Sights in Wadowice

Karol Wojtyła was born and lived up until age 18 in Wadowice (VAH-doh-veet-seh), about 30 miles (a one-hour drive) southwest of Kraków. As it's roughly in the same direction as Auschwitz, a local guide or driver can help you connect both places for one busy day of contrasts. Visiting by public bus or minibus is possible (about 1.25 hours one-way); ask the TI for details.

The lovely town of Wadowice (about 20,000 people) has a quaint and beautifully restored main square with a pretty Baroque steeple. John Paul II pilgrims find it worth a visit to see the **John Paul II Family Home Museum,** which fills four floors of the tenement building where his family lived through his adolescence. You'll explore a multimedia overview of the life and times of one of the newest Catholic saints, including rooms of the family home, a collection of clothing and other articles that belonged to JPII, photographs and video clips of his life and of the tumultuous period in which he lived, and plenty of interactive displays to bring the entire story to life. Admission is limited, and you'll be accompanied the entire time. Ideally, time your visit to go with an English guide (typically 2/day, likely at 11:00 and 14:00—confirm in advance); otherwise, you'll join the Polish tour. Either way, the tour can be a bit rushed, with less time to linger over the exhibits than you might like (20 zł with a Polish guide, 30 zł with English guide, free and crowded on Tue—book 2 weeks ahead; open daily May-Sept 9:00-19:00, April and Oct until 18:00, Nov-March until 16:00, closed last Tue of each month; last entry 1.5 hours before closing, across the street from the town church at ulica Kościelna 7, tel. 33-823-2662, www.homejp2.com).

Sights Outside Kraków

These interesting sights—an impressive salt mine, a purpose-built communist town, and an unusual earthwork—require a bus, tram, or train ride to reach.

▲▲Wieliczka Salt Mine (Kopalnia Soli Wieliczka)

Wieliczka (veel-EECH-kah), a salt mine southeast of Kraków, is beloved by Poles. Hundreds of feet beneath the ground, the mine is filled with sculptures that min-

ers have lovingly carved out of the salt. You'll explore this unique gallery—learning both about the art and about medieval mining techniques—on a required tour. Though the sight is a bit overrated, it's unique and practically obligatory if you're in Kraków for a few days. In my experience, about half of those who visit love Wieliczka, while half feel it's a waste of time—but it can be hard to predict which half you're in. Read this description before you decide. And expect a lot of walking.

Cost and Hours: The standard "tourist route" costs 89 zł and is by guided tour only. English-language tours leave April-Oct 8:00-19:00 and Nov-March 9:00-17:00 (these are first and last tour times). Other routes are more in-depth (such as the interactive "Miner's Route," where visitors wear coveralls and helmets and operate some of the old equipment); for details see the website.

Information: The mine is in the town of Wieliczka at ulica Daniłowicza 10 (tel. 12-278-7302, www.kopalnia.pl).

Crowd-Beating Tips: This popular sight can be plagued by crowds, and there's a strict limit on how many people can be in the mine at once (due to the ventilation system). It's busiest between 10:00 and 16:00—try to arrive before or after those times (the ticket office opens at 7:30; since the last English tour leaves at 19:00 in summer, arriving in the afternoon can be a good way to stretch your sightseeing day). It's most crowded on weekends and in the summer, and overrun on long holiday weekends.

If you're coming on a summer weekend, any day during peak hours, or anytime you anticipate crowds, it's smart to book ahead online (no extra charge). You can also buy your tickets—and get an appointed entry time—at the **Wieliczka Promotion Office,** in Kraków's Old Town (Mon-Fri 9:00-18:00, closed Sat-Sun, Wiślna 12a). However, reservations are only possible up until three days before; after that, you'll have to show up and take your chances. At any time, it's possible to call ahead to the mine to ask about how busy it is, and to get advice about the best time to show up.

Getting There: The salt mine is 10 miles from Kraków. By far the easiest option is to hop on the **train** at Kraków's main train station (2/hour, 4 zł, 20 minutes, get off at Wieliczka Rynek-Kopalnia; from there, walk up through the parking lot and follow signs to the Daniłowicza shaft and entrance, about 5 minutes). In a pinch, you can take **bus #304** (at Kurniki stop, across from church near Galeria Krakowska mall) or a **minibus,** but these take longer (40 minutes)—get details at the TI, or review your options at the www.jakdojade.pl/krakow route finder. **Private drivers** also make this trip (see page 37).

Getting In: You'll begin at the bustling area around the Daniłowicz shaft. If you reserved a ticket online, follow signs to online tickets pickup point. If you need to buy a ticket on the spot, find the ticket sales line. Once you have a ticket, line up at the English tour area. This waiting area is outdoors, with flimsy canopies to protect from the elements (if it's wet, bring rain gear); they're hoping to build a new indoor waiting area soon.

Visitor Information: You'll pay an extra 10 zł to use your camera—but be warned that flash photos often don't turn out, thanks to the irregular reflection of the salt crystals. Dress warmly—the mine is a constant 57 degrees Fahrenheit. Before entering, you'll have to check large bags.

Eating: There's a good little **$ cafeteria** deep down in the mine, at the end of the tour route. Up at the surface is a wide range of eateries, from snack stands to sit-down restaurants.

Background: Going all the way back to Neolithic times, prehistoric tribes gathered salt from springs in this area. In the 1280s,

Wieliczka Salt Mine began producing salt in earnest. Under Kazimierz the Great, one-third of Poland's income came from these precious deposits—back in an age when salt was called "white gold" and was extremely valuable for its ability to preserve foods. (The Romans even paid workers in salt—*salarium,* the origin of our word "salary.") The mines were so valuable that Kazimierz the Great enacted laws protecting the miners—the first known instance of worker-protection laws in Europe. Wieliczka was controlled by the Polish crown and, after the Partitions, by the Austro-Hungarian Empire (which outfitted miners with military-style uniforms). During this time, around the Industrial Revolution (and under efficient Austrian management), the mine hit peak productivity.

Wieliczka miners spent much of their lives underground, leaving for work before daybreak and returning after sundown, rarely emerging into daylight. To pass the time, beginning in the 17th century, miners carved figures, chandeliers, and even entire underground chapels out of the salt. For many modern visitors, these carvings are the most memorable part of Wieliczka.

Until just a few years ago, the mine still produced salt. Today's miners—about 400 of them—primarily work on maintaining the 200 miles of chambers. This entire network is supported by pine beams—over time, the salt strengthens the wood (some you'll see are more than 200 years old), whereas metal would rust. Per tradition, the wood beams are painted white, to reflect the dim light of the miners' oil lamps. Today visitors see only about 1.5 percent of the sprawling mines. (You would not want to visit the original medieval mines, which have tunnels only about three feet tall.)

Visiting the Mine: From the lobby, your guide leads you 380 steps down a winding staircase. If you've always wanted to feel true vertigo, peer between the banisters on your way down. Once at level 1, you begin a 1.5-mile stroll, generally downhill (more than 800 steps down altogether), past 20 of the mine's 2,000 chambers (with signs explaining when they were dug), finishing 443 feet below the surface (at level 3). When you're done, an elevator beams you back up.

As you spelunk, your guide offers a canned commentary about the history of the mines. You'll learn how the miners lived and worked, using horses who spent their entire adult lives without ever seeing the light of day. You'll see the gigantic horse-pulled wheels used to operate lifts within the mines, and find out why igniting pockets of methane gas near the ceiling was the most dangerous part of the job (the mortality rate for miners was about 1 in 10). All along the way, you'll walk through tunnels caved out of the rock salt; although it can be dark in color (mixed with other minerals such as sandstone and gypsum), it's about 90 percent pure salt. To transport the salt out of the mine, the miners would either carve it into big blocks or crush it and pour it into barrels.

The tour takes you through vast underground caverns, past subterranean lakes (32 percent salt—like the Black Sea, the maximum allowed by nature), and introduces you to some of the mine's many sculptures. You'll see Copernicus (who actually visited here in the 15th century), an army of salt elves, the Polish military hero Józef Piłsudski, and this region's favorite son, St. John Paul II.

Your jaw will drop as you enter the enormous **Chapel of St. Kinga,** carved over three decades in the early 20th century. Look for the salt-relief carving of the Last Supper (its 3-D details are astonishing, considering it's just six inches deep). The chapel is still used for services every Sunday morning at 7:30.

From there, you'll see a few more chambers, including one with a big lake and a brief sound-and-light show. Your tour finishes in a deep-down shopping zone about 1.5 hours after you started. From here you can decide to return to the surface, or add on the Mine Museum.

Returning to the Surface: You'll loop around through a handy cafeteria, then present yourself at the exit, where there are three lines. When you're ready to head up, get in the *exit for individual tourists* line, and the attendant will decide which of two elevators you'll use for the ride up: the old-school Daniłowicz shaft, back up to where you began; or the slick, modern Regis shaft, which pops you out closer to the town center of Wieliczka. From there, it's a pleasant 10-minute walk past the town church and castle, and through a park, back to where you started—a guide will take you the whole way, or you can peel off to explore the town (the main square is just uphill from the shaft). Note that you have zero say over which exit you use—it depends entirely on crowds. The line can seem long, but it moves fast—you'll rarely wait more than 10-15 minutes.

Optional Add-On—Mine Museum: If you're not pooped, you can tack on a visit to the museum (included in your ticket)— which adds about an hour and a mile more walking. While overkill for most, the museum is worthwhile for those who enjoyed exploring the mine and would appreciate a little more historical context. Just get in the *museum* line instead of the *exit* line. A guide will take you through the exhibits, showing you the fancy Habsburg-era miner uniforms; historic maps and etchings of the networks of mines, and cutaway scenes of life below the surface; tools and mining equipment (including a variety of Aladdin-style oil lamps, and huge slings used to lower horses into the mines); a photo gallery of famous visitors, including kings, queens, popes, presidents, and Lech Wałęsa; and a remarkably detailed model of the town of Wieliczka circa 1645. Afterwards, you'll head up to the surface on one of the two elevators.

In the winter only, you can pay an extra 8 zł near the entrance to the museum for a little **underground train ride,** about 2.5 km to a station and back again (not possible in high season).

Nearby: Near the parking lot, you'll see the **"Graduation Tower,"** a modern fort-like structure with a wooden walkway up top. The tower is designed to evaporate and then condense the supposedly very healthy brine from deep underground. The resulting moist, salty air is used to treat patients with lung problems. While locals are prescribed visits here, for most tourists it's not worth the extra money.

▲Nowa Huta

Nowa Huta (NOH-vah HOO-tah, "New Steel Works"), an enormous planned workers' town, offers a glimpse into the stark, grand-scale aesthetics of the communists. Because it's five miles east of central Kraków and a little tricky to see on your own, skip it unless you're determined—it can be tricky to appreciate. But architects and communist sympathizers may want to make a pilgrimage here.

Getting There: Tram #4 goes from near Kraków's Old Town (catch the tram on the ring road near Kraków's main train station, at the Dworzec Główny stop) along John Paul II Avenue (aleja Jana Pawła II) to Nowa Huta's main square, plac Centralny (about 30 minutes total), then continues a few minutes farther to the main gate of the Tadeusz Sendzimir Steelworks—the end of the line. From there it returns to plac Centralny and back to Kraków.

Tours: True to its name, Mike Ostrowski's **Crazy Guides** is a loosely run operation that takes tourists to Nowa Huta in genuine communist-era vehicles (mostly Trabants and Polski Fiats). If you've got an interest in the history—and would enjoy spending the day careening around the streets of Kraków in a car that feels like a cardboard box with a lawnmower engine—hire one of their laid-back hipster guides (159 zł/person for 2.5-hour "communism tour" of Nowa Huta; 199 zł/person for 4-hour "communism deluxe" tour that also includes lunch at a milk bar and a visit to their period-decorated communist apartment; other options available—described on website, mobile 500-091-200, www.crazyguides.com, info@crazyguides.com). If you're already hiring a **local guide** in Kraków, consider paying a little extra to add a couple of hours for a short side trip by car to Nowa Huta.

KRAKÓW

Background: Nowa Huta was the communists' idea of paradise. It's one of only three towns outside the Soviet Union that were custom-built to showcase socialist ideals. (The others are Dunaújváros—once called Sztálinváros—south of Budapest, Hungary; and Eisenhüttenstadt—once called Stalinstadt—near Brandenburg, Germany.) Completed in just 10 years (1949-1959), Nowa Huta was built primarily because the Soviets felt that smart and sassy Kraków needed a taste of heavy industry. Farmers and villagers were imported to live and work in Nowa Huta. Many of the new residents, who weren't accustomed to city living, brought along their livestock (which grazed in the fields around unfinished buildings). For commies, it was downright idyllic: Dad would cheerily ride the tram into the steel factory, mom

would dutifully keep house, and the kids could splash around at the man-made beach and learn how to cut perfect red stars out of construction paper. But Krakovians had the last laugh: Nowa Huta, along with Lech Wałęsa's shipyard in Gdańsk, was one of the home bases of the Solidarity strikes that eventually brought down the regime. Now, with the communists long gone, Nowa Huta remains a major suburb of Poland's cultural capital, with a whopping 200,000 residents.

Touring Nowa Huta: Nowa Huta's focal point used to be known simply as **Central Square** (plac Centralny), but in a fit of poetic justice, it was recently renamed for the anticommunist Ronald Reagan. A map of Nowa Huta looks like a clamshell: a semicircular design radiating from Central/Reagan Square. Numbered streets fan out like spokes on a wheel, and trolleys zip workers directly to the immense factory.

Believe it or not, the inspiration for Nowa Huta was the Renaissance (which, thanks to the textbook Renaissance design of the Cloth Hall and other landmarks, Soviet architects considered typically Polish). Notice the elegantly predictable arches and galleries that would make Michelangelo proud. The settlement was loosely planned on the gardens of Versailles (comparing aerial views of those two very different sites—both with axes radiating from a central hub—this becomes clear). When first built (before it was layered with grime), Nowa Huta was delightfully orderly, primly painted, impeccably maintained, and downright beautiful... if a little boring. It was practical, too: Each of the huge apartment blocks is a self-contained unit, with its own grassy inner courtyard, school, and shops. Driveways (which appear to dead-end at underground garage doors) lead to vast fallout shelters.

Today's Nowa Huta—while gentrifying—is a far cry from its glory days. Wander around. Poke into the courtyards. Reflect on what it would be like to live here. It may not be as bad as you imagine. Ugly as they may seem from the outside, these buildings are packed with happy little apartments filled with color, light, and warmth.

The wide boulevard running northeast of Central/Reagan Square, now called Solidarity Avenue (aleja Solidarności, lined with tracks for tram #4), leads to the **Tadeusz Sendzimir Steelworks.** Originally named for Lenin, this factory was supposedly built using plans stolen from a Pittsburgh plant. It was designed to be a cog in the communist machine—reliant on iron ore from Ukraine and therefore worthless unless Poland remained in the Soviet Bloc. Down from as many as 40,000 workers at its peak, the steelworks now employs only about 10,000. Today there's little to see other than the big sign, stern administration buildings, and smokestacks in the distance. Examine the twin offices flanking the sign—topped with turrets and a decorative frieze inspired by Italian palazzos, these continue the Renaissance theme of the housing districts.

Another worthwhile sight in Nowa Huta is the **Lord's Ark Church** (Arka Pana, several blocks northwest of Central/Reagan

Square on ulica Obrońców Krzyża). Back when he was archbishop of Kraków, Karol Wojtyła fought for years to build a church in this most communist of communist towns. When the regime refused, he insisted on conducting open-air Masses before crowds in fields—until the communists finally capitulated. Consecrated on May 15, 1977, the Lord's Ark Church has a Le Corbusier–esque design that looks like a fat, exhausted Noah's Ark resting on Mount Ararat— encouraging Poles to persevere through the floods of communism. While architecturally interesting, the church is mostly significant as a symbol of an early victory of Catholicism over communism.

Kościuszko Mound (Kopiec Kościuszki)

On a sunny day, the parklands west of the Old Town are a fine place to get out of the city and commune with Krakovians at play. On the outskirts of town is the Kościuszko Mound, a nearly perfectly conical hill erected in 1823 to honor Polish and American military hero Tadeusz Kościuszko. The mound incorporates soil that was brought here from battlefields where the famous general fought, both in Poland and in the American Revolution. Later, under Habsburg rule, a citadel with a chapel was built around the mound, which provided a fine lookout over this otherwise flat terrain. And more recently, the hill was reinforced with steel and cement to prevent it from eroding away. You'll pay to enter the walls and walk to the top—up a curlicue path that makes the mound resemble a giant soft-serve cone—and inside you'll find a modest Kościuszko museum. While not too exciting, this is a pleasant place for an excursion on a nice day.

Cost and Hours: 14 zł, includes museum, mound open daily 9:00-dusk, museum open daily 9:30-19:00—shorter hours off-season, café, tel. 12-425-1116, www.kopieckosciuszki.pl.

Getting There: Ride tram #1 or #6 (from in front of the Wyspiański Pavilion or the main post office) to the end of the line, called Salvator. From here, you can either follow the well-marked path uphill for 20 minutes, or hop on bus #100 to the top (runs at :10 past each hour).

Shopping in Kraków

Two of the most popular Polish souvenirs—amber and pottery—come from areas far from Kraków. You won't find any great bargains on those items here, but several shops specializing in them are listed next. Somewhat more local are the many wood carvings you'll see.

The **Cloth Hall,** smack-dab in the center of the Main Market Square, is the most convenient place to pick up any Polish souvenirs. It has a great selection at respectable prices (summer Mon-Fri 9:00-18:00, Sat-Sun until 15:00—but many stalls remain open later; winter Mon-Fri 9:00-16:00, Sat-Sun until 15:00).

Here are some other souvenir ideas, and neighborhoods or streets that are particularly enjoyable for browsing.

Jewelry

The popular **amber** *(bursztyn)* you'll see sold around town is found on northern Baltic shores; if you're also heading to Gdańsk, wait until you get there (for more on amber, see page 252). One unique alternative that's a bit more local is **"striped flint"** *(krzemień pasiasty)*, a stratified stone that's polished to a high shine. It's mined in a very specific subregion near Kraków, and has become popular among Hollywood celebrities. Each piece has its own unique wavy, sandy patterns.

Jewelry shops abound in the Old Town. For a good selection

of striped flint, amber, and other jewelry, try the no-name shop on **plac Mariacki,** the little square facing the side entrance of St. Mary's Church; they also have a selection of Polish folk costumes in the basement (at #9). A few more jewelry and design shops cluster along Sławkowska street, which runs north from the Main Market Square.

Polish Pottery

"Polish pottery," with distinctive blue-and-white designs, is made in the region of Silesia, west of Kraków (in and around the town of Bolesławiec). But, assuming you won't be going there, you can browse one of the shops in Kraków. **Ceramika Bolesławiecka,** on a busy urban street between the Old Town and Kazimierz, has a tasteful, affordable selection of pottery that's oriented more for locals than tourists (closed Sun, Starowiślna 37). In the Old Town—and with inflated prices to match—two places face each other across Sławkowska street, just a block north of the Square: **Dekor Art** at #11 and **Mila** at #14.

Foods, Drinks, and Cosmetics

Krakowski Kredens is a handy, well-curated shop for overpriced but good-quality traditional foods from Kraków and the surrounding region, Galicia. While the deli case in the back is a pricey place to shop for a picnic (head for a supermarket instead), this is a good chance to stock up on souvenir-quality Polish foods for the folks back home. They have several locations around Kraków—and elsewhere in Poland—but one handy branch is just in front of the Florian Gate at Floriańska 42 (www.krakowskikredens.pl).

Szambelan, a block south of the Main Market Square, is a fun concept for vodka lovers: Peruse the giant casks of three dozen different flavored vodkas, buy an empty bottle, and they'll fill and seal it to take home (Gołębia 2 at the corner with Bracka).

Mydlarnia u Franciszka, with a few locations around Kraków (including a handy one just south of the Main Market Square at Gołębia 2), sells a variety of fragrant soaps, lotions, shampoos, and other cosmetics, some produced locally.

T-Shirts

Two creative shops in the Old Town sell souvenir T-shirts that are a step up in quality (and price) from the generic shops on the square. **Chrum** specializes in locally themed ironic T-shirts (closed Sun, across the street from the Barbican at plac Matejki 3, www. chrum.com), while **Red is Bad** sticks with tasteful, classic Polish eagles and flags on quality materials (closed Sun, just west of the Square at Szewska 25, www.redisbad.pl).

Kraków's Old Town Shopping & Entertainment

KRAKÓW

Shopping

1. Cloth Hall
2. Plac Mariacki Jewelry
3. Ceramika Bolesławiecka
4. Dekor Art
5. Mila & Chopin Gallery/Royal Chamber Orchestra Hall
6. Krakowski Kredens
7. Szambelan & Mydlarnia u Franciszka
8. Chrum
9. Red is Bad
10. To Ulica Józefa Shops
11. Kacper Global Shoes
12. Galeria Krakowska
13. Galeria Kazimierz
14. Pasaż 13 Mall

Entertainment

15. Sts. Peter and Paul Church
16. St. Adalbert Church
17. St. Bernadino's/Bernardynów
18. St. Idziego/Giles Church
19. Polonia House/Dom Polonii
20. Jama Michalika
21. Hotel Royal (bus to Skansen Smaków)
22. Jazz Club u Muniaka
23. Harris Piano Jazz Bar
24. Buddha Nightclub
25. Vodka Café Bar
26. Staropolskie Trunki (Vodka Tasting)
27. To Forum Przestrzenie

KRAKÓW

Designer Shops along Ulica Józefa, in Kazimierz

As the epicenter of Kraków's hipster scene, Kazimierz is the best place in town to browse one-off boutiques (both design and fashion). Several good options line up along ulica Józefa, mostly concentrated along a two-block stretch. Head just one block south from plac Nowy on Estery street, turn right, and keep an eye out for these shops (mostly on the left side of the street): **Blazko,** at #11, has some modern, colorful jewelry, handmade right on the premises. A few doors down **Galerie d'Art Naïf** features fascinating works by untrained artists, and (next door) **Deccoria Galeria** feels like a junk shop, cluttered with handmade jewelry, art, accessories, and vintage clothes. Next are **Paon Nonchalant,** with Polish fashion, and a vintage shop. **Art Factory,** at #9, is worth a browse for colorful jewelry, accessories, and housewares by local designers. **Pracownia** ("Lab"), farther down and also at #9, sells handmade art, jewelry, and clothes. And more clothes by Polish designers are across the street at **Nuumi Boutique** (#14).

A couple of blocks away, just off plac Wolnica, is another great spot for local design, housewares, jewelry, and casual fashion (i.e., creative T-shirts): **Idea Fix** and **The Hive Store,** which share a storefront at Bocheńska 7 (daily).

Up closer to Kazimierz's main drag, ulica Szeroka, **Kacper Global** has a large outlet selling made-in-Poland shoes in styles from athletic to casual to stylish (Miodowa 33).

Shopping Malls

Two enormous shopping malls lie just beyond the tourist zone. The gigantic **Galeria Krakowska,** with nearly 300 shops, shares a square with the train station (Mon-Sat 9:00-22:00, Sun 10:00-21:00, has a kids' play area upstairs from the main entry). Only slightly smaller is **Galeria Kazimierz** (daily 10:00-21:00, just a few blocks east of the Kazimierz sights, along the river at Podgórska 24). A small but swanky mall called **Pasaż 13** is a few steps off the southeast corner of the Main Market Square, where Grodzka street enters the Square. Enter the mall under the balcony marked *Pasaż 13.* You'll find a cool brick-industrial interior, with upscale international chains...and not much that's Polish (Mon-Sat 11:00-21:00, Sun until 17:00).

Entertainment in Kraków

As a town full of both students and tourists, Kraków has plenty of fun options, especially at night.

IN THE OLD TOWN

For locations of the following places, see the map on page 116.

Main Market Square

Intoxicating as the Square is by day, it's even better at night...pure enchantment. Have a meal or sip a drink at an outdoor café, or just grab a bench and enjoy the scene. There's often live al fresco music coming from somewhere (either at restaurants, at a temporary stage set up near the Town Hall Tower, or from talented buskers). You could spend hours doing slow laps around the Square after dark, and never run out of diversions. For a great view over the Square at twilight, nurse a drink at **Café Szał**—on the Cloth Hall's upper terrace (long hours, enter through Gallery of 19th-Century Polish Art).

Concerts

You'll find a wide range of musical events, from tourist-oriented Chopin concerts and classical "greatest hits" selections in quaint old ballrooms and churches, to folk-dancing shows, to serious philharmonic performances. Several companies offer competing concerts; some of the best established include www.cracowconcerts. com, www.newculture.pl, and www.facebook.com/orkiestrasm. The free, monthly *Karnet* cultural-events book lists everything (also online at www.karnet.krakow.pl). Because the offerings change from week to week, inquire locally about what's on during your visit. Hotel lobbies are stocked with fliers, but to get all of your options, visit the TI north of the Square on ulica Św. Jana, which specializes in cultural events (they can book tickets for most concerts with no extra fee and can tell you how to get tickets for the others).

Popular Classical Concerts: The three main choices are organ concerts in churches (usually at 17:00); orchestral or chamber music; or Chopin (either can happen anytime between 18:00 and 20:00). The going rate for most concerts is around 65 zł. Many are held in churches (such as **Sts. Peter and Paul** on ulica Grodzka, **St. Adalbert** on the Square, **St. Bernadino's/Bernardynów** near Wawel Castle, or **St. Idziego/Giles** near Wawel Castle). You'll also find concerts in fancy mansions on or near the Main Market Square (including the **Polonia House/Dom Polonii** upstairs from Wierzynek restaurant at #14, near ulica Grodzka; and the **Chopin Gallery**—also billed as the **Royal Chamber Orchestra Hall**—just up Sławkowska street from the Square at #14). Occasionally in summer, they're also held in various gardens around town (July-Aug only, as part of a festival).

Folk Music: Various venues present dinner shows in the old center. At any of these, a small, hardworking ensemble of colorfully costumed Krakovian singers, dancers, and musicians put on a fun little folk show. While the food, the space, and the clientele are all quite tired, it's a nice taste of Polish folk traditions—and the performers try hard to involve members of the audience in the polkas and circle dances. Options include the historic **Jama Michalika,** with its dusty old Art Nouveau interior right along Floriańska street (120 zł includes dinner; Wed and Sat at 19:00; Floriańska 45, tel. 12-422-1561, www.cracowconcerts.com); or two restaurants right on the Square: **Pod Złotym Karpiem** (at #10; 120 zł for dinner and show, Thu-Fri and Sun at 18:00, tel. 604-093-570, www.cracowconcerts.com) or **Tradycyja Restaurant** (at #15; 60 zł for just the show, 120 zł to add dinner; Sat at 19:00; mobile 602-850-900, www.newculture.pl).

For a more serious folk music performance—and to really make an evening of it—consider a show in a more rustic setting just outside of town. The restaurant **Skansen Smaków,** filling a log cabin-like building, has shows each Thursday night. You'll meet the bus at the Hotel Royal near Wawel Castle at 18:30, ride to the restaurant, have a traditional Polish feast during the show, then be brought back home to the Old Town by 22:00 (150 zł, book ahead, tel. 12-357-1006, www.skansensmakow.pl).

Jazz

Kraków has a surprisingly thriving jazz scene. Several popular clubs hide on the streets surrounding the Main Market Square (open nightly, most shows start around 21:30, sometimes free or a cover of 15-30 zł for better shows). **Jazz Club u Muniaka** is the most famous and best for all-around jazz in a sophisticated cellar environment (ulica Floriańska 3, tel. 12-423-1205). **Harris Piano Jazz Bar,** right on the Square (at #28), is more casual and offers a mix of traditional and updated "fusion" jazz, plus blues (tel. 12-421-5741, www.harris.krakow.pl).

Nightlife in the Old Town

The entire Old Town is crammed with nightclubs and discos pumping loud music on weekends. On a Saturday, the pedestrian streets can be more crowded at midnight than at noon. However, with the exception of the jazz clubs mentioned earlier, most of the nightspots in the Old Town are garden-variety dance clubs, completely lacking the personality and creativity of the Kazimierz nightspots described next. Worse, to save money, young locals stand out in front of nightclubs to drink their own booze (BYOB) rather than pay high prices for the drinks inside—making the streets that much more crowded and noisy. For low-key hanging out, people choose a café on the Square; otherwise, they head for Kazimierz.

In addition to the Harris Piano Jazz Bar (listed earlier), two places on the Square worth checking out are near the southeast corner. At #6, head into the passage to find the **Buddha** nightclub, with comfy lounge sofas under awnings in an immaculately restored old courtyard. For something funkier and even more

KRAKÓW

Kazimierz Entertainment & Nightlife

1. Klezmer-Hois Restaurant
2. Hotel Ester
3. Awiw Restaurant
4. Plac Nowy 1 Bar
5. Alchemia
6. Kolory
7. Mleczarnia
8. Nova Resto Bar & Taawa
9. Singer
10. Eszeweria

local, go down the passage at #19, which runs a surprisingly long distance through the block. Soon you'll start to see tables for the **Herring Embassy;** you'll eventually emerge at **Stolarska street,** a still-enjoyable but far less touristy scene (for more on the Herring Embassy and Stolarska, see page 133).

If you have (or would like to cultivate) an appreciation for vodka, stop by the **Vodka Café Bar,** serving more than 100 types of vodkas, liquors, and hard drinks. You can buy a tasting flight board with six small shots; they'll help you narrow down your options (usually around 33-50 zł for the flight, more for top-shelf vodkas). It's a mellow, uncluttered space that lets you focus on the vodka and the company (Mon-Thu 14:00-24:00, Fri-Sun 13:00-24:00, Mikołajska 5).

Tytano Dolne Młyny Cultural Complex

For lively evening and late-night drinking and dining near the Old Town, don't miss this trendy cultural complex, filling an old tobacco factory about a 10-minute walk west of the Square. For details, see page 136 under "Eating in Kraków."

IN KAZIMIERZ

Aside from the Old Town's gorgeous Square, Kraków's best area to hang out after dark is Kazimierz. Although this is also the former Jewish quarter, the Jewish Sabbath has nothing to do with the bar scene here. You can, however, still hear traditional Jewish music called klezmer. For tips on enjoying a concert of klezmer music, see the sidebar.

Bars and Clubs

Squeezed between centuries-old synagogues and cemeteries are wonderful hangouts running the full gamut from sober and tasteful to wild and clubby. The classic recipe for a Kazimierz bar: Find a dilapidated old storefront, fill it with ramshackle furniture, turn the lights down low, pipe in old-timey jazz music from the 1920s, and sprinkle with alcohol. Serves one to two dozen hipsters. After a few clubs of this type caught on, a more diverse cross-section of nightspots began to move in, including some loud dance clubs. The whole area is bursting with life.

On and near Plac Nowy: The highest concentration of bars ring the plac Nowy market square. Do a loop to browse your options. **Plac Nowy 1** specializes in Polish microbrews and upmarket pub grub in a bright, sleek (and arguably "un-Kazimierz") setting. Across the square, **Alchemia,** one of the first—and still one of the best—bars in Kazimierz, is candlelit, cluttered, and claustrophobic, with cave-like rooms crowded with rickety old furniture, plus a cellar used for live performances (Estery 5, www.alchemia.com. pl). Between these two is **Kolory,** with a pleasant Parisian brasserie ambience (Estery 10). Late at night, the little windows in the plac Nowy **market hall** do a big business selling *zapiekanki* (baguette with toppings) to hungry bar-hoppers.

On Rabina Meiselsa street, just a half-block off plac Nowy, under the arch to a characteristic courtyard is **Mleczarnia,** a top-notch beer garden with rickety tables squeezed under the trees and its cozy old-fashioned pub across the street (at #20).

Klezmer Music in Kazimierz

On a balmy summer night, Kazimierz's main square, ulica Szeroka, is filled with the haunting strains of klezmer—traditional Jewish music from 19th-century Poland, generally with violin, string bass, clarinet, and accordion. Skilled klezmer musicians can make their instruments weep or laugh like human voices. There are two main ways to enjoy some klezmer music: at a restaurant or at a concert.

Restaurants: Several eateries on ulica Szeroka offer klezmer music, typically starting between 19:00 and 20:00. The musicians move from room to room, and the menus tend to be a mix of traditional Jewish and Polish cuisine (which are quite similar). But don't come here just for the food—it's an afterthought to the music. While most places claim to do concerts "nightly year-round," they can be canceled anytime it's slow (especially off-season)—confirm ahead.

Some old-school restaurants offer reasonably priced food but charge 30 zł per person for the music. Probably your best choice is the well-established **$$$ Klezmer-Hois,** filling a venerable former Jewish ritual bathhouse and making you feel like you're dining in a rich grandparent's home (daily 8:00-22:00, at #6, tel. 12-411-1245, www.klezmer.pl).

A newer trend is for restaurants with outdoor seating on ulica Szeroka to offer "free" al fresco klezmer music for customers (though the food tends to be that much more expensive). Because the music is free, anybody (at neighboring restaurants, or simply strolling past) can enjoy a taste of klezmer. Just show up, comparison-shop music and menus, and—if you like what you hear—pick a place for dinner or a drink. Eateries offering this option include **$$ Hotel Ester** (at #20, with relatively reasonable prices and live music that begins in the early afternoon rather than evening) and **$$$ Awiw** (at #13, overpriced food).

Concerts: To really focus on klezmer as an art form, pay a bit more to attend a concert. Popular options include the **Jascha Lieberman Trio** (schedule at www.jaschalieberman.com); or a performance in arguably the most powerful space, the giant old prayer hall of **Isaac Synagogue** (60 zł, Sun-Mon and Wed-Thu at 18:00, Kupa 18, www.sibelia.pl). There are also concerts in season in Kraków's Old Town, near the Main Market Square (most afternoons at 17:30, Sławkowska 14, www.cracowconcerts.com). For the latest lineup, check for fliers around town, or ask at any TI.

Don't worry too much about seeking out a particular musician—they are equally good, and each brings a unique style to the music. Many venues share musicians, so on any given night it's hard to predict who's performing where. Bottom line: If you're interested in klezmer music, you can't go wrong in Kazimierz.

Near Isaac Synagogue: A block east of plac Nowy, a few more places cluster on the wide street in front of Isaac Synagogue. The huge **Nova Resto Bar** dominates the scene with a long covered terrace, a vast interior, and seating in their courtyard—all with a cool color scheme, Las Vegas polka-dot style. This feels upscale and a bit pretentious compared to many of the others, but it's the place to be seen (25-40-zł meals, Estery 18). Upstairs is the similarly trendy music club **Taawa** (http://taawa.pl). Facing this double-decker wall of style are some smaller, more accessible options: **Singer** is classy and mellow, with most of its tables made of old namesake sewing machines (Estery 20), while **Warsztat** has an exploding-instruments-factory ambience (Izaaka 3; also recommended later, under "Eating in Kraków").

On Józefa Street: More good bars are just a short block south. Along Józefa, you'll find a pair of classic Kazimierz joints: **Eszeweria,** which wins the "best atmosphere" award, feels like a Polish speakeasy that's been in mothballs for the last 90 years—a low-key, unpretentious, and inviting hangout (Józefa 9). A block up, look for **Kolanko No. 6,** with a cozy bar up front, a pleasant beer garden in the inner courtyard, and a fun events hall in back (Józefa 17, www. kolanko.net; also recommended later, under "Eating in Kraków").

Beach Bar on the Riverbank

South of the river, roughly between Kazimierz and Wawel Castle, **Forum Przestrzenie** fills a dilapidated concrete hotel—a mostly abandoned dinosaur from communist times, today used primarily as an extra-large billboard. But in recent years, the ground floor has been taken over by a lively hipster bar—especially appealing in the balmy summer months, when comfy low-slung chairs sprawl across a tidy lawn and a pebbly "beach"

with views across the Vistula to Wawel Castle. They serve coffee, wine, beer, summery cocktails, and cheap bar snacks. A few artists and designers also have boutiques here (open daily in good weather 10:00-late, skip the trip if it's not nice out, ulica Marii Konopnickiej 28, mobile 515-424-724, www.forumprzestrzenie.com).

Sleeping in Kraków

Kraków is popular, with lots of accommodations options. Healthy competition keeps Kraków's prices reasonable and makes choosing a hotel fun rather than frustrating. Rates are soft; hoteliers don't need much of an excuse to offer discounts, especially on weekends or off-season. I've focused my accommodations in two areas: in and near the Old Town; and in Kazimierz, a hipper, more affordable neighborhood that is home to both the old Jewish quarter and a thriving dining and nightlife zone.

Both zones can suffer from discos that thump loud music on weekend nights to attract roving gangs of rowdy drinkers. The "quiet after 22:00" law is flagrantly ignored. I've tried to avoid the areas most plagued by noise, but my accommodations do come with some risk of noise; to help your odds, ask for a quiet room when you reserve...and bring earplugs.

KRAKÓW

IN AND NEAR THE OLD TOWN

Most of my listings are inside (or within a block or two of) the Planty park that rings the Old Town. Sleeping inside the Old Town comes with pros (maximum atmosphere; handy location for sightseeing and dining) and cons (high prices; the potential for noise—especially on weekends—as noted earlier). Places just outside the Old Town are still handy, but quieter and cheaper. If you need a room in a pinch, several slick, international chains (Ibis, Mercure, Puro) have branches near the train station.

Guesthouses

These good-value pensions come with lots of stairs (no elevators) and are located in the heart of the Old Town along busy pedestrian streets. Many lack air-conditioning, so they can be noisy with the windows open in the summer, especially on weekends. Don't expect a 24-hour reception desk; it's always smart to tell them your arrival time, especially if it's late in the day.

$$ Tango House, run by dance instructor Marcin Miszczak, is in a well-located building with an ancient-feeling stairwell decorated with faded Art Nouveau paintings. Its eight long, skinny, retro-stylish rooms have parquet floors (ask for quieter courtyard room to avoid weekend noise, ulica Szpitalna 4, tel. 12-429-3114, www.tangohouse.pl, tangohouse@gmail.com).

$$ Globtroter Guest House offers 17 basic, somewhat stuffy, rustic-feeling rooms with high ceilings and big beams around a serene garden courtyard. Jacek (Jack), who really understands and respects travelers, conscientiously focuses on value—keeping prices reasonable by not offering needless extras (RS%, 2 people can cram into a single to save money, family rooms, breakfast at nearby café extra, pay laundry service, fun 700-year-old brick cellar lounge down below, go down passageway at #7 at the square called plac Szczepański, tel. 12-422-4123, www.globtroter-krakow.com, globtroter@globtroter-krakow.com).

$$ La Fontaine B&B, run by a French-Polish family, offers

KRAKÓW

Sleep Code

Hotels are classified based on the average price of a standard double room with breakfast in high season.

$$$$	**Splurge:**	Most rooms over 550 zł
$$$	**Pricier:**	400-550 zł
$$	**Moderate:**	250-400 zł
$	**Budget:**	100-250 zł
¢	**Backpacker:**	Under 100 zł
RS%	**Rick Steves discount**	

Unless otherwise noted, credit cards are accepted, hotel staff speak basic English, and free Wi-Fi is available. Comparison-shop by checking prices at several hotels (on each hotel's own website, on a booking site, or by email). For the best deal, *book directly with the hotel.* Ask for a discount if paying in cash; if the listing includes **RS%**, request a Rick Steves discount.

26 rooms and apartments just off the Main Market Square. Tastefully decorated with French flair, it's cute as a poodle. Most of the rooms have a little lounge with a microwave and fridge—many in the hall, some inside the room. If you don't mind huffing up lots of stairs, this is a fine value (air-con in some rooms, low slanted ceilings in some rooms, ulica Sławkowska 1, tel. 12-422-6564, www. bblafontaine.com, biuro@bblafontaine.com).

Outside the Old Town: $$ Cracowdays is the farthest of my listings from the center of town, about a 15-minute walk away (a tram can cut a few minutes off the trek). But it's also a notch more refined than the guesthouses listed previously. It sits in a pleasant residential neighborhood west of the Main Market Square, with eight beautifully decorated and thoughtfully tended rooms, all sharing a central kitchen (two stand-alone studio apartments in another building, air-con, Grabowskiego 7, mobile 604-460-860, www.cracowdays.com, reservation@cracowdays.com).

Hotels

$$$$ Donimirski Boutique Hotels, with three locations in or near Kraków's Old Town, set the bar for splurge hotels in Kraków (www.donimirski.com). All Donimirski hotels come with friendly staff, discounts for my readers, and classy little extras that add up to a memorable hotel experience. **Hotel Polski Pod Białym Orłem** has 60 classic rooms conveniently located near the Florian Gate just inside the Old Town walls (RS%, apartments available, air-con, elevator, ulica Pijarska 17, tel. 12-422-1144, hotel.polski@ donimirski.com). **Hotel Gródek** offers 23 rooms a three-minute walk behind St. Mary's Church, on a quiet dead-end street overlooking the Planty park (RS%, pay parking, Na Gródku 4, tel.

12-431-9030, grodek@donimirski.com). And **Hotel Pugetów,** with six small but plush rooms, is in the workaday neighborhood between the Main Market Square and Kazimierz (RS%, air-con, pay parking, ulica Starowiślna 15A, tel. 12-432-4950, pugetow@ donimirski.com).

$$$$ Hotel Senacki is a business-class place renting 20 comfortable rooms between Wawel Castle and the Main Market Square. The staff is warm, professional, and conscientious, and the location is perfect, making this an ideal splurge in the center. Top-floor "attic" rooms have low beams, skylight windows, and a flight of stairs after the elevator (air-con, elevator—but doesn't go to "attic" rooms, ask about nearby pay parking, ulica Grodzka 51, tel. 12-422-7686, www.hotelsenacki.pl, senacki@hotelsenacki.pl).

$$$$ Hotel Wawel has 39 rooms on a well-located street that's quieter than the Old Town norm. It's colorful and serene; above the swanky marble lobby are hallways creatively painted with the history of the building and images from around Kraków. Out back, a fountain gurgles in a cute little courtyard (air-con, elevator—but doesn't go to top floor, steam room and whirlpool bath extra, ulica Poselska 22, tel. 12-424-1300, www.hotelwawel.pl, hotel@hotelwawel.pl).

$$$ Bracka 6, wonderfully located just one short block off the Main Market Square, is a sort of a hybrid between a hotel and an apartment house. The 16 stylish rooms—with sleek lines, lots of glass, and exposed brick—each have a kitchen, so breakfast is extra. It's on the second and third floors with no elevator, and the reception is open limited hours (daily 8:00-22:00 or so)—but the lack of full hotel amenities keeps the prices affordable for this level of modern elegance (air-con, Bracka 6, tel. 12-341-4011, www. bracka6.pl, info@bracka6.pl).

$$$ Hotel Wielopole sits a block outside the Planty, on the way to the lively Kazimierz district. Its 35 tight rooms are tucked down a side street just past the main post office, facing a big Holiday Inn. The staff are proud of their attentive service, and they circulate a informative little newsletter daily (air-con, elevator, vegetarian restaurant in cellar, Wielopole 3, tel. 12-422-1475, www. wielopole.pl, office@wielopole.pl).

$$$ Hotel Amber sits on a dreary urban street just outside the Planty park, but still less than a 10-minute walk from the Square. Run by the same company as Hotel Wielopole (described above), it has an equally pleasant emphasis on welcoming service. The hotel has two parts: 18 perfectly fine, if smallish, rooms in the original building; and 20 slightly more upscale rooms in the newer "design" section. Both parts share a small gym, sauna, and garden in back (air-con, elevator, Garbarska 8-10, tel. 12-421-0606, www.hotel-amber.pl, office@hotel-amber.pl).

Kraków's Old Town Hotels & Restaurants

KRAKÓW

Accommodations

① Tango House
② Globtroter Guest House
③ La Fontaine B&B
④ To Cracowdays
⑤ Hotel Polski Pod Białym Orłem
⑥ Hotel Gródek
⑦ Hotel Pugetów
⑧ Hotel Senacki & Bar Grodzki
⑨ Hotel Wawel
⑩ Bracka 6
⑪ Hotel Wielopole
⑫ Hotel Amber
⑬ Kraków City Apartments
⑭ Kraków for You Apartments

Eateries

⑮ Restauracja pod Aniołami
⑯ Pod Nosem
⑰ Miód Malina
⑱ Pod Baranem
⑲ Ed Red
⑳ Charlotte
㉑ Café Bunkier
㉒ Ambasada Śledzia
㉓ Pod Wawelem Beer Hall
㉔ Cyklop Pizza & Jadłodajnia "U Stasi"
㉕ Moa Burger
㉖ Krowarzywa
㉗ Lajkonik Sandwiches
㉘ Milkbar Tomasza
㉙ U Babci Maliny (2)
㉚ Bar Mleczny pod Temidą
㉛ Restauracja Samoobsługowa Polakowski
㉜ Chimera Cafeteria
㉝ Krupnicza Street Eateries

Apartments

Apartments aren't just for long stays—these places welcome even one-nighters. As reception times are limited, be sure to clearly communicate your arrival time. A wide variety of apartments is easy to find at online booking sites, but both of these places have a reception desk that manages several units, making them a bit more hotelesque than the norm. Still, you're on your own for breakfast, and don't expect your room to be cleaned during your stay.

$$ Kraków City Apartments has six straightforward, modern studio apartments tucked away in a quiet courtyard at the corner of the Old Town (self check-in—arrange details in advance, ulica Szpitalna 34, mobile 507-203-050, www.krakowapartments.info, info@krakowapartments.info, Andrzej and Katarzyna).

$$ Kraków for You Apartments offers 12 modern, well-decorated studios and one- and two-bedroom units with kitchenettes around a courtyard along one of Kraków's most happening streets, just a few steps off the Main Market Square (reception open daily 10:00-20:00, request quieter courtyard room, lots of stairs with no elevator, go down the passage at Grodzka 4, tel. 12-421-4835, mobile 660-541-085, www.krakowforyou.com, info@krakowforyou.com, Mikołaj).

IN KAZIMIERZ

Kazimierz is both Kraków's Jewish heart and soul, and its trendiest eating and nightlife zone. Sleeping here puts you in close proximity to synagogues and klezmer concerts, as well as to food trucks and hip nightclubs (expect some noise, especially on weekends). Keep in mind that, while pleasant in its own right, Kazimierz is a 20-minute walk or a 5-minute tram ride from Kraków's atmospheric old center (for details on getting to Kazimierz from the Old Town, see page 82). For locations, see the map on page 138.

$$$$ Metropolitan Boutique Hotel is an upscale refuge, just a block before the heart of Kazimierz (just off the busy road on the way to Kraków's Old Town). Its 59 rooms—with exposed brick and slick modern style—sit along a somewhat dreary but conveniently located side street (air-con, elevator, gym, Joselewicza 19, tel. 12-442-7500, www.hotelmetropolitan.pl).

$$$ Rubinstein Residence sits right in the middle of ulica Szeroka—surrounded by klezmer restaurants and synagogues, in the heart of the neighborhood. It fills a painstakingly restored old townhouse (parts of it dating to the 15th century) with heavy wood beams and 30 swanky rooms—some of them palatial suites that incorporate old features like frescoes and pillars. The rooftop terrace—with views over Kazimierz and to the Old Town—sets this place above, and is open to the public after 17:00 (air-con, eleva-

tor, Szeroka 12, tel. 12-384-0000, www.rubinstein.pl, recepcja@
rubinstein.pl).

$$ Karmel Hotel, with 11 rooms above an Italian restaurant,
sits on a pleasant side street near the heart of Kazimierz. It offers
elegance at a reasonable price (some rooms have air-con, upstairs
with no elevator, some night noise on weekends, ulica Kupa 15, tel.
12-430-6697, www.karmel.com.pl, hotel@karmel.com.pl).

$ Residence Tournet, well run by friendly Piotr and Sylwia
Działowy, is your cheap-and-cheery option, offering 18 colorful,
overly perfumed rooms near the edge of Kazimierz toward Wawel
Castle (elevator plus a few stairs, reception open 7:00-22:00, ulica
Miodowa 7, tel. 12-292-0088, www.accommodation.krakow.pl,
tournet@nocleg.krakow.pl).

Eating in Kraków

Kraków has a wide array of great restaurants—for each one I've
listed, there are two or three nearly as good. As the restaurant
scene changes constantly, I've chosen established places that have
a proven track record for reliably good food. In my listings, you'll
find a mix of old-school Polish eateries and modern foodie alterna-
tives (which are still rooted in the local tradition). You could also
consider a food tour (see "Tours in Krakow" near the beginning of
this chapter).

IN THE OLD TOWN

Kraków's Old Town is loaded with dining options. Prices are
often reasonable even on the Main Market Square. And a half-
block away, they get even better. All of these eateries (except the
milk bars) are likely to be booked up on weekends—always reserve
ahead. You'll find plenty of expensive, tourist-oriented restaurants
on the Main Market Square, though I haven't recommended any
here—while they vary in quality, all are overpriced. To enjoy the
same experience more affordably, have just a drink on the Square
and dine elsewhere.

$$$ Restauracja pod Aniołami ("Under Angels") offers
a dressy, candlelit atmosphere on a wonderful covered patio or
in a deep, steep, romantic cellar with rough wood and medieval
vaults. Peruse the elaborately described menu of medieval noble-
men's dishes. The cuisine is traditional Polish, with an emphasis on
grilled meats and trout (on a wood-fired grill). Every meal begins
with *smalec* (spread made with lard, fried onion, bacon, and apple).
Don't go here if you're in a hurry—only if you want to really slow
down and enjoy your dinner. Reservations are smart (daily 13:00-
24:00, ulica Grodzka 35, tel. 12-421-3999, www.podaniolami.pl).

$$$$ Pod Nosem ("Under the Nose") is a smart choice for

Restaurant Price Code

I've assigned each eatery a price category, based on the average cost of a typical main course. Drinks, desserts, and splurge items (steak and seafood) can raise the price considerably.

$$$$	**Splurge:**	Most main courses over 60 zł
$$$	**Pricier:**	45-60 zł
$$	**Moderate:**	25-45 zł
$	**Budget:**	Under 25 zł

In Poland, a milk bar or takeout spot is **$**; a basic sit-down eatery is **$$**; a casual but more upscale restaurant is **$$$**; and a swanky splurge is **$$$$**.

refined, updated Polish cuisine in a sophisticated, less touristy atmosphere. It's tucked at the far end of sleepy Kanonicza lane, just beyond the tourists and before Wawel Castle. In a tight dining room that skips the kitsch, they offer an extensive wine list and a short menu of artfully executed Polish dishes (daily 12:00-22:00, Kanonicza 22, tel. 12-376-0014, www.kanonicza22.com).

$$$ Miód Malina ("Honey Raspberry") is a delightful, acceptably kitschy Polish-Italian fusion restaurant filled with the comforting aroma of its wood-fired oven. The menu is mostly Polish, with a few Italian dishes thrown in. Sit in the cozy, warmly painted interior or out in the courtyard (reservations smart, daily 12:00-23:00, ulica Grodzka 40, tel. 12-430-0411, www.miodmalina.pl).

$$ Pod Baranem ("Under the Ram") is a solid midrange bet for well-executed, traditional Polish food. Respected by locals, it sits just outside the tourist chaos, quietly facing the Planty near Wawel Castle. Several cozy rooms—tasteful but not stuffy—sprawl through a homey old building (daily 12:00-22:00, lighter meals before 19:00, Św. Gertrudy 21, tel. 12-429-4022, www.podbaranem.com).

Steak House: $$$$ Ed Red, by acclaimed local chef Adam Chrząstowski, serves up the best steaks in Kraków. He carefully sources his beef from Poland and dry-ages it himself (21 or 45 days). A short walk from the Main Market Square, the space is classy but not stuffy, with exposed brick, leather benches, and a busy open kitchen. They have a long list of top-quality, dry-aged steaks, as well as a short menu of affordably priced alternatives. Reservations are smart (daily 12:00-23:00, Sławkowska 3, mobile 690-900-555, www.edred.pl).

Youthful Style at Plac Szczepański: While seemingly every corner of the Old Town is jammed with tourists, the pleasant square called plac Szczepański feels more like the terrain of university students—a carefully protected bastion of the local upscale art culture. While just two blocks from the Square, this small array of cafés and galleries has a vibe that's more Warsaw-urbane than ye olde Kraków.

$ Charlotte is a winner—it's a classy, French-feeling bakery/café/wine bar. They make their own breads and pastries in the basement (with lots of seating—you can watch the bakers work if you come early enough in the morning), cultivate a stay-awhile coffeehouse ambience upstairs, and throw in a few square-facing sidewalk tables to boot. And it's affordable, serving up sandwiches, pastries, and salads. While the food is light café fare rather than a filling dinner, after 18:00 they redecorate to give it a more sophisticated flair (Mon-Fri 7:00-24:00, Sat from 9:00, Sun 9:00-22:00, plac Szczepański 2, tel. 12-431-5610).

Just around the corner, facing the Planty park, is the delightful **$$ Café Bunkier.** It belongs to the hulking Bunkier Sztuki contemporary art gallery, but—in contrast to that building's concrete vibe—the café sits under a glass canopy that faces the lush greenbelt, with well-worn wooden tables and an almost Parisian ambience. While it's not the place for a filling meal, it's worth coming here for some light food and drinks while enjoying Kraków's greenery. It's especially cozy on a rainy day. And when it's nice out, they open up the walls and put you right in the heart of the park (daily 9:00-24:00, food from 12:00, plac Szczepański 3a, tel. 12-431-0585).

On Stolarska Street: Stolarska street, a neatly pedestrianized, oddly untrammeled "embassy row" just a block away from the Main Market Square, is worth exploring for a meal or a drink. Stolarska has a fun variety of more locals-oriented bars and cafés. Begin at the Small Market Square (Mały Rynek) behind St. Mary's Church and head south. On the left, look for the ridiculously long sign that perfectly identifies the business: Pierwszy Lokal Na Stolarskiej Po Lewej Stronie Idąc Od Małego Rynku ("The first pub on the left side of Stolarska coming from the Small Market Square"). Notice that this once-sleepy street is lined with embassies and consulates—it's easy to spot the flags of Germany, the US, and France.

On the left, in the stretch of cafés under canopies, you'll see the **$ Ambasada Śledzia** ("Herring Embassy"), with a divey, youthful atmosphere and a "Polish tapas" approach: A dozen different types of herring and other light meals, plus a variety of vodka to wash it down, are posted on the menu. You'll order at the bar, then find a table or take it to go (open long hours daily, Stolarska 8). Across the street and 50 paces back up, the Pasaż Bielaka (look for the low-profile stone doorway at #5) runs through the middle of the block all the way out to the Main Market Square (emerging at Rynek Główny #19); partway along is another sprawling branch of the Herring Embassy.

Beer Hall: $$ Pod Wawelem ("Under Wawel") is a rollicking Czech-style beer hall right on the Planty park near Wawel Castle. It's packed with locals seeking big, sloppy, greasy portions of meaty fare, with giant mugs of various beers on tap (including Polish and Bavarian). Choose between the bustling interior and the outdoor terrace right on the Planty. Locals come here not for a romantic dinner but for a rowdy evening out with friends (different specials every day—such as giant schnitzel, pork ribs, or roasted chicken; daily 12:00-24:00, ulica Św. Gertrudy 26-29, tel. 12-421-2336).

Pizza: $ Cyklop, with 10 tables wrapped around the cook and his busy oven, has good wood-fired pizzas and a cozy, charming ambience (daily 11:00-23:00, near St. Mary's Church at Mikołajska 16, tel. 12-421-6603).

Burgers (and Vegan Burgers): Gourmet hamburgers are all the rage in Poland. One of the best options in the center is **$ Moa Burger,** with a dozen different types of big, sloppy, "New Zealand-style" hamburgers. Order at the counter, then find a seat at a shared table (daily 11:00-23:00, Mikołajska 3, tel. 12-421-2144). Another fad is vegan "burgers"; a handy place in the center is **$ Krowarzywa** (a pun roughly meaning both "Cow Alive" and "Cow Vegetable")—with a hip atmosphere and an enticing menu of meatless options (daily 12:00-23:00, Sławkowska 8, mobile 531-777-136).

Quick Sandwich: If you need a break from milk bars (described next) but want to grab a sandwich on the go, stop by **$ Lajkonik,** a modern bakery/coffee shop *(piekarnia i kawiarnia)* that sells fresh takeout sandwiches (Mon-Fri 7:00-21:00, Sat from 8:00, Sun 8:00-22:00, handy location right in front of the Dominican Church at Dominikański 2, others are just outside the Old Town).

Milk Bars and Other Quick, Cheap, Traditional Eats

Kraków is a good place to try the cheap cafeterias called "milk bars." For pointers on eating at a milk bar, review the sidebar on page 18.

$ Milkbar Tomasza is an upgraded milk bar popular with local students. Modern and relatively untouristy, it serves big, split-table portions of high-quality food—a mix of Polish and international—plus breakfast dishes all day (cheap soup and salad deals, great big salads, Tue-Sun 8:00-20:00, closed Mon, ulica Tomasza 24, tel. 12-422-1706).

$ U Babci Maliny ("Granny Raspberry"), with a grinning Granny on the sign, is well established and much appreciated for its big portions of flavorful traditional food. One location, frequented almost entirely by Krakovians, is designed for university students and staff and is tucked into an inner courtyard of the Science Academy. Find the door at Sławkowska 17, then make your way into the inner courtyard, with an entrance to a rustic cellar where it looks like a kitschy cottage bomb went off (Mon-Fri 11:00-22:30, Sat-Sun from 12:00). Another location is across the street from the National Theater building at Szpitalna 38. The main floor, also done up in a kitschy cottage style, is self-service and budget priced, while the cellar—with a drawing-room vibe—has table service and is about 20 percent more expensive (daily 11:00-23:00). Both locations have walls of photos of the owner posing with bodybuilders and ultimate fighters...not quite in keeping with the country theme.

$ Jadłodajnia "U Stasi" is a throwback that makes you feel like you're in on Kraków's best-kept secret. Its hidden location—tucked at the far end of the passage with the recommended Cyklop pizzeria—attracts a wide range of loyal local clientele, from hardscrabble seniors to politicians, artists, and actors. They're all here for well-executed, unpretentious, home-style Polish lunch grub. There can be a bit of a language barrier, so go with the flow: Pick up the English menu as you enter, find a table, wait for them to take your order, enjoy your meal, then pay as you leave. This is an excellent value and a real, untouristy Polish experience. The short menu changes every day—and when they're out, they're out (Mon-Fri 12:00-17:00, closed Sat-Sun, Mikołajskiej 16).

Throwback Milk Bars on Grodzka Street: Just a couple of blocks south of the Main Market Square, on busy ulica Grodzka, two classic milk bars somehow survive the onslaught of the modern world. First, at the corner with Senacka, is the remarkably basic and traditional milk bar, **$ Bar Mleczny pod Temidą.** The next best thing to a time machine to the communist era, this place has grumpy monolingual service, a mostly

local clientele, and cheap but good food (daily 9:00-20:00). A few more steps down, also on the right (just before the two churches), **$ Bar Grodzki** is a single tight little room with shared tables. They specialize in tasty potato pancake dishes *(placki ziemniaczane).* Order high on the menu and try the rich and hearty "Hunter's Delight"—potato pancake with sausage, beef, melted cheese, and spicy sauce. The English menu posted by the counter makes ordering easy. Order, sit, and wait to be called to fetch your food (daily 9:00-19:00).

$ Restauracja Samoobsługowa Polakowski is a glorified milk bar with country-kitchen decor and cheap, tasty Polish fare. The tongue-twisting samoobsługowa simply means "self-service"— as at other milk bars, you'll order at the counter and bus your dishes when done. Curt service...cute hats (daily 11:00-21:00, facing St. Francis Basilica and the Wyspiański Pavilion at plac Wszystkich Świętych 10).

$ Chimera Cafeteria, just off the Main Market Square, is a handy spot for a quick lunch in the center. It serves fast traditional meals to a steady stream of students. You'll order at the counter— choose a big plate (6 items) or medium plate (4 items), and select from an array of salads and main dishes by pointing to what looks good. Then eat outside on their quiet garden courtyard (good for vegetarians, daily 9:00-22:00, near university at ulica Św. Anny 3). I'd skip their expensive full-service restaurant (in the basement), which shares an entryway.

Lively Student Zone Just West of the Old Town

A few minutes' walk west of the Old Town is a trendy, energetic neighborhood with more students than tourists. If ye olde Kraków is getting a little olde, this area is a closer, easier escape than Kazimierz.

Krupnicza Street: This street, which begins just across the ring road from the Planty, is a handy strip to browse for affordable eateries, as it's lined with student-oriented places with more interesting food than in the Old Town. To get here, head out Szewska street from the middle of the Square (to the west), cross the busy ring road, and bear left at the Teatr Bagatela. Several eateries along here are worth considering: **$$ Sisi** is a cellar café with international and Austrian fare (think Wiener schnitzel, at #3 on the right); **$$ Pod Norenami** has a pan-Asian menu that includes sushi, ramen, curries, gyoza, and wok dishes (at #6 on the left); **$$ Dynia** features a hip brick interior and an inviting garden courtyard (at #20 on the left); and **$$ Meho Café,** with a short menu of international-Polish fusion dishes, is the eatery attached to the Józef Mehoffer House Museum. In summer, the interior garden courtyard is a delightful escape from the city bustle (at #26 on the left). At the end of the street, hook right to find the best place in the area for a sweet treat: **$ Café Lisboa,** which serves great coffee and excellent *pastéis de nata,* the national dessert of Portugal—made by a Pole who went to Belém to learn how to make it just right (Dolnych Młynów 3).

Just a block beyond Café Lisboa is...

Tytano Dolne Młyny Cultural Complex: This former tobacco factory has recently been developed into a cultural complex—a fun-to-explore collection of bars and restaurants. Still run-down and funky, but bursting with creative energy, it's the youthful yin to Kraków's venerable yang. While sleepy during the day, the Tytano complex is well worth walking through in the evening, especially on weekends—and it really gets rolling late at night. Enter the complex through the gate at Dolnych Młynów 10, near **$$ Veganic**—a restaurant with beautifully presented, mostly vegan fare in a casual yet sophisticated setting. You'll pass a few cafés and bars as you angle ahead to the right, then around the biggest building, to the heart of the complex just behind. You'll pass **$$ Tao,** with pan-Asian food and themed cocktails; and the cozy **$ Bonjour Çava,** a coffee-and-cakes eatery with outdoor tables in a low-key garden setting, and some light meals. Anchoring the center of the complex is the industrial-sized **$$ Międzymiastowa** ("Long Distance") restaurant—the most yuppie-feeling choice here, with a big, inviting terrace, an extensive list of gin drinks, and a menu of serviceable international dishes. Nearby is a lane leading to a trio of popular bars: **Strefa,** a tight cocktail bar with a good wine list and interesting bites; **Weźże Krafta,** a taproom with 25 different microbrews on tap and outdoor wood-pallet benches; and—at the lane's dead end—Hala Główna, a student dive bar with ramshackle tables spilling out under twinkle lights, a dozen craft beers on tap, hard drinks, and pizza. Around the corner, a parallel alley is home to **Zet Pe Te,** with lots of outdoor white-wooden-pallet benches under twinkle lights; their vast, industrial interior often hosts DJs or live music. And tucked down a little courtyard nearby is **$ Grill Garaż,** a casual eatery with meat sizzling on the open hood compartment of a vintage VW Beetle.

IN KAZIMIERZ

The entire district is bursting with lively cafés and bars—it's a happening night scene. And, beyond the Jewish-themed places along ulica Szeroka (see the sidebar on page 123), Kazimierz's restaurants are less touristy and more diverse than the Old Town's. For locations, see the map on page 138.

Fast and Cheap

Kazimierz has some great takeout and street food—handy for a lunch break from daytime sightseeing here, or for an affordable dinner break from bar-hopping.

$ Food Trucks: Kazimierz has three vacant lots filled with

KRAKÓW

Kazimierz Hotels & Restaurants

Accommodations
1 To Metropolitan Boutique Hotel
2 Rubinstein Residence
3 Karmel Hotel
4 Residence Tournet

Eateries
5 Judah Square Food Trucks
6 Isaac Synagogue Food Trucks
7 Dajwór 21 Food Trucks
8 Plac Nowy Eateries
9 Nova Krova
10 Good Lood
11 Pod Ursa Maior
12 Bagelmama
13 Hummus Amamamusi
14 Stara Zajezdnia
15 Craftownia
16 Bottiglieria 1881
17 Hamsa Restaurant
18 Alchemia & Alchemia od Kuchni
19 Kolanko No. 6
20 Warsztat (3)
21 Lody Tradycyjna Receptura

fun-to-browse food trucks—most open daily for lunch and dinner.
Each one comes with about a half-dozen entirely different options.
The first and best is at **Judah Square.** Named for its big graffiti
mural (by an Israeli street artist), it's tucked at the southern fringe
of the tourists' Kazimierz, near the old tram depot (corner of Św.
Wawrzyńca and Wąska). Mainstays here include Andrus (super-
decadent and gooey roasted pork sandwiches); Boogie Truck burg-

ers; Yatai sushi; Belgian-style fries; Pan Kumpir baked potatoes; and the beloved Chimney Cake Bakery, which rotisserie-roasts dough and sugar into a sweet and crunchy cake, then fills it with ice cream and other toppings.

Right in the heart of the tourist zone, another food truck pod fills a vacant lot **behind Isaac Synagogue,** just steps from ulica Szeroka. Here you'll find painted-wooden-pallet furniture, hammocks, twinkle lights, and a mellow vibe. Likely options here include hot dogs, Mexican tacos, açaí smoothies, burgers, veggie wraps, Thai ice cream, and—of course—more chimney cakes. Another pod of food trucks—called **Truckarnia**—is at Dajwór 21, across the street from the Galicia Jewish Museum. Trucks here include updated Polish dishes, burgers, tacos, and paella. Note that any and all of these could reshuffle their carts—or be gone entirely, replaced by a ritzy new building—at any moment. But it's clear that, in general, Kazimierz's food-truck scene is here to stay.

Polish Fast Food on Plac Nowy: The centerpiece of the plac Nowy market is a circular brick slaughterhouse, which has recently been taken over by Kazimierz foodies. Each of the shop windows—which once housed butchers and basic Polish grub—is now operated by a different pop-up eatery, from burgers to kebabs to Belgian fries. But the real specialty here is the Poles' beloved *zapiekanek*—a toasted baguette with cheese, ketchup, and a bewildering array of other toppings. You can take a spin around the building to survey your options—noting where the lines are longest (locals know which *zapiekanek* is best). For dessert, line up at Good Lood, top-quality ice cream that's made fresh each morning and available until it's sold out (this is an outpost of the main branch a few blocks away on plac Wolnica—see next).

Foodie Favorites on Plac Wolnica: The big main square of Kazimierz (a couple of blocks south of plac Nowy) has a few locally beloved eateries. **$ Nova Krova** ("New Cow") sells entirely vegan and organic "burgers" and other sandwiches in a hip, woody atmosphere (Mon-Sat 12:00-21:00, Sun from 10:00, at #12). And just kitty-corner, on hot days you'll see a long line at **Good Lood** (a pun on lody—ice cream), with scoops of fresh and flavorful homemade ice cream (daily 11:00-22:00 or until the flavors run out—since it's made fresh daily, at #11). **Pod Ursa Maior**—highly respected by local beer lovers—is a microbrew pub serving the six types of beer they brew in the mountains southeast of Kraków. Each beer comes with a complex backstory, and some of the profits go to wildlife causes—like nursing injured bears and wolves back to health (long hours daily, at #10).

Creative Bagels: $$ Bagelmama, run by an American named Nava (who has worked as a private chef for tennis star John McEnroe), is a casual bagel shop that's popular with expats and locals. The bagels come dressed with a wide variety of spreads, and they also sell sandwiches, soups, salads, desserts, and fresh juices. You can eat in or get it to go (daily 9:00-17:00, ulica Dajwór 10, tel. 12-346-1646).

Hummus Bar: Hole-in-the-wall **$ Hummus Amamamusi** is a bar selling creamy, top-quality homemade hummus with various toppings, bread, and veggies. They also make homemade soft drinks and great coffee (Mon-Fri 9:00-20:00, Sat-Sun from 10:00, Meiselsa 4, tel. 533-306-288).

Beer: Beer lovers find two different experiences along Św. Wawrzyńca. **$$ Stara Zajezdnia** ("Old Tram Depot") fills exactly that—a cavernous old industrial hall—with tables and happy drinkers, draining huge mugs of the five different types of beer brewed on the premises. (You can also order a sampler.) In good weather, the vast courtyard out front becomes an idyllic, self-service beer garden filled with relaxing lounge chairs (Św. Wawrzyńca 12, mobile 664-323-988). For craft beer aficionados, **Craftownia** has 18 Polish microbrews on tap (and many more by the bottle) in a nondescript setting (Mon-Thu 14:00-late, Fri-Sun from 12:00, Św. Wawrzyńca 22, mobile 515-010-565). And to complete your beer crawl, don't miss **Pod Ursa Maior,** nearby on plac Wolnica and described earlier.

Ice Cream: Lody Tradycyjna Receptura has, true to its name, some of the best "ice cream from a traditional recipe" in Kraków—if not in Poland. The straightforward, seasonal flavors—just a few varieties—are made fresh each morning and sold until they run out. Locals line up here—and if you have a sweet tooth, you should, too (daily 9:00-19:00, Starowiślna 83). **Good Lood,** a newer version offering essentially the same concept, has an equally loyal following at its two locations—one on plac Wolnica, and the other in the plac Nowy market hall (both described earlier).

Dining in Kazimierz

For a good-quality sit-down meal, consider these options.

$$$$ Bottiglieria 1881 is a chic, sophisticated wine bar tucked unassumingly just off plac Wolnica. The cellar is stocked with wines from all over the world (with an emphasis on Italian), all complemented by the short, seasonal, thoughtfully designed menu with modern Polish and international dishes. Come for a glass or for a full meal (Tue-Sat 12:00-23:00, closed Sun-Mon, Bochenska 5, mobile 660-661-756).

$$$ Hamsa, with a prime location at the top of ulica Szeroka, offers "hummus and happiness," with an updated take on Israeli food (that's Middle Eastern, not traditional Jewish fare). Don't come here for matzo balls and klezmer music, but for an enticing menu of *mezes* (small plates, like hummus and various dips) and grilled meat dishes in a modern, hip atmosphere (daily 9:00-24:00, ulica Szeorka 2, mobile 515-150-145).

Kazimierz Bars and Cafés with Food

Some of my favorite atmospheric Kazimierz bars also serve food. It's not high cuisine—the food is an afterthought to the busy bar.

$$ Alchemia od Kuchni is an inviting little subway-tiled street-food restaurant—a sleek space around the corner from the ramshackle main branch. You can order at the counter for a bite to go, or opt for table service (daily 8:00-23:00, Estery 5).

$$ Kolanko No. 6 is a great spot for classic Kazimierz atmosphere. The bar up front is filled with old secondhand furniture. Walking toward the back, you discover an inviting garden with tables and, beyond that, a hall where they host events. They serve light meals, specializing in crêpes, toasted sandwiches, salads, and international dishes (daily 10:00-24:00, Józefa 17, tel. 12-292-0320).

$$ Warsztat ("Workshop") is littered with musical instruments: The bar is a piano, and the tight interior is crammed with other instruments and rakishly crooked lampshades. The menu is an odd hybrid of Italian, Middle Eastern, and Polish cuisine, and the portions are big (salads, pizzas, pastas, and meats; daily 9:00-24:00, Izaaka 3, tel. 12-430-1451). They also have two other locations: a small one (focusing on Polish dishes) by the front door of the Tempel Synagogue, and a bigger one on Bożego Ciała street.

Kraków Connections

For getting between Kraków and **Auschwitz,** see page 159 in the next chapter. To confirm rail journeys, check specific times online (www.rozklad-pkp.pl) or at the main train station. You can also buy tickets on this website; you'll be sent a PDF, which you can show the conductor onboard the train.

From Kraków by Train to: Warsaw (hourly, about 2.5 hours, slick EIC express train, requires seat reservation), **Gdańsk** (6/day direct, 5.5 hours on EIC express, plus night train, 8.5 hours), **Toruń** (7/day, 5.5 hours, most transfer at Warsaw's Zachodnia station), **Prague** (1/day direct, 7.5 hours, plus 1 night train, 10 hours; additional connections may be possible with change in Katowice and other points), **Berlin** (2-3/day, 9-10 hours with change at Warsaw's Zachodnia station, more options with multiple changes; plus 1 direct and handy Deutsche Bahn IC bus, 7.5 hours, www.bahn.com), **Budapest** (1/day, 9 hours, change in Katowice, longer connections with more changes; night train connection requires change in Vienna, 1/night, 11.5 hours; also consider long-distance bus—7 hours, www.flixbus.com), **Vienna** (2/day, 8-9 hours, 1-2 changes;

plus direct night train, 8.5 hours). In addition to traditional trains (run by the Polish Railways or the main rail operators in neighboring countries), the private Czech rail company Leo Express may be running some trains between Kraków and the Czech Republic (see www.leoexpress.com).

By Bus: For certain long-distance trips, you can save time and money by taking a bus instead of a train. The dominant company is Flixbus (www.flixbus.pl), but others have come and gone in recent years.

AUSCHWITZ-BIRKENAU

The unassuming regional capital of Oświęcim (ohsh-VEENCH-im) was the site of one of humanity's greatest crimes: the systematic murder of at least 1.1 million innocent people. From 1941 until 1945, Oświęcim was the home of Auschwitz, the biggest, most notorious concentration camp in the Nazi system. Today, Auschwitz is the most poignant memorial anywhere to the victims of the Holocaust.

"Auschwitz" (OWSH-vits) actually refers to a series of several camps in Poland—most importantly Auschwitz I, in the village of Oświęcim (50 miles west of Kraków), and Auschwitz II, a.k.a. Birkenau (about 1.5 miles west of Oświęcim). Auschwitz visitors generally start with Auschwitz I, then ride a shuttle bus to Birkenau. **Auschwitz I,** where public transportation from Kraków arrives, has the main museum building, the *Arbeit Macht Frei* gate, and indoor museum exhibits in former prison buildings. **Birkenau** (BEER-keh-now), on a much bigger scale and mostly outdoors, has the infamous guard tower, a vast field with ruins of barracks, a few tourable rough barracks, the notorious "dividing platform," a giant monument flanked by remains of destroyed crematoria, and a prisoner processing facility called "the Sauna."

A visit here is obligatory for Polish 14-year-olds; students usually come again during their last year of school. And it's an important pilgrimage for school groups from other countries. Many visitors leave flowers and messages; one message—from a German visitor—reads, "Nations who forget their own history are sentenced to live it again."

GETTING THERE

To reach Auschwitz from Kraków, it's easiest to join a package tour or hire a private guide or driver (75-minute drive each way). But the trip is also doable by public transportation (1.75-2.5 hours). For details, see "Auschwitz Connections," at the end of this chapter.

Orientation to Auschwitz

Cost: Free to enter grounds during nonpeak times (donations accepted); 50 zł to join a tour at Auschwitz I—required April-Oct 10:00-16:00 and off-season 10:00-13:00. (Alternatively, you could join a "study tour," or hire your own guide—see the "Guided Tours at Auschwitz" sidebar.) At other times, you're allowed to visit Auschwitz I on your own—though the tour is still well worth considering. Any time of year, Birkenau grounds can be toured without a guide, though you'll likely need a guide to climb the guard tower.

Hours: The museum opens daily at 7:30. Closing times change with the season: June-Aug at 19:00, April-May and Sept at 18:00, March and Oct at 17:00, Feb at 16:00, Jan and Nov at 15:00, and Dec at 14:00. These are "last entry" times; the grounds at Auschwitz I stay open 1.5 hours later (though many buildings—including the national memorials—close promptly at these times). The grounds at Birkenau, where many groups end their visits, may stay open even later.

Information: Tel. 33-844-8100, www.auschwitz.org.

Mandatory Reservations: With more than 2 million visitors each year, Auschwitz struggles with crowds. Reservations are free

Why Visit Auschwitz?

Why visit a notorious concentration camp on your vacation?

Auschwitz-Birkenau is one of the most moving sights in Europe, and certainly the most important of all the Holocaust memorials. Seeing the camp can be difficult: Many visitors are overwhelmed by sadness and anger, as well as inspiration at the remarkable stories of survival. Auschwitz survivors and victims' families want tourists to come here and experience the scale and the monstrosity of the place. In their minds, a steady flow of visitors will ensure that the Holocaust is always remembered—so nothing like it will ever happen again.

Auschwitz isn't for everyone. But I've never met anyone who toured Auschwitz and regretted it. For many, it's a profoundly life-altering experience—at the very least, it will forever affect the way you think about the Holocaust.

and required—whether visiting on your own or with a tour. Book as soon as your dates are set—ideally weeks or even months in advance—at http://visit.auschwitz.org.

Entrance slots for individuals typically become available three months before the date of visit, at noon Poland time (and can fill quickly, especially for May and June, when school groups flood the site). Online reservations are no longer available five days before the visit. These details can change—confirm on the website.

If an English tour isn't available for your preferred date, consider booking one in a foreign language (once inside, you can split off and use this chapter's self-guided tour).

After you've booked your reservation online, print out or save your **eticket barcode** to your phone or tablet. To get in, you'll need both the bar code and ID for each person in your group.

Without Reservations: If you arrive without an advance ticket, there are a couple of last-minute options: You can book a **day tour** through a private company in Kraków, which includes both transportation and a tour of the camp (see the "Guided Tours at Auschwitz" sidebar). Or take your chances and **just show up**—a few tickets are reserved for same-day visitors. A white booth in front of the main building (facing the parking lot, opens at 7:30) lists available spaces on upcoming tours (typically, the later you arrive, the longer the wait). You can pass any wait time by first going to Birkenau, which has less strict timing requirements.

Getting from Auschwitz I to Birkenau: Buses shuttle visitors two miles between the camps (free, every 10 minutes; Nov-March 2/hour, schedule posted at bus stops outside the main building of each site, timed to correspond with tours). Taxis are also standing by (about 15 zł). Or you can walk the 30 minutes between the camps, which gives you a chance for reflection. Along the way, you'll pass the Judenrampe, an old train car like the ones used to transport prisoners.

Services: Auschwitz I's main building has a helpful information desk, bookshops, exchange offices, baggage storage (large bags must be checked), and WCs. You'll also find the theater and posted maps of the camp. The guard tower at Birkenau has another bookshop and more WCs.

Film: The 17-minute movie (too graphic for children) was shot by Ukrainian troops days after the Red Army liberated the camp (included in tours, otherwise 4 zł, ask for the schedule for showings in English when you arrive).

Eating: A café and decent cafeteria are at the main Auschwitz building. More options are in the commercial complex across the street.

Expect Changes: The Auschwitz museum is continually maintained and updated. Some things may be different than described here, but everything is well-signposted.

Etiquette: The camp encourages visitors to remember that Auschwitz is the place where more than a million people lost their lives. Behave and dress here as you would at a cemetery.

Auschwitz Tour

AUSCHWITZ I

• *From the entrance building, step out and look over the grassy field to get oriented.*

Before World War II, this camp was a base for the Polish army. When Hitler occupied Poland, he took over these barracks and turned it into a concentration camp for his Polish political enemies. The location was ideal, with a nearby rail junction and rivers providing natural protective boundaries. An average of

(sidebar, vertical text) AUSCHWITZ-BIRKENAU

Guided Tours at Auschwitz

Visiting Auschwitz on your own works well, given the abundance of English descriptions (and this chapter's self-guided tour). However, due to crowds, to enter Auschwitz I during peak times (April-October 10:00-16:00; off-season 10:00-13:00), you must either join one of the museum's organized tours or reserve a private guide. Even during these busy times, you can enter Birkenau without a guide.

Organized Museum Tours: The Auschwitz Museum's excellent guides are serious and frank historians, who feel a strong sense of responsibility about sharing the story of the camp. The regularly scheduled 3.5-hour English tour covers Auschwitz, Birkenau, and the film (50 zł; 90 zł for 6-hour "study tour"). These tours must be prebooked at http://visit.auschwitz.org. Arrive for your scheduled tour 30 minutes early.

Private Official Museum Guides: If you have a special interest or a small group, it's affordable and worthwhile to hire one of the museum's guides for a private tour. Choose between the basic 3.5-hour tour (430 zł) or a longer "study tour" (610 zł/6 hours, 700 zł/8 hours—possible all in one day, or spread over two days; rates are higher for more than 10 people). Because English-speaking guides are limited, reserve as far ahead as possible (ideally up to 6 months) at http://visit.auschwitz.org.

Day Tours from Kraków: Various Kraków-based companies sell round-trip tours from Kraków to Auschwitz, which include a guided tour of the camp (typically around 160-180 zł). I can't vouch for their quality, but the main outfits are **See Kraków** (www.seekrakow.com), **Discover Cracow** (www.discovercracow.com), and **Cracow City Tours** (www.cracowcitytours.com)—for details, see page 40.

Local Guides and Drivers from Kraków: For easy transportation to the camp and help with booking an organized English tour, hire a Kraków-based guide or driver. These aren't officially registered museum guides, so aren't allowed to show you around the site, but it can be worth the splurge to have someone else deal with the logistics. They can usually make a reservation for you—but the reservation still needs to be booked well ahead of time. I've listed my favorite guides and drivers on page 37.

AUSCHWITZ-BIRKENAU

14,000 prisoners were kept at this camp at one time. (Birkenau could hold up to 100,000.) In 1942, Auschwitz became a death camp for the extermination of European Jews and others whom Hitler considered "undesirable." By the time the camp was liberated in 1945, at least 1.1 million people had been murdered here—approximately 960,000 of them Jewish.

• *Go closer to the camp entrance, approaching the notorious...*

"Arbeit Macht Frei" Gate

Although this gate imparts the message "Work Sets You Free," it's cruelly ironic. The only way out of the camp for the prisoners was through the crematorium chimneys. Note that the "B" was welded on upside down by belligerent inmates, who were forced to make this sign (and much of the camp). This is actually a replica; the original was stolen one night in December 2009, then recovered two days later, cut up into several pieces. The original is now safely in the museum's possession, but no longer displayed.

Just inside the gate and to the right, the camp orchestra (made up of prisoners) used to play marches; having the prisoners march made them easier to count.

• *From the gate, proceed straight up the "main street" of the camp.*

You'll pass two rows of barracks. The first one holds a variety of national memorials. We'll circle back here later, if you'd like to enter some of them. The second row of barracks holds the main museum exhibitions. Blocks 4 and 5 focus on how Auschwitz prisoners were killed. Blocks 6, 7, and 11 explore the conditions for prisoners who survived here a little longer than most. In each block, arrows guide you on a one-way route through the numbered rooms; in many cases, exhibits are both downstairs and upstairs—don't miss these.

• *Start with...*

Block 4: Extermination

In Room 1, a map identifies the countries from which Auschwitz prisoners were brought—as far away as Norwegian fjords and Greek isles. In an alcove along the side of the room is an urn filled with ashes, a symbolic memorial to all the camp's victims.

Room 2 shows photographs of Jewish ghettos from all over Europe being "liquidated"— that is, its residents assembled and deported to various concentration camps. Thanks to its massive occupancy, Auschwitz was a destination for many.

Room 3 displays rare photos of scenes inside the camp. To prevent a riot, the Nazis claimed at first that this was only a transition camp for resettlement in Eastern Europe. At the far end of Room 3, a helpful orientation map for visitors shows the town of Oświęcim, Auschwitz I, Auschwitz II (Birkenau), and other parts of the camp network.

Upstairs in Room 4 is a model of a Birkenau crematorium. People entered on the left, then undressed in the underground

Auschwitz I

To Oświęcim Town →
← LEGIONÓW
To Bielsko-Biała →

WALL

MUSEUM EXHIBITS

NATIONAL MEMORIALS

ARBEIT MACHT FREI GATE

TOUR BEGINS

TOUR ENDS

ENTRY BUILDING

ENTRANCE

100 Meters
100 Yards

To Bus Stop at Edge of Camp

To Bielsko-Biała

Shuttle Bus to Birkenau

To Oświęcim Train Station & Auschwitz II - Birkenau

AUSCHWITZ-BIRKENAU

- **A** Arbeit Macht Frei Gate
- **B** Block 4: Extermination
- **C** Block 5: Material Evidence
- **D** Block 6: Everyday Life
- **E** Block 7: Camp Conditions
- **F** Execution Courtyard
- **G** Block 11: "Death Block"
- **H** Block 27: Jewish Memorial
- **I** Block 21: Netherlands
- **J** Block 20: Belgium & France
- **K** Block 18: Hungary
- **L** Block 17: Austria & Former Yugoslavia
- **M** Block 16: Czechia & Slovakia
- **N** Block 15: Poland
- **O** Block 14: Russia
- **P** Block 13: Roma (Gypsy)
- **Q** Crematorium
- **R** Gallows
- **S** Camp Commander's Home
- **T** Theater (Graphic Film)

rooms (hanging their belongings on numbered hooks and encouraged to remember their numbers to retrieve their clothes later). They then moved into the "showers" and were killed by Zyklon-B gas (hydrogen cyanide), a German-produced cleaning agent that is lethal in high doses. This efficient factory of murder took about 20 minutes to kill 8,000 people in four gas chambers. Elevators brought the bodies up to the crematorium. Members of

AUSCHWITZ-BIRKENAU

Chilling Statistics: The Holocaust in Poland

The majority of people murdered by the Nazis during the Holocaust were killed right here in Poland. For centuries, Poland was known for its relative tolerance of Jews, and right up until the beginning of World War II, Poland had Europe's largest concentration of Jews: 3,500,000. Throughout the Holocaust, the Nazis murdered 4,500,000 Jews in Poland (many of them brought in from other countries) at camps, including Auschwitz, and in ghettos such as Warsaw's.

By the end of the war, only 300,000 Polish Jews had survived—less than 10 percent of the original population. Many of these survivors were granted "one-way passports" (read: deported) to Israel, Western Europe, and the US by the communist government in 1968 (following a big student demonstration with a strong Jewish presence). Today, only about 10,000 Jews live in all of Poland.

the *Sonderkommand*—Jewish inmates who were kept isolated and forced by the Nazis to work here—removed the corpses' gold teeth and shaved off their hair (to be sold) before putting the bodies in the ovens. It wasn't unusual for a *Sonderkommand* worker to discover a wife, child, or parent among the dead. A few of these workers committed suicide by throwing themselves at electric fences; those who didn't were systematically executed by the Nazis after a two-month shift. Across from the model of the crematorium are canisters of Zyklon-B.

Across the hall in the dimly lit Room 5 is one of the camp's most powerful exhibits: a wall of actual victims' hair—4,400 pounds of it. Also displayed is cloth made of the hair, used to make Nazi uniforms. The Nazis were nothing if not efficient...nothing, not even human body parts, could be wasted.

Back downstairs in Room 6 is an exhibit on the plunder of victims' personal belongings. People being transported here were encouraged to bring luggage—and some victims had even paid in advance for houses in their new homeland. After they were killed, everything of value was sorted and stored in warehouses that prisoners named "Canada" (after a country they associated with great wealth). Although the Canada warehouses were destroyed, you can see a few of these items in the next building.

• *Head next door.*

Block 5: Material Evidence of the Nazis' Crimes

The exhibits in this block consist mostly of piles of the victims' goods, a tiny fraction of everything the Nazis stole. As you wander through the rooms, you'll see eyeglasses; fine Jewish prayer shawls; crutches and prosthetic limbs (the first people the Nazis exterminated were mentally and physically ill German citizens); and a pile of pots and pans. Then, upstairs, you'll witness a seemingly endless mountain of shoes; children's clothing; and suitcases with names of victims—many marked *Kind,* or "child." Visitors often wonder if the suitcase with the name "Frank" belonged to Anne, one of the Holocaust's most famous victims. After being discovered in Amsterdam by the Nazis, the Frank family was transported here to Auschwitz, where they were split up. Still, it's unlikely this suitcase was theirs. Anne Frank and her sister Margot were sent to the Bergen-Belsen camp in northern Germany, where they died of typhus shortly before the war ended. Their father, Otto Frank, survived Auschwitz and was found barely alive by the Russians, who liberated the camp in January 1945.

• *Proceed to the next block.*

Block 6: Everyday Life

Although the purpose of Auschwitz was to murder its inmates, not all were killed immediately. After an initial evaluation, some prisoners were registered and forced to work. (This did not mean they were chosen to live—just to die later.) This block shows various aspects of daily existence at the camp.

The halls are lined with photographs of victims, each identified with a name, birthdate, occupation, date of arrival at Auschwitz, date of death, and camp registration number. The dates reveal that these people survived here an average of two to three months. (Flowers are poignant reminders that these victims

are survived by loved ones.) Similar photographs hang in several other museum buildings, as well; as with the plundered items in the last block, keep in mind that these represent only a tiny fraction of the masses of people murdered at Auschwitz.

Room 1 (on the left as you enter the front door) displays drawings of the arrival process. After the initial selection, those chosen to work were showered, shaved, and photographed. After a while, photographing each prisoner got to be too expensive, so prisoners were tattooed instead (see photographs): on the chest, on the arm, or—for children—on the leg. A display shows the symbols that prisoners had to wear to show their reason for internment—Jew,

AUSCHWITZ-BIRKENAU

St. Maksymilian Kolbe (1894-1941)

Among the many inspirational stories of Auschwitz is that of a Polish priest named Maksymilian Kolbe. Before the war, Kolbe traveled as a missionary to Japan, then worked in Poland for a Catholic newspaper. While he was highly regarded for his devotion to the Church, some of his writings had an unsettling anti-Semitic sentiment. But during the Nazi occupation, Kolbe briefly ran an institution that cared for refugees—including Jews.

In 1941, Kolbe was arrested and interned at Auschwitz. When a prisoner from Kolbe's block escaped in July of that year, the Nazis punished the remaining inmates by selecting 10 of them to be put in the Starvation Cell until they died—based on the Nazi "doctrine of collective responsibility." After the selection had been made, Kolbe offered to replace a man who expressed concern about who would care for his family. The Nazis agreed. (The man Kolbe saved is said to have survived the Holocaust.)

All 10 of the men—including Kolbe—were put into Starvation Cell 18. Two weeks later, when the door was opened, only Kolbe had survived. The story spread throughout the camp, and Kolbe became an inspiration to the inmates. To squelch the hope he had given the others, Kolbe was executed by lethal injection.

In 1982, Kolbe was canonized by the Catholic Church. Some critics—mindful of his earlier anti-Semitic rhetoric—still consider Kolbe's sainthood controversial. But most Poles feel he redeemed himself for his earlier missteps through this noble act at the end of his life.

Roma (Gypsy), homosexual, political prisoner, and so on. At the end of the room, a display case holds actual camp uniforms.

Across the hall, Room 4 shows the starvation that took place here. The 7,500 survivors that the Red Army found when the camp was liberated were essentially living skeletons (the "healthier" inmates had been forced to march to Germany). Of those liberated, one-fifth died soon after of disease and starvation.

In Room 5, you can see scenes from the prisoner's workday (sketched by survivors after liberation). Prisoners worked as long as the sun shone—8 hours in winter, up to 12 hours in summer—mostly on farms or in factories.

Room 6 is about Auschwitz's child inmates, 20 percent of the camp's victims. Blond, blue-eyed children were either "Germanized" in special schools or, if younger, adopted by German families. Dr. Josef Mengele conducted gruesome experiments here on children, especially twins and triplets, ostensibly to find ways to increase fertility for German mothers. Also in this room, look for a display of the prisoners' daily ration (in the glass case): a pan of tea or coffee in the morning; thin vegetable soup in the afternoon; and a piece of bread (often made with sawdust or chestnuts) for dinner. This makes it clear that Auschwitz was never intended to be a "work camp," where people were kept alive, healthy, and efficient to do work. Rather, people were meant to die here—if not in the gas chambers, then through malnutrition and overwork.

• *Block 7 shows living and sanitary conditions at the camp, which you'll see in more detail later at Birkenau. Blocks 8-10 are vacant (medical experiments were carried out in Block 10). And Block 11 was the most notorious of all.*

Block 11: The Death Block

Step into the walled-in **courtyard** between Blocks 10 and 11. The wall at the far end is where the Nazis shot several thousand po-

litical prisoners, leaders of camp resistance, and religious leaders. Notice that the windows are covered, so that nobody could witness the executions. Also take a close look at the memorial—the back of it is made of a material designed by Nazis to catch the bullets without a ricochet. Inmates were shot at short range—about three feet. The pebbles represent prayers from Jewish visitors.

Now head into the **"Death Block"** (#11), from which nobody ever left alive. Death here required a "trial"—but it was never a fair trial. Room 2 (on the left as you enter) is where these sham trials were held, lasting about two minutes each. In Room 5, you can see how prisoners lived in these barracks—three-level bunks, with three prisoners sleeping in each bed (they had to sleep on their sides so they could fit). In Room 6, people undressed before they were executed.

In the **basement,** you'll see several types of cells. The Starvation Cell (#18) held prisoners selected to starve to death when a fellow prisoner escaped; Maksymilian Kolbe spent two weeks here to save another man's life (see sidebar on Kolbe). In the Dark Cell (#20), which held up to 30, people had only a small window for ventilation—and if it became covered with snow, the prisoners suffocated. In the Standing Cells (#22), four people would be forced to stand together for hours at a time (the bricks went all the way to the ceiling then).

Upstairs, you'll find gallows and a bench used for administering lashes. Filling this floor are exhibits on various forms of punishment, mostly focusing on resistance within the camp, escapees, and local Poles who were executed—either for trying to assist the prisoners, or for fighting with Nazi officers.

• *Leaving Block 11, proceed straight ahead, between the buildings, to the other row of barracks. Several of these blocks house...*

National Memorials

These exhibits were created not by museum authorities, but by representatives of the home countries of the camps' victims. As these memorials overlap with the general exhibits, and are designed for Europeans to learn more about the victims from their own home countries, most visitors skip this part of the site. On the other hand, while the main museum exhibits await renovation and modernization, the displays in these national memorials tend to be slicker and better-presented than the ones we just saw. (Some of these may be works in progress, as old exhibits are routinely upgraded.) As you walk along this street toward our next stop (the crematorium), consider stepping into the ones that interest you.

The first one you see is the memorial to **Jewish** victims (Block 27). It's compelling and thoughtfully presented, relying heavily on video clips, evocative music, and sound effects.

Most of the other national memorials are on the right side of the street. Across from the Jewish memorial, Block 21 honors **Dutch Jews;** including perhaps the most famous Dutch victim of the concentration camp, Anne Frank.

Block 20, a former hospital block, is shared by **Belgium** and **France.** A room near the entrance explains how some prisoners were killed by lethal injection, with portraits and biographical sketches of victims. Upstairs is the powerful Belgium exhibit, with a room featuring victims' portraits. Block 18 holds a very modern, conceptual exhibit about **Hungary**'s victims, with an eerie heartbeat sound pervading the space. Block 17, which is likely a work in progress, is intended to memorialize victims from **Austria** and the **former Yugoslavia.** Across from this block, notice the long gallows used for mass hangings. Block 16 contains a new and well-presented exhibit about **Czech** and **Slovak** victims.

Block 15 honors victims from **Poland,** focusing on the 1939 Nazi invasion of the country, which resulted in the immediate internment of Polish political prisoners. Exhibits explain the process of "Germanization"—such as renaming Polish streets with German names—and (upstairs) the underground resistance that fought to get back some control over Poland.

Block 14 is the **Russian** national memorial. However, this one's a bit controversial: While Russia claims to have lost "Russian" Jews to the Holocaust, virtually all of them were technically Polish

AUSCHWITZ-BIRKENAU

Jews who had been living within Russia. (They spoke Polish, not Russian.) To sidestep the hot topic of how to identify these victims, this memorial focuses not on victims, but on the Russian liberation of the camp.

Block 13 houses the **Roma (Gypsy)** exhibit. You'll learn that the Roma, along with the Jews, were considered no better than "rats, bedbugs, and fleas," and explore elements of the so-called *Zigeunerfrage*—the "Gypsy question" about what to do with this "troublesome" population.

• *At the end of this row of barracks, you reach a guard tower and a barbed-wire fence. Jog a few steps to the right, through the hole in the fence, then angle left toward the earthen mound with the giant, ominous brick chimney. The entrance is at the far end of the building.*

Crematorium

Up to 700 people at a time could be gassed here. People undressed outside, or just inside the door. As you enter, bear right and find your way into the big "shower room." Look for the vents in the ceiling—this is where the SS men dropped the Zyklon-B. In the adjacent room is a replica of the furnace. This facility could burn 340 bodies a day—so it took two days to burn all of the bodies from one round of executions. (The Nazis didn't like this inefficiency, so they built four more huge crematoria at Birkenau.)

• *Turning left as you exit the crematorium takes you back to the entrance building. But first, circle around to the opposite side of the crematorium for the closest thing this story has to a happy ending.*

Shortly after the war, camp commander Rudolf Höss was tried, convicted, and sentenced to death. Survivors requested that he be executed at Auschwitz, and in 1947, he was hanged here. The **gallows** are preserved behind the crematorium (about a hundred yards from his home where his wife—who is said to have loved her years here—raised their children in a villa maintained by slaves and furnished with possessions of the dead).

• *Take your time with Auschwitz I. When you're ready, continue to the second stage of the camp—Birkenau.*

AUSCHWITZ II—BIRKENAU

In 1941, realizing that the original Auschwitz camp was too small to meet their needs, the Nazis began a second camp in some nearby farm fields. The original plan was for a camp that could hold 200,000 people, but at its

AUSCHWITZ-BIRKENAU

Auschwitz II – Birkenau

TOUR ENDS

MONUMENT

Creek

CREMATORIA

FORMER RAIL LINE

FORMER

BARRACKS

GUARD TOWER

200 Meters
200 Yards

MIECZESNIWA MARDOW

To Auschwitz I
& Oświęcim Town

CREMATORIA

TOUR BEGINS

☐ Foundations
▬ Existing Buildings

❶ Guard Tower, Viewpoint, WC & Bookstore
❷ Latrine & Restored Barracks
❸ Dividing Platform
❹ Brick Barracks
❺ Crematoria Ruins (4)

❻ Monument
❼ "The Sauna"
❽ "Canada" Foundations
❾ Shuttle Bus to Auschwitz I

peak, Birkenau (Brzezinka) held only about 100,000. They were still adding onto it when the camp was liberated in 1945.

• *Train tracks lead past the main building and into the camp. The first sight that greeted prisoners was the...*

Guard Tower

If you've seen *Schindler's List*, the sight of this icon of the Holo-caust—shown in stirring scenes from the movie—may make you queasy.

Climb to the top of the entry building (also houses WCs and bookstore) for an overview of the massive camp. As you look over the camp, you'll see a vast field of chimneys and a few intact wooden and brick barracks. Some of the barracks were destroyed by Germans. Most were dismantled to be used for fuel and build-ing materials shortly after the war. But the first row has been reconstructed (using components from the original structures). The train tracks lead straight back to the dividing platform, and then dead-end at the ruins of the crematorium and camp monument at the far side.

• *Descend the tower, enter the camp, turn right, and walk through the barbed-wire fence to reach the...*

Wooden Barracks

The first of these barrack buildings was the **latrine:** The front half of the building contained washrooms, and the back was a row of toilets. There was no running water, and prisoners were in charge of keeping the latrine clean. Because of the resulting unsanitary conditions and risk of disease, the Nazis were afraid to come in here—so the latrine became the heart of the black market and the inmates' resistance movement.

The third barrack was a **bunkhouse.** Each inmate had a personal number, a barrack number, and a bed number. Inside, you can see the beds (angled so that more could fit). An average of 400 prisoners—but up to 1,000—would be housed in each of these buildings. These wooden structures, designed as stables by a German com-

pany (look for the horse-tying rings on the wall), came in prefab pieces that made them cheap and convenient. Two chimneys connected by a brick duct provided a little heat. The bricks were smoothed by inmates who sat here to catch a bit of warmth.

• *Return to the train tracks, and follow them toward the monument about a half-mile away, at the back end of Birkenau. At the intersection of these tracks and the perpendicular gravel road (halfway to the monument)—now marked by a lonely train car—was the gravel pitch known as the...*

Dividing Platform

A Nazi doctor would stand facing the guard tower and evaluate each prisoner. If he pointed to the right, the prisoner was sentenced to death, and trudged—unknowingly—to the gas chamber. If he pointed to the left, the person would be registered and live a little longer. It was here that families from all over Europe were torn apart forever.

• *Photographs near the wooden building—on the left-hand side as you face the back of the camp complex—show the sad scene. Just beyond that building is a field with some...*

Brick Barracks

Enter one of these buildings. The supervisors lived in the two smaller rooms near the door. Farther in, most barracks still have the wooden bunks that held about 700 people per building. Four or five people slept on each bunk, including the floor—reserved for new arrivals. There were chamber pots at either end of the building. After a Nazi doctor died of typhus, sanitation improved, and these barracks got running water.

Now head back to the train tracks. As you walk along the camp's only road, which leads along the tracks to the crematorium, imagine the horror of this place—no grass, only mud, and all the barracks packed with people, with smoke blowing in from the busy crematoria. This was an even worse place to die than Auschwitz I.

• *The train tracks lead to the camp memorial and crematorium. At the end of the tracks, go 50 yards to the left and climb the three concrete steps to view the ruin of the...*

Crematorium

This is one of four crematoria here at Birkenau, each with a capacity to cremate more than 4,400 people per day. At the far-right end of the ruins, see the stairs where people entered the rooms to undress. They were given numbered lockers, conning them into thinking they were coming back. (The Nazis didn't want a panic.) Then they piled into the "shower room"—the underground passage branching away from the memorial—and were killed. Their bodies were burned in the crematorium (on the left), giving off a scent of sweet almonds (from the Zyklon-B). Beyond the remains of the crematorium is a hole—once a gray lake where tons of ashes were dumped. This efficient factory of death was destroyed by the Nazis as the Red Army approached, leaving the haunting ruins you see today.

When the Soviets arrived on January 27, 1945, the nightmare of Auschwitz-Birkenau was over. The Polish parliament voted to turn these grounds into a museum, so that the world would understand, and never forget, the horror of what happened here.

• *At the back of the camp stands the...*

Monument

Built in 1967 by the communist government in its heavy "Socialist Realist" style, this monument represents gravestones and the chimney of a crematorium. The plaques, written in each of the languages spoken by camp victims (including English, far right), explain that the memorial is "a cry of despair and a warning to humanity."

• *With more time, you could continue deeper into...*

The Rest of the Camp

There's much more to see for those who are interested—Birkenau sprawls for a frightening distance. One worthwhile extension is the reception and disinfection building that prisoners called **"the Sauna"** (the long building with four tall chimneys). It was here that prisoners would be forced to strip and be deloused; their belongings were seized and taken to the "Canada" warehouses

(described earlier) to be sorted. Walking through here (on glass floors designed to protect the original structure below), you'll see artifacts of the grim efficiency with which prisoners were "processed"—their heads were shaved, they were tattooed with a serial number, and they were assigned uniforms and wooden clogs to wear. Portraits at the end of the building humanize those who passed through here. Look for the cart, which was used to dispose of ashes.

In front of the Sauna is a field of foundations of the **"Canada" warehouses.** Nearby are the other two destroyed **crematoria.**

Auschwitz Connections

The Auschwitz Museum is in the town of Oświęcim, about 50 miles west of Kraków. By bus or minibus, the journey takes 1.75 hours each way (longer by train); driving shaves off about 10-20 minutes.

FROM KRAKÓW TO AUSCHWITZ

The easiest way to reach Auschwitz is with a **package tour** (about 160-180 zł/person) or **private guide or driver** (around 400 zł/carload); both of these options are described on page 37. While the package tours are more convenient than going on your own, three people can hire their own driver for less and have a more intimate experience.

If you're using public transportation, here are your choices (each one of these costs around 10-15 zł):

The most comfortable public-transit option is to take one of the frequent **buses,** mostly run by PKS Oświęcim (at least hourly, 1.75 hours, get schedule at any Kraków TI, buses depart from Kraków's main bus station behind the train station). Buy a one-way ticket from the bus-station ticket office or from the driver to leave your options open for getting home. Look for buses to "Oświęcim" (not necessarily "Auschwitz"). Note that these buses can be full, and there's no way to reserve a seat—line up early (generally about 15 minutes ahead). If you don't get on a bus, you'll have to wait for the next one (or, if there's a minibus leaving sooner, you can take one of those instead—described next). Once in the town of Oświęcim, buses from Kraków stop first at the train station, then continue on to one of two stops near the museum: About half of the buses go directly into the parking lot at the museum itself (this stop may be called *Auschwitz Museum/ul. Leszczyńskiej*), while the rest use a low-profile bus stop on the edge of the Auschwitz camp grounds (you'll see a small *Muzeum Auschwitz* sign on the right just before the stop, and a blue *Oświęcim Muzeum PKS* sign at the stop itself). From this bus stop, follow the sign down the road and into the parking lot; the main museum building is across the lot on your left. Note that since some buses don't actually go into the museum's parking lot, the Auschwitz stop can be easy to miss—don't be shy about letting your driver know where you want to go: *"Muzeum?"*

Several **minibuses** from Kraków head for Auschwitz (sporadic departures—generally 1-2/hour, 1.75 hours). Like the larger buses, some go directly to the museum, while others use the bus stop at the edge of camp. These generally depart from the lower platform of the main bus station (but confirm the departure point at the TI). While intended for local commuters, these can be crammed with tourists, but they work fine in a pinch.

You could ride the **train** to Oświęcim, but it's less convenient than the bus because it leaves you at the train station, farther from the museum (nearly hourly, fewer Sat-Sun, 2-2.5 hours). If you do wind up at the Oświęcim train station, it's about a 20-minute walk to the camp (turn right out of station, go straight, then turn left at roundabout, camp is several blocks ahead on left). Or you can take a taxi (around 15 zł).

RETURNING FROM AUSCHWITZ TO KRAKÓW

Upon arrival at Auschwitz I, plan your departure by visiting the information window at the main building. They can give you a schedule of departures and explain where the bus or minibus leaves from. (If you intend to stay late into the afternoon, make a point of figuring out the last possible bus or train back to Kraków, and plan accordingly.) Remember to allow enough time to make it from Birkenau back to Auschwitz I to catch your bus.

Although most minibuses and a few buses back to Kraków leave from the camp parking lot itself, if you're taking the bus,

On the Way to Auschwitz: The Polish Countryside

You'll spend about an hour gazing out the window as you drive or ride to Auschwitz. This may be your only real look at the Polish countryside. Ponder these thoughts about what you're passing...

The small houses you see are traditionally inhabited by three generations at the same time. Nineteenth-century houses (the few that survive) often sport blue stripes, which in those days announced that a daughter was eligible for marriage. Once they saw these blue lines, local boys were welcome to come a-courtin'.

Big churches mark small villages. Like in the US, tiny roadside memorials and crosses indicate places where fatal accidents have occurred.

Polish farmers traditionally had small lots that were notorious for not being very productive. These farmers somewhat miraculously survived the communist era without having to merge their farms. For years, they were Poland's sacred cows: producing little, paying almost no tax, and draining government resources. But since Poland joined the European Union in 2004, they're being forced to get up to snuff...and, in many cases, collectivize their farms after all.

Since most people don't own cars, bikes are common and public transit is excellent. There are lots of bus stops, as well as minibuses that you can flag down anywhere for a 2-zł ride. The bad roads are a legacy of communist construction, exacerbated by heavy truck use and brutal winters.

Poland has more than 2,000 counties, or districts, each with its own coat of arms; you'll pass several along the way. The forests are state-owned, and locals enjoy the right to pick berries in the summer and mushrooms in the autumn (you may see people—often young kids—selling their day's harvest by the side of the road). The mushrooms are dried and then boiled to make tasty soups in the winter.

you'll most likely catch it from the stop on the edge of the Auschwitz I grounds. To reach this bus stop, leave the Auschwitz I building through the main entry and walk straight along the parking lot, then turn right on the road near the end of the lot. At the T-intersection, cross the street to the little bus stop with the blue *Oświęcim Muzeum PKS* sign. Don't be distracted by the ads for a nearby travel agency—you can buy tickets on board.

There's no public transportation back to Kraków from Birkenau, where most people end their tours; you'll have to take the shuttle bus back to Auschwitz I first.

WARSAW

Warszawa

Warsaw (Warszawa, vah-SHAH-vah in Polish) is Poland's capital and biggest city. It's huge, famous, and important...but not particularly romantic. If you're looking for Old World quaintness, head for Kraków. If you're tickled by spires and domes, get to Prague. But if you want to experience a truly 21st-century city, Warsaw's your place.

A decade ago, the city was dreary and uninviting. But things have changed here dramatically. The Varsovians (as locals are called) are chic and sophisticated. Young professionals dress and dine as well as the Parisians and Milanese, and they've mastered the art of navigating an urban jungle in heels or a man bun. Today's Warsaw has gleaming new office towers, glitzy shopping malls, swarms of international businesspeople, inviting parks and pedestrian zones, hipster culture to rival Brooklyn or Portland, and a gourmet coffee shop or designer pastry store on every corner.

Stroll down revitalized boulevards that evoke the city's glory days, pausing at an outdoor café to sip coffee and nibble at a *pączek* (the classic Polish jelly doughnut). Drop by a leafy park for an al fresco Chopin concert, packed with patriotic Poles. Commune with the soul of Poland at the city's many state-of-the-art museums—take your pick: Poland's artists (National Museum), its favorite composer (Chopin Museum), its dramatic history (Museum of Warsaw and Warsaw Uprising Museum), its dedication

Warsaw History: Ebbs and Flows

Warsaw has good reason to be a city of the future: The past hasn't been very kind. Historically, Warsaw has seen wave after wave of foreign rulers and invasions—especially during the last hundred years. But in this horrific crucible, the enduring spirit of the Polish people was forged. As one proud Varsovian told me, "Warsaw is ugly because its history is so beautiful."

Founded around 1300, Warsaw gradually gained importance through the late Middle Ages. In the mid-16th century, it became the seat of the Sejm (parliament of nobles), and it took over as seat of the royal court (and therefore Poland's capital) in 1596.

The city's Golden Age was between the World Wars, when Poland—newly reconstituted after a century and a half of foreign rule under the Partitions—was proudly independent. Interwar Warsaw saw a flourishing of commerce, construction, and the arts almost unmatched in Europe at that time, when it was also the largest and most culturally rich Jewish city in Europe.

Sadly, this age of optimism was cut brutally short by the city's darkest days, as the Nazis occupied the city (and all of Poland) at the outbreak of World War II. First, its Jewish residents were forced into a tiny ghetto. They rose up...and were slaughtered (the Ghetto Uprising—see page 204). Then, in the war's waning days, its surviving residents rose up...and were slaughtered (the Warsaw Uprising—see page 212). Fed up with the troublesome Varsovians, Hitler sent word to systematically demolish the entire city, block by block. At the war's end, Warsaw was virtually gone. An estimated 800,000 residents were dead—nearly two out of every three.

The Poles almost gave up on what was then a pile of rubble, planning to build a brand-new capital city elsewhere. But ultimately they decided to rebuild, creating a city of contrasts: painstakingly restored medieval lanes and retrofitted communist apartment blocks (*bloki* in Polish). And its evolution continues. Since the end of communism, Warsaw has become a hub of international trade and diplomacy—adding sleek skyscrapers to its skyline. It's clear that Warsaw is currently living one of its finest moments.

WARSAW

to the sciences (Copernicus Science Center), and its Jewish story (Museum of the History of Polish Jews). You can also dig into one of Europe's most interesting foodie scenes, where a world of wildly creative chefs open new restaurants all the time—at budget prices. If you picture a dreary metropolis, think again. Warsaw is full of surprises.

PLANNING YOUR TIME

One day is the absolute minimum to get a quick taste of Warsaw—but you'll have to sightsee very selectively. The city can easily fill two or three days, and even then you'll need to pick and choose. Review your museum-going options to decide how much time you need.

No matter how long you stay, get your bearings by taking a stroll through Polish history, following my Royal Way Walk from Palm Tree Circle to the Old Town. With more time, extend your stroll on my Old Town Walk for a sampling of Warsaw's historic core. Then visit other sights according to your interests and time: Jewish history, the Warsaw Uprising, Polish artists, royalty, hands-on science gizmos, hipster hangouts, or Chopin. To slow down and take a break from the city, relax in Łazienki Park.

For dinner, buck the tourist trend by leaving the overpriced Old Town and riding a tram, the Metro, a taxi, or Uber to the hip Śródmieście district, which has the highest concentration of quality eateries.

Orientation to Warsaw

Warsaw sprawls with 1.7 million residents. Everything is on a big scale—it seems to take forever to walk just a few "short" blocks.

Get comfortable with public transportation (or taxis or Uber), and plan your sightseeing to avoid backtracking.

The tourist's Warsaw blankets a mild hill on the west bank of the Vistula River (in Polish: Wisła, VEES-wah). To break things into manageable chunks, I think of the city as three major zones (from north to south):

The **Old Town and Royal Way,** at Warsaw's northern edge, is the most touristy area. Here you'll find the Old Town (Stare Miasto, STAH-reh mee-AH-stoh), the adjacent and nearly-as-old New Town (Nowe Miasto, NOH-vay mee-AH-stoh), the Royal Castle on Castle Square (Plac Zamkowy, plahts zahm-KOH-vee), and the historical artery called the Royal Way (Szlak Królewski, shwock kroh-LEHV-skee). This bustling strip has strollable boulevards, genteel cafés, expansive squares and parks, and stately landmarks both historic and faux-historic (much of this area was rebuilt after World War II).

"Palm Tree Circle" is my nickname for the center of the city, near the traffic circle with a fake palm tree—where busy Jerusa-

Warsaw Overview

Accommodations
1 Hotel Rialto
2 Autor Rooms

Eateries & Shopping
3 Hala Koszyki Food Hall
4 Plac Zbawiciela Eateries
5 Beirut & other Poznańska Eateries
6 Atelier Amaro
7 Mokotowska Street (Shopping)

See the Central Warsaw map

WARSAW

CYTADELA

SŁOMIŃSKIEGO

GDAŃSKI BRIDGE

Vistula River

WYBRZEŻE GDAŃSKIE

WYBRZEŻE RATUSZOWA

WYBRZEŻE HELSKIE

JAGIELLOŃSKA

PONIATOWSKA

KONWIKTORSKA

FRANCISZKAŃSKA

SANGUSZKI

FRETA

New Town Square

DEFENSIVE WALL

NEW TOWN

Old Town Square

OKRZEI

SZCZECIŃSKA

WYBRZEŻE

To Mus. of Hist. of Polish Jews & Former Ghetto

ŚWIĘTOJERSKA

BARBICAN

OLD TOWN

Krasińskich Garden

DŁUGA

MIODOWA

Castle Square

ROYAL CASTLE

BŁASKO-DĄBROWSKI BRIDGE

GEN. ANDERS

ŚWIĘTO-JERSKA

St. Anne's

ROYAL WAY

ORLA

Ratusz M

SOLIDARNOŚCI

SENATORSKA

NATIONAL THEATER & OPERA

WIERZBOWA

RADZIWIŁŁ PALACE

KAROWA

BROWARNA

DOBRA

To National Stadium

KRAKOWSKIE PRZEDMIEŚCIE

HOTEL BRISTOL

COPERNICUS SCIENCE CENTER

ŚWIĘTOKRZYSKI BRIDGE

Saxon Garden

Piłsudski Square

WARSAW UNIVERSITY

Centrum Nauki Kopernik

PTASIA

KRÓLEWSKA

CZACKIEGO

OBOŻNA

TAMKA

Świętokrzyska M

ŚWIĘTOKRZYSKA

HOLY CROSS

Nowy Świat-Uniwersytet M

CHOPIN MUSEUM

GRZYBOWSKA

GALERIA CENTRUM MALL

NOWY ŚWIAT

FOKSAL

PONIATOWSKI BRIDGE

To Warsaw Uprising Museum

PALACE OF CULTURE & SCIENCE

CHMIELNA

SMOLNA

JERUSALEM AVE.

ZŁOTA

E. PLATER

Centrum M

WIDOK

JEROZOLIMSKIE

PALM TREE CIRCLE

NATIONAL MUSEUM

LUDNA

CENTRAL TRAIN STATION

NOWOGRODZKA

ŻURAWIA

AL.

Three Crosses Square

ROYAL WAY

CHAŁUBIŃSKIEGO

WSPÓLNA

MARSZAŁKOWSKA

POZNAŃSKA

WILCZA

KRUCZA

AL. UJAZDOWSKIE

RÓŻBRAT

5

HOŻA

7

PIĘKNA

1

KOSZYKOWA

PIĘKNA

MOKOTOWSKA

AL. NIEPODLEGŁOŚCI

3

2

Constitution Square

ŚRÓDMIEŚCIE

AL. ARMII LUDOWEJ

NOWOWIEJSKA

4

Plac Zbawiciela

6

Łazienki Park

N

Politechnika M

CHOPIN MONUMENT & concerts

PALACE ON THE WATER

WAWELSKA

0.5 Kilometer

0.5 Mile

ROYAL WAY

To Wilanów Palace B

BELWEDER

lem Avenue (aleja Jerozolimskie, ah-LAY-uh yeh-ro-zoh-LIM-skyeh) crosses the shopping street called Nowy Świat (NOH-vee SHVEE-aht). Nearby are some good accommodations, trendy upscale eateries, pedestrianized shopping streets and glitzy malls, the National Museum (Polish art), the Palace of Culture and Science (communist-era landmark skyscraper), and the central train station (Warszawa Centralna).

The **Śródmieście** (SHROD-myesh-cheh, "Downtown") district, to the south, is a mostly residential zone with the city's best restaurant and nightlife scene and some good accommodations. The only real sight here is lush Łazienki Park, with its summertime al fresco Chopin concerts.

In sprawling Warsaw, many more sights—including some major ones—lie outside these three areas, but all are within a long walk or a short ride on public transit. These include the Museum of the History of Polish Jews and Warsaw Uprising Museum (to the west) and the Copernicus Science Center (to the east, along the river). Across the river is the hardscrabble but gentrifying Praga district; while a trendy scene is emerging there, it's beyond the scope of a short visit (Śródmieście is similar, more accessible, and easier to reach).

TOURIST INFORMATION

Warsaw's helpful, youthful TI has three branches: on the **Old Town Market Square** (daily May-Sept 9:00-20:00, Oct-April until 18:00), at the **Palace of Culture and Science** (enter on the side facing the train station, on Emilii Plater; daily May-Sept 8:00-19:00, Oct-April until 18:00), and at **Chopin Airport** (daily 9:00-19:00—though this branch may be closing). The general information number for all TIs is 22-19115. All branches offer advice on live music and have piles of free, useful brochures ("city breaks," Jewish heritage, Chopin, mermaids, St. John Paul II, and so on). Everything is also available online (www.warsawtour.pl).

Sightseeing Pass: Busy sightseers might consider the **Warsaw Pass,** which covers admission to most major sights, the best hop-on, hop-off bus tour, and a Chopin concert (119 zł/24 hours, 159 zł/48 hours, 189 zł/72 hours, sold at the TI); you can add public transportation for a little bit more. If your museum-going plans are ambitious, do the math.

ARRIVAL IN WARSAW
By Train

Most trains arrive at the **central train station** (Warszawa Centralna, vah-SHAH-vah tsehn-TRAHL-nah), a communist-era monstrosity that has been renovated with surprising grace. (Don't get off at Warszawa Zachodnia, which is far from the tourist area.)

Warszawa Centralna can be tricky to navigate: Three parallel concourses run across the tracks, accessed by three different sets of escalators from each platform, creating a subterranean maze (with well-signed lockers, ticket windows, and lots of shops

and eateries). Be patient: To get your bearings, ride up on your platform's middle escalator, then look for signs to the wide-open **main hall** (follow signs for *main hall/hala główna*). Here you'll find a row of ticket windows, a railroad service center, a supermarket, eateries, waiting areas (upstairs), and (from outside, near the taxi stand) views of the adjacent Palace of Culture and Science and Złota 44 skyscrapers. If you have a little time to kill, walk across the street to the super-modern Złote Tarasy Shopping Mall (described on page 201).

Getting into Town: To reach the tourist zone and most of my recommended hotels, a taxi/Uber is the easiest choice, while the bus is more economical (but more challenging to find).

Taxis wait outside the main hall. Many are dishonest—look for one with a company logo and telephone number, and ask for an estimate up front (the fare should be no more than about 20-30 zł for most of my recommended hotels). You can also order an **Uber.**

From the station, **bus #175** or **#128** takes you to the Royal Way and Old Town in about 10 minutes (see "Getting Around Warsaw," later). You can catch either bus in front of the skyscraper with the Hotel Marriott, across busy Jerusalem Avenue from the station. Because it's hard to find this stop from the station's mazelike corridors, it's probably simplest to ascend to street level (on the aleja Jerozolimskie side) and cross surface streets to reach the well-marked Marriott tower. Both buses terminate just off Piłsudski Square, a five-minute walk from the Old Town. **Bus #160** also goes to the Old Town (though not via the Royal Way), but it departs from the opposite side of the station: To find its stop from the main hall, go out the side door toward *ul. Emilii Plater.* Before boarding any bus, buy a ticket from the machine near the stop—or get one within the station's underground zone, at any kiosk marked *RUCH.*

Buying Train Tickets: Lining one wall of the main arrival hall *(hala główna)* are 16 **ticket windows.** A more user-friendly **passenger service center** is in the opposite corner (daily 9:10-20:30). While it can be slower to buy tickets or make reservations in the office (take a number as you enter), staff members are more likely to speak English and have patience for clueless tourists. Additional ticket windows are in the maze of corridors under the station. (You can also book most train tickets online at www.rozklad-pkp.pl.) If buying tickets in person, allow yourself plenty of time to wait in line. Remember: Even if you have a rail pass, a reservation is still required on many express trains (including EIC trains to Kraków or Gdańsk). If you're not sure, ask. To get to your train, first find your way to the right platform (*peron*, as noted on schedules), then keep an eye on both tracks *(tor)* for your train. Train info: Tel. 19436 (22-19436 from outside Warsaw), www.rozklad-pkp.pl.

By Plane
Fryderyk Chopin International Airport

Warsaw's Fryderyk Chopin International Airport (Port Lotniczy im. Fryderyk Chopina, airport code: WAW, tel. 22-650-4220, www.lotnisko-chopina.pl) is about six miles southwest of the center. It's relatively small and manageable; outside the arrivals area, you'll find a TI, ATMs, car-rental offices, and exchange desks *(kantor)*.

To get into town, you can take the train or bus (similar prices, around 5 zł). The train is faster, but the bus makes more stops in the city center and may get you closer to your hotel. From the arrivals area, just follow signs to either option.

The **train** departs about every 15 minutes and takes 20-30 minutes. To find it, turn right in the arrivals area and follow the green line on the floor. Exiting the airport, you'll head downstairs (under the big *Stacja Kolejawa* sign) to find the tracks. The line into town is operated by two different companies (SKM and KM)—take whichever one departs first. Be ready for your stop: Half the trains make fewer stops and take you to Centralna station; others make a few more stops and use the Warszawa Śródmieście station—which feeds into the same underground passages as Centralna (these trains also continue one more stop to the Warszawa Powiśle station, which is a bit closer to Nowy Świat and can be more convenient to some hotels). Whether arriving at Centralna station or Warszawa Śródmieście, see the "By Train" arrival instructions, earlier.

Bus #175 departs from the curb in front of arrivals every 15-20 minutes and runs into the city center (Centralna station, the Royal Way, and Piłsudski Square near the Old Town, 30-45 minutes depending on traffic; buy ticket from machine before you board).

For a **taxi,** head to the official taxi stand. Taxis have a fixed rate of about 45 zł to most downtown hotels (trip takes 30 minutes depending on traffic). It's generally cheaper to order an **Uber** (except at very busy times).

Modlin Airport

Modlin Airport (airport code: WMI), about 21 miles northwest of the city center, primarily serves budget airlines (especially Ryanair). The most direct option for getting to downtown Warsaw is by shuttle bus—**ModlinBus** and **OKbus** both connect the airport to downtown (33 zł, 2/hour, one-hour trip, cheaper if you book ahead online—www.modlinbus.com or www.okbus.pl). An alternative is the well-coordinated **bus-plus-train connection:** Take a shuttle bus to Modlin's main train station, then hop on a train to Warszawa Centralna station (19 zł, hourly, 1-1.5 hours total, www.mazowieckie.com.pl). If you want to ride a **taxi** all the way into Warsaw, the maximum legitimate fare is 200 zł (or 250 zł at night). Airport info: www.modlinairport.pl.

GETTING AROUND WARSAW

Sprawling Warsaw can be exhausting to get around. Get comfortable with public transportation and taxis/Uber.

By Public Transit: Warsaw's efficient, affordable public transportation network includes buses, trams, and the two-line Metro (transit info: www.ztm.waw.pl). Everything is covered by the same tickets. Most rides within the tourist zone take less than 20 minutes, so the default is the 3.40-zł "20-minute city travelcard" *(bilet 20-minutowy)*. For longer journeys, a single ticket *(bilet jednora-zowy)* covers any trip up to 75 minutes for 4.40 zł. A 24-hour travelcard *(bilet dobowy)*—which pays for itself if you take at least five trips—costs 15 zł. Ticket machines, which are at most major stops, are easy to use; they have English instructions and take both coins and credit cards. Or you can buy tickets at any kiosk with a *RUCH* sign. While you may find ticket machines on board some buses and trams, it's safest to buy your ticket before boarding. Be sure to validate your ticket as you board by inserting it in the little yellow box.

Most of the city's major attractions line up on a single axis, the Royal Way, which is served by several different buses (but no trams). **Bus #175**—particularly useful on arrival—links Chopin Airport, the central train station, the Royal Way, and Old Town (it terminates at Piłsudski Square, about a five-minute walk from Castle Square). Once you're in town, the designed-for-tourists **bus #180** conveniently connects virtually all the significant sights and neighborhoods: the former Jewish Ghetto and Museum of the History of Polish Jews, Castle Square/Old Town, the Royal Way, Łazienki Park, and Wilanów Palace (south of the center). This particularly user-friendly bus lists sights in English on the posted schedule inside (other buses don't).

Bus routes beginning with "E" (marked in red on schedules) are express, so they go long distances without stopping (these don't run July-Aug). Note that on Saturdays and Sundays in summer

Central Warsaw

WARSAW

Rondo Babka

PARKING LOT WITH FORMER GHETTO WALL

UMSCHLAGPLATZ MONUMENT

MURANÓW (Former Jewish Ghetto)

FORMER SS HQ

BUNKER

MUSEUM OF THE HISTORY OF POLISH JEWS

GHETTO HEROES SQUARE

Plac Krasinskich

Krasińskich Garden

Nalewki

Muranów

Ratusz

Plac Bankowy

Plac Grzybowski

Plac Grzybowski

Muzeum Powstania Warszawskiego

WARSAW UPRISING MUSEUM

Rondo Daszynskiego

Rondo Daszyńskiego

ZŁOTE TARASY MALL

Dworzec Centralny Bus #160

CENTRAL TRAIN STATION

Dw. Centralny

Dworzec Centralny Bus #175

400 Meters

400 Yards

Accommodations
1. Hotel Indigo
2. Between Us B&B
3. Chopin Boutique B&B
4. Zgoda by DeSilva
5. Apple Inn
6. Oki Doki City Hostel
7. Hotel Bristol
8. Hotel Le Régina
9. Castle Inn
10. Duval Apartments

Eateries
11. Kamanda Lwowska
12. Bibenda
13. Butchery & Wine
14. A. Blikle
15. E. Wedel Pijalnia Czekolady
16. Odette
17. Warszawa Powiśle
18. Kawiarnia Kafka
19. Restauracja pod Samsonem
20. Freta 33
21. Zapiecek (5)

Other
22 Observation Deck Entrance
23 Canaletto Paintings (3)
24 Mysia 3 (Mini-Mall)
25 Jazz Club Akwarium

NEW TOWN
20 New Town Square
MARIE CURIE MUSEUM
21 BARBICAN
DEFENSIVE WALL
MUSEUM OF WARSAW
8 ZAKROCZYMSKA
KOŚCIELNA
MOSTOWA
WYBRZEŻE GDAŃSKIE

19 21 ŚWIĘTOJERSKA
SUPREME COURT
MONUMENT TO WARSAW UPRISING
LITTLE UPRISER MONUMENT
ST. MARTIN'S
DŁUGA
MIODOWA
OLD TOWN
10 Old Town Sq.
TOWN
ST. JOHN THE BAPTIST
WC
9 ROYAL CASTLE
SIGISMUND PILLAR
OLD TOWN WALK BEGINS
T Stare Miasto

Vistula River
ŚLĄSKO-DĄBROWSKI BRIDGE

Castle Square
ST. ANNE'S
Plac Zamkowy B
21
25
Plac Teatralny
NATIONAL THEATER & OPERA
MICKIEWICZ STATUE
RADZIWIŁŁ PALACE
7 HOTEL BRISTOL
B Plac Piłsudski
Piłsudski Square
TOMB OF THE UNKNOWN SOLDIER
23 Hotel Bristol
SMOLENSK PLANE CRASH MONUMENT
23
WYSZYŃSKI MONUMENT
WARSAW UNIVERSITY
Saxon Garden
SOFITEL HOTEL
Uniwersytet
B
KRAKOWSKIE PRZEDMIEŚCIE (ROYAL WAY)
KOŚCIUSZKOWSKIE
KAROWA
DOBRA
BEDNARSKA
WARSAW UNIVERSITY LIBRARY
COPERNICUS SCIENCE CENTER

SENATORSKA
WIERZBOWA
TRĘBACKA
SOLIDARNOŚCI
KRÓLEWSKA
MAZOWIECKA
KREDYTOWA
MARSZAŁKOWSKA
ZIELNA

TRAUGUTTA
23
COPERNICUS MONUMENT
18
OBOŹNA
B Centrum Nauki Kopernik
M

HOLY CROSS
WARSAW HOUSE OF MUSIC
M Nowy Świat Uniwersytet
TAMKA
Plac Dąbrowskiego
6 ŚWIĘTOKRZYSKA
RYSIA
JASNA
H. SIENKIEWICZA
ZŁOTA
ZGODA
BODUENA
WARECKA
16
15
4
21 Ordynacka
B
ORDYNACKA
CHOPIN MUSEUM
11
3
17
FOKSAL
SMOLNA
M Świętokrzyska

PALACE OF CULTURE & SCIENCE
22
GALERIA CENTRUM MALL
SZPITALNA
CHMIELNA
14
2
5
1
PALM TREE
B Nowy Świat
Muzeum Narodowe T
NATIONAL MUSEUM
Park Powiśle

WIDOK
ROYAL WAY WALK BEGINS
DE GAULLE MONUMENT
FORMER COMMUNIST HEADQUARTERS

ALEJA JEROZOLIMSKIE
B Centrum
M
NOVOTEL
12
NOWOGRODZKA
13
ŻURAWIA
KRUCZA
BRACKA
24
Plac Trzech Krzyży
THREE CROSSES

E. PLATER
POZNAŃSKA
MARRIOTT
ALEJA JEROZOLIMSKIE (JERUSALEM AVE)
WSPÓLNA
HOŻA
To Śródmieście
To Łazienki Park & Wilanów Palace

(May-mid-Oct), the Nowy Świat-Krakowskie Przedmieście section of the Royal Way is closed to traffic, so the above routes detour along a parallel street.

Trams can be particularly useful for reaching the trendy Śródmieście district in the south. Several trams (including #4, #15, #18, and #35) run along the north-south Marszałkowska corridor, with stops at plac Konstytucji (Constitution Square, the heart of the Śródmieście) and at plac Zbawiciela (with a cluster of great eateries).

Warsaw's two-line **Metro** system, designed for commuters, can be useful for hops between certain sights—especially line 2, which runs east to west; its most convenient stops are Rondo Daszyńskiego (near the Warsaw Uprising Museum), Świętokrzyska (where you can transfer to line 1), Nowy Świat-Uniwersytet (in the middle of the Royal Way, near the Copernicus Monument), Centrum Nauki Kopernik (on the riverbank, near the Copernicus Science Center), and Stadion Narodowy (National Stadium, across the river). The north-south line 1, which stops at the train station (Centrum), is less useful for visitors.

By Taxi: Use only cabs that are clearly marked with a company logo and telephone number; official cabs have a mermaid decal on the front door (or call your own: Locals like City Taxi, tel. 19459; MPT Radio Taxi, tel. 19191; or Ele taxi, tel. 22-811-1111). All official taxis have similar rates: 8 zł to start, then 3 zł per kilometer (4.50 zł after 22:00 or in the suburbs). **Uber** also works well in Warsaw, just like back home; it's typically cheaper than a taxi and can be useful in situations where you're not near a taxi stand or a convenient public-transit stop.

Tours in Warsaw

Walking Tours

Each year, new companies crop up offering walking tours in Warsaw. These tend to have one of two approaches: A "free" tour of the main sights (with generous tipping expected); or communism-themed tours, often with a ride to a gloomy apartment-block area for a taste of the Red old days. The TI and most hotels have brochures. Survey the latest offerings, do some homework (check online reviews), and pick a tour that suits your interests.

Private Guides

Having a talented local historian as your guide in this city, with such a complex and powerful story to tell, greatly enhances your experience. I've worked with two excellent young guides: smart and charming **Monika Oleśko** (350 zł/3 hours, 550 zł/5.5 hours; more for larger groups, by bike, or by car; mobile 535-770-843, warsawteller.wordpress.com, olesko.monika@gmail.com) and professorial **Hubert Pawlik** (520 zł/5-hour city walking tour, 650 zł with his car, other tours—including options by car—are explained on his website, mobile 502-298-105, www.warsaw-citytours.com, guide@warsaw-citytours.com). Both Monika and Hubert offer theme tours and can tailor the time to your interests.

Food Tours
Eat Polska does excellent food and vodka tours around this fast-emerging foodie mecca. A top-quality guide will take your small group to a variety of restaurants and bars around the city, with tasting samples at each one. The guides do an exceptional job of providing insightful context about what you're tasting, making this educational about both Polish cuisine and Polish culture in general. If you have a serious interest in food, this is the most worthwhile tour in town (food tours typically daily at 13:00, 290 zł, 4 hours; vodka tours with food pairings daily at 17:00, 290 zł, 3.5 hours; www.eatpolska.com).

Bus Tours
Warsaw's spread-out landscape makes it a natural for a hop-on, hop-off bus—although heavy traffic may make you wish you'd taken a tram or the Metro instead. The best choice is CitySightseeing, with red buses (60 zł/24 hours, 80 zł/48 hours, two routes). Skip City-Tour (yellow buses), which is more expensive and less frequent.

Walks in Warsaw

I've outlined two self-guided walks in Warsaw. The "Royal Way Walk" covers the most interesting one-mile section of the Royal Way—in the heart of the city, from Palm Tree Circle to Castle Square. It's followed by the "Old Town Walk," which starts in Castle Square and explores Warsaw's Old Town. Allow about 1.75 hours to do both walks back-to-back.

ROYAL WAY WALK
The Royal Way (Szlak Królewski) is the six-mile route that the kings of Poland used to travel from their main residence (at Castle Square in the Old Town) to their summer home (Wilanów Palace, south of the center and not worth visiting). This busy boulevard changes names from Nowy Świat to Krakowskie Przedmieście as it stretches from south to north. Not counting sightseeing stops, figure about 30 minutes to walk along Nowy Świat ("Part 1"), then another 45 minutes along Krakowskie Przedmieście to the Old Town ("Part 2").

Warsaw at a Glance

▲▲▲**Museum of the History of Polish Jews** Exceptional, expansive exhibit on the full Jewish experience through Polish history. **Hours:** Mon and Thu-Fri 10:00-18:00, Wed and Sat-Sun 10:00-20:00, closed Tue. See page 203.

▲▲**Royal Castle** Warsaw's best palace, rebuilt after World War II, but retaining its former opulence and many original furnishings. **Hours:** May-Sept Mon-Sat 10:00-18:00, Fri until 20:00, Sun 11:00-18:00; Oct-April Tue-Sat 10:00-16:00, Sun 11:00-16:00, closed Mon. See page 189.

▲▲**Old Town Market Square** Re-creation of Warsaw's glory days, with lots of colorful architecture. See page 186.

▲▲**National Museum** Collection of mostly Polish art, with unknown but worth-discovering works by Jan Matejko and the Młoda Polska (Art Nouveau) crew. **Hours:** Tue-Sun 10:00-18:00, Fri until 21:00, closed Mon. See page 193.

▲▲**Warsaw Uprising Museum** State-of-the-art space tracing the history of the Uprising and celebrating its heroes. **Hours:** Mon and Wed-Fri 8:00-18:00, Thu until 20:00, Sat-Sun 10:00-18:00, closed Tue. See page 209.

▲▲**Copernicus Science Center** Spiffy new science museum with well-explained, hands-on exhibits in English; Warsaw's best family activity. **Hours:** Tue-Fri 9:00-18:00, Sat-Sun 10:00-19:00, closed Mon. See page 199.

▲**Castle Square** Colorful spot with whiffs of old Warsaw—Royal Castle, monuments, and a chunk of the city wall—and cafés just off the square. See page 184.

▲**Łazienki Park** Lovely, sprawling green space with Chopin statue, peacocks, and Neoclassical buildings. **Hours:** Always open; wonderful outdoor Chopin concerts mid-May-late Sept generally Sun at 12:00 and 16:00. See page 213.

▲**Museum of Warsaw** In-depth treatment of the history of Warsaw, with excellent movie in English. **Hours:** Tue-Sun 10:00-19:00, closed Mon. See page 192.

Palace of Culture and Science Huge "Stalin Gothic" skyscraper with a more impressive exterior than interior, housing theaters, multiplex cinema, observation deck, and more. **Hours:** Observation deck—daily 10:00-20:00, may be open later in summer. See page 200.

WARSAW

Part 1: Palm Tree Circle and Nowy Świat

• *Start this walk at the traffic circle officially named for Charles de Gaulle, but colloquially known as...*

Palm Tree Circle

This is one of the city's main intersections, marked by the iconic palm tree. Stand near the communist-era monument under the spruce trees (on the curb, kitty-corner from the biggest building) and get oriented.

You're standing at the intersection of two major boulevards: **Nowy Świat** (where we're heading next) and **Jerusalem Avenue** (aleja Jerozolimskie, which heads from Warszawa Centralna station across the river). This street once led to a Jewish settlement called New Jerusalem. Like so much else in Warsaw, it's changed names many times. Between the World Wars, it became "May 3rd Avenue," celebrating Poland's 1791 constitution (Europe's first). But this was too nationalistic for the occupying Nazis, who called it simply Bahnhofstrasse ("Train Station Street"). Then the communists switched it back to "Jerusalem," strangely disregarding the religious connotations of that name. (Come on, guys—what about a good, old-fashioned "Stalin Avenue"?) The strikingly wide boulevards were part of the city's post-WWII Soviet rebuilding. Communist urban planners felt that eight- to twelve-lane roads were ideal for worker pageantry like big May Day parades...and, when the workers aren't happy, for Soviet tanks to thunder around, maintaining order.

You can't miss the giant **palm tree** in the middle of Jerusalem Avenue. When a local artist went to the real Jerusalem, she was struck by the many palm trees—and wanted to erect one along Warsaw's own little stretch of "Jerusalem." This artificial palm tree went up in 2002 as a temporary installation. It was highly controversial, dividing the neighborhood. One snowy winter day, the pro-palm tree faction—who appreciated the way the tree spiced up this otherwise dreary metropolis—camped out here in bikinis and beachwear to show their support. They prevailed, and the tree is now a permanent fixture.

The big, blocky building across the street (on the left side of the intersection) was the **headquarters of the Communist Party,** built in 1948. *Nowy Świat* translates as "New World," inspiring a popular communist-era joke: What do you see when you turn your back on the Communist Party? A "New World." Ironically, when the economy was privatized in 1991, this building became home to Poland's stock exchange. And then the country's only dealer-ship for Ferraris—certainly not an automobile for the proletariat—moved in downstairs.

On the corner in front of the former Communist Party HQ, a statue of **Charles de Gaulle** strides confidently up the street. A gift from the government of France, this celebrates the military tacti-cian who came to Warsaw's rescue when the Red Army invaded from the USSR after World War I.

To the left of the Communist Party building is the vast **National Museum**—a good place for a fascinating lesson in Polish art (see the self-guided tour later, under "Sights in Warsaw").

Before walking down Nowy Świat, notice the small but pow-erful **monument** near you. In 1956, this was dedicated to the "Poles who fought for People's Poland"—with a strong communist conno-tation. In a classic example of Socialist Realism, the communists appropriated a religious theme that Poles were inclined to embrace (this pietà composition)...and politicized it. But in 2014, the statue was rededicated to the "*partyzantom* who fought for free Poland in World War II." "Partisan" was a bad word in the 1950s, when it was used to describe the soldiers of the Polish Home Army—which fought against both the Nazis and the Soviets.

• *From here, turn your back to the Communist Party building and head into a new world—down Nowy Świat—to the first intersection. As you stroll, notice how massive, intense Warsaw suddenly becomes more inti-mate and accessible.*

Nowy Świat

This charming shopping boulevard, lined with boutiques, cafés, and restaurants, feels upscale and elegant. Before World War II, Nowy Świat was Warsaw's most popular neighborhood. And today, once again, rents are higher here than anywhere else in town. While most tourists flock into the Old Town, Varso-vians and visiting businesspeo-ple prefer this zone and farther south. The city has worked hard to revitalize this strip with broad sidewalks, flower boxes, old-time lampposts, and strict restrictions on traffic (only buses and taxis—and on summer weekends, it's en-tirely traffic-free).

Look down the street and notice the harmonious architecture. In the 1920s, this street was anything but cohesive: an eclectic and decadent strip of Art Deco facades, full of individualism. Rather than rebuild in that "trouble-causing" style, the communists used an idealized, more conservative, Neoclassical style, which feels more like the 1820s than the 1920s.

Ulica Chmielna, the first street to the left, is an appealing pedestrian boutique street leading to Emil Wedel's chocolate heaven (a five-minute walk away; described later, under "Eating in Warsaw"). Between here and the Palace of Culture and Science stretches one of Warsaw's top shopping neighborhoods (culminating at the Galleria Centrum mall, just across from the Palace).

Across the street from Chmielna (on the right) is the restaurant street called **Foksal.** On a balmy summer evening, this street is filled with chatty al fresco diners.

A few steps farther down Nowy Świat, on the left, don't miss the recommended **A. Blikle** pastry shop and café—a venerable spot for Polish sweets, especially *pączki* (rose-flavored jelly doughnuts). Step inside for a dose of the 1920s: good-life Art Deco decor and historical photos. Or, if you're homesick for Starbucks, drop in to one of the second-wave coffee shops that line this stretch of Nowy Świat—many with American-style lattes "to go" (one of many American customs that the Poles have embraced).

A half-block down the street (on the left, at #39) is a rare surviving bit of preglitz Nowy Świat: Bar Mleczny Familijny, a classic **milk bar**—a government-subsidized cafeteria filled with locals seeking a cheap meal (an interesting cultural artifact, but not recommended for a meal; for more about milk bars, see the sidebar on page 18). But don't be surprised if it's gone by the time you visit; in this high-rent district, it's unlikely that these few remaining holdovers from the old days will survive for much longer.

Eat and shop your way along Nowy Świat. About one more block down, **Ordynacka street** (on the right) leads downhill to the Chopin Museum, worth considering for musical pilgrims.

At the end of the block on the left (at #63), the **Warsaw House of Music** hosts live concerts of various kinds, and sells tickets for nightly Chopin concerts back near Palm Tree Circle (for details, see "Entertainment in Warsaw," later).

• *Continuing along Nowy Świat through a duller stretch, you'll walk alongside a hulking, gloomy building before popping out in a pleasant square with a big statue of Copernicus.*

Part 2: Krakowskie Przedmieście
• *The street name changes to Krakowskie Przedmieście (meaning, roughly, "suburb in the direction of Kraków") at the big...*

Copernicus Statue
This statue, by the great Danish sculptor Bertel Thorvaldsen, stands in front of the Polish Academy of Science. **Mikołaj Kopernik** (1473-1543) was born in Toruń and went to college in Kraków. The

Nazis stole his statue and took it to Germany (which, like Poland, claims Copernicus as its own). Now it's back where it belongs. The concentric circles radiating from the front of the statue represent the course of the planets' orbits, from Mercury to Saturn.

Just to Copernicus' left is a low-profile, black-marble **Chopin bench**—one of many scattered around the center. These benches mark points related to his life (in this case, his sister lived across the street). Each of these benches plays Chopin's music with the push of a button (though because of passing traffic, this one is tough to hear).

Directly in front of the statue, in the glass case, find a replica of a **Canaletto painting** of this same street scene in 1778, and compare it to today's reality. As the national archives were destroyed, city builders referred to historic paintings like these for guidance after WWII. You'll see other Canaletto replicas like this one scattered around the city.

• *Across from Copernicus, the Church of the Holy Cross is worth a look.*

Church of the Holy Cross (Kościół Św. Krzyża)

We'll pass many churches along this route, but the Church of the Holy Cross is unique (and free to enter). Composer **Fryderyk Cho-**

pin's heart is inside one of the pillars of the nave (first big pillar on the left, look for the marker). After two decades of exile in France, Chopin's final wish was to have his heart brought back to his native Poland after his death. During World War II, the heart was hidden away in the countryside for safety.

Check out the bright gold chapel, located on the left as you face the altar, near the front of the church. It's dedicated to a saint whom Polish Catholics believe helps them with **"desperate and hopeless causes."** People praying here are likely dealing with some tough issues. The beads draped from the altarpieces help power their prayers, and the many little brass plaques are messages of thanks for prayers answered.

In the back-left corner (as you face the altar) is a chapel dedicated to Poland's favorite son, **St. John Paul II.** His ghostly image appears out of the wall; beneath him is a rock inscribed with the words *Tu es Petrus* (Latin for "You are Peter"—what Jesus said when he made St. Peter the first-ever pope), embedded with a capsule containing JPII's actual blood.

Just opposite, in the back-right corner, behind the giant barbed wire, is a memorial to the 22,000 Polish POWs—mostly officers and prominent civilians—massacred by Soviet soldiers in 1940 near **Katyń,** a village in today's Russia. Stalin was determined to decapitate Poland's military intelligentsia in a ruthless mass killing, which Poles have never forgotten.

Leaving the church, notice the 19th-century, bronze-and-granite **statue of Christ bearing the cross** along the balustrade. In front, a placard reads, "Lift up your hearts." Even as Warsaw bore the burden of Russian occupation, this statue inspired them to be strong and not lose hope. It was one of many crosses they bore: a Catholic nation pinched between Orthodox Russians and Protestant Germans.

• *Cross the street (appreciating how pedestrian-friendly it is—crossing here used to be a real-life game of Frogger), and continue left.*

Warsaw University

A long block up the street on the right, you'll see the gates (marked *Uniwersytet*) to the main campus of **Warsaw University,** founded in 1816. This lively student district has plenty of bookstores and cafeterias.

Keep strolling, appreciating the fine facades. The 18th century was a time of great political decline for Poland, as a series of incompetent foreign kings mishandled crises and squandered funds. But ironically, it was also Warsaw's biggest economic boom time. Along this boulevard, aristocratic families of the period built **mansions**—most of them destroyed in World War II and rebuilt since. Some have curious flourishes (just past the university on the right, look for the doorway supported by four bearded brutes admiring their overly defined abs...it's supposed to be a six-pack, but I count ten). Over time, many of these families donated their mansions to the university.

• *The bright-yellow church a block up from the university, on the right, is the...*

Church of the Nuns of the Visitation (Kościół Sióstr Wizytek)

This Rococo confection from 1761 is the only church on this walk that survived World War II, and is notable because Chopin was briefly the organist here.

The monument in front of the church commemorates **Cardinal Stefan Wyszyński,** who was the head of the Polish Catholic Church from 1948 to 1981. He took this post soon after the arrival of the communists, who opposed the Church, but also realized it would be risky for them to shut down the churches in such an ardently religious country. The Communist Party and the Catholic Church coexisted tensely in Poland, and when Wyszyński protested a Stalinist crackdown in 1953, he was arrested and imprisoned. Three years later, in a major victory for the Church, Wyszyński was released. He continued to fight the communists, becoming a great hero of the Polish people in their struggle against the regime.

Across the street is another then-and-now Canaletto illustration.

• *Farther up (on the right, past the park) is the elegant, venerable...*

Hotel Bristol

A striking building with a round turret on its corner, the Hotel Bristol was used by the Nazis as a VIP hotel and bordello, and survived World War II. If you wander through any fancy Warsaw lobby...make it this one. Step in like you're staying here and explore its fine public spaces, with fresh Art Deco and Art Nouveau flourishes. The café in front retains its Viennese atmosphere, but the *pièce de résistance* is the stunning Column Bar deeper in, past the dramatically chandeliered lounge.

• *Leave the Royal Way briefly here for a worthwhile detour. With the corner turret of Hotel Bristol at your back, cross the street and bear left between the buildings. You'll pop out at a vast expanse called...*

Piłsudski Square (plac Marszałka Józefa Piłsudskiego)

The vast, empty-feeling Piłsudski Square (pew-SOOD-skee) has been important Warsaw real estate for centuries, constantly changing with the times. In the 1890s, the Russians who controlled this part of Poland began construction of a huge and magnificent Orthodox cathedral on this spot. But soon after it was completed, Poland regained its independence, and anti-Russian sentiments ran hot. So in the 1920s, just over a decade after the cathedral went up, it was torn down. During the Nazi occupation, this square took the name "Adolf-Hitler-Platz." Under the communists, it was Zwycięstwa, meaning "Victory" (of the Soviets over Hitler's fascism).

When the regime imposed martial law in 1981, the people of Warsaw silently protested by filling the square with a giant cross made of flowers. The huge **plaque** in the ground near the road commemorates two monumental communist-era Catholic events on this square: John Paul II's first visit as pope to his homeland on June 2, 1979; and the May 31, 1981 funeral of Cardinal Stefan Wyszyński, whom we met across the street. The cross nearby also honors the 1979 papal visit, with one of his most famous and inspiring quotes to his countrymen: "Let thy spirit descend, let thy spirit descend, and renew the face of the earth—of *this* earth" (meaning Poland, in a just-barely-subtle-enough dig against the communist regime that was tolerating his visit).

Stand in the center, near the giant flagpole, with the Royal Way at your back, for this quick, spin tour orientation: Ahead are the Tomb of the Unknown Soldier and Saxon Garden; 90 degrees to the right is the old National Theater, eclipsed by a modern business center/parking garage; another 90 degrees to the right is a statue of Piłsudski (which you passed to get here); and 90 more degrees to the right is the Sofitel—formerly the Victoria Hotel, the ultimate plush, top-of-the-top hotel where all communist-era VIPs stayed.

In front of the hotel, the monument that resembles a giant black staircase commemorates a recent tragedy: The 2010 crash of a plane carrying 96 top government officials, including President Lech Kaczyński. There were no survivors. (A week later, the funeral for Kaczyński on this square drew more than 100,000 mourners.)

To the right of the hotel, on the horizon, you can see Warsaw's newly emerging skyline. The imposing Palace of Culture and Science, which once stood alone over the city, is now joined by a cluster of brand-new skyscrapers, giving Warsaw a Berlin-esque vibe befitting its important role as a business center of Eastern Europe.

Walk to the fragment of colonnade by the park that marks the **Tomb of the Unknown Soldier** (Grób Nieznanego Żołnierza). The colonnade was once part of a much larger palace built by the Saxon prince electors (Dresden's Augustus the Strong and his son), who became kings of Poland in the 18th century. After the palace was destroyed in World War II, this fragment was kept to memorialize Polish soldiers. The names of key battles over 1,000 years are etched into the columns, the urns contain dirt from major Polish battlefields, and the two soldiers are pretty stiff. Every hour on the hour, they do a crisp Changing of the Guard—which, poignantly, honors those who have perished in this country, so shaped by wars against foreign invaders.

Just behind the tomb is the stately **Saxon Garden** (Ogród Saski), inhabited by genteel statues, gorgeous flowers, and a spurting fountain. This park was also built by the Saxon kings of Poland.

Like most foreign kings, Augustus the Strong and his son cared little for their Polish territory, building gardens like these for themselves instead of investing in more pressing needs. Poles say that foreign kings such as Augustus did nothing but "eat, drink, and loosen their belts" (it rhymes in Polish). According to Poles, these selfish absentee kings were the culprits in Poland's eventual decline. But they do appreciate having such a fine venue for a Sunday stroll.

Walk back out toward the Royal Way, stopping at the statue you passed earlier. In 1995, the square was again renamed—this

time for **Józef Piłsudski** (1867-1935), the guy with the big walrus moustache. With the help of a French captain named Charles de Gaulle (whom we met earlier), Piłsudski forced the Russian Bolsheviks out of Poland in 1920 in the so-called Miracle on the Vistula. Piłsudski is credited with creating a once-again-independent Poland after more than a century of foreign oppression, and he essentially ran Poland as a virtual dictator after World War I. Of course, under the communists, Piłsudski was swept under the rug. But since 1989, he has enjoyed a renaissance as many Poles' favorite prototype anticommunist hero. His name adorns streets, squares, and bushy-mustachioed monuments all over the country.

• *Return to Hotel Bristol, turn left, and continue your Royal Way walk.*

Radziwiłł Palace

Next door to the hotel, you'll see the huge Radziwiłł Palace. The Warsaw Pact was signed here in 1955, officially uniting the Soviet satellite states in a military alliance against NATO. This building has also, from time to time, served as the Polish "White House." Along the

street in front of the palace is another monument to that horrifying 2010 plane crash, which effectively decapitated Poland's leadership.

• *Beyond Radziwiłł Palace, on the right, you'll reach a park with a...*

Statue of Adam Mickiewicz

Poland's national poet, Adam Mickiewicz spearheaded Poland's cultural survival during more than a century when the country disappeared from maps—absorbed by Austria, Prussia, and Russia. This was an age when underdog nations (and peoples without nations) all over Europe had their own national revival movements. The statue was erected in 1898 with permission from the Russian czar, as long as the people paid for it themselves. It's still an important part of community life: Polish high school students have a big formal ball (like a prom) 100 days before graduation. After the ball, if students come here and hop around the statue on one leg, it's supposed to bring them good luck on their finals. Mickiewicz, for his part, looks like he's suffering from a heart attack—perhaps in response to the impressively ugly National Theater and Opera a block in front of him.

• *Continue to the end of the Royal Way, marked by the big pink palace. Just before the castle, on your right, is...*

St. Anne's Church

This Rococo church has playful capitals inside and out and a fine pulpit shaped like the prow of a ship—complete with a big anchor.

The richly ornamented apse, behind the altar, survived World War II. This church offers organ concerts nearly daily in summer (see "Entertainment in Warsaw," later).

For a scenic finale to your Royal Way stroll, climb the 150 steps of the

view tower by the church (6 zł, generally open daily 10:00-18:00, later in summer, closed in bad winter weather). You'll be rewarded with excellent views—particularly of Castle Square and the Old Town. From up top, visually retrace your steps along the Royal Way, and notice the emerging skyline surrounding the Palace of Culture and Science. The tower also affords a good look at the Praga district across the river, where the Red Army waited for the Nazis to level Warsaw during the uprising. Help was so close at hand...but stayed right where it was.

• *Just across from the view tower entrance, look for another Chopin bench (in front of #79). From St. Anne's Church, it's just another block to Castle Square, the TI, and the start of my "Old Town Walk."*

OLD TOWN WALK

In 1945, not a building remained standing in Warsaw's "Old" Town (Stare Miasto). Everything you see here is rebuilt, mostly finished by 1956. Some think the Old Town seems artificial, in a Disney World kind of way. For others, the painstaking postwar reconstruction feels just right, with Old World squares and lanes charming enough to give Kraków a run for its money. Before 1989, stifled by communist repression and choking on smog, the Old Town was an empty husk of its historic self. But now, the outdoor restaurants and market stalls have returned, and tourists (and a few Varsovians) are out strolling.

This concise walk, which can be done in about 30 minutes (and is a natural continuation of the Royal Way Walk outlined earlier), offers a quick overview of Warsaw's rebuilt historic core—starting at Castle Square and ending at the Barbican and New Town, with an optional return through the back streets.

• *Begin by standing on the gateway square to the Old Town, at the base of the tall pillar.*

Castle Square (Plac Zamkowy)

This square (rated ▲) is packed with Polish history. Get comfy for a quick overview:

Historically, the Polish kings called Kraków home. But things began to change in 1572, with the expiration of the second great Polish dynasty—the Jagiellonians. Rather than elevate another Polish aristocratic family to the throne, the Polish nobility decided to keep power in their own hands. From that point on, Poland was ruled by the Sejm, or Republic of Nobles—consisting of the kingdom's wealthiest 10 percent. The Sejm elected various foreign kings for limited stints on their throne. While this system kept Poland under its own control (to a degree), it wound up being unworkable: Poor choices of sovereigns, coupled with infighting among the nobles, paralyzed Poland and ultimately led to it being wiped from the map of Europe for a century and a half.

The guy on the 72-foot-tall **pillar** is Sigismund III, the first Polish king from the Swedish Vasa dynasty (or Waza in Polish). In 1596, it was Sigismund who relocated his royal seat from Kraków to Warsaw: Warsaw was the meeting point of the Sejm, and it was closer to the center of 16th-century Poland (which had expanded to the east).

Turn your attention to the big, pink **Royal Castle.** A castle has stood here since Warsaw was founded around 1300, but it grew much more important after Warsaw became the capital: It was both the meeting place of the Sejm and the residence of the king...sort of like Buckingham Palace and the Houses of Parliament rolled into one. The palace reached its peak under Stanisław

August Poniatowski—the final Polish king—who imported artists and architects to spiff up the interior.

During World War II, Luftwaffe bombs all but obliterated the palace—only one wall remained standing. Reconstruction stalled because Stalin considered it a palace for the high-class elites. It was finally rebuilt in the more moderate 1970s, funded by local donations. The castle's opulent interior—one of the finest in Eastern Europe—is well worth touring, and described on page 189. (I'll wait while you tour the castle...then let's meet out here to resume the walk.)

Along the right side of the castle, notice the **two previous pillars** lying on a lawn. The first one, from 1644, was falling apart and had to be replaced in 1887 by a new one made of granite. In 1944, a Nazi tank broke this second pillar—a symbolic piece of Polish heritage—into the four pieces (still pockmarked with bullet holes) that you see here today. As Poland rebuilt, its citizens put Sigismund III back on his pillar. Past the pillars are views of Warsaw's red-and-white National Stadium across the river—built for the Euro Cup soccer tournament in 2012.

Across the square from the castle, you'll see the partially reconstructed **defensive wall**. This rampart once enclosed the entire Old Town. Like all of Poland, Warsaw has seen invasion from all sides.

Explore the café-lined lanes that branch off Castle Square. Street signs indicate the year that each lane was originally built.

The first street is **ulica Piwna** ("Beer Street"). If you take a little detour up this street, you'll find **St. Martin's Church** (Kościół Św. Martina, on the left). Run by Franciscan nuns, this church has a simple, modern interior. Walk up the aisle and find the second pillar on the right. Notice the partly destroyed crucifix—it's the only church artifact that survived World War II. Across the street and closer to Castle Square, admire the carefully carved doorway of the house called *pod Gołębiami* ("Under Doves")—dedicated to the memory of an old woman who fed birds amidst the Old Town rubble after World War II.

Back on Castle Square, find the white **plaque** on the wall (at plac Zamkowy 15). It explains that 50 Poles were executed by Nazis on this spot on September 2, 1944. You'll see plaques like this all over the Old Town, each one commemorating victims or opponents of the Nazis. The brick planter under the plaque is often filled with fresh flowers to honor the victims.

• *Leave the square at the far end, on* **St. John's Street** *(Świętojańska). On the plaque under the street name sign, you can guess what the dates mean, even if you don't know Polish: This building was constructed from 1433 to 1478, destroyed in 1944, and rebuilt from 1950 to 1953.*

Partway down the street on the right, you'll come to the big brick...

Cathedral of St. John the Baptist (Katedra Św. Jana Chrzciciela)

This cathedral-basilica is the oldest (1370) and most important church in Warsaw. Superficially unimpressive, the church's own archbishop admitted that it was "modest and poor"—but "the historical events that took place here make it magnificent" (much like Warsaw itself). Poland's constitution was consecrated here on May 3, 1791. Much later, this church became the final battle-ground of the 1944 Warsaw Uprising—when a Nazi "tracked mine" (a huge bomb on tank tracks—this one appropriately named *Goliath*) drove into the church and exploded, massacring the rebels. You can still see part of that tank's tread hanging on the outside wall of the church (through the passage on the right side, between the buttresses near the end of the church).

Cost and Hours: Cathedral—free, crypt—5 zł, both open to tourists Mon-Sat 10:00-17:00, Sun from 15:00, closed during services and summertime organ concerts (see "Entertainment in Warsaw," later).

Visiting the Cathedral: Head inside. Typical of brick churches, it has a "hall church" design, with three naves of equal height. In the back-left corner, find the chapel with the tomb of Cardinal Stefan Wyszyński—the great Polish leader who, as Warsaw's archbishop, morally steered the country through much of the Cold War. (Notice the request to pray for his beatification, as Poles would love to see him become a saint.) Nearby, the crypt holds graves of several important Poles, including Stanisław August Poniatowski (the last Polish king) and Nobel Prize-winning author Henryk Sienkiewicz. Then head up the nave to the main altar, which holds a copy of the Black Madonna—proclaimed "everlasting queen of Poland" after a victory over the Swedes in the 17th century. The original Black Madonna is in Częstochowa (125 miles south of Warsaw)—a mecca for Slavic Catholics, who visit in droves in hopes of a miracle. In the chapel left of the high altar, look for the crucifix ornamented with real human hair.

• *Continue up the street and enter Warsaw's grand...*

Old Town Market Square (Rynek Starego Miasta)

For two centuries, this was a gritty market square. Sixty-five years ago, it was a pile of bombed-out rubble. And today, like a phoenix from the ashes, it's risen to remind residents and tourists alike of the prewar glory of the Polish capital (which is why it's rated ▲▲).

Head to the **mermaid fountain** in the middle of the square. The mermaid is an important symbol in Warsaw—you'll see her everywhere. Legend has it that a mermaid *(syrenka)* lived in the Vistula River and protected the townspeople. While this siren supposedly serenaded the town, she's most appreciated for her strength (hence the sword). This square seems to declare that life goes on in Warsaw, as it always has. Children frolic here, oblivious to the turmoil their forebears withstood.

When the fountain gurgles, the kids giggle. People enjoy cranking the old well until it spurts.

Each of the square's four sides is named for a prominent 18th-century Varsovian: Kołłątaj, Dekert, Barss, and Zakrzewski. These men served as "Presidents" of Warsaw (mayors, more or less), and Kołłątaj was also a framer of Poland's 1791 constitution. Take some time to explore the square. Enjoy the colorful architecture. Notice that many of the buildings were intentionally built to lean out into the square—to approximate the higgledy-piggledy wear and tear of the original buildings.

If you'd like to learn more about Warsaw's history, visit the Museum of Warsaw on the Dekert (north) side of the square (described later, under "Sights in Warsaw").

• *Exit the square on Nowomiejska (at the mermaid's 2 o'clock, next to the Museum of Warsaw, under the second-story niche sculpture of St. Anne). After a block, you'll reach the **barbican** (barbakan). This defensive gate of the Old Town, similar to Kraków's, protected the medieval city from invaders. Once you've crossed through the barbican, you're officially in Warsaw's...*

New Town (Nowe Miasto)

This 15th-century neighborhood is "new" in name only: It was the first part of Warsaw to spring up outside the city walls (and is therefore slightly newer than the Old Town). The New Town is a fun place to wander: only a little less charming than the Old Town, but with a more real-life feel—people live and work here. You can walk two blocks to reach its centerpiece—the **New Town Square** (Rynek Nowego

Miasta)—watched over by the distinctive green dome of St. Kazimierz Church.

Scientists might want to pay homage at the museum (and birthplace) of Warsaw native **Marie Skłodowska-Curie,** a.k.a. Madame Curie (1867-1934); it's along the street between the New Town Square and the barbican. This Nobel Prize winner was the world's first radiologist—discovering both radium and polonium (named for her native land) with her husband, Pierre Curie. Since she lived at a time when Warsaw was controlled by oppressive Russia, she conducted her studies in France. The museum—with photos, furniture, artifacts, and a paucity of English information—is a bit of a snoozer, best left to true fans (11 zł, Tue-Sun 9:00-16:30, closed Mon, ulica Freta 16, tel. 22-831-8092, www.muzeum-msc.pl).

• *Our walk is finished. You can head back the way you came to reach the Old Town Square to snap some photos or nurse an overpriced drink. Or, to see a side of the Old Town that many tourists miss, consider this scenic detour back to Castle Square.*

From the Barbican to Castle Square

Go back through the barbican and over the little bridge, turn right, and walk along the houses that line the inside of the wall. You'll pass a leafy garden courtyard on the left—a reminder that people actually live in the tourist zone within the Old Town walls. Just beyond the garden on the right, look for the carpet-beating rack, used to clean rugs (these are common fixtures in people's backyards). Go left into the square called Szeroki Dunaj ("Wide Danube") and look for another mermaid (over the Thai restaurant). Continue through the square and turn right at Wąski Dunaj ("Narrow Danube"). After about 100 yards, you'll pass the city wall. Just to the right (outside the wall), you'll see the monument to the **Little Upriser** of 1944, a child wearing a grown-up's helmet and too-big boots, and carrying a machine gun. Children—especially Scouts (Harcerze)—played a key role in the resistance against the Nazis. Their job was mainly carrying messages and propaganda.

Now continue around the wall (the upper, inner part is more pleasant). Admire more public art as you head back to Castle Square.

Sights in Warsaw

THE OLD TOWN

These sights are linked by my "Old Town Walk," earlier.

▲▲Royal Castle (Zamek Królewski)

Warsaw's Royal Castle, dominating Castle Square at the entrance to the Old Town, has the most opulent interior in Poland. Many of its furnishings are original (hidden away when it became clear the

city would be demolished in World War II). A visit to the castle is like perusing a great Polish history textbook. In fact, you'll likely see grade-school classes sitting cross-legged on the floors. Watching the teachers quizzing eager young history buffs, try to imagine what it's like to be a young Pole growing up in a country with such a tumultuous history. Wednesday is a good day to visit—it's free, and although some royal rooms are closed, enough are open to make a visit worthwhile.

Cost and Hours: 30 zł, free on Wed (when some royal rooms are closed); open May-Sept Mon-Sat 10:00-18:00, Fri until 20:00, Sun 11:00-18:00; Oct-April Tue-Sat 10:00-16:00, Sun 11:00-16:00, closed Mon; last entry one hour before closing; plac Zamkowy 4, tel. 22-355-5170, www.zamek-krolewski.pl.

Tours: The castle has a well-produced audioguide (17 zł, worth the extra cost) and good English information posted throughout. For the basics, use my commentary to follow the one-way route through the castle.

Services: A public WC is on the courtyard just around the corner of the castle, with more inside and downstairs.

Visiting the Castle: Because the castle visitor route often changes, it's possible you won't see the rooms in this exact order; match the labels in each room to the corresponding text below.

Entering the courtyard, go to the right to buy tickets, then cross to the opposite side to enter. In the lobby, turn left, pass the audioguide-rental room, then follow *Castle Route* signs upstairs.

The first big room is the **Council Chamber,** where a "Permanent Council" consisting of the king, 18 senators, and 18 representatives met to chart Poland's course. Next is the **Great Assembly Hall,** heavy with marble and chandeliers. The statues of Apollo and Minerva flanking the main door are modeled after King

Stanisław August Poniatowski and Catherine the Great of Russia, respectively. (The king enjoyed a youthful romantic dalliance with Catherine on a trip to Russia, and never quite seemed to get over her...much to his wife's consternation, I'm sure.)

From here, you'll pass through the Great Antechamber and do a little loop through some opulent apartments with silk wallpaper and fine paintings. The highlight is three giant canvases by historical painter **Jan Matejko,** each showing a different chapter in Polish history (for more on Matejko, see page 195). First is *Stefan Batory at Pskov,* in which the Polish king negotiates with Ivan the Terrible's envoys to break their siege of a Russian town. Notice the hussars—fearsome Polish soldiers wearing winged armor.

Then, in one big room at the end of this wing, two more Matejko canvases show a high point and a low point in Poland's story: On the left wall, the *Constitution of 3 May 1791* shows the giddy procession (with this castle in the background) heading up the street to the Cathedral of St. John the Baptist to consecrate the first constitution in Europe. But from there, Poland's fortunes tumbled dramatically. On the wall near where you entered, *Rejtan—The Fall of Poland* shows the nobleman Tadeusz Rejtan (on the right) lying in front of a door and pulling his shirt open in violent protest against his colleagues in the Sejm debating the First Partition in 1773, which ceded some Polish territory to neighboring Russia, Prussia, and Austria. Two Partitions later, Poland was erased from the map of Europe for a century and a half.

You'll loop back, passing through a long corridor with royal portraits and busts, then cut through the Great Antechamber again. You'll wind up in the **Marble Room,** with more portraits of Polish greats ringing the top of the room. Above the fireplace is a portrait of Stanisław August Poniatowski (the last Polish king).

From here, step into the **Knights' Hall,** with yet more busts and portraits of VIPs—Very Important Poles. The statue of Chronos—God of time, with the globe on his shoulders—is actually a functioning clock, though now it's stopped at 11:15 to commemorate the exact time in 1944 when the Nazis bombed this palace to bits.

Next, step into the **Throne Room.** Notice the crowned white eagles, the symbol of Poland, decorating the banner behind the throne. The Soviets didn't allow anything royal or aristocratic, so postwar restorations came with crownless eagles. Only after 1989 were these eagles crowned again. Peek into the **Conference**

Room, with portraits of Russia's Catherine the Great, England's George III, and France's Louis XVI—in whose esteemed royal league Stanisław August Poniatowski liked to consider himself.

After four more grand rooms (including the King's Bedroom, with a gorgeous silk canopy over the bed), you'll enter the **Canaletto Room,** filled with canvases of late-18th-century Warsaw painted in exquisite detail by this talented artist. (This Canaletto, also known for his panoramas of Dresden, was the nephew of another more famous artist with the same nickname, known for painting Venice's canals.) Paintings like these helped post-WWII restorers resurrect the city from its rubble. To the left, on the lower wall, the biggest canvas features the view of Warsaw from the Praga district across the river; pick out the few landmarks that are still standing (or, more precisely, have been resurrected). The castle you're in dominates the center of the painting, overlooking the river. Notice the artist's self-portrait in the lower left. Opposite, on the right side of the room, is Canaletto's depiction of the election of Stanisław August Poniatowski as king, in a field outside Warsaw (notice the empty throne in the middle of the group). Among the assembled crowd, each flag represents a different Polish province.

From here, head left of the big "view of Warsaw" painting into the **side chapel,** reserved for the king. In the box to the left of the altar is the heart of Tadeusz Kościuszko, a hero of both the American Revolution and the Polish struggle against the Partitions (for more about the Partitions, see page 10).

As you cross over to the other part of the castle, you'll pass through the **Four Seasons Gallery** (with some fine but faded Gobelin tapestries) before entering a few rooms occupied by the houses of parliament—a reminder that this "castle" wasn't just the king's house, but also the meeting place of the legislature. In the **New Deputies' Chambers,** notice the maps showing Poland's constantly in-flux borders—a handy visual aid for the many school groups that visit here.

After several rooms, you'll reach the grand **Senators' Chamber,** with the king's throne, surrounded by different coats of arms. Each one represents a region that was part of Poland during its Golden Age, back when it was united with Lithuania and its territory stretched from the Baltic to the Black Sea (see the map on the wall). In this room, Poland adopted its 1791 constitution (notice the replica in the display case to the left of the throne).

It was the first in Europe, written soon after America's and just months before France's. And, like the Constitution of the United States, it was very progressive, based on the ideals of the Enlightenment. But when the final Partitions followed in 1793 and 1795, Poland was divided between neighboring powers and ceased to exist as a country until 1918—so the constitution was never fully put into action.

On your way back downstairs, you'll likely be routed through the ground-floor **Gallery of Paintings, Sculpture, and Decorative Arts,** which includes a fine cabinet of silver and crystal, and the 36 paintings of the Lanckroński Collection. It's fine to zip through here quickly, but be sure to slow down in the final room to appreciate two canvases by Rembrandt (both from 1641). *Girl in a Picture Frame* is exactly that—except that she's "breaking the frame" by resting her hands on a faux frame that Rembrandt has painted inside the real one...shattering the fourth wall in a way that was unusual for the time. The other, *A Scholar at His Writing Table,* shows the hirsute academic glancing up from his notes. Circle around behind the canvases to see X-rays of the paintings, which have helped experts better understand the master's techniques.

Other Castle Sights: Consider a detour to the **Kubicki Arcades** (Arkady Kubiciego),

the impressively excavated arcades deep beneath the castle. From the entrance lobby, head downstairs to the area with the cloakroom, bathrooms, and bookshop, then find the long escalator that takes you down to the arcades. It's free to wander the long, cavernous, and newly clean and gleaming space, made elegant by grand drapes.

The **"Tin-Roofed Palace"** (Pałac pod Blachą) features an extensive oriental carpet collection and seven unimpressive apartments of Prince Józef Poniatowski, the king's brother; it's not worth the 15 zł extra.

▲Museum of Warsaw (Muzeum Warszawy)

Four adjoining townhouses on the north side of the Old Town Square have been connected and turned into this in-depth museum that tells the story of Warsaw. While there's too much detail for a casual visitor's attention span, it's well presented and offers some interesting insight into this great city.

Cost and Hours: 20 zł, includes audioguide, free on Tue, open Tue-Sun 10:00-19:00, closed Mon, Rynek Starego Miasta 28–42, tel. 22-277-4300, www.muzeumwarszawy.pl.

Visiting the Museum: The permanent collection, called "Warsaw in 23 Rooms," offers exactly that. Pick up the detailed map and the dense-but-informative audioguide, and head down into the cellars for an orientation to the city's history—with a timeline, lots of graphs, maps, and helpful models of key landmarks. Then head upstairs and weave your way through the labyrinthine collection; your geo-tagged audioguide knows (roughly) where you are and offers commentary.

Back up on the ground floor, in the courtyard, you'll find architectural decorations from city buildings, as well as the original mermaid statue from the square. Then work your way up through four floors: Floor 1 has a photography gallery, paintings of Warsaw, and a model of the Old Town in the late 18th century. Floor 2 features bronzes, silverwork, portraits of important Varsovians, and clothing. Floor 3 has a moving collection of "relics" from the difficult WWII days and a more lighthearted exhibit on "Warsaw packaging"—with nostalgic vintage advertising. Floor 4 features antique clocks and the "Schiele Room"—named not for the artist, but for the local merchant family whose furnishings and personal objects you can see here. You can continue all the way up into the attic ("viewing platform") to look down over the square, and to see panoramas of the Old Town's rooftops.

The museum sporadically presents a poignant 20-minute film (in English) tracing the tragic WWII experience of this city—from a thriving interwar metropolis, to a bombed-out wasteland, to the focus of a massive rebuilding effort. Ask at the entrance if an English showing of this film is scheduled during your visit.

NEAR PALM TREE CIRCLE

These sights are in the city center, near Palm Tree Circle—where Jerusalem Avenue crosses Nowy Świat.

East of the Royal Way (Toward the River)
▲▲National Museum (Muzeum Narodowe)

A celebration of underrated Polish artists, this museum offers a surprisingly engaging and—if you follow my tour—concise overview of this country's impressive painters (many of whom are unknown outside their home country). A modern, state-of-the-art exhibition space allows these unsung canvases to really belt it out. Polish and other European artists are displayed side by side, as if to assert Poland's worthiness on the world artistic stage. After seeing a few of the masterpieces here, you won't disagree.

Cost and Hours: 20 zł, more for temporary exhibits, permanent collection free on Tue; Tue-Sun 10:00-18:00, Fri until 21:00, closed Mon, last entry 45 minutes before closing; audioguide-10 zł;

WARSAW

one block east of Nowy Świat at aleja Jerozolimskie 3, tel. 22-629-3093, www.mnw.art.pl.

➲ Self-Guided Tour: The collection fills several separate galleries. The museum's strongest point—and the bulk of this tour—is its 19th-century Polish art. But before diving in, consider some of the other collections.

Overview: To get your bearings, pick up a floor plan as you enter. On the ground floor are Ancient Art (from Greek pieces to artifacts left by early Polish tribes); Gallery Faras (highlighting the museum's fine collection of archaeological findings from that ancient Egyptian city); and a good collection of Medieval Art, which gathers altarpieces from churches around Poland—organized both chronologically and geographically—and displays some of the most graphic crucifixes and pietàs I've seen.

Upstairs is the excellent Gallery of 19th-Century Art (described next), which flows into the Old Polish and European Portrait Gallery. Nearby, through the gift shop, is the worthwhile 20th- and 21st-Century Art collection, with an impressive array of Modern and Postmodern Polish artists, including photographers and filmmakers. The underwhelming Old European Painting collection (pre-19th-century) is split up among all three floors.

To cut to the chase, focus on the **Gallery of 19th-Century Art.** We'll start with the granddaddy of Polish art, Jan Matejko.

• *From the entrance lobby, head up the left staircase, then turn left across the mezzanine and enter the collection. Matejko is hiding at the far end of this wing: Entering the collection, angle right, then straight, heading all the way to the room at the far end, which is dominated by a gigantic battlefield canvas. (If you get lost, ask the attendants, "mah-TAY-koh?")*

Jan Matejko: While not the most talented of artists—he's a fairly conventional painter, lacking a distinctive, recognizable style—Matejko more than made up for it with vision and productivity. His typically super-sized paintings are steeped in proud Polish history. Matejko's biggest work here—in fact, the biggest canvas in the whole building—is the enormous **Battle of Grunwald.** This epic painting commemorates one of Poland's high-water marks: the dramatic victory of a Polish-Lithuanian army over the Teutonic Knights, who had been terrorizing northern Poland for decades (for more on the Teutonic Knights, see page 303). On July 15, 1410, some 40,000 Poles and Lithuanians (led by the sword-waving Lithuanian in red, Grand Duke Vytautas) faced off against 27,000 Teutonic Knights (under their Grand Master, in white) in one of the medieval world's bloodiest battles. Matejko plops us right in the thick of the battle's climax, painting life-size figures and framing off a 32-foot-long slice of the two-mile battle line.

In the center of the painting, the Teutonic Grand Master is about to become a shish kebab. Duke Vytautas leads the final

Jan Matejko (1838-1893)

Jan Matejko (yawn mah-TAY-koh) is Poland's most important painter, period. In the mid- to late-19th century, the nation of Poland had been dissolved by foreign powers, and Polish artists struggled to make sense of their people's place in the world. Rabble-rousing Romanticism seemed to have failed (inspiring many brutally suppressed uprisings), so Polish artists and writers turned their attention to educating the people about their history, with the goal of keeping their traditions alive.

Matejko was at the forefront of this so-called positivist movement. He saw what the tides of history had done to Poland and was determined to make sure his countrymen learned from it. He painted two types of works: huge, grand-scale epics depicting monumental events in Polish history; and small, intimate portraits of prominent Poles. Polish schoolchildren study history from books with paintings of virtually every single Polish king—all painted by the incredibly prolific Matejko.

Matejko is admired not for his technical mastery (he's an unexceptional painter) or for the literal truth of his works—he was notorious for fudging historical details to give his canvases a bit more propagandistic punch. But he is revered for the emotion behind—and inspired by—his works. His paintings are utilitarian, straightforward, and dramatic enough to stir the patriot in any Pole. The intense focus on history by Matejko and other positivists is one big reason why today's Poles are still so in touch with their heritage.

You'll see Matejko's works in Warsaw's National Museum and Royal Castle, as well as in Kraków's Gallery of 19th-Century Polish Art (above the Cloth Hall). You can also visit his former residence in Kraków.

charge. And waaaay up on a hill (in the upper-right corner, on horseback, wearing a silver knight's suit) is Władysław Jagiełło, the first king of the Jagiellonian dynasty...ensuring his bloodline will survive another 150 years.

Matejko spent three years covering this 450-square-foot canvas in paint. The canvas was specially made in a single seamless piece. This was such a popular work that almost as many fans turned out for its unveiling as there are figures in the painting. On the TV nearby, you can see how the vast painting was recently restored.

From Poland's high point in the *Battle of Grunwald*, look on the right wall for another, much smaller Matejko canvas, ***Stańczyk,*** to see how Poland's fortunes shifted drastically a century later. This more intimate portrait depicts a popular Polish figure: the court jester Stańczyk, who's smarter than the king, but not allowed to say so. This complex character, representing the national conscience, is a favorite symbol of Matejko's. Stańczyk slumps in gloom. He's just read the news (on the table beside him) that the city of Smolensk has fallen to the Russians after a three-year siege (1512-1514). The jester had tried to warn the king to send more troops, but the king was too busy partying (behind the curtain). The painter Matejko—who may have used his own features for Stańczyk's face—also blamed the nobles of his own day for fiddling while Poland was partitioned.

More Matejkos fill this room. Just to the right of *Stańczyk* is a self-portrait of the gray-bearded artist (compare their features), then a painting of the hoisting of the Sigismund Bell to the cathedral tower in Kraków (it's still there). Farther right, you'll see Matejko's portraits of his children and his wife.

On the final wall is a smaller but very dramatic scene, *The Sermon of Piotr Skarga.* In the upper-right corner, this charismatic, early-17th-century Jesuit priest waves his arms to punctuate his message: Poland's political system is broken. Skarga is addressing fat-cat nobles and the portly King Sigismund II Vasa (seated and wearing a ruffled collar), who were acting in their own self-interests instead of prioritizing what was best for Poland. Notice that Skarga's audience isn't hearing his ravings—they seem bored, bugged, or both. The king is even taking a nap. They should have listened: Poland's eventual decline is often considered the fault of its unworkable political system. After the Partitions, the ahead-of-his-time Skarga was rehabilitated as a visionary who should have been heeded. Notice that, like Stańczyk, Skarga is a self-portrait of Matejko.

• *Leaving Matejko, we'll pass through several more rooms of lesser-known Polish painters to the opposite wing, where we'll meet several of Matejko's students—each of whom developed his own style and left his mark on the Polish art world. On the way, I'll point out a few canvases worth a pause.*

Other Polish Painters: First, head back down the long corridor the way you came (passing some Matejko copycats), cutting through a corner of the Portrait Gallery. When you reach the door you came in, bear right to stay inside the gallery. At the end of that first, large room, you'll find some battle scenes by **Józef Brandt**—the only painter who rivaled Matejko in capturing epic warfare on canvas. Many of Brandt's scenes focus on confronting an enemy from the east, which was Poland's lot for much of its history. His biggest work here, *Rescue of Tatar Captives,* is typical of his scenes.

Continue straight into the next room, with some fine landscape scenes. This room (the partition in the middle) also has works by the talented **Józef Chełmoński:** *Indian Summer* and (around back) *Storks*—a young boy and his grandfather look to the sky, as a formation of storks flies overhead.

Turn right and go through one more long room, watching for **Aleksander Gierymski**'s small, evocative, personality-filled *Jewish Woman Selling Oranges* (on the left wall).

• *You'll emerge into a big room that kicks off the collection of...*

Młoda Polska: Matejko's pupils took what he taught them and incorporated the Art Nouveau styles that were emerging around Europe to create a new movement called "Young Poland" (see page 49). This room features works by two of the movement's big names.

On the left wall are paintings by **Jacek Malczewski,** some of them depicting the goateed, close-cropped artist in a semisurrealistic, Polish countryside context. Malczewski painted more or less realistically, but enjoyed incorporating one or two subtle, symbolic elements evocative of Polish folkloric tradition—magical realism on canvas. *The Death of Ellenai* (1907) shows the pivotal scene in Juliusz Słowacki's epic 1838 poem, *Anhelli,* in which a young nobleman exiled from Poland during the Partitions is forced to make his way through the wastelands of Siberia. When his young and idealistic travel companion, Ellenai, perishes, Anhelli kisses her feet and abandons all hope.

Most of the works on the opposite wall are by **Józef Mehoffer,** who paints with brighter colors in a more stylized form, with more abstraction. Mehoffer's hypnotic *Strange Garden* is a bucolic vision of blue-clad Mary Poppinses, nude cherubs, lots of flowers... and a gigantic, hovering, golden dragonfly that places the otherwise plausible scene in the realm of pure fantasy. In the middle of the room, the small version of Auguste Rodin's *The Kiss* reminds us how this emotion-conveying style, called Symbolism, was also finding expression elsewhere in Europe.

The next room, at the end of the hall, features some lesser-known painters from the age. Among these, **Olga Boznańska**'s works are worth lingering over: gauzy, almost Impressionistic portraits that skillfully capture the humanity of each subject.

Head back into the Malczewski/Mehoffer room and find the small, darkened adjoining rooms. The first one features additional Malczewski paintings; the second is a treasure trove of works by the founder and biggest talent of Młoda Polska, **Stanisław Wyspiański.** The specific items in this room are subject to change—as Kraków, which owns the best collection of hometown boy Wyspiański, shuffle his works in and out of special exhibitions—but you'll likely see both paintings and pastel works by this Art Nouveau juggernaut. Wyspiański also designed stage sets and redecorated some important churches; some of the large pastel-on-paper works you may see here were used as studies for those proj-

WARSAW

ects. And you'll likely see some self-portraits and portraits of his wife and children.

Pondering the works here—and throughout the museum—think about how such a talented artist from a small country can be left out of textbooks across the ocean.

Chopin Museum (Muzeum Fryderyka Chopina)

The reconstructed Ostrogski Castle houses this slick museum honoring Poland's most famous composer, with manuscripts, letters, and original handwritten compositions by the composer. Unfortunately, the museum's high-tech gadgetry does more to distract from this rich collection of historic artifacts than to bring it to life. While Chopin devotees may find it riveting, those with only a passing familiarity with the composer may leave feeling like they still don't know much about this Polish cultural giant.

Cost and Hours: 22 zł, free (and crowded) on Sun, open Tue-Sun 11:00-20:00, closed Mon, last entry 45 minutes before closing, 3 blocks east of Nowy Świat at ulica Okólnik 1, tel. 22-441-6251, www.chopin. museum.

Visiting the Museum: You'll be given an electronic card; tap it against glowing red dots to access additional information. You'll proceed more or less chronologically through the composer's life, with various opportunities to hear his compositions. Beginning in the cellars, you'll learn about Chopin's early life in Żelazowa Wola and Warsaw, and find listening stations where you can nurture your appreciation of Chopin by listening to his music.

Then you'll head upstairs into the mansion, with a replica of Chopin's drawing room in Paris, and his last piano, which he used for composing during the final two years of his life (1848-1849). Exhibits here trace themes of the composer's life, such as the women he knew (including his older sister Ludwika, his mother, and George Sand—the French author who took a male pseudonym in order to be published, and who was romantically linked with Chopin). The second floor recounts Chopin's travels around Europe.

Concerts: Under the palace is a **concert hall,** which hosts performances by students (call museum to reserve a space—only 70 seats available; usually Oct-July Thu at 18:00, and typically free).

Nearby: The park next to the museum surrounds the Chopin

University of Music; hanging out here, you'll often hear students rehearsing inside.

Other Chopin Sight: The composer's tourable **birth house** is in a park in Żelazowa Wola, 34 miles from Warsaw. While interesting to Chopin devotees, it's not worth the trek for most. On summer weekends, the Chopin Museum sometimes runs a handy bus to the house—ask at the museum (departs from Marszałkowska street, 30 minutes each way; 9 zł for the bus, 23 zł for the park and birth house; birth house open Tue-Sun 9:00-19:00, Oct-March until 17:00, closed Mon year-round, tel. 46-863-3300).

▲▲Copernicus Science Center (Centrum Nauki Kopernik)

This facility, a wonderland of completely hands-on scientific doodads that thrill kids and kids-at-heart, is a futuristic romper room. Filling two floors of an industrial-mod, purpose-built space, this is Warsaw's best family activity. Exhibits are described in both Polish and English, and there are frequent demonstrations and special events—ask when you buy your ticket or check their website.

Cost and Hours: 31 zł, 21 zł for kids 19 and under, slightly more on weekends, open Tue-Fri 9:00-18:00, Sat-Sun 10:00-19:00, closed Mon, typically opens one hour earlier April-June and closes one hour later July-Aug, last entry one hour before closing, Wybrzeże Kościuszkowskie 20, tel. 22-596-4100, www.kopernik.org.pl.

Crowd-Beating Tips: This popular attraction can be busy on weekends and school holidays. If you anticipate crowds, book ahead on their website to secure your preferred entry time. On weekdays, it's generally no problem to walk right in.

Getting There: It's an easy downhill walk from Warsaw's Royal Way, but the hike back up is fairly steep. Near the modern bridge—about a five-minute walk from the museum—are a Metro stop and a bus stop (both called Centrum Nauki Kopernik). From here, bus #102 goes to Nowy Świat, then up the Royal Way (Uniwersytet and Zachęta stops) before heading west to the Warsaw Uprising Museum. Metro line 2 connects the science center to the National Stadium, the Royal Way (near the Copernicus statue), and the Warsaw Uprising Museum.

Visiting the Center: The science center is a sprawling, two-floor playhouse of hands-on, interactive exhibits. The specifics are always in flux, so pick up a map as you enter and just enjoy exploring. Kids love trying out the various tools and machines, playing with the air cannons, looking at themselves in the funhouse mirrors, and running a slinky down an inclined treadmill. On the main floor there's a special area for kids under 5 (called "Buzzz!"). There's also a section for teens called "RE: Generation," which uses touchscreens to investigate the biological underpinnings of emotion—from what makes you laugh to what grosses you out—and examines how cultures around the world are both similar and different.

Attached to the center is the **"Heavens of Copernicus" planetarium.** Inside is an exhibit that's covered by your entry ticket, but you'll pay extra for a show (3-D shows—27 zł for adults, 21 zł for kids 19 and under; cheaper for 2-D shows, in Polish with English headset, show starts at the top of each hour—ask for schedule at ticket desk).

Nearby: The riverside embankment near the center has a few areas that are fun to stroll; it was created when the busy riverfront highway was rerouted into an underground tunnel. From here you have good views of the modern Holy Cross Bridge (Most Świętokrzyski) and the National Stadium, proudly wrapped in the patriotic red and white of the Polish flag. These riverbanks are a popular hangout by day and after dark; in the summer, a stroll along here reveals a world of picnics, family outings, and impromptu parties.

West of the Royal Way (near Centralna Station)
Palace of Culture and Science
(Pałac Kultury i Nauki, or PKiN)

This massive skyscraper, dating from the early 1950s, is the tallest building between Frankfurt and St. Petersburg (760 feet with the spire, though several new buildings are threatening to eclipse that peak). While you can ride the lift to its top for a commanding view, the highlight is simply viewing it up close from ground level.

Viewing the Skyscraper: This building was a "gift" from Stalin that the people of Warsaw couldn't refuse. Varsovians call it "Stalin's Penis"...using cruder terminology than that. (There are seven such "Stalin Gothic" erections in Moscow.) If it feels like an Art Deco Chicago skyscraper, that's because the architect was inspired by the years he spent studying and working in Chicago in the 1930s. Because it was to be "Soviet in substance, Polish in style," Soviet architects toured Poland to absorb local culture before starting the project. Notice the frilly decorative friezes that top each level—evocative of Poland's many Renaissance buildings (such as Kraków's Cloth Hall). The clock was added in 1999 as part of the millennium celebrations. Since the end of communism, the younger generation doesn't mind the structure so much—and some even admit to liking it for the way it enlivens the predictable glass-and-steel skyline springing up around it.

Everything about the Pałac is big. Approach it from the east side (facing the busy Marszałkowska street and the slick Galeria Centrum shopping mall). Stand in front of the granite tribune where communist VIPs surveyed massive May Day parades and pageantry on the once-imposing square, which today holds a sloppy parking lot. From there, size up the skyscraper—its grand entry flanked by massive statues of Copernicus on the right (science) and the great poet Mickiewicz on the left (culture). It's designed to show off the strong, grand-scale Soviet aesthetic and architectural skill. The Pałac contains various theaters (the culture), museums of evolution and technology (the science), a congress hall, a multiplex (showing current movies), an observation deck, and lots of office space. With all this Culture and Science under one Roof, it's a shame that only the ground-floor lobby (which feels like stepping into 1950s Moscow and is free to enter) and the 30th-floor observatory deck are open to the public.

Observation Deck: You can zip up to the "XXX Floor" in 20 seconds on the retrofitted Soviet elevators—but the trip is overpriced and the view's a letdown (20 zł, daily 10:00-20:00, may be open later in summer, enter through main door on east side of Pałac—opposite from Centralna station, tel. 22-656-7600, www.pkin.pl).

Złote Tarasy Shopping Mall

Tucked behind Centralna station, "Golden Terraces" is a supermodern shopping mall with a funky, undulating glass-and-steel roof. No, you didn't come all the way to Poland to visit a shopping mall. But if you're at the station, crossing the street to peek in here offers a taste of Poland's race into the future.

Hours: Mon-Sat 9:00-22:00, Sun 9:00-21:00, lots of designer shops, food court on top level, www.zlotetarasy.pl.

Złota 44

This skyscraper, with its dramatic swooping lines rising high from the Złote Tarasy shopping mall, was designed by world-renowned architect Daniel Libeskind (who also redeveloped the 9/11 site in New York City). Born in Poland, at a very young age Libeskind emigrated with his family to the US, returning only recently to embark on this project. Its shape evokes an eagle (a symbol for Poland) just beginning to take flight. Of all the shiny new towers popping

WARSAW

up in Warsaw's skyline, this is the most architecturally interesting—and offers a striking counterpoint to the Stalinist Palace of Culture and Science nearby. (For more on the building, visit www.zlota44.com/en.)

JEWISH WARSAW

In the early 1600s, an estimated 80 percent of all Jews lived in Poland—then the largest country in Europe. But after centuries of dwelling in relative peace in tolerant and pragmatic Poland, Warsaw's Jews suffered terribly at the hands of the Nazis. Several sights in Warsaw commemorate those who were murdered, and those who fought back. Because the Nazis leveled the ghetto, there is literally nothing left except the street plan, some monuments, and the heroic spirit of its former residents. However, the top-notch Museum of the History of Polish Jews—which opened in 2014—has rejuvenated the area, making it a magnet for those interested in this chapter of Polish history.

Getting There: To reach Ghetto Heroes Square and the museum from the Old Town, you can hop a **taxi** or **Uber** (10 zł) or take a **bus** (to the Nalewki-Muzeum stop; bus #180 is particularly useful; bus #111 reaches this stop from farther south—Piłsudski Square, the university, and the National Museum). You can also **walk** there in about 15 minutes: Go through the barbican gate two blocks into the New Town, turn left on Świętojerska, and walk straight 10 minutes—passing the green-glass Supreme Court building. En route, at the corner of Świętojerska and Nowiniarska, watch for the pattern of bricks in the sidewalk, marking *Ghetto Wall 1940-1943.*

▲Ghetto Heroes Square (Plac Bohaterow Getta)

The square is in the heart of what was the Jewish ghetto—now surrounded by bland Soviet-style apartment blocks. After the uprising, the entire ghetto was reduced to dust by the Nazis, leaving the communists to rebuild to their own specifications. Today the district is called Muranów ("Rebuilt").

The **monument** in the middle of the square commemorates those who fought and died "for the dignity and freedom of the Jewish Nation, for a free Poland, and for the liberation of humankind." The statue features heroic Jewish men who knew that an inglorious death at the hands of the Nazis awaited them. Flames in the background show Nazis burning the ghetto. The opposite side features a sad procession of Jews trudging to concentration camps, with subtle Nazi bayonets and helmets moving things along.

As you face the monument, look through the trees to the right to see a seated statue. **Jan Karski** (1914-2000) was a Catholic Pole and resistance fighter who traveled extensively through Poland during the Nazi occupation, collected evidence, and then reported on the Warsaw Ghetto and the Holocaust to the leaders of the Western Allies (including a personal meeting with FDR). In 1944, while the Holocaust was still going on, Karski published his eyewitness account, *The Story of a Secret State* (which you can see on this statue's armrest). After the war he became a US citizen, and in 2012 President Barack Obama awarded him a posthumous Presidential Medal of Freedom.

• *The huge, glassy building facing the monument from across the square is the...*

▲▲▲Museum of the History of Polish Jews (Muzeum Historii Żydów Polskich, a.k.a. POLIN)

This world-class attraction thoughtfully traces the epic, millennium-long story of Jews in Poland. This is not a "Holocaust museum;" rather, it provides stirring, comprehensive documentation of the very rich Polish Jewish experience across the centuries. In-depth, engaging, vividly illustrated, and eloquently presented, the exhibits present a powerful context for the many Jewish cul-

tural sites around Poland—offering insights both for people familiar with the story and for beginners. The museum is at once expansive and intimate, with ample descriptions, videos, and touchscreens; you could spend all day here, but two hours is the minimum. It wins my vote for the best museum in Poland, and it's easily Europe's best Jewish museum—and a strong contender for the best European historical museum, period. The building also hosts cultural events and temporary exhibits.

Cost and Hours: Core exhibition—25 zł, more for temporary exhibits, Mon and Thu-Fri 10:00-18:00, Wed and Sat-Sun 10:00-20:00, closed Tue, last entry 2 hours before closing, essential audioguide-10 zł, cafeteria, Anielewicza 6, tel. 22-471-0300, www.polin.pl.

Visiting the Museum: Before entering, view the building's striking **exterior** (designed by Finnish architect Rainer Mahlamäki).

Warsaw's Jews and the Ghetto Uprising

From the Middle Ages until World War II, Poland was a relatively safe haven for Europe's Jews. While other kings were imprisoning and deporting Jews in the 14th century, the progressive king Kazimierz the Great welcomed Jews into Poland, even granting them special privileges (see page 47).

By the 1930s, there were more than 380,000 Jews in Warsaw—nearly a third of the population (and the largest concentration of Jews in any European city). The Nazis arrived in 1939. Within a year, they had pushed all of Warsaw's Jews into one neighborhood and surrounded it with a wall, creating a miserably overcrowded ghetto (crammed with an estimated 460,000 people, including many from nearby towns). There were nearly 600 such ghettos in cities and towns all over Poland.

By the summer of 1942, more than a quarter of the Jews in the ghetto had either died of disease, committed suicide, or been murdered. The Nazis started moving Warsaw's Jews (at the rate of 5,000 a day) into what they claimed were "resettlement camps." Most of these people—300,000 in all—were actually murdered at Treblinka or Auschwitz. Finally, the waning population—now about 60,000—began to get word from concentration camp escapees about what was actually going on there. Spurred by this knowledge, Warsaw's surviving Jews staged a dramatic uprising.

On April 19, 1943, the Jews attacked Nazi strongholds. The overwhelming Nazi war machine—which had rolled over much of Europe—imagined they'd be able to put down the rebellion easily. Instead, they struggled for a month to finally crush the Ghetto Uprising. The ghetto's residents and structures were "liquidated." About 300 of Warsaw's Jews survived, thanks in part to a sort of "underground railroad" of courageous Varsovians.

Warsaw's Jewish sights are emotionally moving, but even more so if you know some of their stories. You may have heard of **Władysław Szpilman,** a Jewish concert pianist who survived the war with the help of Jews, Poles, and even a Nazi officer. Szpilman's life story was turned into the highly acclaimed, Oscar-winning film *The Pianist,* which powerfully depicts events in Warsaw during World War II.

Less familiar to non-Poles—but equally affecting—is the story of Henryk Goldszmit, better known by his pen name, **Janusz Korczak.** Korczak wrote imaginative children's books that are still enormously popular among Poles. He worked at an orphanage in the Warsaw ghetto. When his orphans were sent off to concentration camps, the Nazis offered the famous author a chance at freedom. Korczak turned them down, choosing to die at Treblinka with his children.

You'll enter (and go through a security checkpoint) at the large, asymmetrical hole in the side of the building. Once you're inside, the symbolism becomes clear: This represents Moses parting the Red Sea. (While the main exhibit covers the thousand years of Jews in Poland, this sets the stage by going back even further—to the Jewish origin story.)

Buy your tickets for the core exhibition and rent the invaluable 60-stop audioguide, which helps provide a concise structure for your exploration of the sprawling exhibitions. Then head downstairs and follow the one-way route. In this high-tech, interactive space, exhibits in eight galleries mingle with actual artifacts to bring history to life.

You'll begin by passing through a simulated forest—evocative of legends about the Jews' arrival in Poland—to reach the **First Encounters** exhibit. Here you'll learn how Jewish merchants made their way to Poland in the 10th century (with maps of their trade routes and samples of what they sold). The story is told partly from the perspective of Ibrahim ibn Yakub, a Sephardic Jew who penned early travelogues about Europe. Look for the display case that holds a coin from the ninth century, with Hebrew characters, that was minted in Poland. In 1264, Duke Bolesław the Pious—the first of many tolerant Polish rulers—extended rights and protections to his Jewish subjects, allowing them to thrive. In the next room, on the left wall are illustrations of the leading Polish cities of the time, and on the right wall are Polish medieval monarchs, with in-depth explanations of each one's policies toward their Jewish subjects.

Next, the **Paradisus Iudaeorum** explains how, as Jews became more established in Polish society in the 15th and 16th centuries,

they enjoyed better and better living conditions. (Meanwhile, anti-Semites bitterly complained that Poland was becoming a "Jewish Paradise"—the name of this exhibit.) The centerpiece here is a gigantic, interactive model of Kraków and its Jewish quarter, Kazimierz. In the library section, you can flip through virtual pages of books from the era—representing the flourishing of education during this time.

Continuing into the next area, you'll enter a dark hallway that explains the Khmelnytsky Uprising—a mid-17th-century Cossack rebellion against the Polish lords and the Jews who served them. This brought a new wave of pogroms and 10,000 Jewish deaths.

After the uprising, Polish lords invited Jews to privately owned

WARSAW

market towns—called *shtetls*—to help re-establish the economy. **The Jewish Town** offers a fascinating look at different walks of life in a typical Jewish community: the market, where Jews and Christians could mingle at the tavern; the home, where a family would live, work, eat, and sleep in a single room; the cemetery (touchscreens invite you to learn about the symbolism of Jewish tombstones); and the synagogue, with a gloriously colorful replica of a ceiling and bema (prayer platform) from a wooden syna-

gogue from the village of Gwoździec—dripping with symbolism that's explained on nearby touchscreens. An exhibit also traces the mid-18th-century rise of Hasidism—a mystical branch of Judaism—in the eastern Polish lands (today's Ukraine).

With the Partitions of the late 18th century (when Polish territory was divided among neighboring powers), Polish Jews found themselves split among three different empires—symbolized by a room with giant portraits of the rulers of Prussia, Russia, and Austria, all facing the Polish throne. **Encounters with Modernity** examines how Jews in different parts of the Polish lands had very different experiences. You'll see a replica salon of a wealthy Jewish family who mingled with elites, and learn about the debate at that time of what the role of Jews in society should be (illustrated by a fine collection of items from Jewish ceremonies commemorating rites of passage). You'll also learn about the competing movements within Judaism that emerged during this era: Hasidism, led by charismatic Tzadiks who promised a closer spiritual connection to God, and the more reform-minded Haskalah, an intellectual approach inspired by the Enlightenment.

A mesmerizing, painterly film follows a day in the life of a young student at a *yeshiva* (school). A railway station represents the Industrial Revolution, when the world got smaller and brought a new world of opportunities...and of threats. You'll learn how some Jews worked hard to integrate with their dominant cultures (such as the painter Maurycy Gottlieb). This period also saw the emergence of modern anti-Semitism, including a brutal pogrom in Warsaw in 1881. As Jews sought to define a modern Jewish identity in the late 19th century, many emigrated—some to North or South America, and still others to the Holy Land (the beginnings of Zionism).

All of this sets the stage for World War I, when Jews were drafted into various armies—and often forced to fight one another. But at war's end, Poland was reconstituted as an independent nation. You'll step out onto **The Jewish Street,** which re-creates an interwar shopping street from a Jewish community. ("The Jewish Street" was also slang for the Jewish world in general.) It was between the world wars—when a newly independent Poland extended full citizenship and voting rights to its Jewish citizens—that Jewish cultural life flourished as never before. One-third of Poland's population was Jewish—that's three million people. You'll see re-created Warsaw sites relating to newspapers, cinema, writers, and artists; and you'll learn about Jewish tourism of the era (when middle-class Jews would travel around Poland and Europe to visit Jewish cultural sites). Don't miss the mezzanine area upstairs, with exhibits about education and reform—including bilingual schooling (Yiddish and Polish), the beloved educator and author Janusz Korczak, and the debate over "ghetto benches" (segregated seating areas in schools).

However, this was also a time of rising anti-Semitism, segregation, boycotts, and anti-Jewish quotas; during this period, some 140,000 Jews emigrated to the Holy Land. After one more nostalgic stroll down "The Jewish Street," you come to September 1, 1939, when the Nazis invaded Poland. They stripped Jews of their rights and possessions; humiliated, labeled, tortured, and executed them; and eventually implemented the **Holocaust.** The exhibit traces, step by step, the escalation of the Nazis' "Final Solution," with a focus on events here in Warsaw: Forcing Jews into a ghetto (you'll walk across a platform representing the bridge that connected the two parts of the ghetto, offering Jewish people fleeting glimpses of "normal" life going on outside their walls); the liquidation of the ghetto and the movement of Warsaw's Jews to the death camp at Treblinka; and the Ghetto Uprising, a desperate last stand in which the dwindling number or Warsaw's Jews put up a valiant, but ultimately doomed, fight. Making these stories personal are contemporaneous diaries, documents, and photographs.

The exhibit poses difficult questions about how non-Jewish Poles helped—or did not help—the Jews who were gradually disappearing from their cities. And it explains how a sort of "underground railroad" worked at great peril to save as many Jews as possible—as depicted in the movie *The Pianist.* (Look for the chess set carved by a Jew in hiding.) All told, 9 out of every 10 Polish Jews were murdered in the Holocaust. Only about 300,000 survived.

Finally, **The Postwar Years** follows Holocaust survivors in the years just after the war, when, astonishingly, they were scapegoated for war crimes. About 150,000 more (half the total survivors) fled to the newly created state of Israel, and those who remained had to navigate an unfriendly, anti-Semitic communist regime. In 1968, the communists launched an "anti-Zionist" campaign; eventually around 15,000 Polish Jews lost their citizenship and left for Israel, Western Europe, and the US. Not until the fall of communism could the rest finally enter a world of new possibilities. The final room poses a powerful question: Given this rich yet traumatic history, what is the future for Jews in Poland?

The creation of this museum—the first time that the full story of the Jews of Poland has ever been told in such a mainstream way, and in all its epic scope—represents a critical milestone in celebrating a culture that has survived a harrowing history.

Ghetto Walking Tour

For a poignant stroll through what was the ghetto, with faint echoes of a tragic history, take this brief, lightly guided walk for a few blocks. The neighborhood itself is drab and boxy, though increasingly gentrified. It was rebuilt in characterless communist style after it was leveled during the Holocaust. You'll have to work hard to resurrect the memory of what went on here.

Stand along the street facing the monument, with the museum behind it. Turn right and walk along Zamenhofa—which, like many streets in this neighborhood, is named for a hero of the Ghetto Uprising. From here, you'll follow a series of three-foot-tall, black stone memorials to uprising heroes—the **Path of Remembrance.** Like stations of the cross, each recounts an event of the uprising. Every April 19th (the day the uprising began), huge crowds follow this path.

In a block and a half, just beyond the corner of Miła (on the left, partly obscured by some bushes), you'll find a **bunker** where about 100 organizers of the uprising hid (and where they committed suicide when the Nazis discovered them on May 8, 1943).

Continue following the black stone monuments up Zamenhofa (which becomes Dubois), then turn left at the corner, onto broad and busy Stawki. The ugly gray building on your left (a half-block down at #5, near the tram stop) was the **headquarters of the SS** within the ghetto. This is where the transportation of Warsaw's Jews to concentration camps was organized.

Using the crosswalk at the tram stop, cross Stawki and proceed straight ahead into the gap between the two buildings. At the back of this parking lot is a surviving part of the red-brick **ghetto wall,** with a few remaining scraps of 1940s barbed wire.

Farther up Stawki street, on the right, is the finale of this walk: the **Umschlagplatz** monument. That's German for "transfer place," and it marks the spot where the Nazis brought Jewish families to prepare them to be loaded onto trains bound for Treblinka or Auschwitz. This was the actual site of the touching scene in the film *The Pianist* where the grandfather shares bits of chocolate with his family before being forever separated. In the walls of the monument are inscribed the first names of some of the victims.

WARSAW UPRISING SIGHTS

While the 1944 Warsaw Uprising is a recurring theme in virtually all Warsaw sightseeing, two sights in particular—one a monument, the other a museum—are worth a visit for anyone with a special interest. Neither is right along the main tourist trail; the monument is closer to the sightseeing action, while the museum is a subway, tram, or taxi ride away.

Warsaw Uprising Monument

The most central sight related to the Warsaw Uprising is the monument at plac Krasińskich (intersection of ulica Długa and Miodowa, one long block and about a

five-minute walk northwest of the New Town). Larger-than-life soldiers and civilians race for the sewers in a desperate attempt to flee the Nazis. Just behind the monument is the oxidized-copper facade of Poland's Supreme Court.

WARSAW

▲▲Warsaw Uprising Museum
(Muzeum Powstania Warszawskiego)

Thorough, modern, and packed with Polish field-trip groups, this museum celebrates the heroes of the uprising. It's a bit cramped, and finding your way through the exhibits can be confusing, but it works hard to illuminate this complicated chapter of Warsaw's history. The location is inconvenient (a taxi/Uber, Metro, tram, or bus ride west of Centralna station) and, because it takes some time to visit, may not be worth the trek for those with a casual interest. But history buffs find it worthwhile.

Cost and Hours: 25 zł, free on Sun; open Mon and Wed-Fri 8:00-18:00, Thu until 20:00, Sat-Sun 10:00-18:00, closed Tue; tel. 22-539-7947, www.1944.pl.

Audioguide: The informative, two-hour audioguide is ideal if you really want to delve into the whole story (10 zł, rent it in the gift shop). But the museum is so well described, you can just wander aimlessly and be immersed in the hellish events.

Eating: The museum's $ café is oddly pleasant, serving drinks and light snacks amidst genteel ambience from interwar Warsaw. In summer you can dine on a peaceful terrace. You'll also find a few business lunch-type places in the surrounding office zone.

Getting There: The museum is on the western edge of downtown—a long, dull walk through urban gloom—at ulica Przyokopowa 28. The newly opened Rondo Daszyńskiego Metro stop has been a shot in the arm to this area, which has sprouted a sleek, supermodern zone of office blocks. While it's easiest to reach by taxi or Uber (figure about 10 minutes and 20 zł from the Royal Way), you can get close on public transit. Ride the Metro to Rondo Daszyńskiego, exit toward *Muzeum Powstania Warszawskiego*, walk one block (with the huge traffic circle at your back), turn right on Przyokopowa, and walk another long block to the brick wall surrounding the museum (entrance at far end). You can also reach Rondo Daszyńskiego on bus #178 from Castle Square, bus #105 from the Royal Way (Uniwersytet stop), or bus #109 from Centralna station. There's a slightly closer tram stop, called Muzeum Powstania Warszawskiego, which you can reach on tram #22 or #24 from Centralna station or the street in front of the National Museum.

Visiting the Museum: Buy your ticket at the little house at the far end of the entrance courtyard (marked *kasa*), then head into the main hall. The high-tech main exhibit sprawls across three floors. It tells the story of the uprising chronologically, with a keen focus on military history. The exhibit covers several topics, but doesn't provide a big-picture narrative; to fully understand the context of what you're seeing, read the sidebar before your visit.

As you enter, the **Room of the Little Insurgent** on the right is a children's area, reminding visitors young and old that Varsovian kids played a role in the Warsaw Uprising, too.

The **ground floor** sets the stage with Germany's invasion and occupation of Poland. The Generalgouvernement (Nazi puppet government of occupied Poland, ruled by Hans Frank in Kraków) wasted no time in asserting its control over the Poles; you'll learn how they imprisoned and executed priests, professors, and students. You'll also hear the story of the earlier, smaller uprisings that preceded the Warsaw Uprising, including the Poland-wide Operation Tempest (Burza) in 1943. During those earliest rebellions, Warsaw was intentionally left out of the fray...but only for the time being. The print shop shows how propaganda was spread during the occupation, despite the watchful eye of the Nazis.

To keep with the chronological flow, skip the middle floor for now, and ride the elevator to the **top floor** (#2), which covers the main part of the uprising. You'll meet some of the uprising's heroes and learn about their uniforms, weapons, and methods. The room in the middle, with felt drapes, tells the story of the Wola Massacre, in which some 40,000 residents of that Warsaw neighborhood were executed in just three days. Beyond that, the "Kino Palladium" movie screen shows fascinating Home Army newsreel footage from the period (with English subtitles). To the right of the screen, you'll walk through a simulated sewer, reminiscent of the one that many Home Army soldiers and civilians used to evade the Germans. Imagine terrified troops quietly traversing a sewer

The Warsaw Uprising

By the summer of 1944, it was becoming clear that the Nazis' days in Warsaw were numbered. The Red Army drew near, and by late July, Soviet tanks were within 25 miles of downtown Warsaw.

The Varsovians could simply have waited for the Soviets to cross the river and force the Nazis out. But they knew that Soviet "liberation" would also mean an end to Polish independence. The Polish Home Army numbered 400,000—30,000 of them in Warsaw alone—and was the biggest underground army in military history. The uprisers wanted Poland to control its own fate, and they took matters into their own hands. The symbol of the resistance was an anchor made up of a *P* atop a *W* (which stands for *Polska Walcząca,* or "Poland Fighting"—you'll see this icon all around town). Over time, the Home Army had established an extensive network of underground tunnels and sewers, which allowed them to deliver messages and move around the city without drawing the Nazis' attention. These tunnels gave the Home Army the element of surprise.

On August 1, 30,000 Polish resistance fighters launched an attack on their Nazi oppressors. They poured out of the sewers and caught the Nazis off guard. The ferocity of the Polish fighters stunned the Nazis. But the Nazis regrouped, and within a few days, they had retaken several areas of the city—murdering tens of thousands of innocent civilians as they went. In one notorious incident, some 5,500 Polish soldiers and 6,000 civilians who were surrounded by Nazis in the Old Town were forced to flee through the sewers; many drowned or were shot. (This scene is depicted in the Warsaw Uprising Monument on plac Krasińskich.)

Two months after it had started, the Warsaw Uprising was over. The Home Army called a cease-fire. About 18,000 Polish uprisers had been killed, along with nearly 200,000 innocent civilians. An infuriated Hitler ordered that the city be destroyed—which it was, systematically, block by block, until virtually nothing remained.

Through all this, the Soviets stood still, watched, and waited. When the smoke cleared and the Nazis left, the Red Army marched in and claimed the wasteland that was once called Warsaw. After the war, General Dwight D. Eisenhower said that the scale of destruction here was the worst he'd ever seen. The communists later tracked down the surviving Home Army leaders, killing or imprisoning them.

Depending on whom you talk to, the desperate uprising of Warsaw was incredibly brave, stupid, or a little of both. As for the Poles, they remain fiercely proud of their struggle for freedom. In 2004, 60 years after the uprising, the Warsaw Uprising Museum opened to document and commemorate this tragedy.

line like this one more than a mile long (but with lower ceilings)—and doing it while knee-deep in liquid sewage. At the end of the "sewer," stairs lead down to the middle floor.

The **middle floor** focuses on the grueling aftermath of the uprising. The later days of the uprising are outlined, battle by battle. A chilling section describes how Warsaw became a "city of graves," with burial mounds and makeshift crosses scattered everywhere. One room honors the Field Postal Service, which, at great personal risk, continued mail delivery of both military communiqués and civilian correspondences. Many of these brave "mailmen" were actually Scouts who were too young to fight. Nearby, another room recreates a clandestine radio broadcast station set up in a living room.

If you need a break, look for the red corridor leading through the USSR section to the **café** and WC.

End your visit by walking down the stairs into the **main hall,** which is dominated by two large-scale exhibits: a replica of an RAF Liberator B-24 J, used for airborne surveillance of war-time Warsaw; and a giant movie

screen showing more newsreels assembled by the Home Army's own propaganda unit during the uprising. Under the screen, behind the black curtains, an exhibit tells the story of Germans in Warsaw, along with another, more claustrophobic walk-through sewer.

Also in the main hall, look for the entrance to the seven-minute 3-D film *City of Ruins (Miasto Ruin)*, with virtual aerial footage of the postwar devastation. This gives you a look at the reality of the thousand people (nicknamed "Robinson Crusoes") who lived in bombed-out Warsaw immediately after the war. It's worth waiting in line to see this powerful film.

The **park** surrounding the building features several thought-provoking sights. A Chevy truck armored by the Home Army is both a people's tank and an example of how outgunned they were. Along the back is the Wall of Memory, a Vietnam War Memorial-type monument to soldiers of the Polish Home Army who were killed in action. You'll see their rank and name, followed by their code name, in quotes. The Home Army observed a strict policy of anonymity, forbidding members from calling each other by anything but their code names. The bell in the middle is dedicated to the commander of the uprising, Antoni Chruściel (code name "Monter").

SOUTH OF THE CENTER
▲Łazienki Park (Park Łazienkowski)

The huge, idyllic Łazienki Park (wah-ZHYEN-kee) is where Varsovians go to play. The park is sprinkled with fun Neoclassical buildings, strutting peacocks, and young Poles in love. It was built by Poland's very last king (before the final Partition), Stanisław August Poniatowski, to serve as his summer residence and provide a place for his citizens to relax.

On the edge of the park (along Belwederska) is a **monument to Fryderyk Chopin.** The monument, in a rose garden, is flanked

by platforms, where free summer piano **concerts** of Chopin's music are given weekly (mid-May-late Sept only, generally Sun at 12:00 and 16:00—confirm at TI). The statue shows Chopin sitting under a wind-blown willow tree. Although he spent his last 20 years and wrote most of his best-known music in France, his inspiration came from wind blowing through the willow trees of his native land, Poland. The Nazis were quick to destroy this statue, which symbolizes Polish culture. They melted the original (from 1926) down for its metal. Today's copy was recast after World War II. Savor this spot; it's great in summer, with roses wildly in bloom, and in autumn, when the trees provide a golden backdrop for the black, romantic statue.

Venture down into the ravine and to the center of the park, where (after a 10-minute hike) you'll find King Poniatowski's strik-

ing **Palace on the Water** (Pałac na Wodzie)—literally built in the middle of a river. Nearby, you'll spot a clever amphitheater with seating on the riverbank and the stage on an island. The king was a real man of the Enlightenment, host-ing weekly Thursday dinners here for artists and intellectuals. But Poland's kings are long gone, and proud peacocks now rule this roost.

Łazienki Park is also slated to be the future home of the state-of-the-art **Museum of Polish History,** which is being built along the Łazienkowska highway (near Ujazdów Castle, at the northeastern edge of the park). When it opens—likely 2021 or later—this museum will be yet another big draw for visitors (to check on the progress, see www.en.muzhp.pl).

Getting There: The park is just south of the city center on the Royal Way. Buses #116 and #180 run from Castle Square in the Old Town along the Royal Way directly to the park (get off at the stop called Łazienki Królewskie, by Belweder Palace—you'll see Chopin squinting through the trees on your left). Maps at park entrances locate the Chopin monument, Palace on the Water, and other park attractions.

Shopping in Warsaw

You'll notice that many Varsovians are chic, sophisticated, and very well-dressed. To see where they outfit themselves, go window-shopping. **Mysia 3** is a super-hip mini mall with three concise floors dedicated to mostly Polish fashion designers, but also has cutting-edge housewares and decor (Mon-Sat 10:00-20:00, Sun 12:00-18:00, across Jerusalem Avenue from Nowy Świat, inside the former communist propaganda office at Mysia 3, www.mysia3.pl). Warsaw's main "fashion row" is a bit farther south, in the Śródmieście district. **Mokotowska street,** which angles northeast from trendy plac Zbawiciela, is lined with dozens of chichi boutiques, jewelry shops, shoe stores, designer pastry shops, hair salons, and hipster barbers. The highest concentration is a few short blocks north of plac Zbawiciela, north of Piękna. If you enjoy this zone, the area immediately to the west—along Wilcza and Poznańska streets—has more of the same.

Entertainment in Warsaw

Warsaw fills the summer with live music options. In addition to more serious options (opera, symphony, etc.), consider these crowd-pleasing choices.

CHOPIN

My favorite Warsaw music option is to enjoy a Chopin performance. There's nothing like hearing Chopin's compositions passionately played by a teary-eyed Pole who really feels the music. The best option is the outdoor concert in front of the big Chopin statue in **Łazienki Park,** but it is held only one day a week in summer (free, mid-May-late-Sept generally Sun at 12:00 and 16:00, www.lazienki-krolewskie.pl; for more on this option, see the Łazienki Park listing on page 213).

If you're not in town on a Sunday, the next best thing is the **Chopin Salon.** Jarek Chołodecki, who runs the recommended

Chopin Boutique B&B, hosts an intimate piano concert in his delightful salon nightly at 19:30. The performance can cover a range of musical styles and composers—but generally there are piano pieces featuring Chopin. The concert lasts around 45 minutes and is followed by wine, homemade cakes, and social time. A small group of locals and travelers gathers around Jarek's big shiny Steinway grand to hear great music by talented young artists in a great city (50 zł, ulica Smolna 14, reservations required, tel. 22-829-4801, www.bedandbreakfast.pl).

The **Chopin Museum** has a concert series where music academy students recommended by their professors perform an hour-long concert. These are free and typically take place October through July each Thursday at 18:00 (call ahead to reserve a seat, tel. 22-441-6100, www.en.chopin.nifc.pl).

Additionally, various **touristy Chopin concerts** are popping up all over the city; figure 60 zł for a piano performance set in a drawing room or small theater. Ask your hotel or the TI for the latest fliers.

OTHER MUSIC

Warsaw House of Music, in a refurbished town house along the Royal Way, hosts an even wider range of musical events. The lineup does include some Chopin, but goes beyond touristy cliches to delve into other historical musical forms from Warsaw, including Jewish klezmer music, interwar Polish cabaret songs, Slavic folk songs, and traditional and contemporary jazz (50 zł, daily at 17:00, Nowy Świat 63, tel. 22-692-4824).

Two big, historic churches in and near the Old Town put on 30-minute **organ concerts** most days through the summer. Choose between the Cathedral of St. John the Baptist, with an austere brick interior, right in the heart of the Old Town (15 zł, May-Sept Mon-Sat at 14:00, no concerts Sun); or the frilly, Rococo St. Anne's Church, with a more sumptuous interior, just outside the Old Town (15 zł, May-early Oct Mon-Sat at 12:00, no concerts Sun). Both are run by the same company (mobile 501-158-477, www.kapitula.org).

Free outdoor **jazz concerts** take place each Saturday in summer right on the Old Town Square (July-Aug at 19:00). You'll also spot the outdoor **Jazz Club Akwarium** along the Royal Way, in the park next to the Adam Mickiewicz statue; at this casual venue, music lovers relax in slingback chairs, while serious concerts fill the cellar (music most Thu-Sun nights starting sometime between 19:00 and 21:00, Krakowskie Przedmieście 60A, mobile 664-063-050).

LIVELY HANGOUT ZONES

The Old Town and New Town are totally for tourists. To find some more interesting areas to explore and hang out after dark, your first stop should be **plac Zbawiciela** in the Śródmieście and the surrounding streets (see page 223). Locals also enjoy spending a balmy afternoon or evening on the **Vistula riverbanks.** Long ignored by Varsovians, the left (west) bank has undergone a dramatic renovation, with beautiful parklike embankments ideal for strolling. Meanwhile, the right (east) bank is still rugged and undeveloped, with forests and natural beaches—the biggest being around the eastern base of the Poniatowski Bridge (where Jerusalem Avenue crosses the river).

Sleeping in Warsaw

Because Warsaw is a major business destination, its hotel rates fluctuate from day to day. I've categorized hotels based on estimated prices during busy times, but you may find prices much higher or much lower depending on what's happening in town. Regardless, you'll find Warsaw affordable for a European capital—for what you'd spend on a basic room in Rome or Amsterdam, you can get a palatial room in a top-end hotel here. That said, two of my Warsaw favorites—Chopin Boutique B&B and Duval Apartments— are both affordable and characteristic, making them excellent all-around choices.

I've arranged my listings by neighborhood. For locations, see the map on page 170. Keep in mind that in the Old Town, you'll rarely see a local, while in Śródmieście, you'll rarely see a tourist. Choose your Warsaw experience.

NEAR PALM TREE CIRCLE (NOWY ŚWIAT AND JERUSALEM AVENUE)

Considering how spread out Warsaw is, this is a convenient location for reaching various sights around the city. While comfortable inside, these hotels are in big buildings on uninspiring urban streets.

$$$ Hotel Indigo, part of a high-end chain, surrounds a glassy atrium with 60 posh rooms at reasonable prices. This is a great value for elegance in a central location (breakfast extra, air-con, elevator, Smolna 40, tel. 22-418-8900, www.indigowarsaw.com, reservation@indigowarsaw.com).

$$$ Between Us B&B is an inviting home-away-from-home for hipsters in Warsaw. Beata rents three trendy rooms above a youthful café centrally located in downtown Warsaw, near the bottom end of this price range. As this place books up early, reserve far ahead (on second floor, no elevator, check in at Między Nami

Sleep Code

Hotels are classified based on the average price of a standard double room with breakfast in high season.

$$$$	**Splurge:** Most rooms over 550 zł
$$$	**Pricier:** 400-550 zł
$$	**Moderate:** 250-400 zł
$	**Budget:** 100-250 zł
¢	**Backpacker:** Under 100 zł
RS%	**Rick Steves discount**

Unless otherwise noted, credit cards are accepted, hotel staff speak basic English, and free Wi-Fi is available. Comparison-shop by checking prices at several hotels (on each hotel's own website, on a booking site, or by email). For the best deal, *book directly with the hotel.* Ask for a discount if paying in cash; if the listing includes **RS%,** request a Rick Steves discount.

café downstairs, Bracka 20, tel. 22-828-5417, mobile 603-096-701, www.between-us.eu, info@between-us.eu).

$$ Chopin Boutique B&B offers comfort, class, personality, hospitality, and value in an ideal location. Jarek Chołodecki, who lived near Chicago for many years, returned to Warsaw and converted this beautifully renovated apartment building into a bed-and-breakfast with 30 endearingly creaky, creatively decorated, antique-furnished rooms. Quirky, charming Jarek is a good host (you'll feel like you're staying with your Warsaw sophisticate cousin), and his well-trained staff provide a warm professionalism that's rare at this price range. You'll enjoy breakfast (with locally sourced foods) at big communal tables in the cellar restaurant, escape from the city in the garden courtyard, and have the opportunity to take in a nightly Chopin concert in the ground-floor salon—see "Entertainment in Warsaw," earlier (RS%, elevator, bike rental, ulica Smolna 14, tel. 22-829-4801, www.bedandbreakfast.pl, office@bedandbreakfast.pl).

$$ Zgoda by DeSilva, an impersonal but comfortable apartment hotel, has 51 efficient units designed for business travelers on a tight budget (breakfast extra or use the kitchenette, air-con, elevator, Zgoda 6, tel. 22-553-6200, www.desilva.pl, zgoda@desilva.pl).

$$ Apple Inn, with 10 tight, modern rooms in the attic of a hulking building, is your cheap-and-cheery option in the center (breakfast extra, shared kitchen and library, sometimes unstaffed—clearly communicate your arrival time, Chmielna 21, unit 22B—ride elevator to fourth floor, mobile 601-746-006, www. appleinn.pl, Marta).

¢ **Oki Doki City Hostel,** on a pleasant square a few blocks in front of the Palace of Culture and Science, is colorful, creative, and easygoing. Each of its 37 rooms was designed by a different artist with a special theme—such as Van Gogh, Celtic spirals, heads of state, or Lenin. It's run by Ernest—a Pole whose parents loved Hemingway—and his wife Łucja, with help from their sometimes-jaded staff (private rooms available, plac Dąbrowskiego 3, tel. 22-828-0122, www.okidoki.pl, okidoki@okidoki.pl).

IN ŚRÓDMIEŚCIE ("DOWNTOWN")

Foodies, people who hate tourists, and travelers who really want to disappear into Warsaw choose to sleep in Śródmieście. A 10- to 15-minute walk (or quick tram ride) south of Jerusalem Avenue, it feels urban-residential and very local. And if trendy restaurants are on your agenda, sleeping near the culinary hotspots in Śródmieście is an efficient strategy. Compared to most of my other Warsaw listings, these feel a bit chic and trendy...just right for the neighborhood.

$$$$ Hotel Rialto is a professional-feeling boutique hotel with Art Deco flair—both inside (in the lobby, respected restaurant, and 44 rooms) and out. It's a splurge that feels sophisticated, but without pretense. They plan to add another 100 rooms in the adjacent building (air-con, elevator, Wilcza 73, nearest tram/bus stop at Koszykowa, tel. 22-584-8700, www.rialto.pl, info@rialto.pl).

$$$ Autor Rooms is classy and intimate—a third-floor apartment with four rooms (each one different) and a shared breakfast table. It's off a busy street in an urban jungle just off Constitution Square, but once you're settled in, it's a handy home base (elevator, Lwowska 17, nearest tram/bus stop at plac Konstytucji, mobile 797-992-737, www.autorrooms.pl, hello@autorrooms.pl).

IN OR NEAR THE OLD TOWN

The Old Town area has some fine splurges and easy access to the romantic, rebuilt historic core. But it's less handy to Warsaw's trendier side.

$$$$ Hotel Bristol is Warsaw's top splurge—as much a landmark as a hotel (see description on page 180), this classic address on the Royal Way is where you're likely to spot visiting dignitaries and celebrities. (Just inside the round entrance on the corner, find the wall of brass knobs identifying past VIP guests—from

Pablo Picasso to Ed Sheeran.) The public spaces are palatial, with sumptuous Art Deco lounges, bars, and coffee shops that make you want to dress up just to hang out. And the 206 rooms are fresh, elegant, and well-equipped. If you like a posh home base, check the rates here first—you may be surprised at how affordable opulence can be (air-con, classy old vintage elevator, gym, swimming pool, sauna, Krakowskie Przedmieście 42, tel. 22-551-1000, www. hotelbristolwarsaw.pl, bristol@luxurycollection.com).

$$$ Hotel Le Régina is another tempting splurge, buried in the quiet and charming New Town (just beyond the Old Town). From its elegant public spaces to its 61 top-notch rooms, everything here is done with class (pricey breakfast extra, elevator, exercise room, pool, Kościelna 12, tel. 22-531-6000, www.leregina. com, reception.leregina@mamaison.com).

$$$ Castle Inn, sitting on Castle Square at the entrance to the Old Town, is the next rung up the ladder for youth hostelers who've outgrown the grungy backpacker scene. Run by the owners of Oki Doki Hostel (described earlier), it has 22 creative and colorful rooms, each with different decor (breakfast extra, lots of stairs and no elevator, can be noisy—request quiet room, Świętojańska 2, tel. 22-425-0100, www.castleinn.pl, castleinn@castleinn.pl).

$$ Duval Apartments, named for a French woman who supposedly had an affair with the Polish king in this building, offers four beautifully appointed rooms above a restaurant and teahouse (called Same Fusy) a few steps off the square in the Old Town. Each spacious room has a different theme: traditional Polish, Japanese, glass, or retro. Offering B&B comfort with hotel anonymity, this is an excellent value and one of my Warsaw favorites (lots of stairs with no elevator, breakfast extra, some restaurant noise—light sleepers should request a quiet room, Nowomiejska 10, mobile 608-679-346, www.duval.net.pl, duval@duval.net.pl). Arrange a meeting time with Agnieszka or Marcin when you reserve.

Eating in Warsaw

Warsaw is, quite unexpectedly, one of Eastern Europe's best foodie cities...not that the tourists who stick to the kitschy, conventional, Old Town eateries would know. While there are some fine places in the historic center to sample traditional Polish food, that's better done in Old World Kraków; in Warsaw, don't be shy about exploring some local neighborhoods to find a more eclectic, modern, cosmopolitan food scene. Prices are low, so even a "splurge" restaurant lets you experience high-end experimental cuisine for a fraction of the cost of a similar place in a Western European capital.

But be warned: The food scene here changes at a bewildering pace. What's hot and new one year is shuttered the next. Don't

WARSAW

be surprised if some places I list here are closed when you visit. On the upside, that means there's always something new to check out. Ask around, do some online research (try checking www.warsawfoodie. pl), and find out what's trending right now.

Wherever you dine, most restaurants are open until the "last guest," which usually means about 23:00 (sometimes later in summer)—but can be earlier than expected on slow nights. If dining late, call ahead. For locations, see the map on page 170.

NEAR PALM TREE CIRCLE (NOWY ŚWIAT AND JERUSALEM AVENUE)

These practical options are right in the middle of your sightseeing plans—handy for lunch on the go, or worth going out of your way for to enjoy a memorable dinner. The clientele is a mix of local yuppies, savvy business travelers, and casual tourists smart enough to steer clear of Old Town restaurants.

$$$ Kamanda Lwowska is the best spot in central Warsaw for traditional Polish cooking. It's named for the former Polish city that's now in Ukraine (Lwow, a.k.a. Lviv). It has a few outdoor seats in a parklike setting and a charming, cluttered old cellar with just a touch of kitsch. The friendly and fun staff serves up well-executed Polish classics (daily 10:00-24:00, Foksal 10, tel. 22-828-1031). The street between here and Nowy Świat, called Foksal, is lined with an ever-changing lineup of lively, contemporary eateries where diners cram the al fresco tables.

$$ Bibenda is a rustic-trendy bar with cocktails and an enticing seasonal menu of Polish fusion dishes. The creative chefs use Polish classics as a starting point, then jazz them up with elements borrowed from corresponding dishes in other cultures. For example, you might see fried chicken (a Polish staple), marinated in buttermilk (from the American south), with a raspberry/chipotle glaze (from Mexico). Or perhaps a *gołąbki* (Polish cabbage roll) done in the style of a Turkish *dolma* (stuffed grape leaves). It's creative, delicious, and surprisingly affordable; reservations are wise at dinnertime (Tue-Sun 12:00-late, closed Mon, Nowogrodzka 10, mobile 502-770-303, www.bibenda.pl). The street Bibenda is on—Nowogrodzka—is lined with other, nearly-as-appealing bars and casual eateries to suit every taste (craft beer, whisky, wine bar, and so on).

$$$$ Butchery & Wine, in an unassuming location on

> # Restaurant Price Code
>
> I've assigned each eatery a price category, based on the aver-
> age cost of a typical main course. Drinks, desserts, and splurge
> items (steak and seafood) can raise the price considerably.
>
> | | | |
> |---|---|---|
> | **$$$$** | **Splurge:** | Most main courses over 60 zł |
> | **$$$** | **Pricier:** | 45-60 zł |
> | **$$** | **Moderate:** | 25-45 zł |
> | **$** | **Budget:** | Under 25 zł |
>
> In Poland, a milk bar or takeout spot is **$**; a basic sit-down
> eatery is **$$**; a casual but more upscale restaurant is **$$$**; and
> a swanky splurge is **$$$$**.

a drab urban street, serves upscale comfort food, specializing in steaks. The main location is a small, lively room of business travelers; across the alley is a more casual bar-like annex with a similar menu. The wine list is extensive, and reservations are smart (Mon-Sat 12:00-22:00, Sun until 20:00, Żurawia 22 and 20, tel. 22-502-3118, www.butcheryandwine.pl).

Polish Treats—Old and New
These places are on or close to the busy Nowy Świat boulevard.

A. Blikle, Poland's most famous pastry shop, serves a wide variety of delicious treats. This is where locals shop for cakes when they're having someone special over for coffee. The specialty is *pączki* (PONCH-kee), the quintessential Polish doughnut, filled with rose-flavored jam. You can get your goodies "to go" in the shop, or pay double to enjoy them with coffee in the swanky, classic café with indoor or outdoor seating (daily 9:00-21:00, Nowy Świat 35, tel. 22-828-6601). They also have a sit-down restaurant, but I come here only for the *pączki*. You'll see many other A. Blikle branches around town, but this is the original.

E. Wedel Pijalnia Czekolady thrills chocoholics. Emil Wedel made Poland's favorite chocolate, and today, his former residence houses this chocolate shop and genteel café. This is the spot for delicious pastries and a *real* hot chocolate—*czekolada do picia* ("drinking chocolate"), a cup of melted chocolate, not just hot chocolate milk. Or, if you fancy chocolate mousse, try *pokusa*. Wedel's was *the* Christmas treat for locals under communism. Cadbury bought the company when Poland privatized, but they kept the E. Wedel name, which is close to all Poles' hearts...and taste buds (Mon-Fri 8:00-22:00, Sat from 9:00, Sun 9:00-21:00, Szpitalna 8, tel. 22-827-2916, www.wedelpijalnie.pl/en).

Odette, tucked in a sleek, new, mixed-use complex hiding a block behind Nowy Świat, is a good choice for updated treats: pris-

WARSAW

tinely executed designer cakes at reasonable prices. Look through the glass door to the kitchen (Tue-Sun 10:00-20:00, Mon from 13:00, Wojciecha Górskiego 6, unit 7, mobile 604-745-444). These upscale dessert shops are all the rage—keep an eye out for them all over the city.

In Powiśle, near the Riverbank

The low-lying Powiśle neighborhood—squeezed in the little canyon between the Royal Way and the river—is newly trendy, thanks partly to its proximity to the inviting riverbank parks. My recommendations are simply fun hangout cafés, good for a drink or a light meal if you're in the area.

$ **Warszawa Powiśle** is a café/bar occupying the old, communist-style ticket office for the suburban train station of the same name. Tucked along a picturesque bike lane beneath the towering legs of a bridge, its sidewalk is jammed with cool Varsovians and in-the-know visitors. I'd skip the basic food (light sandwiches, dumplings) and instead just enjoy the vibe with a drink (daily 9:00 until late, Kruczkowskiego 3B, tel. 22-474-4084).

$ **Kawiarnia Kafka** combines a used bookstore (with books sold by weight) with a hip, creative café. Inside you'll find comfy chairs, stay-awhile tables, and checkerboard tiles; outside, on the lawn across from the café, guests lounge in slingback chairs (Mon-Fri 9:00-22:00, Sat-Sun 10:00-22:00, Oboźna 3, tel. 22-826-0822).

IN ŚRÓDMIEŚCIE ("DOWNTOWN")

Warsaw's Śródmieście district is the epicenter of Polish hipster/foodie culture—where you'll find young Varsovian foodies digging into affordable dishes at the trendiest new places. This area is a 15-minute walk south of Jerusalem Avenue, and also well-served by public transportation (for example, trams #4, #15, #18, and #35 run frequently along the main north-south Marszałkowska corridor to plac Zbawiciela; of these, tram #4 stops in the middle of the road below Castle Square, where the Royal Way meets the Old Town); the Politechnika Metro stop is also nearby. Listed next are a few different restaurant-hunting zones, with a handful of specific recommendations. For locations, see the map on page 165.

Hala Koszyki

This trendy food hall, which opened in 2016 in a renovated brick market hall from 1906, is your handiest one-stop shop for sampling Warsaw's current
dining scene. Outside—
sandwiched between the
two brick entrances—is
a sprawling zone of al
fresco tables amidst lush
trees strewn with twinkle
lights. Inside you'll find
more than a dozen entirely
different eateries, cover-

ing all of the culinary bases: Spanish tapas, sushi, Indian, Latin American, Italian, Thai, hummus bar, beer hall, tea salon, gourmet chocolates, *gelateria,* and more (most are **$$-$$$**). It's anchored by the big bar in the middle, surrounded by communal seating. Nearby, look for the Bazar Koszyki—a tight row of nine differ-ent international street food stalls (udon, hot dogs, *Flammkuchen,* pierogi, pho). The upper level, ringed by design studios, has quieter seating and views over the action. The complex also has some seri-ous sit-down eateries, including **$$$ Ćma** ("Moth"), with updated Polish fare and occasional live DJs. The complex, and most of its eateries, is open daily (Mon-Sat 8:00-22:00, Sun 9:00-20:00, Ko-szykowa 63, www.koszyki.com). They also have live performances (concerts for kids on Sun afternoons, Polish stand-up comedy on Wed nights, and so on)—check the website for details.

On Plac Zbawiciela

Named "Holiest Savior Square" for the looming church, this is a dizzying six-way intersection with a big traffic circle ringed by hulk-ing old colonnades. To get a quick taste of the Śródmieście scene,
come here first and just do a slow
loop around the circle, surveying
your options. Starting to the right
of the steeple and moving clockwise,
here are a few options you'll see:
$$ Izumi Sushi, $ Karma coffee
shop, and **$$ Tuk Tuk** Thai street
food are all popular, with great seat-
ing out on the square. Continuing
two crosswalks around the circle,
you'll cross Mokotowska; look-
ing left here, you may spot a line of
people at **Sucré**—an unpretentious
hole-in-the-wall serving all-natural,

homemade ice cream. The next section (after Mokotowska) has **Pałaszowanie,** serving cheap but creative *zapiekanki* (French bread pizza), followed by the trendy **$$ Charlotte** designer bakery and wine bar, with homemade treats and tables spilling out all over the square. Up above, **Plan B** is a hipster dive bar with drinks, snacks, and views down over the square; this is where revelers head at 2 in the morning, after the restaurants are closed (find the graffiti-slathered staircase up, just past Charlotte).

On and near Poznańska Street

A few short blocks west of plac Zbawiciela, this street is also lined with trendy and youthful eateries (especially around the intersection with Wilcza street; the nearest tram/bus stop is Hoża, and it's also not far from plac Konstytucji). Strolling this strip, you'll find several enticing options. **$$ Beirut,** a rustic and casual bar serving up excellent Middle Eastern food, is the culinary anchor of this neighborhood—always packed and lively. The hummus bar, on the left, has a wide variety of *mezes* (small plates) and grilled meats, while the "Kraken Rum Bar" on the right has fish dishes (portions are modest—plan to share a few, order at the counter then find a table, daily, Poznańska 12). **$$ Tel Aviv,** with gluten-free and vegan Middle Eastern food across the street, is the upscale answer to Beirut...and enjoys handling its overflow (daily, Poznańska 11). A few steps away, two more options are at the intersection with Wilcza: **$$$$ Nolita** is one of Warsaw's splurges—top-end, white-tablecloth fine dining, but still affordable on a European scale (closed Sat lunch and all day Sun, Wilcza 46, www.nolita.pl). **$$$ Wilcza 50** is a big, glitzy, crank-'em-out place offering international fare in a modern and spacious setting (daily, Wilcza 50).

Fine Dining near Łazienki Park

$$$$ Atelier Amaro, which has two Michelin stars, is a worthwhile splurge for foodies. If you're going to spend $100 on dinner anywhere in Poland...do it here. Filling an otherwise unexceptional brick building at the corner of Łazienki Park, the restaurant comes with high-end service and top-quality cuisine. Influenced by the New Nordic school, chef Wojciech Modest Amaro (who hosts the Polish versions of *Top Chef* and *Hell's Kitchen*) sources his ingredients as locally as possible, and creates a multicourse meal that feels like a journey through the forests and farms of Poland—with abundant earthy, savory, smoky flavors. You'll pay around 300 zł per person, depending on how many "moments" (courses) you choose, plus wine and vodka, but it's worthwhile for foodies who want to experience how a talented chef interprets the Polish culinary tradition at a very high level. Reservations are essential (Wed-Fri 12:00-

15:00 & 18:00-24:30, Tue and Sat 18:00-24:30 only, closed Sun-Mon, Agrykola 1, tel. 22-628-5747, www.atelieramaro.pl).

IN OR NEAR THE OLD TOWN

The restaurants in the Old Town and surrounding streets are 100 percent for tourists. Dining right on the Old Town Market Square is exorbitantly expensive, but could be worth it for those who treasure a romantic memory. Still, I'd rather walk a block or two to one of these options, which are as good as it gets in this area. For locations, see the map on page 170.

$$ Restauracja pod Samsonem ("Under Samson") is a quirky throwback and a sentimental favorite. The menu is affordable, well-executed, unfussy Jewish and Polish comfort food. The outdoor seating, on the New Town's main drag just outside the barbican, is enjoyable in good weather. And the staff is old-school: gruff, playfully opinionated, and stingy (you'll have to pay to check your coat or use the bathroom—yes, even if you're dining here). But nostalgic locals appreciate this as a stubborn remnant of the old days—a time before service with a smile, fine dining for business travelers, and hipster fusion restaurants (daily 10:00-23:00, Freta 3, tel. 22-831-1788).

$$ Freta 33—a block farther into the New Town, facing the serene New Town Square—has decent international fare (such as pastas), fine outdoor seating, and a contemporary subway-tile interior (daily 12:00-23:00, Freta 33, tel. 22-635-0931).

$$ Zapiecek, with a half-dozen locations in and near the Old Town, is a kitschy chain serving up cheap and cheery traditional Polish dishes. Yes, it's something of a tourist trap. But the prices are reasonable, and the food is better and more authentic than it has any right to be. They proudly make their prizewinning pierogi by hand every morning. If you need a quick, traditional meal anywhere near the Old Town...you could do much worse (handiest location faces the Cathedral of St. John the Baptist at Świętojańska 13, others are on the main drag through the New Town at Freta 1 and Freta 18, two more on the Royal Way at Nowy Świat 64 and Krakowskie Przedmieście 55, all open long hours daily).

Warsaw Connections

Almost all trains into and out of Warsaw go through hulking Warszawa Centralna station (described earlier, under "Arrival in Warsaw," including ticket-buying tips). If you're heading to Gdańsk, note that the red-brick Gothic city of Toruń and the impressive Malbork Castle are both on the way, but are on separate train lines—making it difficult to do both en route (see the Gdańsk and Pomerania chapters). Also be aware that EIC and IC express

WARSAW

trains to many destinations—including Kraków and Gdańsk—require seat reservations, even if you have a rail pass.

You can buy most tickets online (www.rozklad-pkp.pl)—saving you a trip to Centralna station. To confirm rail journeys, check specific times online or at the station.

From Warszawa Centralna Station by Train to: Kraków (hourly, about 2.5 hours), **Gdańsk** (hourly, 3 hours), **Malbork** (hourly, 2.5 hours), **Toruń** (every 2 hours direct, 3 hours on express IC train, more with changes), **Prague** (2/day direct, including 1 night train, more with change in Ostrava, 8 hours), **Berlin** (4/day direct, 6.5 hours, no direct night train), **Budapest** (1/day direct, 10 hours; 1/day overnight, 13 hours; also 2/day with change in Břeclav, Czech Republic, 10 hours), **Vienna** (2/day direct, 7 hours; plus 1 night train, 10 hours).

By Bus: Flixbus—described on page 142—runs bus routes throughout Poland and to international destinations (www.flixbus.pl).

GDAŃSK & THE TRI-CITY

Gdańsk (guh-DAYNSK) is a true find on the Baltic Coast of Poland. Some travelers may associate Gdańsk with dreary images of striking dockworkers from the nightly news in the 1980s. But there's more to this city than shipyards, Solidarity, and smog. Gdańsk may be *the* great undiscovered Eastern European destination—rich with history and culture, slathered with gorgeous architecture old and new, loaded with world-class museums and great restaurants, and just plain fun.

Exploring Gdańsk is a delight. The historical center is a gem, with block after block of red-brick churches and narrow, colorful, ornately decorated Hanseatic burghers' mansions. The riverfront embankment, with its trademark medieval crane, oozes salty maritime charm. Gdańsk's history is also fascinating—from its 17th-century Golden Age to the headlines of the late 20th century, big things happen here. You might even see ol' Lech Wałęsa still wandering the streets. And yet Gdańsk is also unmistakably a city of the future, with state-of-the-art construction projects popping up all over. In many areas, it feels more Scandinavian than Polish.

Gdańsk and two nearby towns (Sopot and Gdynia) together form an area known as the "Tri-City," offering several day-trip opportunities north along the coast (see page 285). The belle-époque seaside resort of Sopot beckons to tourists, while the modern burg of Gdynia sets the pace for today's Poland. Beyond the Tri-City, the sandy Hel Peninsula is a popular spot for summer sunbathing, and Malbork Castle (covered in the next chapter) is an easy half-hour train ride away.

PLANNING YOUR TIME

Gdańsk, with more than its share of great sights (and tempting side-trips), demands two full days—which also makes the long trip up here more worthwhile. If you're in a rush, those with a limited appetite for sightseeing could squeeze it into one day. If you have more time, Gdańsk will fill it.

Gdańsk sightseeing has three major components: the Royal Way (historic main drag with good museums); the river embankment, leading to the WWII history museum; and the modern shipyard where Solidarity was born (with a fascinating museum). If you have just one (very busy) day, follow my self-guided walk through the Main Town and then out to the Solidarity sights, followed by a spin through the WWII museum (closed Mon) and a stroll along the riverfront back into town.

With two days, I'd devote one day to the Main Town, riverbank, and WWII museum, and a second day to the Solidarity sights, rounding out your time with other attractions: Art lovers enjoy the National Museum (with a stunning altar painting by Hans Memling), history buffs make the pilgrimage to Westerplatte (where World War II began), castle fans side-trip to Malbork, and church and pipe-organ fans might visit Oliwa Cathedral in Gdańsk's northern suburbs (on the way to Sopot).

If you have more time, consider the wide variety of side-trips. The most popular option is the half-day round-trip to Malbork Castle (30-45 minutes each way by train, plus two or three hours to tour the castle—see next chapter). It only takes a quick visit to enjoy the resort town of Sopot (25 minutes each way by train), but on a sunny day, the town's beaches may tempt you to laze around longer. Gdynia is skippable, but it does have one great sight (the Emigration Museum) and rounds out your take on the Tri-City. And if you have a full day and great weather, and you don't mind fighting the crowds for a patch of sandy beach, go to Hel.

Gdańsk gets busy in late June, when school holidays begin, and it's crowded with (mostly German, Norwegian, and Swedish) tourists from July to mid-September—especially during St. Dominic's Fair (Jarmark Św. Dominika, three weeks from late July to mid-Aug), with market stalls, concerts, and other celebrations.

Several Gdańsk museums are closed Monday—especially outside summer. Monday is a good day to visit churches or the European Solidarity Center, or to take a side-trip to Sopot (but not to Malbork Castle or Gdynia's Emigration Museum, which are also closed Monday).

Orientation to Gdańsk

With 460,000 residents, Gdańsk is part of the larger urban area known as the Tri-City (Trójmiasto, total population of 1 million).

But the tourist's Gdańsk is compact, welcoming, and walkable—virtually anything you'll want to see is within a 20-minute stroll of everything else.

Focus on the Main Town (Główne Miasto), home to most of the sights described, including the spectacular Royal Way main drag, ulica Długa. The Old Town (Stare Miasto) has a handful of old brick buildings and faded, tall, skinny houses—but the area is mostly drab and residential, and not worth much time. Just beyond the northern end of the Old Town (about a 20-minute walk from the heart of the Main Town) is the entrance to the Gdańsk Shipyard, with the excellent European Solidarity Center and its top-notch museum. From here, shipyards sprawl for miles.

The second language in this part of Poland is German, not English. As this was a predominantly German city until the end of World War II, German tourists flock here in droves. But you'll win no Polish friends if you call the city by its more familiar German name, Danzig. You'll also find that Gdańsk is becoming an increasingly popular cruise destination, with about 100 ships calling here each year (most dock at the nearby city of Gdynia, and passengers take a bus or train in). During summer daytime hours, the town is filled with little excursion groups.

TOURIST INFORMATION

Gdańsk has two different TI organizations. Most helpful is the **regional TI,** which occupies the Upland Gate, at the start of my self-guided walk (Mon-Fri 9:00-20:00, Sat-Sun until 18:00; Oct-mid-May daily 9:00-18:00; tel. 58-732-7041, www.pomorskie. travel). The **city TI** has three branches—one conveniently located at the bottom end of the main drag, at Długi Targ 28 (just to the left as you face the river gate; daily 9:00-19:00, Sept-April until 17:00; tel. 58-301-4355, www.visitgdansk.com), with satellite TIs at the Madison shopping center (across from the train station) and at the airport.

Sightseeing Pass: Busy sightseers should consider the **Tourist Card,** which includes entry to several sights in Gdańsk, Gdynia, and Sopot, and discounts at others (such as 20 percent off the European Solidarity Center). Check the list of what's covered, and do the arithmetic (50 zł/24 hours, 65 zł/48 hours, 80 zł/72 hours, pay more to add local transit, sold only at TIs).

ARRIVAL IN GDAŃSK

By Train at Gdańsk's Main Train Station (Gdańsk Główny): If you're on a PKP train, get off at the Gdańsk Główny stop. This station is a pretty brick palace on the western edge of the old center. (To save money, architects in Colmar, France copied this exact design to build their city's station.) Trains to other parts of Poland (marked *PKP*) typically use platforms 1 or 2; regional trains with connections to the Tri-City (marked *SKM*) use the shorter platform 3.

Inside the terminal building, you'll find lockers, ATMs, ticket windows, and ticket machines. Outside, the pedestrian underpass by the McDonald's leads you beneath the busy road—a TI is in the Madison shopping center just beyond.

The easiest choice for reaching your hotel is to hop in a **taxi** or request an **Uber** (about 15 zł to any of my recommended hotels). Or it's a 15-minute walk to the heart of the Main Town and many recommended hotels: Go through the underpass, exit to the right, circle around the right side of Cinema City, and follow the busy road until you see the brick towers on your left.

By Train at Gdańsk Śródmieście: If you're arriving in Gdańsk on a commuter SKM train, consider staying on one more stop to the Gdańsk Śródmieście station, which is a slightly shorter walk to the start of my Gdańsk Walk. From Gdańsk Śródmieście, use the underpass to reach the gigantic Forum shopping mall. Walk straight through the mall to the far end; after exiting, if you look to the right, you'll see a pedestrian underpass leading to the Upland Gate and the start of my walk.

By Plane: Gdańsk's architecturally impressive, user-friendly airport, named for Lech Wałęsa, is about five miles west of the city center (airport code: GDN, tel. 58-348-1163, www.airport.gdansk. pl). The 25-minute **taxi** ride into town should cost no more than 60 zł; an **Uber** costs about half that much (except during peak times). Public **bus** #210 heads into the center and stops near the main train station and at Brama Wyżynna, near the heart of the Main Town (3.20 zł, buy ticket at machine at stop or on board for a bit more; 2/hour Mon-Fri, hourly Sat-Sun, 40 minutes).

Gdańsk at a Gdlance

▲▲▲Gdańsk Walk Stroll down the city's colorful showpiece main drag, ending at the famous shipyards and the European Solidarity Center. See page 232.

▲▲▲Solidarity Sights and Gdańsk Shipyard Home to the beginning of the end of Eastern European communism, with a towering monument and excellent museum. **Hours:** Memorial and shipyard gate—always open. European Solidarity Center exhibit—May-Sept Mon-Fri 10:00-19:00, Sat-Sun until 20:00; Oct-April Mon and Wed-Fri 10:00-17:00, Sat-Sun until 18:00, closed Tue. See page 257.

▲▲Main Town Hall Ornate meeting rooms, town artifacts, and tower with sweeping views. **Hours:** Mon 10:00-13:00, Tue-Sat until 18:00, Sun 11:00-18:00; Oct-April Tue until 13:00, Wed and Fri-Sun until 16:00, Thu until 18:00, closed Mon. See page 253.

▲▲Artus Court Grand meeting hall for guilds of Golden Age Gdańsk, boasting an over-the-top tiled stove. **Hours:** Same as Main Town Hall. See page 254.

▲▲St. Mary's Church Giant red-brick church crammed full of Gdańsk history. **Hours:** Mon-Sat 9:00-17:30, Sun from 13:00, tower open until 20:00 or 21:00 in summer but closed in winter. See page 244.

▲▲Museum of the Second World War Poland's definitive museum on the most devastating conflict in human history. **Hours:** June-Sept Tue 10:00-19:00, Wed-Sun 10:00-20:00; Oct-May Tue-Fri until 19:00, Sat-Sun until 20:00; closed Mon year-round. See page 268.

▲Amber Museum High-tech exhibit of valuable golden globs of petrified tree sap. **Hours:** Same as Main Town Hall, above. See page 251.

▲Uphagen House Tourable 18th-century interior, typical of the pretty houses that line ulica Długa. **Hours:** Same as Main Town Hall. See page 252.

▲National Maritime Museum Sprawling exhibit on all aspects of the nautical life, housed in several venues connected by a ferry boat. **Hours:** July-Aug daily 10:00-18:00; Sept-Oct and March-June Tue-Sun until 16:00, closed Mon; Nov-Feb Tue-Sun until 15:00, closed Mon. See page 256.

GETTING AROUND GDAŃSK

Nearly everything is within easy walking distance of my recommended hotels, but public transportation can be useful for reaching outlying sights such as Oliwa Cathedral, Westerplatte, Sopot, Gdynia, and Hel (specific transportation options for these places are described in each listing).

By Public Transportation: Gdańsk's trams and buses work on the same tickets: single-ride ticket—3.20 zł, one-hour ticket—3.80 zł, 24-hour ticket—13 zł. Major stops have user-friendly ticket machines, which take credit cards. Otherwise, buy tickets *(bilety)* at kiosks marked *RUCH,* or buy one on board from the driver (single-ride not available—you have to buy the one-hour ticket). In the city center, the stops worth knowing about are Plac Solidarności (near the European Solidarity Center), Gdańsk Główny (in front of the main train station), and Brama Wyżynna (near the Upland Gate and the Gdańsk Śródmieście commuter train station).

By Taxi or Uber: Taxis cost about 8 zł to start, then 2-3 zł per kilometer (a bit more at night). However, taxis waiting at stands often have inflated rates; it's safer to call a cab (try Neptun, tel. 19686 or 585-111-555; EcoCar, tel. 123-456-789; or Dajan, tel. 58-19628). Uber works well in Gdańsk and is typically cheaper than a taxi.

Tours in Gdańsk

Private Guides

Hiring a local guide is an exceptional value. **Agnieszka Syroka**—personable and knowledgeable—is a wonderful guide (450 zł/up to 4 hours, more for all day, mobile 502-554-584, www.tourguidegdansk.com, syroka.agnieszka@gmail.com). **Jacek "Jake" Podhorski,** who teaches economics at the local university, guides in the summer and enjoys sharing fascinating memories of the communist days (400 zł/3 hours, 100 zł extra with his car, mobile 603-170-761, ekojpp@ug.edu.pl).

Gdańsk Walk

In the 16th and 17th centuries, Gdańsk was Poland's wealthiest city, with gorgeous architecture (much of it in the Flemish Mannerist style) rivaling that in the two historic capitals, Kraków and Warsaw. During this Golden Age, Polish kings would visit this city of well-to-do Hanseatic

League merchants and gawk along the same route trod by tourists today.

The following self-guided walk—rated ▲▲▲—introduces you to the best of Gdańsk. It bridges the two historic centers (the Main Town and the Old Town), dips into St. Mary's Church (the city's most important church), and ends at the famous shipyards and Solidarity Square (where Poland began what ultimately brought down the USSR). I've divided the walk into two parts (making it easier to split up, if you like): The first half focuses on a loop through the Main Town (with most of the high-profile sights), while the second part carries on northward, through the less-touristy Old Town to the shipyards.

PART 1: THE MAIN TOWN
• *Begin at the west end of the Main Town, just beyond the last gate at the edge of the busy road.*

❶ Upland Gate (Brama Wyżynna)
The Main Town's fortifications were expanded with a Renaissance wall bound by the Upland Gate (built in 1588). "Upland" refers to the hills you see beyond—considered high country in this flat region. Standing with your back to the busy arterial (which traces the old moat), study the gate. Find its three coats of arms (the black eagle for Royal Prussia, the crowned white eagle for Poland, and the two crosses for Gdańsk). Recall that this city has, for almost the entirety of its history before the mid-20th century, been bicultural: German and Polish, coexisting more or less peacefully. Also notice the little wheels that once hoisted a drawbridge.

Now look across the busy street, to the supermodern **Forum shopping center.** While controversial for its over-the-top design (and for covering over a historic canal), this replaced a ragtag old flea market area—so, like many things in Gdańsk, it's a melding of new and old. A lion—symbol of Gdańsk—perches high on the corner of the rust-colored main building. I'm not in the habit of telling travelers to visit shopping malls...but this one really is worth a look.
• *It's a straight line from here to the river. Walk through the arch (which houses a TI) to the next arch, just a few steps ahead.*

❷ Torture Chamber (Katownia) and Prison Tower (Wieża Więzienna)
The tall, Gothic brick gate before you was part of an earlier protective wall made useless after the Renaissance walls were built in 1588. While today these structures house the Amber Museum (described later), it's free to walk through the evocative passage. Inside, find gargoyles (on the left, a town specialty) and the shackles from which prisoners were hung (on the right). Look up at the

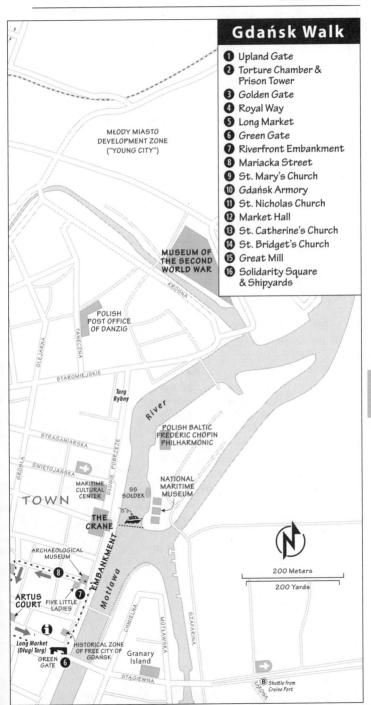

Gdańsk Walk

1. Upland Gate
2. Torture Chamber & Prison Tower
3. Golden Gate
4. Royal Way
5. Long Market
6. Green Gate
7. Riverfront Embankment
8. Mariacka Street
9. St. Mary's Church
10. Gdańsk Armory
11. St. Nicholas Church
12. Market Hall
13. St. Catherine's Church
14. St. Bridget's Church
15. Great Mill
16. Solidarity Square & Shipyards

MŁODY MIASTO DEVELOPMENT ZONE ("YOUNG CITY")

MUSEUM OF THE SECOND WORLD WAR

KROSNA

POLISH POST OFFICE OF DANZIG

TANECZNA

OLEJARNA

STAROMIEJSKIE

Targ Rybny

River

POLISH BALTIC FRÉDÉRIC CHOPIN PHILHARMONIC

STRAGANIARSKA

GROBLA

ŚWIĘTOJAŃSKA

MARITIME CULTURAL CENTER

DŁUGIE POBRZEŻE

SS SOŁDEK

NATIONAL MARITIME MUSEUM

TOWN

THE CRANE

EMBANKMENT

ARCHAEOLOGICAL MUSEUM

Motława

8

7

ARTUS COURT

FIVE LITTLE LADIES

Long Market (Długi Targ)

GREEN GATE

6

HISTORICAL ZONE OF FREE CITY OF GDAŃSK

CHMIELNA

MOTŁAWSKA

Granary Island

STĄGIEWNA

SZAFARNIA

ŁĄKOWA

B Shuttle from Cruise Port

200 Meters

200 Yards

inside of the high gable to the headless man, identifying this as the torture chamber. This old jail—with its 15-foot-thick walls—was used as a prison even in modern times, under Nazi occupation.

Leaving the Torture Chamber and Prison Tower through the far end, look to your left (100 yards away) to see a long, brick building with four fancy, uniform gables. This is the **armory** *(zbrojownia)*, one of the finest examples of Dutch Renaissance architecture anywhere. Though this part of the building appears to have the facades of four separate houses, it's an urban camouflage to hide its real purpose from potential attackers. But there's at least one clue to what the building is really for: Notice the exploding cannonballs at the tops of the turrets. (We'll get a better look at the armory from the other side, later in this walk.)

The round, pointy-topped tower next to the armory is the **Straw Tower** (Baszta Słomiana). Gunpowder was stored here, and the roof was straw—so if it exploded, it could easily blow its top without destroying the walls.

• *Straight ahead, the final and fanciest gate between you and the Main Town is the...*

❸ Golden Gate (Złota Brama)

While the other gates were defensive, this one's purely ornamental. The four women up top represent virtues that the people of Gdańsk should exhibit toward outsiders (left to right): Peace, Freedom, Prosperity, and Fame. The gold-lettered inscription, a psalm in medieval German, compares Gdańsk to Jerusalem: famous and important. Directly above the arch is the Gdańsk coat of arms: two white crosses under a crown on a red shield. We'll see this symbol all over town. Photographers love the view of the Main Town framed in this arch. Inside the arch, study the old photos showing the 1945 bomb damage. On the left is the glorious view you just enjoyed...ravaged by war. And on the right is a heartbreaking aerial view of the city in 1945, when 80 percent of its buildings were in ruins.

• *Passing through the Golden Gate, you reach the Main Town's main drag.*

❹ The Royal Way

Before you stretches ulica Długa (cleverly called the "Long Street")—the main promenade of what, 600 years ago, was the biggest and richest city in Poland, thanks to its profitable ties to the Hanseatic League of merchant cities. This promenade is nick-named the "Royal Way" because (just as in Warsaw and Kraków) the king would follow this route when visiting town.

Walk half a block, and then look back at the Golden Gate. The women on top of this side represent virtues the people of Gdańsk should cultivate in themselves (left to right): Wisdom, Piety, Justice, and Concord (if an arrow's broken, let's take it out of the quiver and fix it). The inscription—sharing a bit of wisdom as apropos today as it was in 1612—reads, "Concord makes small countries develop, and discord makes big countries fall." Gdańsk was cosmopolitan and exceptionally tolerant in the Middle Ages, attracting a wide range of people, including many who were perse-cuted elsewhere: Jews, Scots, Dutch, Flemish, Italians, Germans, and more. Members of each group brought with them strands of their culture, which they wove into the tapestry of this city—dem-onstrated by the eclectic homes along this street. Each facade and each gable was different, as nobles and aristocrats wanted to display their wealth. On my last visit, a traveler seeing this street for the first time gasped to me, "It's like stepping into a Fabergé egg."

During Gdańsk's Golden Age, these houses were taxed based on frontage (like the homes lining Amsterdam's canals)—so they were built skinny and deep. The widest houses belonged to the super-elite. Different as they are from the outside, every house had the same general plan inside. Each had three parts, starting with the front and moving back: First was a fancy drawing room, to show off for visitors. Then came a narrow corridor to the back rooms—often along the side of an inner courtyard. Because the houses had only a few windows facing the outer street, this court-yard provided much-needed sunlight to the rest of the house. The residential quarters were in the back, where the family actually lived: bedroom, kitchen, office. To see the interior of one of these homes, pay a visit to the interesting **Uphagen House** (at #12, on the right, a block and a half in front of the Golden Gate; described later).

This lovely street wasn't always so lively and carefree. At the end of World War II, the Royal Way was in ruins. That epic war actually began here, in what was then the "Free City of Danzig." Following World War I, nobody could decide what to do with this influential and multiethnic city. So, rather than assign it to Ger-many or Poland, it was set apart as its own little autonomous state-let. In 1939, Danzig was 80 percent German-speaking—enough for Hitler to consider it his. And so, on September 1 of that year, the Nazis seized it in one day with relatively minor damage (though the attack on the Polish military garrison on the city's Westerplatte peninsula lasted a week).

But six years later, when the Soviets arrived (March 30, 1945), the city was devastated. This was the first traditionally German city that the Red Army took on their march toward Berlin. And, while it was easy for the Soviets to seize the almost empty city, the commander then insisted that it be leveled, building by building—in retaliation for all the pain the Nazis had caused in Russia. (Soviets didn't destroy nearby Gdynia, which they considered Polish rather than German.) Soviet officers turned a blind eye as their soldiers raped and brutalized residents. An entire order of horrified nuns committed suicide by throwing themselves into the river.

It was only thanks to detailed drawings and photographs that these buildings could be so carefully reconstructed. Notice the cheap plaster facades done in the 1950s—rough times under communism, in the decade after World War II. (Most of the town's medieval brick was shipped to Warsaw for a communist-sponsored "rebuild the capital first" campaign.) While the fine facades were restored, the buildings behind the facades were completely rebuilt to modern standards.

Just beyond Uphagen House, **Cukiernia Sowa** ("The Owl," on the right at #13) is *the* place for cakes and coffee. Directly across the street, **Grycan** (at #73) has been a favorite for ice cream here for generations.

Just a few doors down, on the left, are some of the most striking **facades** along the Royal Way. The blue-and-white house with

the three giant heads is from the 19th century, when the hot style was eclecticism—borrowing bits and pieces from various architectural eras. This was one of the few houses on the street that survived World War II.

At the next corner on the right is the huge, blocky, red **post office,** which doesn't quite fit with the skinny facades lining the rest of the street. Step inside. With doves fluttering under an airy glass atrium, the interior's a class act. Directly across the street, the candy shop **(Ciuciu Cukier Artist)** is often filled with children clamoring to see lollipop-making demos. Step in and inhale a universal whiff of childhood.

A few doors farther down, on the left at #62, pop into the **Millennium Gallery** amber shop (which would love to give you an educational amber polishing demo) to see the fascinating collection of old-timey photos, letting you directly compare Gdańsk's cityscape before and after the WWII destruction.

Above the next door, notice the colorful **scenes.** These are slices of life from 17th-century Gdańsk: drinking, talking, shopping, playing music. The ship is a *koga*, a typical symbol of Hanseatic ports like Gdańsk.

Across the street and a few steps down are the fancy facades of three houses belonging to the very influential medieval **Ferber family,** which produced many burghers, mayors, and even a bishop. On the house with the little dog over the door (#29), look for the heads in the circular medallions. These are Caesars of Rome. At the top of the building is Mr. Ferber's answer to the constant question, "Why build such an elaborate house?"—*PRO INVIDIA,* "For the sake of envy."

A few doors down, on the right, is Gdańsk's most scenically situated milk bar, the recommended **Bar Mleczny Neptun.** Back in communist times, these humble cafeterias were subsidized to give workers an affordable place to eat out. To this day, they offer simple and very cheap grub.

Next door (at #35) is the **Russian Culture Center,** with Russian movies and art exhibits. Poland has no love lost for Russia, but in this multicultural city, this just fits.

Before you stands the **Main Town Hall** (Ratusz Głównego Miasta) with its mighty brick clock tower. Consider climbing its observation tower and visiting its superb interior, which features ornately decorated meeting rooms for the city council (described later).

• *Just beyond the Main Town Hall, ulica Długa widens and becomes...*

❺ Long Market (Długi Targ)

Step from the Long Street into the Long Market, and do a slow, 360-degree spin to appreciate the amazing array of proud architecture here in a city center that rivals the magnificent Grand Place in Brussels. The centerpiece of this square is one of Gdańsk's most important landmarks, the statue of **Neptune**—God of the sea. He's a fitting symbol for a city that dominates the maritime life of Poland. Behind him is another worthwhile museum, the **Artus Court.** Step up to the magnificent door on the right side and study the golden relief just above, celebrating the Vistula River (in so many ways the lifeblood of the Polish nation): Lady Vistula is exhausted after her heroic journey, and is finally carried by Neptune to her ultimate destination, the Baltic Sea. (This is just a preview of the ornate art that fills the interior of this fine building—described later.)

Midway down the Long Market (on the right, across from the Hard Rock Café) is a glass case with the **thermometer and barometer of Daniel Fahrenheit.** Although that scientist was born here, he did his groundbreaking work in Amsterdam.

• *At the end of the Long Market is the...*

Gdańsk History

Visitors to Gdańsk are surprised at how "un-Polish" the city's history is. In this cultural melting pot of German, Dutch, and Flemish merchants (with a smattering of Italians and Scots), Poles were only a small part of the picture until the city became exclusively Polish after World War II. However, in Gdańsk, cultural backgrounds traditionally took a back seat to the bottom line. Wealthy Gdańsk was always known for its economic pragmatism—no matter who was in charge, merchants here made money.

Gdańsk is Poland's gateway to the waters of Europe, where its main river (the Vistula) meets the Baltic Sea. The town was first mentioned in the 10th century, and was seized in 1308 by the Teutonic Knights (who called it "Danzig"; for more on the Teutonic Knights, see page 303). The Knights encouraged other Germans to settle on the Baltic coast, and gradually turned Gdańsk into a wealthy city. In 1361, Gdańsk joined the Hanseatic League, a trade federation of mostly Germanic merchant towns that provided mutual security. By the 15th century, Gdańsk was a leading member of this mighty network, which virtually dominated trade in northern Europe (and also included Toruń, Kraków, Lübeck, Hamburg, Bremen, Bruges, Bergen, Tallinn, Novgorod, and nearly a hundred other cities).

In 1454, the people of Gdańsk rose up against the Teutonic Knights, burning down their castle and forcing them out of the city. Three years later, the Polish king borrowed money from wealthy Gdańsk families to hire Czech mercenaries to take the Teutonic Knights' main castle, Malbork (described in the next chapter). In exchange, the Gdańsk merchants were granted special privileges, including exclusive export rights. Gdańsk now acted as a middleman for much of the trade passing through Polish lands, and paid only a modest annual tribute to the Polish king.

The 16th and 17th centuries were Gdańsk's Golden Age. Now a part of the Polish kingdom, the city had access to an enormous hinterland of natural resources to export—yet it maintained a privileged, semi-independent status. Like Amsterdam, Gdańsk became a progressive and booming merchant city. Its mostly Germanic and Dutch burghers imported Dutch, Flemish, and Italian architects to give their homes an appropriately Hanseatic flourish. At a time of religious upheaval in the rest of Europe, Gdańsk became known for its tolerance—a place that opened its doors to all visitors (many Mennonites and Scottish religious refugees emigrated here). It was also a haven for great thinkers, including philosopher Arthur Schopenhauer and scientist Daniel Fahrenheit (who invented the mercury thermometer).

Along with the rest of Poland, Gdańsk declined in the late 18th century and became part of Prussia (today's northern Germany) during the Partitions. But the people of Gdańsk—even those of German heritage—had taken pride in their independence and weren't enthusiastic about being ruled from Berlin. After World War I, in a unique compromise to appease its complex ethnic makeup, Gdańsk did not fall under German or Polish control, but once again became an independent city-state: the Free City of Danzig (about 750 square miles, populated by 400,000 ethnic Germans and 15,000 Poles). The city, along with the so-called Polish Corridor connecting it to Polish lands, effectively cut off Germany from its northeastern territory. On September 1, 1939, Adolf Hitler started World War II when he invaded Gdańsk in order to bring it back into the German fold. Later, nearly 80 percent of the city was destroyed when the Soviets "liberated" it from Nazi control.

After World War II, Gdańsk officially became part of Poland, and was painstakingly reconstructed (mostly replicating the buildings of its Golden Age). In 1970, and again in 1980, the shipyard of Gdańsk witnessed strikes and demonstrations that would lead to the fall of European communism. Poland's great anticommunist hero and first postcommunist president, Lech Wałęsa, is Gdańsk's most famous resident, and still lives here. When he flies around the world to give talks, he leaves from Gdańsk's "Lech Wałęsa Airport."

A city with a recent past that's both tragic and uplifting, Gdańsk celebrated its 1,000th birthday in 1997. Very roughly, the city has spent about 700 years as an independent entity, and about 300 years under Germanic overlords (the Teutonic Knights, Prussia, and the Nazis). But today, Gdańsk is decidedly its own city. And, as if eager to prove it, Gdańsk is making big improvements at a stunning pace: new museums (the European Solidarity Center and WWII museum), cultural facilities (the Shakespeare Theater), sports venues (a stadium that resembles a blob of amber, built for the 2012 Euro Cup tournament), and an ongoing surge of renovation and refurbishment that has the gables of the atmospheric Hanseatic quarter gleaming once again.

❻ Green Gate (Zielona Brama)

This huge gate (named for the Green Bridge just beyond) was built as a residence for visiting kings...who usually preferred to stay back by Neptune instead (maybe because the river, just on the other side of this gate, stank). It might not have been good enough for kings and queens, but it's plenty fine for a former president: Lech Wałęsa's office is upstairs. A few steps down the skinny lane to the left is the endearing little **Historical Zone of the Free City of Gdańsk** museum, which explains the interwar period when "Danzig" was an independent and bicultural city-state (described later).

• *Now go through the gate, walk out onto the Green Bridge, anchor yourself in a niche on the left, and look downstream.*

❼ Riverfront Embankment

The Motława River—a side channel of the mighty Vistula—flows into the nearby Baltic Sea. This port was the source of Gdańsk's phenomenal Golden Age wealth. This embankment was jam-packed in its heyday, the 14th and 15th centuries. It was so crowded with boats that you would hardly have been able to see the water, and boats had to pay a time-based moorage fee for tying up to a post.

Look back at the Green Gate and notice that these bricks are much smaller than the locally made ones we saw earlier on this walk. These bricks are Dutch: Boats from Holland would come here empty of cargo, but with a load of bricks for ballast. Traders filled their ships with goods for the return trip, leaving the bricks behind.

The old-fashioned **galleons** and other tour boats moored nearby depart hourly for a fun cruise to Westerplatte (where on September 1, 1939, Germans fired the first shots of World War II) and back. Though kitschy, the galleons are a fun way to get out on the water (details under "Gdansk Connections—By Boat" on page 284).

Across the river is **Granary Island** (Wyspa Spichrzów), where grain was stored until it could be taken away by ships. Before World War II, there were some 400 granaries here; almost all were destroyed...and this island remained rubble until just a few years ago, when developers began erecting a passel of modern new buildings (evoking the old Gdańsk gables) and wrapped the island in a scenic boardwalk—a wonderful place for a stroll. The three older-looking granaries downstream, in the distance on the next island, house exhibits for the National Maritime Museum (described later).

From your perch on the bridge, look down the embankment (about 500 yards, on the left) and find the huge wooden **crane**

(żuraw) bulging over the water. This monstrous 15th-century crane—a rare example of medieval port technology—was once used for loading and repairing ships...beginning a shipbuilding tradition that continued to the days of Lech Wałęsa. The crane mechanism was operated by several workers scrambling around in giant hamster wheels. Treading away to engage the gears and pulleys, they could lift 4 tons up 30 feet, or 2 tons up 90 feet.

• *Walk along the embankment about halfway to the crane, passing the lower embankment, with excursion boats heading to the Westerplatte monument. Pause when you reach the big brick building with green window frames and a tower. This red-brick fort houses the **Archaeological Museum** (described later). Its collection includes the five ancient stones in a small garden just outside its door (on the left). These are the **Prussian Hags**—mysterious sculptures from the second century AD (a.k.a. "Five Little Ladies," each described in posted plaques).*

Turn left through the gate in the middle of the brick building. You'll find yourself on the most charming lane in town...

❽ Mariacka Street

The calm, atmospheric "Mary's Street" leads from the embankment to St. Mary's Church. Stroll the length of it, enjoying the most romantic lane in Gdańsk. (If you need a coffee break, the recommended Drukarnia—on the right—is tops.) The **porches** extending out into the street, with access to cellars underneath, were a common feature in Gdańsk's Golden Age. For practical reasons, after the war, these were restored only on this street. Notice how the porches are bordered with fine stone relief panels and gargoyles attached to storm drains. If you get stuck there in a hard rainstorm, you'll understand why in Polish these are called "pukers." Enjoy a little amber comparison-shopping. As you stroll up to the towering brick St. Mary's Church, imagine the entire city like this cobbled lane of proud merchants' homes, with street music, delightful facades, and brick church towers high above.

Look up at the church tower viewpoint—filled with people who hiked 409 steps for the view. Our next stop is the church, which you'll enter on the far side under the tower. Walk around the left side of the church, appreciating the handmade 14th-century bricks on the right and the plain post-WWII facades on the left. (Reconstructing the Royal Way was better funded. Here, the priority was simply getting people housed again.) In the distance is the fancy facade of the armory (where you'll head after visiting the church).

• *But first, go inside...*

❾ St. Mary's Church (Kościół Mariacki)

Of Gdańsk's 13 medieval red-brick churches, St. Mary's (rated ▲▲) is the one you must visit. It's the largest brick church in the world—with a footprint bigger than a football field (350 feet long and 210 feet wide), it can accommodate 20,000 standing worshippers.

Cost and Hours: 4 zł, 10 zł with tower climb, Mon-Sat 9:00-17:30, Sun from 13:00, tower open until 20:00 or 21:00 in summer but closed in winter.

❍ **Self-Guided Tour:** Inside, sit directly under the fine carved and painted 17th-century Protestant pulpit, two-thirds of the way down the nave (on the left side), to get oriented.

Overview: Built from 1343 to 1502 by the Teutonic Knights (who wanted a suitable centerpiece for their newly captured main city), St. Mary's remains an important symbol of Gdańsk. The church started out Catholic, became Lutheran in the mid-1500s, and then became Catholic again after World War II. (Remember, Gdańsk was a Germanic city before World War II and part of the big postwar demographic shove, when Germans were sent west, and Poles from the east relocated here. Desperate, cold, and homeless, the new Polish residents moved into what was left of the German homes.) While the church was originally frescoed from top to bottom, the Lutherans white-

washed the entire place. Today, some of the 16th-century whitewash has been peeled back (behind the high altar—we'll see this area soon), revealing a bit of the original frescoes. The floor is paved with 500 grave-stones of merchant families. Many of these were cracked when bombing sent the brick roof crashing down in 1945.

Most Gothic churches are built of stone in the basilica style—with a high nave in the middle, shorter aisles on the side, and flying buttresses to support the weight. (Think of Paris' Notre-Dame.) But with no handy source of stone available locally, northern Polish churches are built of brick, which won't work with the basilica design. So, like all Gdańsk churches, St. Mary's is a "hall church"—with three naves the same height and no exterior buttresses.

Also like other Gdańsk churches, St. Mary's gave refuge to the Polish people after the communist government declared martial law in 1981. When a riot broke out and violence seemed imminent, people flooded into churches, knowing that the ZOMO riot police wouldn't dare follow them inside.

Most of the church decorations are original. A few days before the Soviets arrived to "liberate" the city in 1945, locals—knowing what was in store—hid precious items in the countryside. Take some time now to see a few of the highlights.

• *From this spot, you can see most of what we'll visit in the church: As you face the altar, the astronomical clock is at 10 o'clock, the Ferber family medallion is at 1 o'clock, the Priests' Chapel is at 3 o'clock (under a tall, colorful window), and the magnificent 17th-century organ is directly behind you (it's played at each Mass and during free concerts on Fri in summer).*

Pulpit: For Protestants, the pulpit is important. Designed as an impressive place from which to share the Word of God in the people's language, it's located midnave, so all can hear.

• *Opposite the pulpit is the moving...*

Priests' Chapel: The 1965 statue of Christ weeping commemorates 2,779 Polish chaplains executed by the Nazis. See the grainy black-and-white photo of one about to be shot, above on the right.

• *Head up the nave to the...*

High Altar: The main altar, beautifully carved in 1517, is a triptych showing the coronation of Mary. She is surrounded by the Trinity: flanked by God and Jesus, with the dove representing the Holy Spirit overhead. The church's medieval stained glass was destroyed in 1945. Poland's biggest stained-glass window, behind the altar, is from 1980.

• *Start circling around the right side of the altar. Look right to find (high on a pillar) the big, opulent family marker.*

Ferber Family Medallion: The falling baby (under the crown) is Constantine Ferber. As a precocious child, li'l Constantine leaned out his window on the Royal Way to see the king's processional come through town. He slipped and fell, but landed in a salesman's barrel of fish. Constantine grew up to become the mayor of Gdańsk.

• *As you continue around behind the altar, search high above you, on the walls to your right, to spot those restored pre-Reformation frescoes. Behind the altar, look for an...*

Empty Glass Case: This case was designed to hold Hans Memling's *Last Judgment* painting, which used to be in this church, but is currently being held hostage by the National Museum (described later, under "Sights in Gdansk"). To counter the museum's claim that the church wasn't a good environment for such a precious work, the priest had this display case built—but that still wasn't enough to convince the museum to give the painting back. (You'll see a smaller replica of the painting soon.) Because of a recent church renovation, this case may be missing when you visit.

• *Now circle back the way you came to the area in front of the main altar, and proceed straight ahead into the transept. High on the wall to your right, look for the...*

Astronomical Clock: This 42-foot-tall clock is supposedly the biggest wooden clock in the world. Below it is an elaborate circular calendar that, like a medieval computer, calculates on which day each saint's festival day falls in different years (see the little guy on the left, with the pointer). Above are zodiac signs and the time (back then, the big hand was all you needed). Way up on top, Adam and Eve are naked and ready to ring the bell. Adam's been swinging his clapper at the top of the hour since 1473...but sadly, the clock is broken.

• *A few steps in front of the clock is a modern chapel with the...*

Memorial to the Polish Victims of the 2010 Plane Crash: The gold-shrouded Black Madonna honors the 96 victims of an air disaster that killed much of Poland's government—including the president and first lady—during a terrible storm over Russia. The main tomb is for Maciej Płażyński, from Gdańsk, who was leader of the parliament. On the left, the jagged statue has bits of the wreckage and lists each victim by name.

• *Head a few steps back toward the entrance, then look back at one of the nearby pillars to find a large painting (facing the back of the church).*

Replica of *Last Judgment* Altarpiece: This is a smaller, mustier replica of the exquisite, priceless altarpiece housed in the National Museum. If you're not planning to go see it at the National Museum, you could read the description on page 273 now.

• *Near where you entered are stairs leading to the...*

Church Tower: You can climb 409 steps to burn off some pierogi and earn a grand city view. It's a long hike (and you'll know it—every 10th step is numbered). But because the viewpoint is surrounded by a roof, the views are distant and may not be worth the effort. The first third is up a tight, medieval spiral staircase. Then you'll walk through the eerie, cavernous area between the roof and the ceiling, before huffing up steep concrete steps that surround the square tower (as you spiral up, up, up around the bells). Finally you'll climb a little metal ladder and pop out at the viewpoint.

• *Leaving the church, angle left and continue straight up atmospheric ulica Piwna ("Beer Street") toward the sprightly facade of the armory.*

❿ The Gdańsk Armory (Zbrojownia)

The 1605 armory, which we saw from a distance at the start of this walk, is one of the best examples of Dutch Renaissance architecture in Europe. Athena, the goddess of war and wisdom, stands in the center, amid motifs of war and ornamental pukers.

• *If you want to make your walk a loop, you're just a block away from where we started (to the left). Or, to continue through the Old Town to the European Solidarity Center's fine museum, follow the second part of this walk, next.*

PART 2: THROUGH THE OLD TOWN TO THE SHIPYARDS

The second part of this walk works its way out of the Main Town and heads into the Old Town, toward Solidarity Square and the shipyards. We'll walk along this street (which changes names a couple of times) nearly all the way. The walk ends at the European Solidarity Center's fine museum. You'll want plenty of time to tour the museum and linger over its exhibits, so if you're already pooped or it's getting late in the day, consider finishing this walk another time.

• *Facing the armory, turn right and head up Kołodziejska, which quickly becomes Węglarska. After two blocks (that is, one block before the big market hall), detour to the right down Świętojańska and use the side door to enter the brick church.*

⓫ St. Nicholas Church (Kościół Św. Mikołaja)

Near the end of World War II, when the Soviet army reached Gdańsk on its march westward, they were given the order to burn all the churches. Only this one survived—because it happened to be dedicated to Russia's patron saint. As the best-preserved church in town, it has a more impressive interior than the others, with lavish black-and-gold Baroque altars.

• *Backtrack out to the main street and continue along it, passing a row of seniors selling their grown and foraged edibles. Immediately after the church is Gdańsk's...*

⓬ Market Hall

Built in 1896 and renovated in 2005, Gdańsk's market hall is fun to explore. Appreciate the delicate steel-and-glass canopy overhead. This is a totally untouristy scene: You'll see everything from skintight *Polska* T-shirts, to wedding gowns, to maternity wear. The meat is downstairs, and the veggies are outside on the adjacent square. As this was once the center of a monastic community, the basement has the graves of medieval Dominican monks, which were exposed when the building was refurbished: Peer over the glass railing, and you'll see some of those scant remains.

Across the street from the Market Hall, a round, red-brick

tower, part of the city's protective wall back in 1400, marks the end of the Main Town and the beginning of the Old Town.

• *Carry on. For an ice cream break, watch on the right (after crossing the street) for the recommended Paolo Gelateria. Another block up the street, on the right, is the huge...*

⓭ St. Catherine's Church (Kościół Św. Katarzyny)

"Katy," as locals call it, is the oldest church in Gdańsk. In May of 2006, a carelessly discarded cigarette caused the church roof to burst into flames. Local people ran into the church and pulled everything outside, so nothing valuable was damaged; even the carillon bells were saved. However, the roof and wooden frame were totally destroyed. The people of Gdańsk were determined to rebuild this important symbol of the city. Within days of the fire, fundraising concerts were held to scrape together most of the money needed to raise the roof once more. Step inside. On the left side of the gate leading to the nave, photos show bomb damage. Farther in, on the left, are vivid photos of the more recent conflagration. The interior is evocative, with still-bare-brick walls that almost seem intentional—as if they're trying for an industrial-mod look.

• *The church hiding a block behind Katy—named for Catherine's daughter Bridget—has important ties to Solidarity and is worth a visit. Go around the right side of Katy and skirt the parking lot to find the entrance, on the side of the church, near the far end.*

⓮ St. Bridget's Church (Kościół Św. Brygidy)

This was the home church of Lech Wałęsa during the tense days of the 1980s. The church and its priest, Henryk Jankowski, were particularly aggressive in supporting the ideals of Solidarity. Jankowski became a mouthpiece for the movement. In gratitude for the church's support, Wałęsa named his youngest daughter Brygida.

Cost and Hours: 4 zł, daily 10:00-18:00.

Visiting the Church: Head inside. For your visit, start at the high altar, then circle clockwise back to the entry.

The enormous, unfinished **high altar** is made entirely of amber—more than a thousand square feet of it. Features that are already in place include the Black Madonna of Częstochowa, a royal Polish eagle, and the Solidarity symbol (tucked below the Black Madonna). The structure, like a scaffold, holds pieces as they are completed and added to the ensemble. The video you may see playing overhead gives you a close-up look at the amber elements.

The wrought-iron gate of the adjacent **Chapel of Fatima** (right of main altar) recalls great battles and events in Polish history from 966 to 1939, with important dates boldly sparkling in gold. Some say the Polish Church is too political. But it was only through a politically engaged Church that this culture survived the Partitions of Poland over a century and a half, plus the brutal antireligious policies of the communist period. The national soul of the Polish people—whether religious or not—is tied up in the Catholic faith.

Henryk Jankowski's tomb—a white marble box with dark-red trim—is along the same wall, but closer to the back of the church. Jankowski was a key figure during Solidarity times; the tomb proclaims him *Kapelan Solidarności* ("Solidarity Chaplain"). But his public standing took a nosedive near the end of his life—thanks to ego-driven projects like his amber altar, as well as accusations of anti-Semitism and corruption. Forced to retire in 2007, Jankowski died in 2010.

In the rear corner, where a figure lies lifeless on the floor under a wall full of wooden crosses, is the tomb of Solidarity martyr **Jerzy Popiełuszko.** A courageous and famously outspoken Warsaw priest, in 1984 Popiełuszko was kidnapped, beaten, and murdered by the communist secret police. Notice that the figure's hands and feet are bound—as his body was found. The crosses on the wall above are historic—each one was carried at various strikes against the communist regime. The communists believed they could break the spirit of the Poles with brutality—like the murder of Popiełuszko. But it only made the rebels stronger and more resolved to ultimately win their freedom.

Under the choir loft, step into the evocative chapel with **memorials** to other 20th-century Polish martyrs.

Near the exit, on a monitor, a fascinating 12-minute **video** shows great moments of this church, with commentary by Lech Wałęsa himself.

• *Return to the main street, turn right, and continue on. The big brick building ahead on the left, with the many windows in its roof, is the Great Mill. Walk past that and look down at the canal that once powered it.*

⓯ The Great Mill

This huge brick building dates from the 14th century. Look at the waterfalls and imagine standing here in 1400—with the mill's 18 wheels spinning 24/7, powering grindstones that produced 20 tons of flour a day. Like so much else here, the mill survived until 1945. Until recently it housed a shopping mall; now it's slated to be the new home of the Amber Museum (described later).

The **park** just beyond the mill is worth a look. In the distance is the Old City Town Hall (Dutch Renaissance style, from 1595). The monument in the middle honors the 17th-century astronomer Jan Haweliusz. He's looking up at a giant, rust-colored wall with a map of the heavens. Haweliusz built the biggest telescopes of his era to better appreciate and understand the cosmos. Behind the mill stands the miller's home—its opulence indicates that, back in the Middle Ages, there was a lot of money in grinding. Just steps into the family-friendly park is a fountain that brings shrieks of joy to children on hot summer days.

• *To get to the **shipyards**, keep heading straight up Rajska. You'll pass the modern Madison shopping mall. After another long block, jog right, passing to the right of the big, ugly, and green 1970s-era skyscraper. On your right, marked by the famous red logo on the roof, is today's **Solidarity headquarters** (which remains the strongest trade union in Poland, with 700,000 members, and is also active in many other countries). On the corner in front of the Solidarity building, you may see two big chunks of **wall**: a piece of the Berlin Wall and a stretch of the shipyard wall that Lech Wałęsa scaled to get inside and lead the strike. The message: What happened behind one wall eventually led to the fall of the other Wall.*

From here, hike on (about 200 yards) toward the huge, rust-colored building in the distance, angling left to reach the trio of tall, skinny crosses in front of it.

⓰ Solidarity Square and the Shipyards
Three tall crosses mark Solidarity Square and the rust-colored European Solidarity Center (with an excellent museum). For the exciting story of how Polish shipbuilders set in motion events that led to the end of the USSR, turn to page 257.

Sights in Gdańsk

MAIN TOWN (GŁÓWNE MIASTO)
The following sights are all in the Main Town, listed roughly in the order you'll see them on the self-guided walk of the Royal Way.

Museum of Gdańsk
The Museum of Gdańsk has four excellent branches—the Amber Museum, Uphagen House, Main Town Hall, and Artus Court—and a few lesser ones. Along with St. Mary's Church (described earlier), these are the four most important interiors in the Main Town. All have the same hours, but you must buy a separate ticket for each.

Cost and Hours: 12 zł for Amber Museum and Main Town Hall, 10 zł for Uphagen House and Artus Court, likely free Mon in summer and Tue off-season; hours are notoriously changeable, but here's my best guess: May-Sept Mon 10:00-13:00, Tue-Sat until 18:00, Sun 11:00-18:00; Oct-April Tue until 13:00, Wed and Fri-Sun until 16:00, Thu until 18:00, closed Mon.

Information: The museums share a phone number and website (central tel. 58-767-9100, www.muzeumgdansk.pl).

▲Amber Museum (Muzeum Bursztynu)

Housed in a pair of connected brick towers (the former Prison Tower and Torture Chamber) just outside the Main Town's Golden Gate, this museum has two oddly contradictory parts. One shows off Gdańsk's favorite local resource, amber, while the other focuses on implements of torture. You'll follow the one-way route through four exhibits on amber (with lots of stairs), and then walk the rampart to the other tower for a little torture. Note: The amber collection will likely be moved to the Great Mill, perhaps in 2020. For a primer before you visit, read the "All About Amber" sidebar.

Visiting the Museum: The exhibit has four parts: First, head up to the **second floor** for a look at amber in nature. View inclusions (organic items trapped in resin) through a magnifying glass and microscope, and see dozens of samples showing the full rainbow of amber shades. Interactive video screens explain the creation of amber. The **third-floor** exhibit explains amber in culture: the "Amber Route" (the ancient Celtic trade road connecting Gdańsk to Italy) and its medicinal uses. This floor also displays a wide range of functional items made from amber: clocks, pipe stems, candlesticks, chandeliers, jewelry boxes, and much more. Take a whiff—what's that smell? It's a cathedral. Amber is an ingredient in incense. The **fourth floor** shows off more artistic items made of amber: sculptures, candelabras, beer steins, chessboards, and a model ship with delicately carved sails. At the **top floor,** you'll find a modern gallery showing more recent amber craftsmanship and displays about amber's role in fashion today, particularly in jewelry.

Then, walking along the upper rampart level of the courtyard, you'll enter an exhibit about the building itself and the town's fortifications. This leads to the **Prison Tower** and the torture exhib-

All About Amber

Poland's Baltic seaside is known as the Amber Coast. You can see amber *(bursztyn)* in Gdańsk's Amber Museum, in the collection at Malbork Castle (see the Pomerania chapter), and in shop windows everywhere. This fossilized tree resin originated here on the north coast of Poland 40 million years ago. It comes in as many different colors as Eskimos have words for snow: 300 distinct shades, from yellowish white to yellowish black, from opaque to transparent. (I didn't believe it either, until I toured Gdańsk's museum.) Darker-colored amber is generally mixed with ash and sand—making it more fragile, and generally less desirable. Lighter amber is mixed with gasses and air bubbles.

Amber has been popular since long before there were souvenir stands. Archaeologists have found Roman citizens (and their coins) buried with crosses made of amber. Almost 75 percent of the world's amber is mined in northern Poland, and it often simply washes up on the beaches after a winter storm. Some of the elaborate amber sculptures displayed at the museum are joined with "amber glue"—melted-down amber mixed with an adhesive agent. More recently, amber craftsmen are combining amber with silver to create artwork—a method dubbed the "Polish School."

Some Poles believe that, in addition to being good for the economy, amber is good for their health. A traditional cure for arthritis pain is to pour strong vodka over amber, let it set, and then rub it on sore joints. Other remedies call for mixing amber dust with honey or rose oil. It sounds superstitious, but users claim that it works.

it—with sound effects, scant artifacts, and mannequins helpfully demonstrating the grisly equipment.

▲Uphagen House (Dom Uphagena)

This interesting place, at ulica Długa 12, is your chance to glimpse what's behind the colorful facades lining this street. It's the only grand Gdańsk mansion rebuilt as it was before 1945, and it has the typical configuration of three parts: dolled-up visitors' rooms in front, a corridor along the courtyard, and private rooms in the back. The finely decorated salon was used to show off for guests. You'll see several examples of **"Gdańsk-style furniture,"** characterized by three big, round feet along the front, lots of ornamentation, and usually a virtually impossible-to-find lock (sometimes hidden behind a movable decoration). Passing into the dining room, note the knee-high paintings of hunting and celebrations. Along the passage to the back, each room has a theme: butterflies in the smoking room, flowers in the next room, birds in the music room. In the private rooms at the back, the decor is simpler.

Back downstairs, you'll see the rustic working rooms: a humble bedroom, the kitchen, and the pantry. Step out into the courtyard to appreciate how it carves a little fresh air and sunshine out of a densely packed city. Back inside, look for the cross-section model showing the three parts of the house you just walked through. You'll exit through a room with photos of the house before the war, which were used to reconstruct what you see today.

▲▲Main Town Hall (Ratusz Głównego Miasta)

This landmark building contains remarkable decorations from Gdańsk's Golden Age. You can also climb 293 concrete steps to the top of the **tower** for commanding views (5 zł extra, mid-June–mid-Sept only).

Visiting the Main Town Hall: After buying your ticket, walk through the courtyard, then up the stairs to the first historic room. Ogle the finely crafted spiral staircase. The ornately-carved wooden **door,** which we'll pass through in a minute, is all-original, from the 1600s. Above the door are two crosses under a crown. This seal of Gdańsk is being held—as it's often depict-

ed—by a pair of lions. The felines are stubborn and independent, just like the citizens of Gdańsk. The surface of the door is carved with images of crops. Around the frame of the door are mermen, reminding us that this agricultural bounty, like so many of Poland's resources, is transported on the Vistula and out through Gdańsk.

Step into the **Great Weta Hall,** a meeting room with big portraits and big windows. Then go back through the first room and through the ornate door into the **Red Hall,** where the Gdańsk city council met in the summertime. (The lavish fireplace, with another pair of lions holding the coat of arms of Gdańsk, was just for show. There's no chimney.) City council members would sit in the seats around the room, debating city policy. Marvel at the 17th-century inlaid wood panels (just overhead) showing slices of local life. Paintings on the wall above represent the seven virtues that the burghers meeting in this room should possess.

The exquisite ceiling—with 25 paintings in total—is all about theology. Including both Christian and pagan themes, the ceiling was meant to inspire the decision makers in this room to make good choices. Study the oval painting in the middle (from 1607)—

the museum's highlight. It shows the special place Gdańsk occupies between God, Poland, and the rest of the world. In the foreground, the citizens of Gdańsk go about their daily lives. Above them, high atop the arch, God's hand reaches down (from within clouds of Hebrew characters) and grasps the Main Town Hall's steeple. The rainbow arching above also symbolizes God's connection to Gdańsk. Mirroring that is the Vistula River, which begins in the mountains of southern Poland (on the right), runs through the country, and exits at the sea in Gdańsk (on the left, where the rainbow ends).

Continue into the less-impressive **Winter Hall,** with another fireplace (this one actually hooked up to a chimney) and another coat of arms held by lions. Keep going through a few more rooms with historical artifacts. Then head upstairs, past a floor with temporary exhibits. Higher up is a fascinating exhibit about Gdańsk's time as a **"free city"** between the World Wars—when, because of its delicate ethnic mix of Poles and Germans, it was too precarious to assign it to either country. You'll see border checkpoints, uniforms, signs in German (the predominant language of "Danzig"), and reconstructed rooms (homes and shops) from the era. Near the end of this room, you have the option to climb up to the top of the tower. Otherwise, you'll head back out the way you came.

▲▲Artus Court (Dwór Artusa)

In the Middle Ages, Gdańsk was home to many brotherhoods and guilds (like businessmen's clubs). For their meetings, the city provided this elaborately decorated hall, named for King Arthur— a medieval symbol for prestige and power. Just as in King Arthur's Court, this was a place where powerful and important people came together. Of many such halls in Baltic Europe, this is the only original one that survives (in tall, white, triple-arched building behind Neptune statue at Długi Targ 43). Note:

On days when it's free (Mon in summer, Tue in winter), you have to enter at the top and bottom of each hour.

Visiting the Artus Court: In the grand hall, various **cupboards** line the walls. Each organization that met here had a place to keep its important documents and office supplies. Suspended from the ceiling are seven giant **model ships** that depict Baltic vessels, symbolic of the city's connection to the sea.

In the far-back corner is the museum's highlight: a gigantic **stove** decorated with 520 colorful tiles featuring the faces of kings, queens, nobles, mayors, and burghers—a mix of Protestants and Catholics, as a reminder of Gdańsk's religious tolerance. Almost all the tiles are original, having survived WWII bombs.

Notice the huge **paintings** on the walls above, with 3-D animals emerging from flat frames. Hunting is a popular theme in local artwork. Like minting coins, hunting was a privilege usually reserved for royalty, but it was extended in special circumstances to the burghers of special towns...like Gdańsk. These "paintings" are new, digitally generated reproductions of the originals, which were damaged in World War II.

The next room—actually in the next building—is a typical **front room** of the burghers' homes lining ulica Długa. Ogle the gorgeously carved wooden staircase and the Gdańsk-style cupboards.

Other Museums in the Main Town
Historical Zone of the Free City of Gdańsk
(Strefa Historyczna Wolne Miasto Gdańsk)

In a city so obsessed with its Golden Age and Solidarity history, this charming little collection illuminates a unique but often-overlooked chapter in the story of Gdańsk: The years between World Wars I and II, when—in an effort to find a workable compromise in this ethnically mixed city—Gdańsk was not part of Germany or Poland, but a self-governing "free city" *(wolne miasto)*. Like a holdover from medieval fiefdoms in modern times, the city-state of Gdańsk even issued its own currency and stamps. This modest museum, up a tight spiral staircase, earnestly shows off artifacts from the time—photos, stamps, currency (the Gulden), maps, flags, promotional tourist leaflets, and other items from the free city, all marked with the Gdańsk symbol of two white crosses under a crown on a red shield. The brochure explains that four out of five people living in the free city identified themselves not as Germans or Poles, but as "Danzigers." While some might find the subject obscure, this endearing collection is a treat for WWII history buffs. Be sure to borrow the English translations at the entrance.

Cost and Hours: 8 zł, Tue-Sun 12:00-18:00, Sept-April until 17:00, closed Mon year-round, down the little alley just in front of the Green Gate at Warzywnicza 10A, tel. 58-320-2828, www.strefahistorycznawmg.pl.

Archaeological Museum (Muzeum Archeologiczne)

This museum is worth a quick peek for those interested in archaeology. Highlights include distinctive urns with cute faces (which date from the Hallstatt Period and were discovered in slate graves around Gdańsk); Bronze and Iron Age tools; before-and-after photos of WWII Gdańsk; and a reconstructed 12th-century Vikinglike Slavonic longboat. You can also climb the building's tower, with good views up Mariacka street toward St. Mary's Church.

Cost and Hours: Museum—8 zł (free on Sat), tower—5 zł; July-Aug Tue-Fri 9:00-17:00, Sat-Sun 10:00-17:00; Sept-June Tue and Thu-Fri 8:00-16:00, Wed 9:00-17:00, Sat-Sun 10:00-16:00; closed Mon year-round; ulica Mariacka 25, tel. 58-322-2100, www.archeologia.pl.

▲National Maritime Museum
(Narodowe Muzeum Morskie)

Gdańsk's history and livelihood are tied to the sea. This collection, spread among several buildings on either side of the river, examines all aspects of this connection. Nautical types may get a thrill out of the creaky, sprawling museum, but most visitors find it little more than a convenient way to pass some time and enjoy a cruise across the river. The museum's lack of English information is frustrating; fortunately, some exhibits have descriptions you can borrow.

Cost and Hours: Each part of the museum has its own admission (6-8 zł; ask about combo-tickets). The Maritime Cultural Center is worth neither the time nor the money for grown-ups. The hours fluctuate, but it's usually open July-Aug daily 10:00-18:00; Sept-Oct and March-June Tue-Sun until 16:00, closed Mon; Nov-Feb Tue-Sun until 15:00, closed Mon; ulica Ołowianka 9, tel. 58-301-8611, www.nmm.pl.

Visiting the Museum: The exhibit has four parts. The first two parts—the crane and the Maritime Cultural Center—are on the Main Town side of the river. The landmark medieval **crane** (żuraw), Gdańsk's most important symbol, houses a humble exhibit on living in the city during its Golden Age (16th-17th centuries). For more on the crane itself, see page 243.

The **Maritime Cultural Center,** a modern exhibit right next door to the crane, is not worth the exercise unless you are leading a school group. For adults, the most interesting part is "Working Boats," on the second floor.

The rest of the museum—the Old Granaries and the *Sołdek* steamship—is across the river on Ołowianka Island, which you can reach via the little **ferry** (named the *Motława*, like the river; 1.50 zł one-way). The ferry runs about every 15 minutes in peak season (during museum hours only), less frequently in shoulder season, and not at all in the winter.

Once on the island, visit the three rebuilt **Old Granaries** (*Spichlerze*). These make up the heart of the exhibit, tracing the history of Gdańsk—particularly as it relates to the sea—from prehistoric days to the present. Models of the town and region help put things in perspective. Other exhibits cover underwater exploration, navigational aids, artifacts of the Polish seafaring tradition, peekaboo cross-sections of multilevel ships, and models of the modern-day shipyard where Solidarity was born. This place is home to more miniature ships than you ever thought you'd see, and the Nautical Gallery upstairs features endless rooms with paintings of boats.

Finally, crawl through the holds and scramble across the deck of a decommissioned steamship called the *Sołdek,* docked permanently across from the crane (ship generally closed in winter). This was the first postwar vessel built at the Gdańsk shipyard. Below decks, you can see where the crew shoveled the coal; wander through a maze of pipes, gears, valves, gauges, and ladders; and visit the rooms where the sailors lived, slept, and ate. You can even play captain on the bridge.

SOLIDARITY AND THE GDAŃSK SHIPYARD

Gdańsk's single most memorable experience is exploring the shipyard (Stocznia Gdańska) that witnessed the beginning of the end of communism's stranglehold on Eastern Europe. Taken together, the sights in this area are worth ▲▲▲. Here in the former industrial wasteland that Lech Wałęsa called the "cradle of freedom," this evocative site tells the story of the brave Polish shipyard workers who took on—and ultimately defeated—an Evil Empire. A visit to the Solidarity (Solidarność) sights has two main parts: Solidarity Square (with the memorial and gate in front of the shipyard), and the outstanding museum inside the European Solidarity Center.

Getting to the Shipyard: These sights cluster around Solidarity Square (Plac Solidarności), at the north end of the Old Town, about a 20-minute walk from the Royal Way. For the most interesting approach, follow Part 2 of my self-guided walk (earlier), which ends here. Or take tram #7 or #8 from the Brama Wyżynna stop (near the Upland Gate) or the train station to the Plac Solidarości stop.

Background: After the communists took over Eastern Europe at the end of World War II, oppressed peoples throughout the Soviet Bloc rose up in different ways. The most dramatic uprisings— Hungary's 1956 Uprising and Czechoslovakia's 1968 "Prague Spring"—were brutally crushed under the treads of Soviet tanks. The formula for freedom that finally succeeded was a patient, near-ly decade-long series of strikes and protests spearheaded by Lech Wałęsa and his trade union, called Solidarność—"Solidarity." (The movement also benefited from good timing, as it coincided with the *perestroika* and *glasnost* policies of Soviet premier Mikhail Gorbachev.) While politicians tussled from their plush offices, imagine the courage it took for Wałęsa and his fellow workers to fight communism on the front lines—armed with nothing more than guts.

Solidarity Square (Plac Solidarności) and the Monument of the Fallen Shipyard Workers

The seeds of August 1980 were sown a decade before. Since becoming part of the Soviet Bloc, the Poles staged frequent strikes, protests, and uprisings to secure their rights, all of which were put down by the regime. But the bloodiest of these took place in December of 1970—a tragic event memorialized by the **three-crosses monument** that towers over what's now called Solidarity Square.

The 1970 strike was prompted by price hikes. The communist government set the prices for all products. As Poland endured drastic food shortages in the 1960s and 1970s, the regime frequently announced what it called "regulation of prices." Invariably, this meant an increase in the cost of essential foodstuffs. (To be able to claim "regulation" rather than "increase," the regime would symbolically lower prices for a few select items—but these were always nonessential luxuries, such as elevators and TV sets, which nobody could afford anyway.) The regime was usually smart enough to raise prices on January 1, when the people were fat and happy after Christmas, and too hungover to complain. But on December 12, 1970, bolstered by an ego-stoking visit by West German Chancellor Willy Brandt, Polish premier Władysław Gomułka increased prices. The people of Poland—who cared more about the price of Christmas dinner than relations with Germany—struck back.

A wave of strikes and sit-ins spread along the heavily industrialized north coast of Poland, most notably in Gdańsk, Gdynia, and Szczecin. Thousands of angry demonstrators poured through the gate of this shipyard, marched into town, and set fire to the Communist Party Committee building. In an attempt to quell the riots, the government-run radio implored the people to go back to work. On the morning of December 17, workers showed up at shipyard gates across northern Poland, and were greeted by the army and police. Without provocation, the Polish army opened fire on the workers. While the official death toll for the massacre stands at 44, others say the true number is much higher. The monument, with a trio of 140-foot-tall crosses, honors those lost to the regime that December.

Go to the middle of the **wall** behind the crosses, to the monument of the worker wearing a flimsy plastic work helmet, attempting to shield himself from bullets. Behind him is a list—pock-marked with symbolic bullet holes—of workers murdered on that day. *Lat* means "years old"—many teenagers were among the dead. The quote at the top of the wall is from St. John Paul II, who was elected pope eight years after this tragedy. The pope was known for his clever way with words, and this very carefully phrased quote—which served as an inspiration to the Poles during their darkest hours—skewers the regime in a way subtle enough to still be tolerated: "Let thy spirit descend, and renew the face of the earth—of *this* earth" (that is, Poland).

Stretching to the left of this center wall are plaques representing labor unions from around Poland—and around the world (look for the Chinese characters)—expressing solidarity with these workers. To the right is an enormous Bible verse: "May the Lord give strength to his people. May the Lord bless his people with the gift of peace" (Psalms 29:11).

Inspired by the brave sacrifice of their true comrades, shipyard workers rose up here in August of 1980, formulating the **"21 Points"** of a new union called Solidarity. Their demands included the right to strike and form unions, the freeing of political prisoners, and an increase in wages. The 21 Points are listed in Polish on the panel at the far end of the right wall, marked *21 X TAK* ("21 times yes"). An unwritten precondition to any agreement was the right for the workers of 1980 to build a memorial to their comrades slain in 1970. The government agreed, marking the first time a communist regime ever allowed a monument to be built to honor its own victims. Wałęsa called it a harpoon in the heart of the communists. The towering monument, with three crucified anchors on top, was designed, engineered, and built by shipyard workers. The monument was finished just four months after the historic agreement was signed.

• *Now continue to the gate and peer through into the birthplace of Eastern European freedom.*

Gdańsk Shipyard (Stocznia Gdańska) Gate #2

When a Pole named Karol Wojtyła was elected pope in 1978—and visited his homeland in 1979—he inspired his 40 million countrymen to believe that impossible dreams can come true. Prices continued to go up, and the workers continued to rise up. By the summer of 1980, it was clear that the dam was about to break.

In   August,   Anna

Lech Wałęsa

In 1980, the world was turned on its ear by a walrus-mustachioed shipyard electrician. Within three years, this seemingly run-of-the-mill Pole had precipitated the collapse of communism, led a massive 10-million-member trade union with enormous political impact, been named *Time* magazine's Man of the Year, and won a Nobel Peace Prize.

Lech Wałęsa was born in Popowo, Poland in 1943. After working as a car mechanic and serving two years in the army, he became an electrician at the Gdańsk Shipyard in 1967. Like many Poles, Wałęsa felt stifled by the communist government, and was infuriated that a system that was supposed to be for the workers clearly wasn't serving them.

When the shipyard massacre took place in December of 1970 (see page 258), Wałęsa was at the forefront of the protests. He was marked as a dissident, and in 1976, he was fired. Wałęsa hopped from job to job and was occasionally unemployed—under communism, a rock-bottom status reserved for only the most despicable derelicts. But he soldiered on, fighting for the creation of a trade union and building up quite a file with the secret police.

In August 1980, Wałęsa heard news of the beginnings of the Gdańsk strike and raced to the shipyard. In an act that has since become the stuff of legend, Wałęsa scaled the shipyard wall to get inside.

Before long, Wałęsa's dynamic personality won him the unofficial role of the workers' leader and spokesman. He negotiated with the regime to hash out the August Agreements, becoming a rock star-type hero during the so-called 16 Months of Hope... until martial law came crashing down in December 1981. Wałęsa was arrested and interned for 11 months in a country house. After

Walentynowicz—a Gdańsk crane operator and known dissident—was fired unceremoniously just short of her retirement. This sparked a strike in the Gdańsk Shipyard (then called the Lenin Shipyard) on August 14, 1980. An electrician named Lech Wałęsa had been fired as an agitator years before. But on hearing news of the strike, Wałęsa went to the shipyard and climbed over the wall to get inside. The strike now had a leader.

These were not soldiers, nor were they idealistic flower children. The strike participants were gritty, salt-of-the-earth manual laborers: forklift operators, welders, electricians, machinists. Imagine being one of the 16,000 workers who stayed here for 18 days being released, he continued to struggle underground, becoming a symbol of anticommunist sentiment.

Finally, the dedication of Wałęsa and Solidarity paid off, and Polish communism dissolved—with Wałęsa rising from the ashes as the country's first postcommunist president. But the skills that made Wałęsa a rousing success at leading an uprising didn't translate well to the president's office. Wałęsa proved to be a stubborn, headstrong politician, frequently clashing with the parliament. He squabbled with his own party, declaring a "war at the top" of Solidarity and rotating higher-ups to prevent corruption and keep the party fresh. He also didn't choose his advisors well, enlisting old friends as staffers who wound up immersed in scandal. His overconfidence was his Achilles' heel, and his governing style verged on authoritarian.

Unrefined and none too interested in scripted speeches, Wałęsa was a simple man who preferred playing ping-pong with his buddies to attending formal state functions. Though lacking a formal education, Wałęsa had unsurpassed drive and charisma... but that's not enough to lead a country—especially during an impossibly complicated, fast-changing time.

Wałęsa was defeated at the polls, by the Poles, in 1995, and when he ran again in 2000, he received a humiliating one percent of the vote. Since leaving office, Wałęsa has kept a lower profile, but still delivers speeches worldwide. Many poor Poles grumble that Lech, who started life simple like them, has forgotten the little people. But his fans point out that he gives much of his income to charity. And on his lapel, he still always wears a pin featuring the Black Madonna of Częstochowa—the most important symbol of Polish Catholicism.

Poles say there are at least two Lech Wałęsas: the young, bombastic, working-class idealist Lech, at the forefront of the Solidarity strikes, who will always have a special place in their hearts; and the failed President Wałęsa, who got in over his head and tarnished his legacy.

during the strike—hungry, cold, sleeping on sheets of Styrofoam, inspired by the new Polish pope, excited about finally standing up to the regime...and terrified that at any moment you might be gunned down, like your friends had been a decade before.

Workers, afraid to leave the shipyard, communicated with the outside world through this gate—wives and brothers showed up here and asked for a loved one, and those inside spread the word until the striker came forward. Occasionally, a truck pulled up inside the gate, with Lech Wałęsa standing atop its cab with a megaphone. Facing the thousands of people assembled outside the gate, Wałęsa gave progress reports on the negotiations and pleaded for supplies. The people of Gdańsk responded, bringing armfuls of bread and other food to keep the workers going. Solidarity.

During the strike, two items hung on the fence. One of them (which still hangs there today) was a picture of Pope John Paul II—a reminder to believe in your dreams and have faith in God (for more on the Pope and his role in Solidarity, see page 56). The other item was a makeshift list of the strikers' 21 Points—demands scrawled in red paint and black pencil on pieces of plywood.

• *Walk through the passage at the right end of the gate and enter the former shipyard.*

There's not much to see today, but during its peak from 1948 to 1990, the **shipyard** churned out over a thousand ships and employed 16,000 workers. About 60 percent of these ships were exported to the USSR—and so, when the Soviet Bloc broke apart in the 1990s, they lost a huge market. Today the facilities employ closer to 1,200 workers...who now make windmills.

Before entering the museum, take a look around. This part of the shipyard, long abandoned, is slated for redevelopment into a **"Young City"** (Młode Miasto)—envisioned as a new city center for Gdańsk, with shopping, restaurants, offices, and homes. Rusting shipbuilding equipment is being torn down, and old brick buildings are being converted into gentrified flats. The nearby boulevard called Nowa Wałowa will be the spine connecting this area to the rest of the city. Farther east, plans call for the harborfront to be rejuvenated, creating a glitzy marina and extending the city's delightful waterfront people zone to the north (see www.ycgdansk.com). Fortunately, the shipyard gate, monument, and other important sites from the Solidarity strikes—now considered historical monuments—will remain.

• *The massive, rust-colored European Solidarity Center, which faces Solidarity Square, houses the museum where we'll learn the rest of the story.*

▲▲▲European Solidarity Center (Europejskie Centrum Solidarności)

Europe's single best sight about the end of communism is made even more powerful by its location: in the very heart of the place where those events occurred. Filling just one small corner of a huge, purpose-built educational facility, the permanent exhibition uses larger-than-life photographs, archival footage, actual artifacts, interactive touchscreens, and a state-of-the-art audioguide to eloquently tell the story of the end of Eastern European communism.

Cost and Hours: 20 zł, includes audioguide; May-Sept Mon–Fri 10:00–19:00, Sat–Sun until 20:00; Oct–April Mon and Wed–Fri 10:00–17:00, Sat–Sun until 18:00, closed Tue; last entry one hour before closing, Plac Solidarności 1, tel. 58-772-4000, www.ecs.gda.pl.

◑ Self-Guided Tour: First, appreciate the architecture of the **building** itself. From the outside, it's designed to resemble the rusted hull of a giant ship—seemingly gloomy and depressing. But step inside to find an interior flooded with light, which cultivates a surprising variety of life—in the form of lush gardens that make the place feel like a very expensive greenhouse. You can interpret this symbolism a number of ways: Something that seems dull and dreary from the outside (the Soviet Bloc, the shipyards themselves, what have you) can be full of brightness, life, and optimism inside.

In the lobby, buy your ticket and pick up the essential, included audioguide. The exhibit has much to see, and some of it is arranged in a conceptual way that can be tricky to understand without a full grasp of the history. I've outlined the basics in this self-guided tour, but the audioguide can illuminate more details—including translations of films and eyewitness testimony from participants in the history.

• *The permanent exhibit fills seven lettered rooms—each with its own theme—on two floors. From the lush lobby, head up the escalator and into...*

The Birth of Solidarity (Room A): This room picks up right in the middle of the dynamic story we just learned out on the square. It's August of 1980, and the shipyard workers are rising up. You step straight into a busy shipyard: punch clocks, workers' lockers, and—up on the ceiling—hundreds of plastic helmets. A big **map** in the middle of the room shows the extent of the shipyard in 1980. Nearby stands a **truck;** Lech Wałęsa would stand on top of the cab of a truck like this one to address the nervous locals who had amassed outside the shipyard gate, awaiting further news.

In the middle of the room, carefully protected under glass, are those original **plywood panels** onto which the strikers scrawled their 21 demands, then lashed to the gate. Just beyond that, a giant video screen and a map illustrate how the strikes that began here spread like a virus across Poland. At the far end of the room, behind the partition, stand **two tables** that were used during the talks to end the strikes (each one with several actual items from that era, under glass).

After 18 days of protests, the communist authorities finally agreed to negotiate. On the afternoon of August 31, 1980, the Governmental Commission and the Inter-Factory Strike Committee (MKS) came together and signed the August Agreements, which legalized Solidarity—the first time any communist government permitted a workers' union. As Lech Wałęsa sat at a big table and signed the agreement, other union reps tape-recorded the proceedings and played them later at their own factories to prove that the unthinkable had happened. Take a moment to linger over the rousing **film** that plays on the far wall, which begins with the strike, carries through with the tense negotiations that a brash young Lech Wałęsa held with the authorities, and ends with the triumphant acceptance of the strikers' demands. Lech Wałęsa rides on the shoulders of well-wishers out to the gate to spread the good news. The gate opens, the strikers file out, and the crowd cheers: "Leszek! Leszek!" (Lech-y! Lech-y!)

• *Back by the original 21 demands, enter the next exhibit...*

The Power of the Powerless (Room B): This section traces the roots of the 1980 strikes, which were preceded by several far less successful protests. It all begins with a kiss: a giant photograph of Russian premier Leonid Brezhnev mouth-kissing the Polish premier Edward Gierek, with the caption **"Brotherly Friendship."** Soviet premiers and their satellite leaders really did greet each other "in the French manner," as a symbolic gesture of their communist brotherhood.

Working your way through the exhibit, you'll see the door to a **prison cell**—a reminder of the intimidation tactics used by the Soviets in the 1940s and 1950s to deal with their opponents as they exerted their rule over the lands they had liberated from the Nazis.

The typical **communist-era apartment** is painfully humble. After the war, much of Poland had been destroyed, and population shifts led to housing shortages. People had to make do with tiny spaces and ramshackle furnishings. Communist propaganda blares from both the radio and the TV.

A map shows **"red Europe"** (the USSR plus the satellites of Poland, Czechoslovakia, Hungary, and East Germany), and a **timeline** traces some of the smaller Soviet Bloc protests that led up to Solidarity: in East Germany in 1953, in Budapest and Poznań in 1956, the "Prague Spring" of 1968, and other 1968 protests in Poland.

In the wake of these uprisings, the communist authorities cracked down even harder. Peek into the **interrogation room,** with a wall of file cabinets and a lowly stool illuminated by a bright spotlight. (Notice that the white Polish eagle on the seal above the desk is missing its golden crown—during communism, the Poles were allowed to keep the eagle, but its crown was removed.)

The next exhibit presents a day-by-day rundown of the **1970 strikes,** from December 14 to 22, which resulted in the massacre of the workers who are honored by the monument in front of this building. In the glass case, the leather jacket with bullet holes was worn by a 20-year-old worker who was killed that day. A wall of mug shots gives way to exhibits chronicling the steady rise of dissent groups through the 1970s, culminating in the June 1976 protests in the city of Radom (prompted, like so many other uprisings, by unilateral price hikes). On your way out of this section, you pass through a mock-up of a grocery store from the period...with empty shelves.

• *Loop back through Room A, and proceed straight ahead into...*

Solidarity and Hope (Room C): While the government didn't take the August Agreements very seriously, the Poles did...and before long, 10 million of them—one out of every four, or effectively half the nation's workforce—joined Solidarity. So began what's often called the **"16 Months of Hope."** Newly legal, Solidarity continued to stage strikes and make its opposition known. Slick Solidarity posters and children's art convey the childlike enthusiasm with which the Poles seized their hard-won kernels of freedom. The communist authorities' hold on the Polish people began to slip. Support and aid from the outside world poured in, but the rest of the Soviet Bloc looked on nervously, and the Warsaw Pact army assembled at the Polish border and glared at the uprisers. The threat of invasion hung heavy in the air.

• *Exiting this room, head up the staircase and into...*

At War with Society (Room D): In this black room, you're greeted by a wall of TV screens delivering a stern message. On Sunday morning, December 13, 1981, the Polish head of state, **General Wojciech Jaruzelski**—wearing his trademark dark glasses—appeared on national TV and announced the introduction of **martial law.** Solidarity was outlawed, and its leaders were arrested. Frightened Poles heard the announcement and looked out their windows to see Polish Army tanks rumbling through the snowy streets. (On the opposite wall, see footage of tanks and heavily armed soldiers intimidating their countrymen into compliance.) Jaruzelski claimed that he imposed martial law to prevent the Soviets from invading. Today, many historians question whether martial law was really necessary, though Jaruzelski remained unremorseful through his death in 2014.

Continuing deeper into the exhibit, you come to a **prisoner transport.** Climb up inside to watch chilling scenes of riots, demonstrations, and crackdowns by the ZOMO riot police. In one gruesome scene, a demonstrator is quite intentionally run over by a truck. From here, pass through a gauntlet of *milicja* riot-gear shields to see the truck crashing through a gate. Overhead are the uniforms of miners from the **Wujek mine** who were massacred on December 16, 1981 (their names are projected on the pile of coal below).

Martial law was a tragic, terrifying, and bleak time for the Polish people. It didn't, however, kill the Solidarity movement, which continued its fight after going underground. Passing prison cells, you'll see a wall plastered with handmade, underground posters and graffiti. Notice how in this era, **Solidarity propaganda** is much more primitive; circle around the other side of the wall to see several presses that were actually used in clandestine Solidarity print shops during this time. The outside world sent messages of support as well as supplies—represented by the big wall of cardboard boxes. This approval also came in the form of a Nobel Peace Prize for Lech Wałęsa in 1983; you'll see video clips of his wife accepting the award on his behalf (Wałęsa feared that if he traveled abroad to claim it, he would not be allowed back into the country). On the other side of the room is an exhibit about Pope John Paul II's visit in the very tense days of 1983.

• *But even in these darkest days, there were glimmers of hope. Enter...*

The Road to Democracy (Room E): By the time the Pope visited his homeland again in 1987, martial law had finally been lifted, and Solidarity—still technically illegal—was gaining momentum, gradually pecking away at the communists. Step into the small inner room with footage of the **Pope's third pilgrimage** to his homeland in 1987, by which time (thanks in no small part to his inspirational role in the ongoing revolution) the tide was turning.

Step into the room with the big, white **roundtable.** With the moral support of the pope and the entire Western world, the brave Poles were the first European country to throw off the shackles of communism when, in the spring of 1989, the "Roundtable Talks" led to the opening up of elections. The government arrogantly called for parliamentary elections, reserving 65 percent of seats for themselves.

In the next room, you can see Solidarity's strategy in those **elections:** On the right wall are posters showing Lech Wałęsa with each candidate. Another popular "get out the vote" measure was the huge poster of Gary Cooper—an icon of America, which the Poles deeply respect and viewed as their friendly cousin across the Atlantic—except that, instead of a pistol, he's packing a ballot. Rousing reminders like this inspired huge voter turnout. The communists' plan backfired, as virtually every open seat went to Solidarity. It was the first time ever that opposition candidates had taken office in the Soviet Bloc. On the wall straight ahead, flashing a V-for-*wiktoria* sign, is a huge photo of Tadeusz Mazowiecki—an early leader of Solidarity, who became prime minister on June 4, 1989.

• *For the glorious aftermath, head into the final room.*

The Triumph of Freedom (Room F): This room is dominated by a gigantic **map of Eastern Europe.** A countdown clock on the right ticks off the departure of each country from communist clutches, as the Soviet Bloc "decomposes." You'll see how the success of Solidarity in Poland—and the ragtag determination of a scruffy band of shipyard workers right here in Gdańsk—inspired people all over Eastern Europe. By the winter of 1989, the Hungarians had opened their borders, the Berlin Wall had crumbled, and the Czechs and Slovaks had staged their Velvet Revolution. (Small viewing stations that circle the room reveal the detailed story for each country's own road to freedom.) Lech Wałęsa—the shipyard electrician who started it all by jumping over a wall—became the first president of postcommunist Poland. And a year later, in Poland's first true elections since World War II, 29 different parties won seats in the parliament. It was a free-election free-for-all.

In the middle of the room stands a white wall with **inspirational quotes** from St. John Paul II and Václav Havel—the Czech poet-turned-protester-turned-prisoner-turned-president—which are repeated in several languages. On the huge wall, the **Solidarity "graffiti"** is actually made up of thousands of little notes left behind by visitors to the museum. Feel free to grab a piece of paper and a pen and record your own reflections.

• *Finally, head downstairs into a peaceful space.*

Culture of Peaceful Change (Room G): Many visitors find that touring this museum—with vivid reminders of a dramatic and pivotal moment in history that took place in their own lifetimes and was brought about not by armies or presidents, but by everyday people—puts them in an emotional state of mind. Designed for silent reflection, this room overlooks the monument to those workers who were gunned down in 1970. It shows footage of Pope John Paul II, Lech Wałęsa, Martin Luther King Jr., and others who dedicated their lives to peaceful change.

• *For an epilogue, continue deeper into the former shipyard to see one more important landmark from 1980. Exit the building the way you came in, and turn left. The path leads to a low-profile, red-brick building about 80 yards ahead, the...*

▲Sala BHP

This is the building where the communists sat down across the table from Lech Wałęsa and his team and worked out a compromise (as seen in the videos inside the European Solidarity Center). Entering, turn left into the Small Hall to view a series of photos that illustrate Solidarity history; these are all the more poignant because they lack the bombastic presentation of the glitzy museum. The images speak for themselves. The other side of the building (right from the entrance) is the actual hall where those fateful meetings took place, with a long table set up on the stage. You'll see a model of the shipyard, circa 1980, and models of the various ships that were built here.

Cost and Hours: Free, daily 10:00-18:00, Oct-April until 16:00, www.salabhp.pl.

NORTH OF THE MAIN TOWN
▲▲Museum of the Second World War
(Muzeum II Wojny Światowej)

In 2017, Poland's definitive WWII museum opened in a state-of-the-art, purpose-build facility a 10-minute walk north of Gdańsk's Main Town. It uses artifacts, creative design, insightful storytelling, and ample archival footage to tell the story of the war that began right at Gdańsk's doorstep—focusing on the Polish experience, but also expanding its focus to other aspects of the conflict. At more than 50,000 square feet, it's one of the biggest historical exhibits in the world. (Pace yourself.) While those with a limited appetite for history may find it overwhelming, even those with a casual interest will be glad they invested two or three hours touring its exhibits.

As impressive as the museum is, it could have been that much better. The original design presented an ambitiously global, yet personal, perspective on the war—carefully calibrated to be even-handed and international in its outlook. But as it neared completion, ruling politicians from the nationalistic Law and Justice Party deemed it too pacifistic and "not Polish enough." They replaced the museum director and his staff, and hired a new director who changed several exhibits to be more singularly patriotic—playing up the "martyrdom" aspect of Poland's role in the war. In the end, it's sad to think that this museum could have been Europe's best WWII museum—if only trained historians had been allowed to control it, rather than politicians. For that reason, I rate it ▲▲ rather than ▲▲▲.

Cost and Hours: 23 zł, essential audioguide-5 zł; June-Sept Tue 10:00-19:00, Wed-Sun 10:00-20:00; Oct-May Tue-Fri until 19:00, Sat-Sun until 20:00; closed Mon year-round; Plac Władysława Bartoszewskiego 1, tel. 58-760-0960, www.muzeum1939.pl.

Getting There: It's a short walk north of the historical center. The most appealing approach is to walk north along the riverfront promenade all the way to its end; you'll see the giant, rust-red, glassy tower on your left.

Visiting the Museum: As you approach, appreciate the symbolic architecture of the site. The ground level—nicely landscaped, with inviting slingback chairs in the summer—represents the present. The museum's exhibit space is entirely underground—representing the past. And the tower rising above represents the future. All of the buildings are clad in rusted steel—the material of choice in this shipbuilding city.

Head down the stairs at the base of the tower, go inside, and take the elevator down to level -3. This area has ticket desks, a cloakroom, WCs, a **$** bistro, a shop, a cinema, temporary exhibits, and the entrance to the permanent exhibition. When you buy your ticket, spring for the audioguide, which helpfully navigates the highlights of the sprawling exhibits and translates some of the films. It's geo-tagged, so it knows where you are and informs you accordingly.

Head through the turnstile. A long **corridor** stretches to your right; 18 clearly numbered exhibition halls weave in and out of this corridor, chronologically telling the story. As you crisscross through the corridor, take a moment to ponder its exhibits about everyday life in wartime, covering such topics as food and cooking, fashion and style, the black market, travel, and music.

Before heading into the main exhibition, consider turning left, into the **Time Travel** exhibit. Designed for Polish kids, it follows two children and their everyday life, before, during, and after the war—with the same apartment re-created for each time period.

The first part of the exhibit is straight ahead from the entrance turnstile: A movie that sets the stage by recapping the events of World War I and the interwar period.

Now proceed down the corridor and work your way chronologically through the numbered exhibits. Section **01** traces the rise of communism in the Soviet Union (the quern stone was used for grinding grain by ethnic Poles in Ukraine, many of whom perished under Stalin's policies); Fascism in Italy (the Fiat embodies the populism—a car in every driveway—that drove Mussolini's propaganda); and Nazism in Germany (with a bust and posters of Hitler, some hateful anti-Semitic propaganda, and a clip from Leni Riefenstahl's *Triumph of the Will*).

Section **02** is a reconstructed Polish street from the interwar period. (Remember this—you'll see it again later.) The nearby hallway outlines the rise of imperialism in Japan, Franco's ascent in Spain, and Germany's dismantling of the Versailles system that ended the conflict of World War I. Gdańsk—then called Danzig—held a unique position: It was a free city, with Germany on one side and Poland on the other. As Hitler rose, Western Europeans already knew that Danzig would be a bulwark against his aggression—giving rise to the slogan "Die for Danzig." You'll see a replica of the secret Molotov-Ribbentrop Pact between the USSR and Nazi Germany, agreeing to divide Poland down the middle—and clearing the way for invasion.

In section **03,** you'll learn how that invasion took place on September 1, 1939, when Hitler invaded Poland (en route to Danzig) and quickly overran the country—the first use of his relentless Blitzkrieg ("Lightning War") strategy. One exhibit explains the first volley of that war, in which 200 Poles defended the military transit depot Westerplatte against 3,000 Nazi troops for seven days. You'll learn about the brutal Nazi atrocities from that first invasion, including photos of bombed-out cities. One of the museum's highlights is the film *Siege,* shot and narrated by American correspondent Julien Bryan, who was in Warsaw during the invasion and witnessed the Nazis bombarding a church during Mass, the bombing of a maternity ward, and a village of peasants machine-gunned from the air while digging up potatoes. You'll learn how soon, the Soviet Union also invaded (per their secret agreement)—meeting the Nazis in the middle and splitting Poland in half.

Across the main corridor, section **04** outlines Soviet conquests in other parts of Europe (Finland, the Baltic states, Romania). Section **05** (with a JU-87 dive bomber suspended from the wall) explains how this was a new kind of war, relying heavily on air warfare (Hitler's Luftwaffe).

Back across the corridor, section **06** documents the ruthlessness of the Nazis, including their starvation of Soviet POWs (the "Hunger Plan" that killed more than three million captured troops); the 871-day Siege of Leningrad (today's St. Petersburg, where one million civilians starved to death); and air raids that killed another one million civilians.

Across the corridor, section **07** considers how totalitarian regimes recruited collaborators in the countries they occupied—employing methods from propaganda to intimidation. You'll see a replica of a "Red Corner"—a workers' meeting hall, draped in communist propaganda, that you'd find in any workplace or institution. A film on Soviet propaganda methods explains Stalin's philosophy of "national in form, Soviet in content"—appropriating locally beloved symbols, but infusing them with a communist agenda.

At section **08,** giant letters spell out TERROR. This exhibit explains how totalitarian regimes rounded up and executed elites (such as the USSR's Katyń Massacre of Polish intelligentsia, close to the heart of every Pole). The room with a vast map on the floor illustrates forced resettlement; the doors lining the walls have exhibits explaining specific examples. You'll learn how heavily the occupying forces relied on forced labor—essentially exploiting 20 million slaves—including workers here in Gdańsk (the metal plates on the walls were used to keep track of workers). This section also has a powerful exhibit on daily life in Nazi concentration camps, with many powerful objects: striped uniforms and wooden clogs; a homemade nativity scene and tiny figures carved from a toothbrush by prisoners; a violin; and a baby's christening gown. You'll also see a wheelchair from a psychiatric hospital near Gdańsk. All of its inmates were executed.

Section **09** explores the methodical implementation of the Holocaust, including a train car used to transport prisoners. A wall of suitcases is a re-

minder of how prisoners were stripped of belong-ings on arrival. You'll walk through a room displaying photographs of hundreds of Holocaust victims. Sec-tion **10** considers other in-stances of ethnic cleansing during World War II, in-cluding Serbs killed in the Nazi puppet state of Croatia, and Poles killed in Ukraine.

Section **11**—with the giant letters *OPÓR* ("Resistance")— explains the various ways that occupied peoples rose up. Poland maintained a government in exile, and a military that participated in Allied offensives (Poles were the first to reach the top of Monte Cassino in Italy)—essentially a continuation of prewar statehood, despite occupation. You'll learn both about civilian resistance movements, and partisan fighting forces on the battlefields (such as Tito's Partisans in Yugoslavia). This section also honors various uprisings against totalitarian regimes.

Section **12** features the clandestine front—spies, espionage, and the battle over secrets. In a room with an actual Enigma ma-chine, you'll learn how it was Polish mathematicians who first broke the Nazis' secret code...then furnished that breakthrough to the British. Today, Alan Turing and the other codebreakers at Britain's Bletchley Park get virtually all of the credit for the tens of thousands of lives that were saved. (Many Poles believe that the breaking of the Enigma code was Poland's single most important contribution to winning the war.)

Section **13** considers the ways that countries mobilize—economically and societally—in times of war. Wartime brought about such innovations as the jet engine, the computer, and the nuclear bomb. While the Nazis relied on slave labor to build armaments, the Allies mobilized female citizens...and outproduced their enemies three-to-one. In this section, you'll see a Sherman Firefly tank (built in the UK).

Section **14** explains how the tide of war turned toward the Allies, while section **15** considers the postwar reality—which was cooked up even before Hitler was dead, when Churchill, FDR, and Stalin met in Yalta, agreeing to divvy up Europe after their victory. (Many Poles still consider this a betrayal: After their suffering and valiant contributions, they were effectively left to the whim of the USSR after the war.) The postwar period was bittersweet: victory parades celebrating the defeat of evil, but also a Poland left in ruins, the rise of a ruthless Soviet empire in Eastern Europe, and a series of forced population resettlements (to match the new borders) that uprooted millions.

Section **16** shows the same city street we saw earlier—but now in ruins, presided over by a Soviet tank. A mockup of a courtroom considers both the triumphs and the failings of the postwar justice system: Yes, high-profile war criminals were prosecuted. But the overflowing file cabinet on the dark side of the room is a reminder of the many lower-level war criminals who were never brought to justice.

Cross the destroyed street to section **17,** with photos of cities that were left in ruins at war's end, and section **18,** divided by a symbolic "Iron Curtain"—a reminder that World War II was only the beginning of a painful chapter for Poland and all of Eastern Europe.

Just before you exit, playing overhead is a cheaply produced, rabble-rousing, nakedly patriotic **movie**...a sad reminder of the way a wonderful museum was mucked up by politics. (Before the right-wing government fired the museum director, this film was very different—ending the exhibit on a pensive note rather than a nationalistic one.)

Despite its shortcomings, the Museum of the Second World War is a powerful and comprehensive look at the most devastating conflict in human history, from the perspective of the country that was perhaps the most devastated by it.

Nearby: A short walk over a canal (across the Więcierze Bridge) from the museum is the **Polish Post Office of Danzig**

(on plac Obrońców Poczty Polskiej). History buffs recognize this landmark as part of the initial Nazi attacks on September 1, 1939, which began World War II. The post office—which was a nerve center for local Polish intelligence officers—was attacked by Nazi forces and defended by Polish officers. After 15 hours of fighting, everyone inside was dead or had fled; those who escaped were later executed. Immortalized in the 1959 Günter Grass historical novel *The Tin Drum,* today this building is a museum suitable only for real history buffs.

SOUTH OF THE MAIN TOWN

A 10- to 15-minute walk south of the Main Town, these sights round out the Gdańsk experience for those with a special interest in art or theater.

National Museum in Gdańsk (Muzeum Narodowe w Gdańsku)

This art collection, housed in what was a 15th-century Franciscan monastery, is worth ▲▲ to art lovers for one reason: Hans Memling's glorious *Last Judgment* triptych altarpiece, one of the two most important pieces of art to be seen in Poland (the other is Leonardo da Vinci's *Lady with an Ermine,* usually in Kraków's Czartoryski Museum). If you're not a purist, you can settle for seeing the much smaller replica in St. Mary's Church. But if medieval art is your bag, make the 10-minute walk here from the Main Town.

Cost and Hours: 10 zł, May-Sept Tue-Sun 10:00-17:00, Oct-April Tue-Sun 9:00-16:00, closed Mon year-round, last entry 45 minutes before closing; walk 10 minutes due south from ulica Długa's Golden Gate, after passing the Shakespeare Theater take the pedestrian underpass beneath the big cross street, then continue down the busy street until you see signs for the museum; ulica Toruńska 1, tel. 58-301-6804, www.mng.gda.pl.

Visiting the Museum: From the entry, the **altarpiece by Hans Memling** (c. 1440-1494) is at the top of the stairs and to the right. The history of the painting is as interesting as the work itself. It was commissioned in the mid-15th century by the Medicis' banker in Florence, Angelo di Jacopo Tani. The ship delivering the painting from Belgium to Florence was hijacked by a Gdańsk pirate, who brought the altarpiece to his hometown to be displayed in St. Mary's Church. For centuries, kings, emperors, and czars admired it from afar, until Napoleon seized it in the early 19th century and took it to Paris to hang in the Louvre. Gdańsk finally got the painting back, only to have it exiled again—this time into St. Petersburg's Hermitage Museum—after World War II. On its return to Gdańsk in 1956, this museum claimed it—though St. Mary's wants it back.

Have a close look at Memling's well-traveled work. It's the end of the world, and Christ rides in on a rainbow to judge humankind. Angels blow reveille, waking the dead, who rise from their graves. The winged archangel Michael—dressed for battle and wielding the cross like a weapon—weighs the grace in each person, sending them either to the fires of hell (right panel) or up the sparkling-crystal stairway to heaven (left).

It takes all 70 square feet of paneling to contain this awesome scene. Jam-packed with dozens of bodies and a Bible's worth of symbolism, and executed with astonishing detail, the painting can keep even a non-art lover occupied. Notice the serene, happy expressions of the righteous, as they're greeted by St. Peter (with his giant key) and clothed by angels. And pity the condemned, their faces filled with terror and sorrow as they're tortured by grotesque devils more horrifying than anything Hollywood could devise.

Tune in to the exquisite details: the angels' robes, the devils' genetic-mutant features, the portrait of the man in the scale (a Medici banker), Michael's peacock wings. Get as close as you can to the globe at Christ's feet and Michael's shining breastplate: You can just make out the whole scene in mirror reflection. Then back up and take it all in—three panels connected by a necklace of bodies that curves downward through hell, crosses the earth, then rises up to the towers of the New Jerusalem. On the back side of the triptych are reverent portraits of the painting's patron, Angelo Tani, and his new bride, Catarina.

Beyond the Memling, the remainder of the collection isn't too thrilling. The rest of the upstairs has more Flemish and Dutch art, as well as paintings from Gdańsk's Golden Age and various works by Polish artists. The ground floor features a cavernous, all-white cloister filled with Gothic altarpiece sculptures, gold and silver wares, and Gdańsk-style furniture.

Gdańsk Shakespeare Theater (Teatr Szekspirowski)

Gdańsk has a long and proud tradition of staging plays by Shakespeare. As early as the 17th century, theater troupes from England would come to this cosmopolitan trading city to perform. In 1993, local actors revived the tradition with an annual Gdańsk Shakespeare Festival. And in 2014, the city built the state-of-the-art Gdańsk Shakespeare Theater to honor its connection to the Bard.

The building's minimalist, black-brick, blocky architecture—with a few symbolic faux-buttresses to echo the gables of the surrounding buildings—was criticized for not blending in very well with its surroundings. But the celebration of theater that takes place inside is welcomed by all. The main theater can be modified to create three different types of performance spaces (proscenium, thrust stage, and theater in the round)—and even has a retractable roof to wash the actors with direct sunlight.

If you want to take a peek, just follow Pcztowa street south from the middle of ulica Długa; the box office is at Bogusławskiego 1.

Tours and Performances: Theater lovers can take a one-hour guided tour of the building for 18 zł (usually daily at 15:00). Call or check their website for details on the tour and upcoming performances (tel. 58-351-0101, www.teatrszekspirowski.pl).

Shakespeare contributes only a tiny piece of the theater's full lineup—it plays host to a wide variety of performances and festivals throughout the year. You're most likely to find Shakespeare performed in English during the annual Shakespeare Festival, which is typically in the summer (details on theater website).

OUTER GDAŃSK

These two sights—worthwhile only to those with a particular interest in them—are each within the city limits of Gdańsk, but they take some serious time to see round-trip.

Oliwa Cathedral (Katedra Oliwska)

The suburb of Oliwa, at the northern edge of Gdańsk, is home to this visually striking church. The quirky, elongated facade hides a surprisingly long and skinny nave. The ornately decorated 18th-century organ over the main entrance features angels and stars that move around when the organ is played. While locals are proud of this place, it's hard to justify the effort it takes to get out here. Skip it unless you just love Polish churches or you're going to a concert.

Concerts: The animated organ performs its 20-minute show frequently, especially in summer (in high season, concerts at the top of most hours—confirm schedule online or at Gdańsk TI before making the trip, www.archikatedraoliwa.pl). Note that on Sundays and holidays, there are no concerts before 15:00.

Getting There: Oliwa is about six miles northwest of central Gdańsk, on the way to Sopot and Gdynia. To reach Oliwa from Gdańsk's main train station, you have two options: Ride **tram #6** or #12, get off at the Oliwa stop and walk a few minutes through the park to the church (about 30 minutes total); or take an **SKM commuter train** to the Gdańsk Oliwa stop (15 minutes), then walk 15 minutes (or take a 10-zł taxi ride) to Oliwski Park and the cathedral.

Westerplatte

World War II began on September 1, 1939, when Adolf Hitler sent the warship *Schleswig-Holstein* to attack this Polish munitions depot, which was guarding Gdańsk's harbor. Though it may give serious WWII history buffs goosebumps, most visitors will find little to see here aside from a modest museum, a towering monument, and some old bunkers.

Getting There: The most enjoyable approach is on a cruise—either on a modern boat, or on a fun old-fashioned galleon (45 minutes each way; see page 284). You can also take **bus** #106, #138, or (in summer) #606 from the main train station (about 30 minutes).

Shopping in Gdańsk

The big story in Gdańsk is amber *(bursztyn)*, a fossil resin available in all shades, shapes, and sizes (see the "All About Amber" sidebar, earlier). The best place to browse and buy amber is along the atmospheric ulica Mariacka (between the Motława River and St. Mary's Church). This pretty street, with old-fashioned balconies and dozens of display cases, is fun to wander even if you're not a shopper. Other good places to buy amber are along the riverfront embankment and on ulica Długa.

To avoid rip-offs—such as amber that's been melted and re-shaped—always buy it from a shop, not from someone standing on the street. (But note that most shops also have a display case and salesperson out front, which are perfectly legit.) Prices everywhere are about the same, so instead of seeking out a specific place, just window shop until you see what you want. Styles range from gaudy necklaces with huge globs of amber, to tasteful smaller pendants in silver settings, to cheap trinkets. All shades of amber—from near-white to dark brown—cost about the same, but you'll pay more for inclusions (bugs or other objects stuck in the amber).

Gdańsk also has several modern shopping malls, most of them in the Old Town or near the main train station. The most impressive is the Forum, across the street from the Upland Gate; the Madison shopping center is between the Main Town and the Solidarity shipyard.

Sleeping in Gdańsk

The high season is generally May through September; at all of these places, you'll pay a bit less in the off-season. Many hotels are booked up (mostly with German and Scandinavian tourists) in peak season—reserve ahead.

IN THE MAIN TOWN

The Main Town is convenient for sightseeing, but can come with nighttime noise—particularly in summer, when loud bars and discos keep things lively. Request a quiet room...and pack earplugs.

$$$ Hotel Wolne Miasto ("Free City") offers lush, wood-carved public spaces with photos of old Gdańsk and 68 richly

Sleep Code

Hotels are classified based on the average price of a standard double room with breakfast in high season.

$$$$	**Splurge:** Most rooms over 550 zł
$$$	**Pricier:** 400-550 zł
$$	**Moderate:** 250-400 zł
$	**Budget:** 100-250 zł
¢	**Backpacker:** Under 100 zł
RS%	**Rick Steves discount**

Unless otherwise noted, credit cards are accepted, hotel staff speak basic English, and free Wi-Fi is available. Comparison-shop by checking prices at several hotels (on each hotel's own website, on a booking site, or by email). For the best deal, *book directly with the hotel.* Ask for a discount if paying in cash; if the listing includes **RS%**, request a Rick Steves discount.

decorated rooms on the edge of the Main Town, just two blocks from the main drag. It's above a popular disco that gets noisy on weekends (Thu-Sat nights), so it's especially important to request a quieter room when you reserve (elevator, ulica Świętego Ducha 2, tel. 58-322-2442, www.hotelwm.pl, rezerwacja@hotelwm.pl).

$$$ Hotel Admirał is simply practical: a big, solidly built, business-class place with 44 comfortable rooms tucked in a quiet residential alley at the north end of the embankment, just a few steps off the old fish market. Their rates are soft, so the hotel is especially worth considering if you can get a deal (air-con, elevator, Tobiasza 9, tel. 58-320-0320, www.admiralhotel.pl, recepcja@admiralhotel.pl).

$$ Gotyk House, a good value, is run with warmth and pride by Andrzej, an energetic armchair historian who works hard to make his little hotel comfortable while still respecting the sanctity of Gdańsk's oldest house (and supposedly the residence of Copernicus' longtime lover). The chimes from St. Mary's Church, next door, provide a pleasant soundtrack. The original, historic building has five rooms; a modern annex out back holds six additional rooms with air-conditioning and more refined touches. Neither building has an elevator, so be ready for stairs (ulica Mariacka 1, tel. 58-301-8567, www.gotykhouse.eu, reservation@gotykhouse.eu).

$$ Aparthotel Neptun lacks personality, but owns a great location—on a slightly dreary side street between delightful Mariacka and the bustling Royal Way. While it's just a few steps to most of the town's big sights, it's just far enough away to avoid crowds and weekend noise. The 39 rooms and apartments are modern, efficient, well-equipped, and forgettable...but well-priced for the

GDAŃSK & THE TRI-CITY

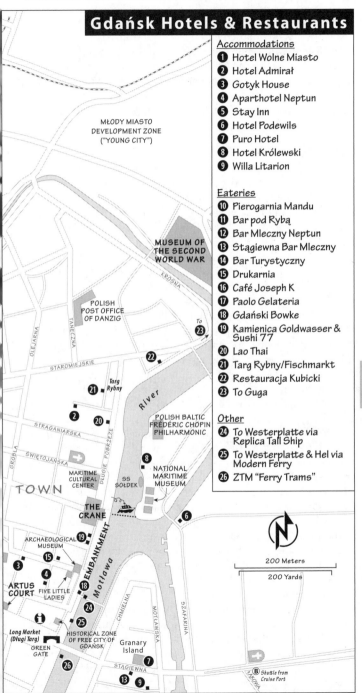

Gdańsk Hotels & Restaurants

Accommodations
1. Hotel Wolne Miasto
2. Hotel Admirał
3. Gotyk House
4. Aparthotel Neptun
5. Stay Inn
6. Hotel Podewils
7. Puro Hotel
8. Hotel Królewski
9. Willa Litarion

Eateries
10. Pierogarnia Mandu
11. Bar pod Rybą
12. Bar Mleczny Neptun
13. Stągiewna Bar Mleczny
14. Bar Turystyczny
15. Drukarnia
16. Café Joseph K
17. Paolo Gelateria
18. Gdański Bowke
19. Kamienica Goldwasser & Sushi 77
20. Lao Thai
21. Targ Rybny/Fischmarkt
22. Restauracja Kubicki
23. To Guga

Other
24. To Westerplatte via Replica Tall Ship
25. To Westerplatte & Hel via Modern Ferry
26. ZTM "Ferry Trams"

MŁODY MIASTO DEVELOPMENT ZONE ("YOUNG CITY")

MUSEUM OF THE SECOND WORLD WAR

KROSNA

POLISH POST OFFICE OF DANZIG

TANECZNA

OLEJARNA

STAROMIEJSKIE

To 23

Targ Rybny

River

POLISH BALTIC FRÉDÉRIC CHOPIN PHILHARMONIC

STRAGANIARSKA

GROBLA

ŚWIĘTOJAŃSKA

MARITIME CULTURAL CENTER

TOWN

SS SOŁDEK

NATIONAL MARITIME MUSEUM

THE CRANE

Motława

DŁUGIE POBRZEŻE

ARCHAEOLOGICAL MUSEUM

ARTUS COURT

FIVE LITTLE LADIES

EMBANKMENT

Long Market (Długi Targ)

GREEN GATE

HISTORICAL ZONE OF FREE CITY OF GDAŃSK

Granary Island

STAGIEWNA

CHMIELNA

MOTŁAWSKA

SZAFARNIA

ŁĄKOWA

200 Meters

200 Yards

Ⓑ Shuttle from Cruise Port

GDAŃSK & THE TRI-CITY

central location (breakfast extra, elevator, spa, Grzaska 1, mobile 604-466-466, www.apartneptun.com, info@apartneptun.com).

$$ Stay Inn couldn't be more central—facing the side of St. Mary's Church, right in the heart of the Main Town. Although the street it's on is quieter than most, a downstairs pub can be noisy on weekends. Its 42 rooms are stylish and colorful (breakfast extra, air-con, elevator, Piwna 28, tel. 58-354-1543, www.stayinngdansk.com, booking@stayinngdansk.com).

ACROSS THE RIVER

These hotels are across the river from the Main Town. That puts you a bit farther from the sightseeing action, but it's a relatively short walk (no more than 10 minutes from any of these).

$$$$ Hotel Podewils is the top choice for a friendly splurge. Filling a storybook-cute house from 1728, overlooking the marina and across the river from a fine panorama of the Gdańsk embankment, it's classy. The public spaces and 10 rooms have all the modern amenities, but with plush, almost Baroque, decor (air-con, Szafarnia 2, tel. 58-300-9560, www.podewils.pl, gdansk@podewils.pl).

$$$ Puro Hotel, just a short walk from Gdańsk's main drag in the middle of Granary Island, is part of a Norwegian chain. It's big (eight floors), splashy, and fills brand-new buildings with towering glass atriums, a big restaurant, and a top-floor bar. The 211 rooms are modern, practical, and stylish; for the quality and location, it's a great value for those wanting a big hotel (air-con, elevator, spa, Stągiewna 26, tel. 58-563-5000, www.purohotel.pl, gdansk@purohotel.pl).

$$ Hotel Królewski fills a renovated red-brick granary with 30 rooms sitting right along the river, facing classic Gdańsk embankment views. As it's across the river from the landmark crane—a long walk from the heart of town—the location isn't entirely convenient. But it's well priced for the quality, and the Polish Baltic Philharmonic is right next door (apartments, try asking for a view room for no extra charge, elevator, good restaurant, ulica Ołowianka 1, tel. 58-326-1111, www.hotelkrolewski.pl, office@hotelkrolewski.pl). To get into town, hop on the ferry across the river offered by the Maritime Museum; if it's not running, it's a scenic 15-minute walk along the river, past the marina, and over the bridge into the Main Town.

$$ Willa Litarion, run by the Owsikowski family, sits on the back side of a charmingly restored row of colorful houses on the island just across the river from the main drag. It's tall and skinny, with no elevator, and faces a gloomy parking lot, but the location is handy. Each of the 13 small rooms is different (pay parking garage, ulica Spichrzowa 18, tel. 58-320-2553, www.litarion.pl, recepcja@

Restaurant Price Code

I've assigned each eatery a price category, based on the average cost of a typical main course. Drinks, desserts, and splurge items (steak and seafood) can raise the price considerably.

$$$$ **Splurge:** Most main courses over 60 zł
$$$ **Pricier:** 45-60 zł
$$ **Moderate:** 25-45 zł
$ **Budget:** Under 25 zł

In Poland, a milk bar or takeout spot is $; a basic sit-down eatery is $$; a casual but more upscale restaurant is $$$; and a swanky splurge is $$$$.

litarion.pl). Several other, similar (but less appealing) "villas" line this same street—if you're in a pinch for a room, this is a handy place to go ringing doorbells.

Eating in Gdańsk

In addition to traditional Polish fare, Gdańsk has some excellent Baltic seafood. Herring *(śledź)* is popular here, as is cod *(dorsz)*. Natives brag that their salmon *(łosoś)* is better than Norway's. For a stiff drink, sample *Goldwasser* (similar to Goldschlager). This sweet and strong liqueur, flecked with actual gold, was supposedly invented here in Gdańsk. The following options are all in the Main Town, within three blocks of the Royal Way.

AFFORDABLE RESTAURANTS IN THE CITY CENTER

These places are well priced, tasty, quick, and wonderfully convenient—on or very near the Royal Way (ulica Długa). They're worth considering even if you're not on a tight budget.

$$ Pierogarnia Mandu, serving a wide variety of pierogi—all handmade (see them working through the window), with modern flourish—is *the* foodie hotspot in Gdańsk. Hiding in a nondescript residential zone between the train station and the main tourist area, it's worth seeking out for pierogi, plus a variety of other international dumplings. As it's popular, be prepared to wait for a table; it can take 30-45 minutes for your dumplings to be made fresh (daily 11:00-22:00, Elżbietańska 4, tel. 58-300-0000).

$$ Bar pod Rybą ("Under the Fish") is nirvana for fans of baked potatoes *(pieczony ziemniak)*. They offer more than 20 varieties, piled high with a wide variety of toppings and sauces, from Mexican beef to herring to Polish cheeses. They also serve fish dishes with salad and potatoes, making this a cheap place to sample local seafood. The interior has big, comfy couches, and the outdoor seating fills a big stone balcony on atmospheric Piwna street (daily 10:00-22:00, Piwna 61, tel. 58-305-1307). Piwna street is lined with other tempting options—it's a fun street to browse for a meal.

$ Bar Mleczny Neptun is your handiest milk-bar option in the Main Town. A hearty meal, including a drink, runs about $5. This popular place has outdoor seating along the most scenic stretch of the main drag, and an upstairs dining room overlooking it all. The items on the counter are for display—point to what you want, and they'll dish it up fresh (Mon-Fri 7:30-20:00, Sat-Sun 10:00-20:00, may have shorter hours off-season, ulica Długa 33, tel. 58-301-4988). For more on milk bars, see page 18.

$ Stągiewna Bar Mleczny, in the middle of Granary Island just beyond the Royal Way, is a classy, updated, modern milk bar with appealing outdoor seating—good for lunch or an early dinner (daily 9:00-18:00, Stągiewna 15, mobile 570-112-222).

$ Bar Turystyczny is misnamed—not just for tourists, it has become beloved by locals as the central area's favorite milk bar. Easy to miss on the way between the Main Town and the Solidarity sights, it's always jammed (daily 8:00-18:00, Szeroka 8, tel. 58-301-6013).

Coffee: Drukarnia ("Printer") is the best spot in town for gourmet coffee in a modern, trendy setting that still melds well with the tradition all around it. The interior is industrial-mod, and the outdoor seating fills two levels of a stone balcony on Gdańsk's loveliest street, Mariacka. In addition to coffee and creative tea drinks, they have craft beers, breakfast, and other light bites—sandwiches and cakes (daily 10:00-22:00, Mariacka 36, mobile 510-087-064).

Hipster Bar/Café: Café Joseph K, on charming Piwna street, is a popular hangout for coffee, craft beer, and creative cocktails. Similar to Drukarnia (but edgier and less coffee-focused), they have a modern interior and stay-awhile outdoor tables (daily 10:00-24:00, Piwna 1, mobile 572-161-510).

Ice Cream: The people of Gdańsk—and its many visitors—seem obsessed with ice cream *(lody)*. For high quality, creative flavors and generous portions, stop by **Paolo Gelateria,** on the way between the Main Town and the Solidarity sights (Mon-Fri 10:00-20:00, Sat-Sun until 21:00, across from the Great Mill at Podwale Staromiejskie 96, mobile 504-222-651).

ON THE RIVERFRONT EMBANKMENT

Perhaps the most appealing dining zone in Gdańsk stretches along the riverfront embankment near the landmark medieval crane. On a balmy summer evening, the outdoor tables here are enticing. This area is popular—consider scouting a table during your sightseeing, and reserve your choice for dinner later that night. While these places are mostly interchangeable, I've listed a few to consider, in the order you'll reach them as you walk north along the embankment. These places are more expensive than other options in town, but the views are worth it.

$$$ Gdański Bowke is kitschy, but fun and lively. The menu of classic local dishes looks like a big, vintage newspaper. They brew their own beer, and often have live music out on the embankment (daily 10:00-23:00, Długie Pobrzeże 11, tel. 58-380-1111).

$$$$ Kamienica Goldwasser is a classy choice, offering high-quality Polish and international cuisine. Choose between cozy, romantic indoor seating on several levels, or scenic outdoor seating (daily 10:00-24:00, occasional live music, Długie Pobrzeże 22, tel. 58-301-8878).

Just beyond Goldwasser, **$$$ Sushi 77** (Długie Pobrzeże 30, tel. 58-682-1823) and **$$$ Lao Thai** (ulica Targ Rybny 11, www.laothai.pl) are good-quality Asian eateries and also have riverfront seating. Or carry on farther for more Asian cuisine at Guga, described later.

$$$$ Targ Rybny/Fischmarkt ("The Fish Market") has less appealing outdoor seating that overlooks a park (the onetime fish market that it's named for) and parking lot. But the warm, mellow-yellow nautical ambience inside is pleasant, making this a good option in bad weather. It features classy but not stuffy service, and the expected emphasis on fish (daily 10:00-23:00, ulica Targ Rybny 6C, tel. 58-320-9011).

$$$ Restauracja Kubicki, along the water just past the Hilton, has a long history (since 1918), but a recent remodel has kept the atmosphere—and its food—feeling fresh. This is a good choice for high-quality Polish and international cuisine in a fun, sophisticated interior that's a clever mix of old and new (daily 12:00-23:00, Wartka 5, tel. 58-301-0050).

$$ Guga, all the way at the end of the embankment (past the drawbridge, near the WWII museum), has a modern ambience and a short menu of Asian fusion dishes. There are two parts: "Salty" for a snack or meal, or "Sweet" for dessert (Mon-Thu 9:00-20:00, Fri-Sun until 22:00, Stara Stocznia 2, mobile 533-272-642).

GDAŃSK & THE TRI-CITY

Gdańsk Connections

BY TRAIN

Gdańsk is well-connected to the Tri-City via commuter SKM trains (explained later, under "Getting Around the Tri-City"). It's also connected to Warsaw and Kraków by the high-speed EIC line (which requires reservations). Given the distance between Gdańsk and other Polish destinations, also consider domestic flights: LOT has easy flights between Gdańsk and Kraków for not much more than a train ticket.

From Gdańsk by Train to: Hel (town on Hel Peninsula, 3/day direct July-Aug only, 2 hours; otherwise about hourly with change in Gdynia), **Malbork** (2/hour, about half are express EIC trains that take 30 minutes, the rest are slower regional trains that take around 45 minutes), **Toruń** (4/day direct, 2.5 hours; more with a change in Bydgoszcz or Iława, 3 hours), **Warsaw** (hourly, 3 hours on express EIC train), **Kraków** (6/day direct, 5.5 hours, 1 more with change in Warsaw; plus 8.5-hour night train), **Berlin** (1/day direct, 6 hours; 3/day, 7.5 hours, change in Poznań).

BY BOAT

Boats depart from Gdańsk's embankment to nearby destinations, including **Westerplatte** (the monument marking where World War II started) and **Hel** (the beachy peninsula, described later). As schedules change often, confirm your plans carefully at the TI. All boat trips are weather permitting, especially faster hydrofoils. In shoulder season (April-June and Sept-Oct), most boats stop running from Gdańsk, but several routes still run between Sopot, Gdynia, and Hel. Boats generally don't run in winter (Nov-March).

To Westerplatte: To travel by boat to the monument at Westerplatte, you have three options. Most enjoyable is to ride a replica **17th-century galleon,** either the *Galeon Lew* ("Lion Galleon") or the *Czarna Perła* ("Black Pearl"). These over-the-top, touristy boats depart hourly from the embankment just outside the Green Gate for a lazy 1.5-hour round-trip cruise to Westerplatte and back. (You can choose to get off at Westerplatte and take a later boat back.)

You'll see more industry than scenery, but it's a fun excuse to set sail, even if you don't care about Westerplatte (45 zł round-trip, 30 zł one-way, the two boats take turns departing at the top of each hour 10:00-19:00 in July-Aug, fewer departures May-June and Sept, from the embankment near the landmark crane, mobile 601-629-191, www.galeony.pl). Two other, duller alternatives leave from right nearby: big, modern **Żegluga Gdańska** boats (www.zegluga.pl); or cheaper but less frequent city-run **ZTM "ferry trams"** *(tramwaj wodny)*, which depart from the embankment on the south side of the bridge (3-4/day).

To Hel: Various boats zip out to Hel in two hours during the summer. This route is most likely run by Żegluga Gdańska (May and Sept weekends only, June-Aug 3/day, 35 zł one-way, www.zegluga.pl).

BY CRUISE SHIP

A few cruise ships (under 800 passengers) dock in **Gdańsk,** near the Westerplatte monument (described earlier; connected to the center by 45-minute pleasure-boat trip or 30-minute ride on bus #106, #138, and—in summer—#606). But most cruises advertising a stop in Gdańsk actually dock in the nearby town of **Gdynia.** For details on this town, see page 289.

The Tri-City (Trójmiasto)

Gdańsk is the anchor of the three-part metropolitan region known as the Tri-City (Trójmiasto). The other two parts are as different as night and day: Sopot, a swanky resort town, and Gdynia, a practical, nose-to-the-grindstone business center. The Tri-City as a whole is home to bustling industry and a sprawling university, with several campuses and plenty of well-dressed, English-speaking students. Beyond the Tri-City, the long, skinny Hel Peninsula—a sparsely populated strip of fishing villages and fun-loving beaches—arches dramatically into the Baltic Sea.

Sopot—boasting sandy beaches, tons of tourists, and a certain elegance—is clearly the most appealing day-trip option. Gdynia is less romantic, but comes with an excellent Emigration Museum and offers a glimpse into workaday Poland. Hel, which requires the better part of a day to visit, is worthwhile only if you've got perfect summer weather and a desire to lie on the beach.

GETTING AROUND THE TRI-CITY

Gdańsk, Sopot, and Gdynia are connected by two different types of trains: regional commuter trains *(kolejka,* operated by SKM) use track 3 at Gdańsk's main train station, while trains operated by Poland's national railway (PKP) use tracks 1 and 2. The SKM trains are cheaper, a bit slower, and more frequent than long-distance PKP trains—they go in each direction about every 10-15 minutes

Gdańsk Day Trips

To Karlskrona, Sweden

Władysławowo

Jastarnia

To Szczecin & Berlin — Jurata — Hel Peninsula

Hel

Gdynia

Sopot

Oliwa — TRI-CITY

WESTERPLATTE

Gdańsk

Pruszcz Gdański

E-75

Motława River

Vistula River

To Poznań & Berlin

Starogard Gdański

To Toruń & Warsaw

E-77

Tczew

Malbork

20 Kilometers
20 Miles

Baltic Sea

Baltijsk — RUSSIA (Kaliningrad)

Wiślany Lagoon — A-194

To Kaliningrad & Vilnius, Lithuania

Braniewo

POLAND

Elbląg

Orneta

Pasłęk

E-77

To Warsaw

(less frequently after 19:30 and Sun). Trains to Hel are always operated by PKP.

Buying Tickets: Confusingly, SKM trains and PKP trains are covered by different tickets, and the fastest PKP trains (marked *IC, EIC,* or *TLK*) require reservations—effectively a third type of ticket. Prices are comparable between systems, typically around 4-6 zł one-way between Gdańsk and Gdynia (though trains requiring reservations can be much more).

It can be challenging to figure out which train is leaving next, and to buy a ticket for the right train. First, check posted schedules (or look online) to establish which train you want. For an SKM train, you can buy tickets at machines labeled *SKM Bilety* (English instructions), or at the SKM ticket office (outside the station, facing the SKM tracks). SKM tickets purchased at a machine come already validated, but if you buy one at the office, you'll need to stamp your ticket in the easy-to-miss yellow slots at the platform.

For a PKP train, you can stand in line at the ticket windows; however, English-speaking staff can be limited.

Another option is to look for the general ticket machines inside the station, which typically inform you about all upcoming trains and sell you tickets for any type (English instructions, take Polish cash; American credit cards may not work).

Using the Right Stop: Each city has multiple stops. Remember, in Gdańsk, use either Gdańsk Główny (the main station for SKM and PKP) or Gdańsk Śródmieście (SKM only). For Sopot, use the stop called simply Sopot. For Gdynia, it's Gdynia Główna (the main station).

Boat Alternative: For a more romantic—and much slower—approach, consider a boat (see "Gdańsk Connections," earlier).

Sopot

Sopot (SOH-poht), dubbed the "Nice of the North," was a celebrated haunt of beautiful people during the 1920s and 1930s, and it remains a popular beach getaway to this day.

Sopot was created in the early 19th century by Napoleon's doctor, Jean Georges Haffner, who believed Baltic Sea water to be therapeutic. By the 1890s, it had become a fashionable seaside resort. This gambling center boasted enough high-roller casinos to garner comparisons to Monte Carlo.

The casinos are gone, but the health resorts remain, and you'll still see more well-dressed people here per capita than just about anywhere else in the country. While it's not quite Cannes, Sopot feels relatively high class, which is unusual in otherwise unpretentious Poland. But even so, a childlike spirit of summer-vacation fun pervades this St-Tropez-on-the-Baltic, making it an all-around enjoyable place.

You can get the gist of Sopot in just a couple of hours. Zip in on the train, follow the main drag to the sea, wander the pier, get your feet wet at the beach, then head back to Gdańsk. Why not come here in the late afternoon, enjoy those last few rays of sunshine, stay for dinner, then take a twilight stroll on the pier?

Orientation to Sopot

The main pedestrian drag, Monte Cassino Heroes street (ulica Bohaterów Monte Cassino), leads to the Molo, the longest pleasure pier in Europe. From the Molo, a broad, sandy beach stretches in each direction. Running parallel to the surf is a tree-lined, people-filled path made for strolling.

Tourist Information: The TI is near the base of the Molo at

GDAŃSK & THE TRI-CITY

Plac Zdrojowy 2 (daily 10:00-18:00, mobile 790-280-884, www. sopot.pl).

Arrival in Sopot: From the SKM station, exit to the left and walk down the street. After a block, you'll see the PKP train station on your left. Continue on to the can't-miss-it main drag, ulica Bohaterów Monte Cassino (marked by the big red-brick church steeple). Follow it to the right, down to the seaside.

Sights in Sopot

▲Monte Cassino Heroes Street
(Ulica Bohaterów Monte Cassino)

Nicknamed "Monciak" (MOHN-chak) by locals, this in-love-with-life promenade may well be Poland's most manicured street (and is named in honor of the Polish soldiers who helped the Allies pry Italy's Monte Cassino monastery from Nazi forces during World War II). Especially after all the suburban and industrial dreck you passed through to get here, it's easy to be charmed by this pretty drag. The street is lined with happy tourists, trendy cafés, al fresco restaurants, movie theaters, and late-19th-century facades (known for their wooden balconies).

The most popular building along here (on the left, about half-way down) is the so-called **Crooked House** (Krzywy Domek), a trippy, Gaudí-inspired building that looks like it's melting. Hard-partying Poles prefer to call it the "Drunken House," and say that when it looks straight, it's time to stop drinking.

Molo (Pier)

At more than 1,600 feet long, this is Europe's longest wooden entertainment pier. While you won't find any amusement-park rides, you will be surrounded by vendors, artists, and Poles having the time of their lives. Buy a *gofry* (Belgian waffle topped with whipped cream and fruit) or an oversized cloud of *wata cukrowa* (cotton candy), grab your partner's hand, and stroll with gusto (8 zł, free Oct-April, open long hours daily, www.molo.sopot.pl).

Climb to the top of the Art Nouveau lighthouse for a waterfront panorama. Scan the horizon for sailboats and tankers. Any pirate ships? For a jarring reality check, look over to Gdańsk. Barely visible from the Molo are two of the most important sites in 20th-century history: the towering monument at Westerplatte, where World War II started, and the cranes rising up from the Gdańsk Shipyard, where Solidarity was born and European communism began its long goodbye.

In spring and fall, the Molo is a favorite venue for pole vaulting—or is that Pole vaulting?

The Beach

Yes, Poland has beaches. Nice ones. When I heard Sopot compared to places like Nice, I'll admit that I scoffed. But when I saw those stretches of inviting sand as far as the eye can see, I wished I'd packed my swim trunks. (You could walk from Gdańsk all the way to Gdynia on beaches like this.) The sand is finer than anything I've seen in Croatia...though the water's not exactly crystal-clear. Most of the beach is public, except for a small private stretch in front of the Grand Hotel Sopot. Year-round, it's crammed with locals. At these northern latitudes, the season for bathing is brief and crowded.

Overlooking the beach next to the Molo is the **Grand Hotel Sopot.** It was renovated to top-class status just recently, but its history goes way back. They could charge admission for a multiroom suite that has hosted the likes of Adolf Hitler, Marlene Dietrich, and Fidel Castro (but not all at the same time). With all the trappings of Sopot's belle époque—dark wood, plush upholstery, antique furniture—this room had me imagining Hitler sitting at the desk, looking out to sea, and plotting the course of World War II.

Gdynia

Compared to its flashier sister cities, straightforward Gdynia (guh-DIN-yah) is all business. Gdynia is less historic than Gdańsk or Sopot, as it was built almost entirely in the 1920s to be Poland's main harbor after "Danzig" became a free city. Called "The Gateway to Poland," the waterfront is built on large concrete piers (a communist-style fountain in the middle of the park marks the original coastline). Although nowhere near as attractive as Gdańsk or Sopot, Gdynia has an upscale, modern feel and a lovely waterfront promenade (www.gdynia.pl).

Gdynia is a major business center, and—thanks to its youthful, progressive city government—has edged ahead of the rest of Poland economically. It enjoys one of the highest income levels in the country. The fine Modernist architecture of the downtown has been renovated, and Gdynia is becoming known for its top-tier shopping—all the big designers have boutiques here. If a local has been shopping on Świętojańska street in Gdynia, it means that he or she has some serious złoty.

Because Gdańsk's port is relatively shallow, the biggest cruise ships must put in at Gdynia...leaving confused tourists to poke around town looking for some medieval quaintness, before coming to their senses and heading for Gdańsk. Gdynia is also home to a major military harbor and an important NATO base.

To get a taste of Gdynia, take the train to the Gdynia Główna station, follow signs to *wyjście do miasta,* cross the busy street, and walk 15 minutes down Starowiejska. When you come to the intersection with the broad Świętojańska street, turn right (in the direction the big statue is looking) and walk two blocks to the tree-lined park on the left. Head through the park to the Southern Pier (Molo Południowe). This concrete slab—not nearly as charming as Sopot's wooden-boardwalk version—features a modern shopping mall and a smattering of sights, including an aquarium and a pair of permanently moored museum boats.

The big sightseeing draw in Gdynia is at the fairly distant Nabrzeże Francuskie (French Quay, where cruise ships arrive—handy for cruisers but a taxi ride away for tourists coming on the train). Here you'll find the excellent Emigration Museum, telling the story of Poles who left through Gdynia to find a better life in the New World (described next).

Sights in Gdynia

▲▲Emigration Museum (Muzeum Emigracji)

This museum, right next to Gdynia's cruise terminal, fills the former Marine Station building at the address Polska 1. This building opened in 1933, becoming the main port of departure for Polish American Lines passenger steamers to New York City and Quebec. For a time, vast numbers of Poles emigrated to the New World through right here. (Before that time, they mostly went through Hamburg or Bremen.) After World War II, the

Iron Curtain slammed shut, the line was severed, and the Marine Station remained bombed-out for decades. Now it has been renovated and hosts a high-tech, engaging museum that tells the story of the 3.5 million Poles who left their homeland in search of a better life between the mid-19th century and World War II. Concise yet informative, engaging, and all in English, the exhibit is a delight for anyone, and worth ▲▲▲ for patriotic Polish-Americans.

Cost and Hours: 10 zł, free on Wed, open Tue 12:00-20:00, Wed-Sun 10:00-18:00, closed Mon, good 5-zł audioguide, www.polska1.pl.

Getting There: It's a·25-minute, dreary walk from Gdynia's main train station. A taxi makes things easier. Unfortunately, the ones out front charge about 25 zł, but if you call a legitimate taxi or order an Uber, the fair rate is closer to 10-15 zł (try Hallo Express, tel. 19190). Or you can take a bus: #119, #133, #137, or #147 go from along Władysława IV avenue (between the train station and the waterfront) to the Dworzec Morski/Muzeum Emigracji stop.

Visiting the Museum: Buy your ticket on the main floor, where you'll also find WCs, a café, and a museum shop. Then head upstairs, through the middle of the cavernous building, to find the exhibit entrance. Inside, the permanent exhibition tells the story of Polish emigration. You'll see photos of famous Poles who left (from Kościuszko to Chopin), and learn about the various waves of emigration throughout Polish history, and what sparked each one: the Partitions in the late 18th century; failed uprisings in 1830 and 1864; and the potato famine (Poland suffered like Ireland did—the wall of potatoes symbolizes how important this staple was to peasant life). The Industrial Revolution sparked a different kind of (internal) emigration, as rural farming families moved into the cities for work.

The exhibit introduces the Sikora family, and follows their emigration from Chmielnik to Chicago, by way of the port of Bremen. You'll learn how the "emigration industry" operated: Steamer lines conducted a medical examination of each passenger before they left Europe—because if they were rejected upon examination once they arrived in the New World, the company had to pay to ship them back. Exhibits include a mock-up of a train station, the deck of an Atlantic steamship, a cross-section of life below decks, and a peek into a tight sleeping quarters, crammed with bunks where the poorest passengers would spend 10 days on turbulent seas. Finally you arrive in New York City. Imagine seeing a wall of skyscrapers after a long journey from a thatched village. The train car is a reminder that from New York, new arrivals spread out across North America. Chicago is famous for its huge Polish émigré population, but you'll learn that many Poles also went to Brazil ("Brazilian Fever").

You'll learn about the history of Gdynia (a purpose-built port, created entirely after World War I) and see a giant replica of the MS

Stefan Bathory—a passenger steamer that was built here. (Sadly, when trans-atlantic travel ended after World War II, ships like this one were scrapped.) In the World War II section, trees cut down to their stumps represent the forced displacement of populations during and after the war. You'll learn about the "Polish diaspora" around the world (Chicago, Rio, Britain, Australia). At the end of World War II, Polish officers who had fought alongside the Western Allies were warned not to return to Poland—where they'd be executed as potential rabble-rousers against the Soviet regime. So they stayed where they were, creating a new wave of "emigration." The exhibit ends with a kitschy look at Poland under communism (and Solidarity).

Exiting the exhibit, step out onto the long terrace that looks out over the cruise port. While it serves tourists today, this port evokes the millions of brave Poles who left behind everything they knew, set sail across a dangerous ocean, and had the courage to seek a new life in a New World.

ARRIVING BY CRUISE IN GDYNIA

Many Northern European cruises include a stop at "Gdańsk"; most of these actually put in at Gdynia's sprawling port. And, while Gydnia's town center is relatively manicured and pleasant, its port area is the opposite—like a Soviet Bloc bodybuilder, it's muscular and hairy. Cruise ships are shuffled among hardworking industrial piers with few amenities.

Each of the port's many piers is named for a country or region. Most cruise ships use **French Quay** (Nabrzeże Francuskie), which is surrounded by heavy industry. Smaller ships can use the convenient **Pomeranian Quay** (Nabrzeże Pomorskie, part of the Southern Pier), which is an easy walk from the center. Port information: www.port.gdynia.pl.

The French Quay is home to Gdynia's best sight, the **Emigration Museum.** It deserves at least an hour of your time—or more, if you have Polish ancestry. This is a good place to spend any remaining time before "all aboard."

To get from your cruise ship to Gdańsk, the best option is a **shuttle bus-plus-train connection.** The shuttle drops you off at Skwer Kociuski, in downtown Gdynia (5-10 minute trip). From here, it's about a 15-minute walk to the train station (Dworzec Główna). From here you can ride the train into Gdańsk, which takes 30-40 minutes (for details on your various train options, see "Getting Around the Tri-City," earlier). Returning to Gdynia on the train, you want the Gdynia Główna stop.

Taxi drivers line up to meet arriving cruise ships. Cabbies here are usually unofficial (and therefore can set their own, inflated rates). It's worth ordering an Uber or calling for a taxi to get legitimate rates: 10-15 zł to Gdynia's train station (*Dworzec*, DVOH-zhets); 125 zł to Gdańsk's Main Town; and 60-80 zł to Sopot (typically cheaper by Uber). Taxi drivers generally take euros, though their off-the-cuff exchange rate may not be favorable.

For more details on Gdynia's port—and several others on the Baltic, North Sea, and beyond—pick up the *Rick Steves Scandinavian and Northern European Cruise Ports* guidebook.

Hel Peninsula (Mierzeja Helska)

Out on the edge of things, this slender peninsula juts 20 miles into the ocean, providing a sunny retreat from the big cities—even as it shelters them from Baltic winds. Trees line the peninsula, and the northern edge is one long, sandy, ever-shifting beach.

On hot summer days, Hel is a great place to frolic in the sun with Poles. Sunbathing and windsurfing are practically religions here. Small resort villages line Hel Peninsula: Władysławowo (at the base), Chałupy, Kuźnica, Jastarnia, Jurata, and—at the tip—a town also called Hel. Beaches right near the towns can be crowded in peak season, but you're never more than a short walk away from your own stretch of sand. There are few permanent residents, and the waterfront is shared by budget campgrounds, hotels hosting middle-class families, and mansions of Poland's rich and famous (former president Aleksander Kwaśniewski has a summer home here).

The easiest way to go to Hel—aside from coveting thy neighbor's wife—is by boat (see "Gdańsk Connections," earlier). Trains from Gdańsk also reach Hel (summer only), and from Gdynia, you can take a train, bus, or minibus. But overland transit is crowded and slow—especially in summer, when Hel is notorious for its hellish traffic jams.

POMERANIA

Malbork Castle • Toruń

The northwestern part of Poland—known as Pomerania (Pomorze)—has nothing to do with excitable little dogs, but it does offer two attractions worth singling out. Malbork, the biggest Gothic castle in Europe, is one of the best castles in Eastern Europe. Farther south, the Gothic town of Toruń—the birthplace of Copernicus, and a favorite spot of every proud Pole—holds hundreds of red-brick buildings...and, it seems, even more varieties of tasty gingerbread. The story of this region—which was part of the German world for much of its history—is tied inexorably to the Teutonic Knights, who ruled over this northern swath of present-day Poland (see the sidebar later in this chapter) and fortified their holdings with elegant red brick...still the hallmark of Pomerania.

Be prepared for a higher language barrier here; unlike Kraków and Warsaw, English is not the default.

PLANNING YOUR TIME

Malbork works well as a side trip from Gdańsk (frequent trains, 30-45 minutes each way), and it's also on the main train line from Gdańsk to Warsaw. While Toruń doesn't merit a long detour, it's worth a stroll or an overnight if you want to sample a smaller Polish city. Unfortunately, Toruń is on a different train line than Malbork—if you visit both in one day, it'll be a very long one. Ideally, if traveling round-trip from Warsaw, see one of these destinations coming to Gdańsk, and visit the other on the way back. Or do Malbork as a side trip from Gdańsk, then visit Toruń on the way to or from Warsaw. Malbork isn't worth an overnight (since it's so close to Gdańsk), but Toruń can be a delightful place to settle in for the night.

Malbork Castle

Malbork Castle is soaked in history. The biggest brick castle in the world, the largest castle of the Gothic period, and one of Europe's most imposing fortresses, it sprawls on a marshy plain at the edge of the town of Malbork, 35 miles southeast of Gdańsk. This was the headquarters of the Teutonic Knights, the Germanic band of ex-Crusaders who dominated northern Poland in the Middle Ages.

Touring the massive castle, you'll see good exhibits on amber and armor; walk though vast halls with graceful Gothic arches and fan vaulting; learn a bit about the Teutonic Knights; and see enough red brick to last a lifetime. Visiting the whole place is a bit exhausting, but this chapter's self-guided tour helps you focus on the highlights.

GETTING THERE

Malbork is conveniently located right on the express train line between Gdańsk and Warsaw. Coming by train from Gdańsk, you'll enjoy views of the castle on your right as you cross the Nogat River. Store your luggage at the station's lockers (next to the exit doors) and head into town.

To get from the station to the castle, it's an easy, 10-minute, mostly downhill **walk:** Leave the station to the right, walk straight past the bus stops, and go through the pedestrian underpass beneath the busy road (by the red staircase). Ascending the stairs on the other side, turn right and follow the busy road (noticing peek-a-boo views on your right of the castle's main tower). Take the first right and head down Kościuszki, the main shopping street (partway down on the right, a fancy peach-colored building houses the TI). Near the bottom of Kościuszki, at the fountain and the McDonald's, jog right, then—at the roundabout—turn left to cross the moat. The castle ticket office will be on your right.

The fair metered price for a **taxi** to the castle is no more than 12 zł, but the cabbies waiting at the station charge 20 zł.

To return to the station, just reverse the walking directions. To avoid the uphill walk, ask the info desk clerk in the castle ticket office to call a (fairly priced) taxi for you.

ORIENTATION TO MALBORK CASTLE

Cost and Hours: Mid-April-Sept—40 zł, open Tue-Sun 9:00-19:00; Oct-mid-April—30 zł, open Tue-Sun 10:00-15:00; closed Mon year-round; grounds stay open an hour later than the castle.

Information: Tel. 55-647-0978, www.zamek.malbork.pl.

Crowd-Beating Tips: The castle is busiest at midday, when there can be a line for tickets. If so, you can buy a ticket on their website with your phone.

Tours: Your ticket includes a good **audioguide,** but supply is limited—they may run out during peak times (11:00-14:00). While informative, the system's location-detection doesn't always work well. This chapter's self-guided tour is more concise and lets you go at your own pace.

If they're out of audioguides, you may be required to enter the castle with a guided tour in Polish—but you can split off on your own as soon as you're inside. In summer, there's usually an **English tour** (included in ticket price) at 10:30. Any time of year, you can pay 240 zł for a private English tour (ideally book ahead, tel. 55-647-0902, kasa@zamek.malbork.pl). If you show up and there's no scheduled English tour, ask whether an English-speaking guide is available. If so, take the initiative to play "tour organizer" and gather a group of English speakers to split the cost of a private tour.

Services and Eating: **WCs** are downstairs from the ticket office and scattered within the castle complex. Several cheap **$ food stands** cluster outside the castle (by the river). For a good meal inside the castle complex, the **$$$ Gothic Café,** in a cellar under the stairs to the armory in the Middle Castle, is a serious restaurant with surprisingly high-quality food by a renowned chef. Dishing up traditional Polish fare inspired by historic dishes, it's handy for its 50-zł lunch deal that includes a main dish and soup (tel. 55-647-0889, www.gothic.com.pl). Immediately across the courtyard, **$$ Restauracja Piwniczka** is cheaper and simpler, with stick-to-your-ribs beer-hall fare served in atmospheric cellars or at outdoor tables.

Best Views: The views of massive Malbork are stunning—especially at sunset, when its red brick glows. Be sure to walk out across the footbridge over the Nogat River. The most scenic part of the castle is the twin-turreted, riverside Bridge

Gate, which used to be connected by a bridge to the opposite bank.

BACKGROUND

When the Teutonic Knights were invited to Polish lands in the 13th century to convert neighboring pagans, they found the perfect site for their new capital here, on the bank of the Nogat River. Construction began in 1274. After the Teutonic Knights conquered Gdańsk in 1308, the order moved its official headquarters from Venice to northern Poland, where they remained for nearly 150 years. They called their main castle Marienburg, the "Castle of Mary," in honor of the order's patron saint. Poles call it "Malbork."

At its peak in the early 1400s, Malbork was both the imposing home of a seemingly unstoppable army and Europe's final bastion of chivalric ideals. Surrounded by swamplands, with only one gate in need of defense, it was a tough nut to crack. Malbork Castle was never taken by force in the Middle Ages, though it had to withstand various sieges by the Poles during the Thirteen Years' War (1454-1466)—including a campaign that lasted more than three years. Finally, in 1457, the Polish king gained control of Malbork by buying off Czech mercenaries guarding the castle. Malbork became a Polish royal residence for 300 years. But when Poland was partitioned in the late 18th century, this region went back into German hands. The castle became a barracks, windows were sealed up, delicate vaulting was damaged, bricks were quarried for new buildings, and Malbork deteriorated.

In the late 19th century, Romantic German artists and poets rediscovered the place. An architect named Konrad Steinbrecht devoted 40 years of his life to Malbork, painstakingly resurrecting the palace's medieval splendor. A half-century later, the Nazis used the castle to house POWs. Hitler—who, like many Germans, had a soft spot for Malbork's history—gave the order to defend it to the last man. About half of the castle was destroyed by the Soviet army, who saw it as a symbol of long-standing German domination. But it was restored once again, and today Malbork has been returned to its Teutonic glory.

⊘ SELF-GUIDED TOUR

The official tour of Malbork lasts about three hours; my tour of the highlights takes about half that long, unless you linger. Use the map in this section to navigate. The castle complex is a bit of a maze, with multiple entrances and exits for each room, often behind closed (but unlocked) doors. Don't be shy about grabbing a medieval doorknob and letting yourself in.

POMERANIA

Malbork Castle

ST. JOHN

TERRACES

N
o
g
a
t

To Town &
Train Station

P

PIASTOWSKA

TICKET OFFICE
(MEET TOURS)

HIGH
CASTLE

❻

❼

BRONZE
MODEL

STAROŚCIŃSKA

❽

DRAW-
BRIDGE

WC

❷

❺

❹

BRIDGE
GATE

❸

❶

MIDDLE
CASTLE

ENTRANCE
FOR GRAND
MASTER'S
PALACE

❾

To
Best
Views

DRAW-
BRIDGE

ENTRANCE
GATE

FOOD
STANDS

LOWER
CASTLE

R
i
v
e
r

100 Meters

100 Yards

POMERANIA

❶ Amber Exhibition (downstairs)
❷ Armory (upstairs) & Gothic
   Café (downstairs)
❸ "Boiler Room" (downstairs)
   & Grand Refectory (upstairs)
❹ Grand Master's Palace

❺ Grand Master Statues
❻ Well
❼ Dansker Tower
❽ St. Mary's Church
❾ Restauracia Piwniczka

Entering the Castle Complex

From the ticket office, exit straight ahead and belly up to the brick wall by the bronze model for a panoramic view of the giant complex. Slowly pan across one of Europe's most intimidating fortresses—home to the Grand Master, monks, and knights of the Teutonic Order. The High Castle (where the monks lived) is on the left, marked by the 30-foot-tall statue of Mary at the end of St. Mary's Church. To the right is the Middle Castle, where the knights lived. We'll loop around the right end (Middle Castle), working our way inside, and ending at the High Castle.

The bronze **model** shows the realm of the Teutonic Knights at their peak—stretching from Gdańsk in the north to Toruń to the south, and, waaaay up on the northeast, the city of Kłajpeda, today part of Lithuania. For more than a century (1308-1410), the Teutonic Knights were a formidable presence. For more on this history, see the sidebar later in this chapter.

• *Now turn right and cross the drawbridge under the brick tower. Keep going alongside the moat, turning left to cross another drawbridge into the castle ward. Ahead and to the right, the long, low-lying building was the Lower Castle, where servants and support staff lived. Just before that, on the left, is yet another drawbridge. Show your ticket here and cross partway over the bridge—pausing just outside the brick gate.*

Entrance Gate

Above the door to the brick gate is a sculpture of the Virgin Mary with Baby Jesus, next to a shield and helmet. The message is two-fold: This castle is protected by Mary, and the Teutonic Knights are here to convert pagans—by force, if necessary.

From the drawbridge, look right to observe the formidable fortifications. The Teutonic Knights connected nearby lakes to create a system of canals, forming a moat around the castle that could be crossed only by drawbridge. The rooster-capped corner tower (which contains a toilet) is connected by a sky bridge to the fancy Gothic 14th-century facade of the brick infirmary—kept at a distance for disease control.

Continue farther, until you're inside the gate structure itself. Imagine the gate behind you slamming shut. Look up to see wooden chutes where archers are preparing to rain arrows down on you. Your last thought: Maybe we should have left the Teutonic Knights alone after all.

Before you're pierced by arrows, read the castle's history in its walls: The foundation is made of huge stones—rare in these marshy lands—brought from Sweden. But most of the castle, like so many other buildings in northern Poland, was built with handmade red brick. Throughout the castle, the darker-colored, rougher brick is original, and the lighter-colored, smoother brick was used during

POMERANIA

later restorations (in the 19th century, and again after World War II). Marvel at the ironclad doors and the heavy portcullis.

Venture through two more enclosed spaces, watching for the holes in the wall (for more guards and soldiers). Ponder the fact that you must pass through five separate, well-defended gates to reach the...

Middle Castle (Zamek Średni)

This part of Malbork, built at an uphill incline to make it even more imposing, was designed to impress. Knights and monks lived here.

Let's get oriented: To your left is the east wing, where visiting monks would sleep. Today this houses the Amber Exhibition (ground floor) and the armory (upstairs). To the right (west) as you enter the main courtyard is the Grand Refectory (closer to the entrance) and the Grand Master's Palace (the taller, squarer building at the far end).

• *Enter the ground floor of the building on the left (go through the small door, and take a few steps down). Here you'll tour the...*

Amber Exhibition

Amber, precious petrified tree sap, is found here in Poland; for a primer, read the "All About Amber" sidebar on page 252. You'll start 42 million years ago and follow the story of amber, then walk down the dimly lit corridor, checking out huge chunks of raw amber and illuminated displays of inclusions (bugs and other organic objects stuck in the amber, à la *Jurassic Park*). Some of the ancient amber artifacts displayed here are up to 3,000 years old, found in graves.

At the end of the corridor, U-turn and work your way back up a parallel hall, lined with all manner of exquisite amber creations: boxes, brooches, necklaces, chess sets, pipes, miniature ships, wine glasses, and belts for skinny-waisted, fashion-conscious women. Many of the finely decorated jewelry boxes and chests have ivory, silver, or shell inlays—better for contrast than gold. The portable religious shrines and altars allowed travelers to remain reverent on the road and still pack light. Notice the wide range of amber colors—from opaque white to transparent yellow to virtually black.

• *Exit at the far end, passing the recommended Gothic Café on your way back outside. As you emerge into the Middle Castle courtyard, go up the wooden staircase on your right, go inside, turn left and walk to the end of the long hall, and go up the stairs. Here you'll find the...*

Armory

This enjoyable, well-displayed collection includes an impressive array of swords, armor, and other armaments. Look for the 600-year-old "hand-and-a-half" swords—too big to be held in one hand. Tucked behind the cannons is a giant shield. A row of these shields could be lined up to form a portable wall—called a phalanx—to protect the knights. In the big room with the decoratively hilted swords, look for the terrifying "flame-bladed sword." You'll also see pikes, maces, crossbows, rifles, and horse armor. And in the room with the body armor, the centerpiece is a suit of armor from the Hussars—Polish horseback knights. Equipped with wings, it created a ter-

rifying sound when the horses were galloping.

• At the end of the armory, head down the modern stairs and back outside (noticing the handy WC straight ahead). Cross the main courtyard, angling downhill, and enter the smaller courtyard through the passage next to the stubby, dark-wood-topped tower. Find the (unlabeled and sometimes closed) door to a dark, steep flight of stairs that leads down into the...

"Boiler Room"

The Teutonic Knights had a surprisingly sophisticated method for heating this huge complex. You see a furnace down below and a holding area for hot rocks above. The radiant heat given off by the rocks spread through the vents without also filling them with smoke (illustrated by a chart on the wall). This is one of 11 such "boiler rooms" in the castle complex. As you tour the rest of the castle, keep an eye out for saucer-sized heating vents in the floor.

• Climb back up the stairs, take an immediate left through a tiny arch, and then go left again, up through the second door (not down through the first door, which takes you out of the castle). This leads into the...

Grand Master's Palace

This was one of the grandest royal residences in medieval Europe, used in later times by Polish kings and German kaisers. (Today it's sometimes used for special exhibitions.)

• From the kitchen—with its huge chimney (wow!)—turn left into the big and bright...

Grand Refectory: With remarkable palm vaulting and grand

POMERANIA

frescoes, this dining hall hosted feasts for up to 400 people to celebrate a military victory or to impress visiting dignitaries. In the floor, notice the 36 heating vents—which are directly above the boiler room you just visited—designed to keep the VIPs warm.

• *At the far end of the refectory, climb the stairs into the...*

Private Rooms of the Grand Master: Though the Teutonic Order dictated that the monks sleep in dormitories, the Grand Master made an exception for himself—with this suite of private rooms. This area is a bit of a maze, so stick with me (or just wander around looking for each of these rooms): From the hall where you enter, turn left into another hall, with show-off decor—including some 15th-century original frescoes of wine leaves and grapes. The door on your left leads to the Grand Master's private **chapel,** dedicated to St. Catherine. Head back into the ivy-draped hall, and go through the door on the left, where a narrow hallway leads past the Grand Master's **private bedroom,** decorated with (now very faint) frescoes of four virgins—female martyrs. Continue past the bedroom to the end of this passage, angle left past the columns and a coin collection (on your right—the knights minted their own coins), then go through the door on the right, into the green-walled **private study** of the Grand Master.

Continue through the study, and you'll step into the Top Knight's private dining room, the **Winter Refectory,** with fewer windows (better insulation) and more of the little heating vents in the floor. The walls are draped with tapestries, which also helped warm things up a bit.

For a dramatic contrast, continue into the next room—the **Summer Refectory.** With big stained-glass windows and delicate vaulting supported by a single central pillar, this room was clearly not designed with defense in mind. In fact, medieval Polish armies focused their attacks on this room. On one legendary occasion, the attackers—tipped off by a spy—knew that an important meeting was going on here and fired a cannonball into the room. It just missed the pillar. (You can see where the cannonball hit the wall, just above the fireplace.) The ceiling eventually did collapse during World War II.

Continue through the

POMERANIA

The Teutonic Knights

The Order of the Teutonic Knights began in the Holy Land in 1191, during the Third Crusade. These militarized German monks built hospitals and cared for injured knights. When the Crusades ended in the 12th century, the knights returned to Europe and reorganized as a chivalric order of Christian mercenaries—pagan-killers for hire.

In 1226, a northern Polish duke called in the Teutonic Knights to subdue a tribe of pagans who had been attacking his lands. Clad in their white cloaks with skinny black crosses, the Teutonic Knights spent 60 years "saving" the pagans by turning them into serfs or massacring them.

Job done, the Teutonic Knights decided to stick around. With the support of the pope and the Holy Roman Emperor (who were swayed by the knights' religious zeal), the knights built one of Europe's biggest and most imposing fortresses: Malbork. In 1308, they seized large parts of northern Poland (including Gdańsk), cutting off Polish access to the Baltic Sea. The knights grew rich from Hanseatic trade, specializing in amber, grain, and timber. By the late 14th century, the Teutonic Knights had grown to become Europe's largest-ever monastic state and were threatening to overtake Lithuania.

Inspired by a mutual desire to oust the Teutonic Knights, the Poles and the Lithuanians teamed up. In 1386, Polish Princess Jadwiga married Lithuanian Prince Władysław Jagiełło, kick-starting a grand new dynasty: the Jagiellonians.

Every Pole knows the date July 15, 1410: the Battle of Grunwald. King Władysław Jagiełło and Lithuanian Grand Duke Vytautas the Great led a ragtag army of some 40,000 soldiers—Lithuanians, Poles, other Slavs, and even speedy Tatar horsemen—against 27,000 Teutonic Knights. At the end of the day, some 18,000 Poles and Lithuanians were dead—but so were half of the Teutonic Knights, and the other half had been captured. Poland and Lithuania were victorious.

The Battle of Grunwald marked the beginning of the end for the Teutonic Knights, who were conclusively defeated during the Thirteen Years' War (1454-1466). The order officially dissolved in 1575, when they converted to Protestantism and much of their land was folded into Prussia. Later, 19th-century Polish Romantics reimagined the Teutonic Knights as an early symbol of Germanic oppression—poignant among Poles, who suffered through a new round of German abuse in World War II. Some conspiracy theorists believe the Teutonic Knights are still very much active...but that's another story.

POMERANIA

Summer Refectory, stepping out into a hallway. Turn right, noticing the washbasin and trough along the corridor. Anyone wanting an audience with the Grand Master had to wash both his hands and his feet. Farther along, find the stairs down (on your left).

• *Take those stairs back out in the courtyard. On your right are four...*

Grand Master Statues

Though this was a religious order, these powerful guys look more like kings than monks. From left to right, shake hands with Hermann von Salza (who was Grand Master when the Teutonic Knights came to Poland); Siegfried von Feuchtwangen (who actually moved the T. K. capital from Venice to Malbork, and who conquered Gdańsk for the knights—oops, can't shake his hand, which was supposedly chopped off by Soviet troops); Winrich von Kniprode (who oversaw Malbork's Golden Age and turned it into a castle fit for a king); and Markgraf Albrecht von Hohenzollern (the last Grand Master before the order dissolved and converted to Protestantism).

• *We're heading into the final section of the castle. Before we do, it's a good time for a break—WCs and eateries are on this courtyard. When you're ready, continue into the High Castle. To the right of the Grand Masters, cross over the...*

Drawbridge

As you cross, notice the extensive system of fortifications and moats protecting the innermost part of the castle just ahead. Once inside the gate, on your left is a door leading to a green zone that runs around the High Castle. Here you'll see a collection of stone catapult balls that were actually fired at this castle when it was under siege. (Look high above to see the dents such stones can make.) This is a fun area to explore on your way back out of the castle...if you're not castled out by that point.

Continue straight ahead from the drawbridge, into a passage that's lined with holes to the sides (for surveillance) and with chutes up above (to pour scalding water or pitch on unwanted visitors). It's not quite straight—so a cannon fired here would hit the side wall of the passage, rather than enter the High Castle and its central courtyard. Which is what you're about to do now.

High Castle (Zamek Wysoki)

This is the heart of the castle, and its oldest section. From this spot, the Teutonic Knights governed their vast realm—the largest monk-ruled territory in European history. As much a monastery as a fortress, the High Castle was off-limits to all but 60 monks of the Teutonic Order and their servants. (The knights stayed in the Middle Castle.) Here you'll find the monks' dormitories, chapels, church, and refectory. As this was the nerve center of the Teutonic

Knights, it was also their last line of defense. They stored enormous amounts of food here in case of a siege.

In the middle of the High Castle courtyard is a **well**—an essential part of any inner castle, especially one as prone to sieges as Malbork. At the top is a sculpture of a pelican. Because this noble bird was believed to kill itself to feed its young (notice that it's piercing its own chest with its beak), it was often used in the Middle Ages as a symbol for the self-sacrifice of Jesus.

• *Take some time to explore the...*

Ground Floor

Immediately to your left is a door leading to the **prison,** with small "solitary confinement" cells near the entrance. Diagonally across the courtyard, hiding in the far corner, is an exhibit on **stained-glass windows** from the castle church.

Back near where you entered the courtyard, step into the **kitchen.** This exhibit—with a long table piled with typical ingredients from that time—gives you a feel for medieval monastery life. The monks who lived here ate three meals a day, along with lots of beer (made here) and wine (imported from France, Italy, and Hungary). A cellar under the kitchen was used as a simple refrigerator—big chunks of ice were cut from the frozen river in winter, stored in the basement, and used to keep food cool in summer. Behind the long table, see the big dumbwaiter (with shelves for hot dishes), which connects this kitchen with the refectory upstairs. Step into the giant stove and peer up into the biggest chimney in the castle.

• *Now go back out into the courtyard and climb up the stairs near where you first entered.*

Middle Floor

• *From the top of the stairs, the first door on the left (with the colorfully painted arch) leads to the most important room of the High Castle, the...*

Chapter Room: Monks gathered here after Mass, and it was also the site for meetings of Teutonic Knights from throughout the realm. If a Grand Master was killed in battle, the new one would be elected here. Carvings above each chair indicated the status of the man who sat there. The big chair belonged to the Grand Master. Notice the little windows high on the wall above his chair, connecting this room to the church next door. Ecclesiastical music

POMERANIA

would filter in through these windows; imagine the voices of 60 monks bouncing around with these acoustics.

While monks are usually thought to pursue simple lives, the elegant vaulting in this room is anything but plain. The 14th-century frescoes (restored in the 19th century) depict Grand Masters. In the floor are more vents for the central heating.

• *Leave the Chapter Room and walk straight ahead, imagining the monk-filled corridors of Teutonic times. The first door on the right is the...*

Treasury: As you explore the five rooms of the tax collector and the house administrator, notice the wide variety of safes and other lock boxes. Documents, amber, and coins were kept behind heavily armored and well-locked doors.

• *Continue around the cloister. At the end of the corridor, spot the little devil at the bottom of the vaulting (on the right, just above your head). He's pulling his beard and crossing his legs—pointing you down the long corridor leading about 100 yards away from the cloister to the...*

Dansker Tower: From the devil's grimace, you might have guessed that this tower houses the latrine. Four wooden toilet stalls filled this big room. Where one is missing, you can look down to see how the "toilets" simply dropped the waste into the moat. For obvious sanitary (and olfactory) reasons, this potty tower is set apart from the main part of the castle. The bins above the toilets were filled with cabbage leaves, to be used by the T. K. as TP (and as an organic form of Preparation H). This tower could also serve as a final measure of defense—it's easier to defend than the entire castle. Food was stored above, just in case. More info on this grand castle WC is on the wall.

• *Return down the long corridor. Before the end, on the right-hand side of the long passage, a door leads into the...*

Church Exhibition: Once dormitories for the monks, these three rooms now display a wide range of relics from the church. In the last room, on the far wall, is the artistic highlight of the castle: a finely carved and gilded three-panel altarpiece from 1504 featuring the coronation of Mary. Mary's face is mesmerizing. Characteristic of the late Gothic period, the robes seem to fly unrealistically (as if they were bent metal).

• *Back out in the main cloister, turn right, and continue to the end, arriving at the...*

Golden Gate: This elaborate doorway—covered in protective glass—marks the entrance to St. Mary's Church. Before entering, examine this rare original **door.** Ringed with detailed carvings from the New Testament, and symbolic messages about how monks of the Teutonic Order should live their lives, it's a marvelous example of late-13th-century art. At the bottom-left end of the arch, find the five wise virgins who, having filled their lamps with oil and conserved it wisely, are headed to heaven. On the right, the five foolish virgins who overslept and used up all their oil are damned, much to their dismay.

Step inside **St. Mary's Church** to appreciate a glorious Gothic interior—recently reopened after a lengthy restoration. Straight

ahead from where you entered, look for the 14th-century cross, which was partly burned when the castle was destroyed. Throughout the space, notice how the restorers intentionally used different materials to distinguish repairs from different eras: the brighter plaster dates from the recent work, while the darker plaster (closer to the area where you entered) is from the 19th century.

• *Back outside, go through the narrow door next to the Golden Gate and hike up the tight spiral staircase to the final set of exhibits.*

Top Floor

Walk through a space with temporary exhibits. At the end, descend into the **monks' common room** (left, at the bottom of the stairs). Over the fireplace is a relief depicting the Teutonic Knights fighting the pagans. To the left and above (see the stone windows) is a balcony where musicians entertained the monks after a meal.

The next, very long room, with seven pillars, is the **refectory,** where the monks ate in silence. Along the right-hand wall are lockable storage boxes for tableware. At the end of this room, just beyond another ornate fireplace, notice the grated hole in the wall. This is where the dumbwaiter comes up from the kitchen (which we saw below). Beyond this room is an exhibit about the architectural renovation of the castle.

• *Your Malbork tour ends here. You leave the way you came. En route, you can walk around terraces lining the inner moat, between the castle walls (stairs lead down off the drawbridge, by the catapult balls). It's hardly a must-see, but it's pleasant enough, with the Grand Master's garden, a cemetery for monks, and the remains of the small St. Anne's Chapel (with Grand Master tombs).*

MALBORK CONNECTIONS

From Malbork by Train to: Gdańsk (2/hour, 30 minutes on express EIC train, 45 minutes on slower regional train), **Toruń** (about every 2 hours, 2.5 hours, change in Iława), **Warsaw** (hourly, 2.5 hours on express EIC train).

Toruń

Toruń (TOH-roon) is a pretty, lazy Gothic town conveniently located about halfway between Warsaw and Gdańsk. It's worth a few hours to stroll the lively streets, ogle the huge red-brick buildings, and savor the flavor of perhaps Poland's most livable city.

With about 210,000 residents and 30,000 students (at Copernicus University), Toruń is a thriving burg. Like Kraków (and unlike most other Polish cities), Toruń escaped destruction during World War II and remains well-preserved today. Locals brag that their city is a "mini Kraków." But that sells both cities short. Toruń lacks Kraków's over-the-top romanticism, and its sights are quickly exhausted. On the other hand, Toruń may well be Poland's most user-friendly city: tidy streets with a sensible grid plan, wide pedestrian boulevards crammed with locals who greet each other like they're long-lost friends, and an easygoing ambience that seems to say, "Hey—relax." And, while the city has its share of tourists, almost none are Americans.

Toruń clings fiercely to its two claims to fame: It's the proud birthplace of the astronomer Copernicus (Mikołaj Kopernik), and home to a dizzying variety of gingerbread treats (*piernika*; pyer-NEE-kah).

Orientation to Toruń

Everything in Toruń worth seeing is in the walled Old Town, climbing up a gentle hill from the Vistula River. The broad, traffic-free main drag, ulica Szeroka (called Różana at the entrance of town), bisects the Old Town, running parallel to the river. You can walk from one end of the town center to the other in about 15 minutes. The helpful **TI** is on the main square, behind the Old Town Hall (Mon-Fri 9:00-18:00, Sat-Sun from 10:00, shorter hours and closed Sun Oct-April, Rynek Staromiejski 25, tel. 56-621-0930, www.visittorun.com).

ARRIVAL IN TORUŃ

Toruń's main train station (Toruń Główny) is across the river from the Old Town, about a mile away. The main hall has ticket windows, ATMs, and lockers (near the bistro).

To reach the Old Town, you can take a **taxi**—they wait out the door from the main hall (15 zł or less to Plac Rapackiego, the start of my Toruń Walk). To go by **bus,** first buy a ticket from the Relay kiosk inside the station, then take the pedestrian underpass outside (look for *ul. Kjawska* sign and bus icon, past platform 4). Surfacing, find the bus stop for bus #22 or #27. Take the bus to Plac Rapackiego, the first stop after the long bridge. To return to the station, catch the bus across the busy road from where you got off. You can return on bus #22 or #27, or on bus #11, #14, or #36, which go to the opposite side of the station. Note: Public transit is free for anyone over age 65 (just show your passport).

Alternate Train Station: Some (but not all) trains also stop at **Toruń Miasto** station, which is a bit closer to the Old Town (about a 15-minute walk along the river). Check schedules carefully to see if your train stops here; those overnighting in town may find it more convenient.

Toruń Walk

This brief self-guided walk takes you through the heart of Toruń—showing you pretty much everything you'd want to see on a brief visit. With no stops, you could do it in 30 minutes.

• *The bus stop is at...*

Plac Rapackiego: The park that rings Toruń—once the site of the medieval city wall—is an inviting people zone. From the bus stop, walk straight ahead through the park, toward town. You'll pass a self-service bike repair station *(stacja naprawy rowerów)* and a futuristic sculpture (labeled *Solimnia Regit*) honoring hometown boy Copernicus' heliocentric theory...more on him later. The big, historic, ornately gabled building on your left is the Collegium

Toruń

Accommodations
1. Hotel 1231 & Restaurant
2. Hotel Karczma Spichrz & Restaurant
3. Solaris Hotel
4. Hotel Retman

Eateries
5. Chleb i Wino
6. Maneken
7. Pierogarnia Stary Młyn

8. Luizjana
9. Tradycyjne Prawdziwe Pierniki Gingerbread Shop

Sights
10. Old Town Hall District Museum
11. Museum of the History of Toruń
12. Museum of Toruń Gingerbread
13. Gingerbread Museum

POMERANIA

Maximum, the historic headquarters of Toruń's prestigious university.

Carry on straight ahead, going below the narrow house marked *1930* and the adjoining local Solidarity headquarters. You'll pop out on the town's main drag.

• *Continue one block straight along the main street to reach the bustling...*

Old Town Market Square (Rynek Staromiejski): This square is surrounded by huge brick buildings and outdoor restaurants buzzing with lively locals (for tips, see "Eating in Toruń," later).

The **Old Town Hall** (Ratusz Staromiejski) fills the middle of the square. Like the similar Cloth Hall in Kraków, this building began life as a general market. Toruń is, at its heart, a trading city, and benefitted tremendously from its membership in the Hanseatic League—a trade union of Northern European maritime cities. Toruń's prime position on the Vistula River, navigable by oceangoing vessels, put it on the map and allowed it to prosper. The Old Town Hall contains a fine, if dated, museum, and you can pay to climb its tower for a town view (described later, under "Sights in Toruń").

The building with the pointy spires on the right (across from the Old Town Hall) is the **Artus Court,** where the medieval town council and merchants' guilds met. While the town was founded in 1231, the current building is Neo-Gothic, dating from 1891.

The guy playing his violin in front of the Old Town Hall is a **rafter**—one of the medieval lumberjacks who lashed tree trunks together and floated them down the Vistula to Gdańsk. This particular rafter came to Toruń when the town was infested with frogs. He wooed them with his violin and marched them out of town. (Hmm...sounds like a certain pied piper...)

Walk in front of the Old Town Hall (passing the ticket desk for the museum and tower climb). At the far end, the bigger statue depicts **Mikołaj Kopernik,** known internationally as Nicolaus Copernicus (1473-1543). This Toruń-born son of aristocrats turned the world on its ear when he suggested that the sun, not the earth, is the center of the universe (the "heliocentric theory"). Toruń is seriously proud of this local boy done good—he's the town mascot, as well as the namesake of the local university. Among its fields of study, Copernicus U. has a healthy astronomy program. There's a planetarium in the Old Town (just past the far corner of the square) and a giant radio telescope on the outskirts. Despite all the local fuss over Copernicus, there's some dispute about his "nationality": He was born in Toruń, but at a time when it was the predominantly German town of "Thorn." So is he Polish...or German? (For more on Copernicus, you can visit his birth house—now a museum—just two blocks away and described later, under "Sights in Toruń.")

Copernicus faces a shiny **donkey** at the corner of Szeroka and Żeglarska streets. Notice the sharp ridge on the donkey's back, which recalls a humiliating punishment. Centuries ago, delinquents and petty criminals needing to be set straight would be forced to straddle this donkey—after townspeople had tied heavy stones to their feet, weighing them down painfully.

• *But you're on vacation—and, rather than humiliation, you get gingerbread. Follow your nose to the right, down Żeglarska street, which is lined with...*

Gingerbread Shops: For Poles, Toruń is synonymous with gingerbread *(piernika)*—you'll smell its heavenly scent all over town. When Chopin visited, most of his impressions of Toruń revolved around gingerbread. Today, this Toruń treat can be topped with different kinds of jams or glazes, and/or dipped in chocolate. But historically, gingerbread was more straightforward—and a valuable commodity. The honey used in its dough and for glazing acted as a preservative, allowing gingerbread to be traded far and wide. And its spices aid digestion, so it served a medicinal purpose as well. Thanks to Hanseatic League connections, Toruń's bakers had access to exotic, imported spices such as white ginger, cinnamon, clove, anise, citrus skins, cardamom, and peppercorns (for which *piernika* is named). Traditionally, gingerbread dough was pressed into wooden molds, giving each cookie a distinctive shape.

While you'll spot a half-dozen options for buying gingerbread within a few steps of here, I like the one marked **Tradycyjne Prawdziwe Pierniki** (on the right, at #25). This shop has a fun system: All the varieties cost the same, so you can assemble just the mix you like by pointing. *Róża* is rose, *malina* is raspberry, *czarna porzeczka* is black currant, *morela* is apricot, and—of course—*czekolada* is chocolate.

• *A few steps down and across the street is the...*

Cathedral of Two Saint Johns (Katedra Św. Jana Chrzciciela i Jana Ewangelisty): Dedicated in the 12th century to both John the

Baptist and John the Evangelist, this is the parish church of the Old Town. Its massive bulk dominates the view of Toruń from across the river. From here at street level, appreciate the architectural heaviness: The marshy land lacked big stones, so instead of flying buttresses, medieval engineers designed an overbuilt brick structure so they could go big.

Stepping inside, you find graceful Gothic austerity—with delicate ribs and whitewashed walls. The gravestones of big shots pave the floor. Each trade guild had its own chapel, with its own fancy altar. On the wall to the left of the main altar, notice the finely restored 13th-century *Last Judgment* fresco. As you leave, head to the back-right corner (opposite where you came in) and find the colorful baptismal font where, in 1473, Copernicus was baptized (free entry, tower climb extra, open Mon-Sat 9:00-17:30, Sun from 14:30).

• *Having satisfied your ginger tooth and seen the town's most important church, head back to the square and that painful donkey, turn right, and join the human stream down the appropriately named...*

Ulica Szeroka ("Wide Street"): This enjoyable pedestrian promenade leads through the heart of town. Embedded in the paving bricks are the coats of arms of Toruń's medieval trading partners. And on each side of the street is an eclectic commotion of fun facades.

About 30 yards before the road forks at the stately, white Empik building, look down narrow Przedzamcze street to the right to see fragments of the town wall. This marks the border between the Old Town and the New Town (chartered only about 30 years later—both in the 13th century). While these areas are collectively known today as the unified "Old Town," they were quite different in the Middle Ages—each with its own market square, and separated by a wall. Because the New Town lacked the easy access to the river, most of its residents were craftspeople who supplied the traders in the Old Town. (If you're curious to see the New Town Square and Town Hall, take the left fork at the Empik building and walk two blocks up ulica Królowej Jadwigi.)

• *One of the city's two gingerbread museums is just ahead on the left (described later, under "Sights in Toruń").*

But for now, turn right down Przedzamcze, bear left at the parking lot, and continue under the stubby, standalone brick gate. Emerging on the other side, you'll see an old mill straight ahead, and a crenellated brick tower on your right. You're standing in the middle of what's left of...

Toruń Castle: This castle, built by the Teutonic Knights who were so influential in northern Poland in the Middle Ages (see page 303), was destroyed in the 15th century by the locals—who, aside from a heap of bricks, left only the tower that housed the Teutonic toilets. The ruins nearby—basically just foundations—have nothing much to offer. But what survives is one of the better toilet towers in Europe—which was connected to the castle by an elevated walkway and located far enough away to keep things hygienic. The old mill next to the toilet is now a recommended hotel and restaurant named 1231, for the date the Teutonic Order arrived here.

• *Our walk is over. You can backtrack the way you came and explore more of the city (including the sights listed next). Or you can take a quick riverside stroll: Go under the toilet tower and down to the Vistula River, turn right, and stroll along the castle and 14th-century city walls back to your starting point (and the bus stop back to the station). The road is called Bulwar Filadelfijski—for Toruń's sister city in Pennsylvania.*

POMERANIA

Sights in Toruń

Toruń is more about strolling than it is about sightseeing—the town's museums are underwhelming. Aside from its half-dozen red-brick churches (any of which are worth dropping into), the following attractions are worth considering on a rainy day.

Hours: Almost all of these sights—everything except the second Gingerbread Museum—are operated by the city and have the same hours: Tue-Sun 10:00-18:00, Oct-April until 16:00, closed Mon year-round (www.muzeum.torun.pl).

City History Museums

Toruń operates two different history museums. Both show off intimate bits and pieces of history—from pewter tankards to old gingerbread molds—that show the richness of this traders' city. They're essentially redundant—pick one.

The **Old Town Hall District Museum,** inside the centerpiece building on the main square, has more impressive spaces—including Gothic corridors and royal meeting rooms upstairs. But the collection is dusty and challenging to appreciate. The highlight is the Gothic Gallery on the main floor—featuring medieval church art saved from the region's churches, with lots of Marys (the patron of the Teutonic Order), and a close-up look at some 14th-century stained glass (13 zł, Rynek Staromiejski 1). You can also pay (separately) 13 zł to climb the 176 narrow wooden steps to the top of the **tower,** for great views over the city center.

A few blocks away, the **Museum of the History of Toruń** fills an old red-brick granary with four floors of well-explained artifacts, colorful exhibits, and English translations. While the space is less impressive, it's a more meaningful experience (10 zł, Łazienna 16). You can pay extra to watch an informative, 13-minute 3-D movie (with English subtitles) about the town's history on the top floor.

Gingerbread Museums

Toruń also has two competing museums about gingerbread. Neither is essential—the main Toruń gingerbread experience is simply dropping into a shop and buying some to snack on—but they both, in different ways, teach about this important local product. Unlike cookies, you should choose just one of these museums.

The **Museum of Toruń Gingerbread,** just off the main drag at the far end of town, is more of a traditional museum. It fills the historic red-brick Weese family gingerbread factory, established in 1885. (The company still makes gingerbread, in a modern plant on the outskirts.) After watching a brief film, you'll walk through three floors of quaint, modern exhibits that trace the history of gingerbread: historic artifacts (molds, ovens) in the cellar; a re-created late-19th-century street on the upper floor; and an interesting overview of the gingerbread-making process on the main floor (10 zł, Strumykowa 4). While they also offer hands-on gingerbread demonstrations, they're not reliably in English (though you can book one for 70 zł extra, details on website).

The similarly named **Gingerbread Museum** (Muzeum Piernika), between the main square and the river, is for those wanting an English demonstration rather than a traditional museum. Costumed medieval bakers spend about an hour walking you through the traditional process of rolling, cutting out, baking, and tasting your own batch of gingerbread cookies. After aging for 12 weeks to achieve the proper consistency, the dough bakes for only 12 minutes—or, according to the medieval bakers, about 50 Hail Marys. At the end, they spend another 20 minutes demonstrating how the process changed in the early 20th century, with the advent of modern equipment (17 zł, daily 10:00-18:00, Polish tours start at the top of each hour, English tours run 2/day—usually at 13:00 and 16:00, in peak times it's smart to reserve online in advance, Rabiańska 9, tel. 56-663-6617, www.muzeumpiernika.pl).

Copernicus House (Dom Kopernika)

Filling a pair of gabled brick buildings between the main square and the river, this museum celebrates the hero of Toruń. As much about medieval Toruń as about the famous astronomer, and sprawling over several floors, the exhibits loosely explain Nicolaus Copernicus' life and achievements, with several re-created Gothic rooms. However, it's not engaging and fails to do justice to this very important native son; it's skippable for casual visitors (13 zł, Kopernika 15, tel. 566-605-613). If you visit, skip the "4-D cinema" (which costs extra)—while it provides a weighty introduction to astronomy and astrophysics, from the Big Bang to the plight of Pluto, it barely mentions Copernicus.

Other Toruń Museums

Toruń is a popular destination for Polish families, and the TI loves to suggest attractions for those with more time. The **"Mill of Knowledge"** is a hands-on science museum designed for kids, with six floors of interactive exhibits. The **Travelers Museum** focuses on Toruń native Tony Halik, who hosted a travelogue TV show that was many Poles' gateway to the world. The city has two **open-air folk museums:** one just north of the Old Town, and a better one, called Olender, across the river. And in the park ringing the Old Town, just a two-minute walk from the bus stop, is the **Fontanna Cosmopolis,** a dancing fountain that thrills kids with a little music-and-lights show each evening.

Sleeping in Toruń

$$ Hotel 1231, filling a restored 13th-century mill at the bottom of town, has 22 modern rooms near the top of this price range, and a good restaurant (Przedzamcze 6, tel. 607-553-812, www.hotel1231.pl).

$$ Hotel Karczma Spichrz ("Granary") has 24 rooms in a renovated old granary, and 20 more in a newer annex. Rustic and creaky, it has huge wooden beams around every corner (low ceilings, thin floors and walls can be noisy, elevator, a block off the main drag toward the river at ulica Mostowa 1, tel. 56-657-1140, www.spichrz.pl).

$ Solaris Hotel, just off the main square, has 23 stylish rooms tucked into a historic town house (Panny Marii 9, tel. 56-471-3042, www.hotel-solaris.pl).

$ Hotel Retman ("Rafter") has 29 older but nicely appointed rooms over a restaurant just down the street from the Gingerbread Museum (ulica Rabiańska 15, tel. 56-657-4460, www.hotel-retman.pl).

Eating in Toruń

On the Old Town Market Square: The square surrounding the Old Town Hall is ringed with stay-awhile al fresco tables, any of which is a good choice for a scenic meal; most are open long hours daily. Favorites include **$$ Chleb i Wino** ("Bread and Wine"), which feels a bit more upscale, with Polish and Mediterranean dishes; and **$ Maneken,** the original outpost of a popular chain, which serves crêpes.

Traditional Restaurants in Hotels: The recommended **$$ Spichrz** and **$$$ 1231** hotels both have traditional restaurants in historic spaces, with tempting menus of stick-to-your-ribs traditional fare. Spichrz is a bit ye olde and more casual; 1231 feels more upscale (see contact information earlier).

Hearty Pierogi: Pierogarnia Stary Młyn ("Old Mill"), on a side street near the history museum, has an over-the-top-rustic interior (and some outdoor tables) and a long menu of pierogi—boiled, baked, pan-fried—with various fillings (daily, Łazienna 28, tel. 566-210-309).

Cajun: Luizjana, named for the US state, offers Cajun cooking that's better than it has any right to be (daily for dinner, Mon-Fri also for lunch, ulica Mostowa 10).

POMERANIA

Toruń Connections

Toruń is a natural stopover on the way between Warsaw and Gdańsk. The connection to Warsaw or Gdańsk is quick and easy; to reach Malbork, you'll usually need to change.

From Toruń by Train to: Warsaw (every 2 hours direct, 3 hours on express IC train), **Gdańsk** (4/day direct, 2.5 hours; additional options with a change in Bydgoszcz or Iława, 3 hours), **Malbork** (about every 2 hours, 2.5 hours, change in Iława), **Kraków** (1/day direct, 6.5 hours; more options with a change at Warsaw's Zachodnia station: 7/day, 6 hours), **Berlin** (4/day, 6 hours, change in Poznań).

By Bus: If heading to **Gdańsk,** consider buses operated by Arriva, which are cheaper and faster than the train (about 2 hours; www.arrivabus.pl).

PRACTICALITIES

This section covers just the basics on traveling in Poland (for much more information, see *Rick Steves Eastern Europe*). You'll find free advice on specific topics at www.ricksteves.com/tips.

MONEY

Poland uses a currency called the złoty: 4 Polish złoty (zł) = about $1. To roughly convert Polish złoty into dollars, divide by four (e.g., 40 zł = about $10, 100 zł = about $25, 200 zł = about $50). Check www.oanda.com for the latest exchange rates.

The standard way for travelers to get złoty is to withdraw money from an ATM (known as a *Bankomat* in Poland) using a debit card, ideally with a Visa or MasterCard logo. Before departing, call your bank or credit-card company: Confirm that your card(s) will work overseas, ask about international transaction fees, and alert them that you'll be making withdrawals in Europe.

Also ask for the PIN number for your credit card—you may need it for Europe's "chip-and-PIN" payment machines (see below; allow time for your bank to mail your PIN to you). To keep your valuables safe, wear a money belt.

Using Credit Cards: European cards use chip-and-PIN technology; most chip cards issued in the US instead have a signature option. Some European card readers will accept your card as-is; others may generate a receipt for you to sign or prompt you to enter your PIN (so it's important to know the code for each of your cards). If a cashier is present, you should have no problems.

At self-service payment machines (transit-ticket kiosks, parking, gas pumps, etc.), results are mixed, as US cards may not work in some unattended transactions. If your card won't work, look for a cashier who can process the transaction manually—or pay in cash.

Dynamic Currency Conversion: If merchants or hoteliers offer to convert your purchase price into dollars (called dynamic currency conversion, or DCC), refuse this "service." You'll pay extra for the expensive convenience of seeing your charge in dollars. If an ATM offers to "lock in" or "guarantee" your conversion rate, choose "proceed without conversion." Other prompts might state, "You can be charged in dollars: Press YES for dollars, NO for złoty." Always choose the local currency.

STAYING CONNECTED

The simplest solution is to bring your own device—mobile phone, tablet, or laptop—and use it just as you would at home (following the money-saving tips below, such as connecting to free Wi-Fi whenever possible).

To call Poland from a US or Canadian number: Whether you're phoning from a landline, your own mobile phone, or a Skype account, you're making an international call. Dial 011-48 and then the phone number. (011 is our international access code; 48 is Poland's country code.) If dialing from a mobile phone, you can enter + in place of the international access code—press and hold the 0 key.

To call Poland from a European country: Dial 00-48 followed by the phone number. (00 is Europe's international access code.)

To call within Poland: Just dial the whole number.

To call from Poland to another country: Dial 00 followed by the country code (for example, 1 for the US or Canada), then the area code and number. If you're calling European countries whose phone numbers begin with 0, you'll usually have to omit that 0 when you dial.

Tips: If you bring your own mobile phone, consider signing up for an international plan; most providers offer a global calling plan that cuts the per-minute cost of phone calls and texts, and a flat-fee data plan.

Use Wi-Fi whenever possible. Most hotels and many cafés offer free Wi-Fi, and you'll likely also find it at tourist information offices, major museums, and public-transit hubs. With Wi-Fi you can use your phone or tablet to make free or inexpensive domestic and international calls via a calling app such as Skype, FaceTime, or Google Hangouts. When you can't find Wi-Fi, you can use your cellular network to connect to the Internet, send texts, or make voice calls. When you're done, avoid further charges by manually switching off "data roaming" or "cellular data."

Without a mobile device, you can make calls from your hotel and get online using public computers (there's usually one in your hotel lobby or at local libraries). Most hotels charge a high fee for international calls—ask for rates before you dial.

For more on phoning, see www.ricksteves.com/phoning. For a one-hour talk on "Traveling with a Mobile Device," see www.ricksteves.com/travel-talks.

Sleep Code

Hotels in this book are categorized according to the average price of a standard double room with breakfast in high season.

$$$$	**Splurge:** Most rooms over 550 zł
$$$	**Pricier:** 400-550 zł
$$	**Moderate:** 250-400 zł
$	**Budget:** 100-250 zł
¢	**Backpacker:** Under 100 zł
RS%	**Rick Steves discount**

Unless otherwise noted, credit cards are accepted, hotel staff speak basic English, and free Wi-Fi is available. Comparison-shop by checking prices at several hotels (on each hotel's own website, on a booking site, or by email). For the best deal, *book directly with the hotel.* Ask for a discount if paying in cash; if the listing includes **RS%,** request a Rick Steves discount.

SLEEPING

I've categorized my recommended accommodations based on price, indicated with a dollar-sign rating (see sidebar). In Poland, you can choose from a variety of stylish and charming hotels and guest-houses. Hotel prices are roughly on par with midrange Western European countries. You can uncover some bargains, but I think it's worth paying a little more for comfort and a good location.

I recommend reserving rooms in advance, particularly during peak season. Once your dates are set, check the specific price for your preferred stay at several hotels. You can do this by checking Hotels.com, Booking.com, and hotel websites. Then book directly with the hotel itself. Contact small family-run hotels directly by phone or email (not on their website). When you go direct by phone or email, the owner avoids any third-party commission, giving them wiggle room to offer you a discount, a nicer room, or a deluxe breakfast. If you prefer to book online or are considering a hotel chain, it's to your advantage to use the hotel's website.

For complicated requests, send an email with the following information: number and type of rooms; number of nights; arrival date; departure date; and any special requests. Use the European style for writing dates: day/month/year. Hoteliers typically ask for your credit-card number as a deposit.

Some hotels are willing to make a deal to attract guests: Try emailing several hotels to ask for their best price. In general, hotel prices can soften if you do any of the following: offer to pay cash, stay at least three nights, or travel off-season.

Restaurant Price Code

Eateries in this book are categorized according to the average cost of a typical main course. Drinks, desserts, and splurge items (steak and seafood) can raise the price considerably.

$$$$	**Splurge:**	Most main courses over 60 zł
$$$	**Pricier:**	45-60 zł
$$	**Moderate:**	25-45 zł
$	**Budget:**	Under 25 zł

In Poland, a milk bar or takeout spot is **$**; a basic sit-down eatery is **$$**; a casual but more upscale restaurant is **$$$**; and a swanky splurge is **$$$$**.

EATING

I've categorized my recommended eateries based on the average price of a typical main course, indicated with a dollar-sign rating (see sidebar). Poland offers good food for relatively little money. Polish cuisine has a reputation for being heavy and hearty, with lots of pork, potatoes, and cabbage...which is true. But the food here is also delicious, with more variety than you might expect. For all the details about Polish food, see page 19. Ethnic restaurants provide a welcome change of pace. Seek out Italian, Indian, sushi, and other alternatives (I've recommended several in this book).

Tipping: Good service is relaxed (slow to an American). You won't get the bill until you ask for it: *"Rachunek?"* (rah-KHOO-nehk). To tip at restaurants that have a waitstaff, round up the bill 5 to 10 percent if you're happy with the service.

TRANSPORTATION

Public transportation is the best way to connect the cities in this book.

By Train: Poland has an extensive, if dated, rail network; you can reach most towns and cities by train. Since point-to-point tickets are affordable, a rail pass won't likely save you money (but to review your options, see www.ricksteves.com/rail). To research train schedules and fares, visit the Polish rail site, www.rozklad-pkp.pl, or Germany's excellent online timetable, www.bahn.com. While most short-haul journeys don't require a seat reservation, you must reserve for some high-speed trains (such as the Kraków-Warsaw or Warsaw-Gdańsk express). Schedules will indicate when a seat assignment is required on EuroCity or InterCity long-distance trains. It's also smart to reserve a sleeping berth if you're taking a night train. For more tips, see "Train Station Lingo" on page 6.

By Bus: The dominant outfit in Poland is the German-owned

Flixbus (www.flixbus.com), which offers easy online booking and generally comfortable buses with air-conditioning and Wi-Fi.

By Car: It's cheaper to arrange most car rentals from the US. If you're planning a multicountry itinerary by car, be aware of often-astronomical international drop-off fees. For tips on your insurance options, see www.ricksteves.com/cdw. Bring your driver's license. It's also required to carry an International Driving Permit (IDP), available at your local AAA office ($20 plus two passport-type photos, www.aaa.com). For route planning, consult www.viamichelin.com.

Poland is building a network of new expressways, but they're far from complete (you'll pay tolls to take completed segments—take a toll ticket as you enter the expressway, then pay when you get off, based on how far you've traveled). Locals travel long distances on two-lane country roads. Since each lane is about a lane and a half wide, passing is commonplace. Slower drivers should keep to the far-right of their lane, and not be surprised when faster cars zip past them. A car is a worthless headache in cities—park it safely (get tips from your hotel).

You're required to have your headlights on whenever you're driving—even in broad daylight, and seat belts are mandatory. Road etiquette is similar to that in the US. Ask your car-rental company for details, or check the US State Department website (www.travel.state.gov, select "International Travel," search for your country in the "Learn about your destination" box, then click on "Travel and Transportation").

By Plane: Consider covering long distances on a budget flight, which can be cheaper (and much faster) than a train. Poland's national carrier, LOT Airlines (www.lot.com), generally charges reasonable fares for short-distance trips. Or try some no-frills carriers, such as www.wizzair.com, www.easyjet.com, and www.ryanair.com. To compare several budget airlines, see www.skyscanner.com.

HELPFUL HINTS

Emergency Help: For any emergency—whether **medical** or **police**—dial 112. For passport problems, call the **US Embassy** in Warsaw (tel. 022-504-2784, after-hours emergency tel. 022-504-2000, http://pl.usembassy.gov) or the **US Consulate** in Kraków (tel. 012-424-5100; https://pl.usembassy.gov/embassy-consulate/krakow); or the **Canadian Embassy** in Warsaw (tel. 022-584-3100, www.poland.gc.ca).

If you have a minor illness, do as the locals do and go to a pharmacist for advice. Or ask at your hotel for help—they'll know of the nearest medical and emergency services. For other concerns, get advice from your hotelier.

ETIAS Registration: Beginning in 2021, US and Canadian citizens will be required to register online with the European Travel Information and Authorization System (ETIAS) before entering certain European countries including Poland (quick and easy process, $8 fee, valid 3 years). A useful private website with more details is www.schengenvisainfo.com/etias.

Theft or Loss: To replace a passport, you'll need to go in person to an embassy or consulate (see above). Cancel and replace your credit and debit cards by calling these 24-hour US numbers collect: Visa—tel. 303/967-1096, MasterCard—tel. 636/722-7111, American Express—tel. 336/393-1111. In Poland, to make a collect call to the US, dial 00-800-111-1111; press zero or stay on the line for an operator. File a police report either on the spot or within a day or two; you'll need it to submit an insurance claim for lost or stolen rail passes or travel gear, and it can help with replacing your passport or credit and debit cards. For more information, see www.ricksteves.com/help.

Dress Code: At churches, a modest dress code (no bare shoulders or shorts) is encouraged.

Holidays and Festivals: Poland celebrates many holidays, which can close sights and attract crowds (book hotel rooms ahead). For information on holidays and festivals, check Poland's website: www.poland.travel. For a simple list showing major—though not all—events, see www.ricksteves.com/festivals.

Numbers and Stumblers: What Americans call the second floor of a building is the first floor in Europe. Europeans write dates as day/month/year, so Christmas 2021 is 25/12/21. Commas are decimal points and vice versa—a dollar and a half is 1,50, and there are 5.280 feet in a mile. Poland uses the metric system: A kilogram is 2.2 pounds; a liter is about a quart; and a kilometer is six-tenths of a mile.

RESOURCES FROM RICK STEVES

This Snapshot guide is excerpted from the latest edition of *Rick Steves Eastern Europe,* which is one of many titles in my ever-expanding series of guidebooks on European travel. I also produce a public television series, *Rick Steves' Europe,* and a public radio show, *Travel with Rick Steves.* My website, www.ricksteves.com, offers free travel information, a forum for travelers' comments, guidebook updates, my travel blog, an online travel store, and information on European rail passes and our tours of Europe. If you're bringing a mobile device, my free Rick Steves Audio Europe app features podcasts of my radio shows and travel interviews about Poland. You can get Rick Steves Audio Europe via Apple's App Store, Google Play, or the Amazon Appstore. For more information, see www.ricksteves.com/audioeurope.

Additional Resources

Tourist Information: www.poland.travel
Passports and Red Tape: www.travel.state.gov
Packing List: www.ricksteves.com/packing
Travel Insurance: www.ricksteves.com/insurance
Cheap Flights: www.kayak.com or www.google.com/flights
Airplane Carry-on Restrictions: www.tsa.gov
Updates for This Book: www.ricksteves.com/update

INDEX

Our website enhances this book and turns

Explore Europe

At ricksteves.com you can browse through thousands of articles, videos, photos and radio interviews, plus find a wealth of money-saving travel tips for planning your dream trip. And with our mobile-friendly website, you can easily access all this great travel information anywhere you go.

TV Shows

Preview the places you'll visit by watching entire half-hour episodes of Rick Steves' Europe (choose from all 100 shows) on-demand, for free.